Murder in the Courtroom

American Psychology-Law Society Series

Books in the Series

Murder in the Courtroom

The Cognitive Neuroscience of Violence

Brigitte Vallabhajosula

OXFORD
UNIVERSITY PRESS

OXFORD

UNIVERSITY PRESS

Oxford University Press is a department of the University of
Oxford. It furthers the University's objective of excellence in research,
scholarship, and education by publishing worldwide.

Oxford   New York
Auckland   Cape Town   Dar es Salaam   Hong Kong   Karachi
Kuala Lumpur   Madrid   Melbourne   Mexico City   Nairobi
New Delhi   Shanghai   Taipei   Toronto

With offices in
Argentina   Austria   Brazil   Chile   Czech Republic   France   Greece
Guatemala   Hungary   Italy   Japan   Poland   Portugal   Singapore
South Korea   Switzerland   Thailand   Turkey   Ukraine   Vietnam

Oxford is a registered trademark of Oxford University Press
in the UK and certain other countries.

Published in the United States of America by
Oxford University Press
198 Madison Avenue, New York, NY 10016

© Oxford University Press 2015

Library of Congress Cataloging-in-Publication Data
Vallabhajosula, Brigitte, author.
Murder in the courtroom : the cognitive neuroscience of violence / Brigitte Vallabhajosula.
    p. ; cm. — (American Psychology-Law Society series)
Cognitive neuroscience of extreme violence
Includes bibliographical references and index.
ISBN 978–0–19–999572–1 (pbk. : alk. paper)
I. American Psychology-Law Society, issuing body.   II. Title.   III. Title: Cognitive
neuroscience of extreme violence.   IV. Series: American Psychology-Law
Society series.
[DNLM: 1. Dangerous Behavior.   2. Brain—physiology.   3. Cognitive Science.
4. Jurisprudence.   5. Neuropsychology.   6. Violence—psychology. WM 600]
RC569.5.V55
616.85′82—dc23
2014024193

9 8 7 6 5 4 3 2 1
Printed in the United States of America
on acid-free paper

To Shankar, for being the first to believe

Contents

11. Linking Brain Function and Behavior   226

12. A Cautionary Tale   237

Series Foreword

This book series is sponsored by the American Psychology-Law Society (APLS). APLS is an interdisciplinary organization devoted to scholarship, practice, and public service in psychology and law. Its goals include advancing the contributions of psychology to the understanding of law and legal institutions through basic and applied research; promoting the education of psychologists in matters of law and the education of legal personnel in matters of psychology; and informing the psychological and legal communities and the general public of current research, educational, and service activities in the field of psychology and law. APLS membership includes psychologists from the academic, research, and clinical practice communities, as well as members of the legal community. Research and practice is represented in both the civil and criminal legal arenas. APLS has chosen Oxford University Press as a strategic partner because of its commitment to scholarship, quality, and the international dissemination of ideas. These strengths will help APLS reach its goal of educating the psychology and legal professions and the general public about important developments in psychology and law. The focus of the book series reflects the diversity of the field of psychology and law, as we publish books on a broad range of topics.

In the latest book in the series, *Murder in the Courtroom: The Cognitive Neuroscience of Violence*, Brigitte Vallabhajosula begins by posing the question, "Can brain scans be used to determine whether a person is inclined toward violent behavior or criminality?" This question, asked by Senator Biden at the nomination hearing of John G. Roberts as Chief Justice of the

United States, sets the foundation for the information presented in *Murder in the Courtroom*. Over the course of 12 chapters, Vallabhajosula distills the available literature regarding the use of various neuroimaging techniques in attempting to answer legally relevant questions regarding the link between brain and behavior. Chapter 1 begins with a distillation of the various definitions and conceptualizations of violence and the impact of these on research, policy, and practice. An overview of neurodevelopment, anatomy, organization, biology, and physiology of the human brain is provided in chapter 2, and chapter 3 provides a review of the basics of neuroimaging techniques, followed by a discussion of the various neuropsychological tests and measures in chapter 4. Chapters 5 and 6 focus on the etiology of violent behavior and the relationship between the adolescent brain and violence. An overview of the law related to the admission of scientific evidence and evidentiary reliability is presented in chapters 7 and 8, and chapter 9 is devoted to the issue of malingering and its assessment. Case law related to neuroscience evidence proffered in court is delineated in chapter 10, and chapter 11 describes the multimodal/multidisciplinary approach for the assessment of cognitive dysfunction. The book ends with a cautionary tale regarding the practical and legal concerns that have been raised by advances in the neurosciences.

Vallabhajosula has written an interesting and accessible book that will appeal to a diverse array of mental health professionals and legal scholars. *Murder in the Courtroom* presents a comprehensive and detailed analysis of issues most relevant to answering tough questions regarding the link between brain and behavior and the strengths and weaknesses in the currently available neuroimaging techniques. Practitioners, scholars, and researchers will undoubtedly find that this book has the potential to help shape their thinking and practice in this emerging legal arena.

Patricia A. Zapf
Series Editor

Acknowledgments

Science is a collaborative enterprise, spanning the generations.
When it permits us to see the far side of some new horizon, we
remember those who prepared the way—seeing for them also.

Carl Sagan

No one walks alone on the journey of life, and few, if any, scientific endeavors are undertaken in isolation. This book, like other projects, has greatly benefited from the advice and guidance of many individuals without whose contributions this work would be unintelligible. To all those, I am deeply indebted.

I would like to extend a special thanks to the following individuals:

Dr. Patricia Zapf, professor in the department of psychology at City University of New York and president of the American Psychology-Law Society, for her unwavering dedication and efforts to make my dream a reality;

Dr. P. David Mozley, professor of radiology and chief of nuclear medicine at Weill Medical College of Cornell University, and my technical editor, for his insightful and thought-provoking comments, and expert advice, and guidance; and

Dr. Shankar Vallabhajosula, professor of radiochemistry and radiopharmacy in radiology at Weill Medical College of Cornell University, for sharing much of his wisdom and expertise throughout the writing of this book.

I would also like to thank the following individuals for reviewing specific sections of the manuscript and offering much needed advice: Dr. Lyn Harper-Mozley, associate principal scientist at Merck; Dr. Jonathan Dyke, assistant research professor of physics in radiology at Weill Medical College of Cornell University; and Dr. Shungu Dikoma, professor of physics in radiology at Weill Medical College of Cornell University.

Finally, I would like to express my gratitude to my family and friends, without whose love and support this book may well still be in its infancy.

Namaste
Brigitte Vallabhajosula

SERIES IN EXPLAINED

Murder in the Courtroom

1

Violence, Free Will, and Legal Responsibility

A human being . . . is a part of the whole, called by us "Universe," a part limited in time and space. He experiences himself, his thoughts and feelings as something separated from the rest—a kind of optical delusion of his consciousness.

(Sullivan, 1972, p. 1)

1.1 Introduction

In 1221, the Mongol Tului killed between 700,000 and 1,300,000 people in Meru Chahjan, one of the four major cities of Khorassan on the northern borderland of Persia. Upon capture, the inhabitants were made to evacuate the city and then were distributed among the Mongols and massacred. It took more than 13 days to count the corpses (Howorth, 1965).

On September 8, 1974, a Boeing 707 operating as TWA Flight 841 left Tel Aviv en route to JFK International Airport, New York. After a stopover in Athens, the flight departed for Rome. About 30 minutes after takeoff the plane crashed into the Ionian Sea, brought down by a bomb that was hidden in the cargo hold. All 79 passengers and nine crew members were killed (Werth, 2006).

After the Battle of Nanking, on December 13, 1937, Japanese entered the city virtually resistance free. From then on, for a period of about six weeks, widespread war crimes were committed, including the killing of civilians and prisoners of war. Most estimates put the number of deaths at between 150,000 and 300,000 dead (Coonan, 2007).

On December 14, 2012, 20-year-old Adam Lanza fatally shot six adults and 20 children at Sandy Hook Elementary School in Newtown, Connecticut. Prior to driving to the school, Lanza shot and killed his mother.

As first-responders arrived, he committed suicide by shooting himself in the head (Barron, 2012).

Considering these examples, it is not surprising that the question of why human beings behave violently has preoccupied the minds of philosophers and scholars for centuries. Indeed, trying to understand the etiology of human violence continues to be one of the most pressing tasks of our time. But what is it about a particular behavior that can be called "violent?" Violence has been defined by the World Health Organization as the intentional use of physical force or power, threatened or actual, against a person, group, or community that either results in or has a high likelihood of resulting in injury, death, psychological harm, maldevelopment, or deprivation. Violence has also been variously defined as "the use of power to harm another, whatever form it takes" (Henry, 2000, p. 3), "an act of physical hurt deemed legitimate by the performer and illegitimate by (some) witnesses" (Riches, 1986, p. 8), and "the avoidable impairment of fundamental human needs" (Galtung, 1993, p. 106).

Perhaps one of the most universal ways of defining violence is to consider only criminal violence and argue that violence is the use of force that society has prohibited by law. However, while violence may conventionally mean a physical attack, the term *physical violence* includes a much larger spectrum of behaviors (Waddington, Badger, & Bull, 2004, p. 149). This is evident even within the criminal law, which typically defines violence as

> the actual or threatened, knowing or intentional application of statutory impermissible physical force by one person directly against one or more other persons outside the contexts both of formal institutional or organizational structures and of civil or otherwise collective disorders and movements for the purpose of securing some end against the will or without the consent of the other person or persons. (Weiner, 1989, pp. 37–38)

As the foregoing indicates, inquiries into the phenomenon of violence demonstrate that violence can take on not only many forms but different characteristics. It has also been contended that violence as merely a concept has no significance; violence becomes significant only because of its affect and cultural content (Nordstrom, 2004). Although all societies contend with problems of violence, rules or expectations of behavioral norms can vary widely from one culture to the next, as the following examples illustrate:

- In 2008, a father killed his daughter for chatting with a man on Facebook. The killing became public only when a Saudi cleric referred to the case, not to condemn it but to criticize Facebook for the strife it caused (McElroy, 2008).
- According to the Human Rights Commission of Pakistan, in 2011 at least 943 women were killed "in the name of honor" (Wells, 2012).

- In 2001, Andrea Yates was charged with capital murder in the deaths of her five children, which she had drowned in a bathtub. After her initial conviction was overturned, Yates was found not guilty by reason of insanity in 2006 and was ordered to spend time in a mental hospital.

It has been argued that "a culture, like an individual, is a more or less consistent pattern of thought and action" (Benedict, 1934, p. 46). While societal and cultural norms do not always correspond with individual values and beliefs, if the norms become internalized, they may influence these values and beliefs. In other words, cultures construct the meaning of "proper" and "improper" behaviors and actions, and society imposes these constructs on individuals in an attempt to create deeply ingrained values and beliefs (Reisig & Miller, 2009). As societies construct these cultural meanings, a shared reality is created for members of each society. In order for any society to function and remain stable within the reality that has been created, individuals must adhere to the social norms (Reisig & Miller, 2009). Indeed, as noted centuries ago, all societies, great or small, resemble complex molecules in which the atoms are

> represented by men, possessed of multifarious attractions and repulsions which are manifested in their desires and volitions, the unlimited power of satisfying which we call freedom . . . the social molecule exists in virtue of the renunciation of more or less of this freedom by every individual. (Huxley, 1871, p. 536)

Cultural norms can exist as either informal or formal rules of behavior. Informal norms are the unwritten laws of behavior; they are the practices and customs people follow in their daily lives. For example, adultery is generally thought of as wrong; however, many jurisdictions do not legally prohibit it. In contrast, formal norms are the written laws that are designed to protect the general public and that, if broken, result in some form of punishment (e.g.,. driving while under the influence of alcohol or drugs). The difference between an illegitimate and a legitimate form of violence tends to be ethically and ideologically constructed and thus has more to do with variations in the extent of social outrage than with the seriousness of the actual act (Barak, 2003). Cultural diversity is also clearly evident on matters of morality where one would expect universal agreement. For example, it may be assumed that killing another human being is a universal wrong. However, even in the matter of extreme forms of violence, cultural norms and standards can greatly influence an individual's behavior, as noted previously.

This influence is also clearly illustrated in *People v. Kimura*, (No. A-09133; L.A. Super. Ct. 1985). Mrs. Kimura, when told about her husband's unfaithfulness to her, tried to commit suicide, together with her two children, by drowning in the Pacific Ocean. According to Japanese tradition, she had been taught that her husband's unfaithfulness was her own fault and that she must commit suicide to regain her honor. Both of her two children were killed, but she survived and was consequently accused of double murder. However, more than 25,000 American citizens of Japanese origin sent written statements to the Attorney General in Los Angeles, California, stating that, according to Japanese culture, suicide that results in two motherless children is far more serious than suicide together with the children, because the latter does not expose the children to disgrace (Matsumoto, 1995). As a result, a plea bargain was struck, according to which Mrs. Kimura was given a one-year prison sentence and placed under supervision for five years. Furthermore, as argued by Chief Justice Roberts in his dissenting opinion in *Miller v. Alabama* (2012), when determining whether a punishment is cruel and unusual, the court typically begins with "'objective indicia of society's standards, as expressed in legislative enactments and state practice.'" We look to these "objective indicia" to ensure that we are not simply following our own subjective values or beliefs. Such tangible evidence of societal standards enables us to determine whether there is a "consensus against" a given sentencing practice. If there is, the punishment may be regarded as "unusual" (p. 2).

The influence of culture is further evident when one attempts to define "normal" behavior. It may be argued that there are no universal standards for labeling a behavior as abnormal since specific behaviors can only be abnormal relative to specific cultural norms. For example, symptoms associated with schizophrenia, such as delusions and hallucinations, seem to be clearly pathological and easily definably. However, increased attention to cultural variation has made it very clear that what is considered a delusion (e.g., belief in spirits) or hallucination (e.g., hearing God's voice) in one culture may be accepted as normal in another (Grzywa, Morylowska-Topolska, & Gronkowski, 2012). Indeed, "prior to Western schooling, there used to be eccentric old fools who functioned as entertainers, poets, and religious healers, but there was not a single case of schizophrenia" (Al-Issa, 2000, p. 329). Cultures also may influence the sources and expressions of anxiety and distress. Indeed, ancient scriptures, such as the Ramayana[1] and the Mahabharata,[2] contain descriptions of depression and states of anxiety, mental disorders that were generally thought to reflect abstract metaphysical entities or supernatural agents. Suggested causes included disrespect toward the gods and teachers, faulty bodily activity, or mental shock due to excessive joy, and treatments included the use of charms and prayers and moral or emotional persuasion (Bhugra, 1992).

1.2 Science and the Concept of Free Will

Philosophers and scientists have long sought to explain human behavior in general and abnormal behavior in particular. Historically, psychology assumed that abnormal behavior is the sole result of deficient psychological development while biologists assumed that all abnormal behaviors are the result of purely biological causes. This view dates back to the Hippocratic Corpus, a collection of ancient Greek medical writings in which Hippocrates and his students suggested that the brain is the seat of intelligence, emotion, wisdom, and consciousness and any disorders involving these functions are logically located in the brain (Barlow & Durand, 2004). More specifically, more than two and a half millennia ago, Hippocrates (1886) wrote:

> And men ought to know that from nothing else but thence [from the brain] come joys, laughter, sorrows, and lamentations. And by this, in an especial manner, we acquire wisdom and knowledge, and see and hear, and know what are bad and what are good. (pp. 344–345)

There is no doubt that violence is a deeply emotional subject that affects political and criminal justice responses to violence and to crime in general (Levi & Maguire, 2002). While for many centuries criminal law and neuroscience have been engaged in a contentious dialogue, neuroscience, which has now begun to expose the potential causes attributed to some of the most violent behaviors, has long exerted a tremendous influence over the law. Beginning in the 19th century with the development of phrenology, first expressed by Gall, scientists argued that a person's character can be determined from the bumps and depressions on the outside of the skull (see Figure 1.1). In fact, Gall's conclusion that certain bumps and hollows correspond to an "instinct to kill" (Simpson, 2005, p. 476) profoundly influenced the M'Naghten test

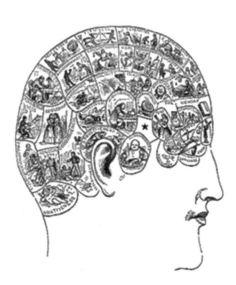

Figure 1.1 Phrenology Chart

Image courtesy of Wikimedia Commons: http://en.wikipedia.org/wiki/File:Phrenology Pix.jpg

for insanity, a test designed to separate the ability to know right from wrong from the rest of an accused's mental state. For example, in *Ferrer v. State* (1853), the Ohio Supreme Court, in considering whether a housekeeper could be held criminally responsible for poisoning a young boy, noted that a phrenologist would just have to look at the shape of her head to know she was criminally insane and had murderous impulses.

While it may be argued that, in principle, all human behavior is the result of causally determined biological events, the idea that violent behavior is determined solely by causes that are beyond an individual's control is hard to reconcile with the concept of free will on which our legal system is based. Indeed, an ongoing debate as to the ultimate causes of human behavior in general and violent behavior in particular has centered on two questions: (a) what constitutes freedom of action, and (b) did the individual have the capacity to do otherwise (Boldt, 1992)? The universality of this discourse is striking, as thinkers ranging from Plato to Kant have all attempted to understand the complexities and perplexities of human behavior and the processes by which individuals carry out particular actions (Boldt, 1992).

One of the legal system's most fundamental assumption is that individuals are able to control their behavior and choose between different actions. In fact, "the belief in freedom of the human will and a consequent ability and duty of the normal individual to choose between good and evil [is a belief that is] universal and persistent in mature systems of law" (*Morissette v. United States*, 1952, p. 250). The law further assumes that it is possible to distinguish individuals who have the capacity of free will from those who do not; however, this assumption may be wrong. While many neuroscientific studies have suggested that behavior is driven by biological mechanisms, neuroscientific research findings cannot, individually, prove that we are mere mechanisms. Indeed, "an understanding of the potential yields of neuroscientific techniques reveals them to be rather impotent for exacerbating the status of the free will problem" (Roskies, 2006, p. 421). In addition, as noted by the American Psychiatric Association in *United States v. Mest* (1986), when an ultimate issue question is presented to the expert witness to which the expert must respond with "yes" or "no," the expert no longer addresses medical issues but instead must infer what is in fact impossible to infer—the likely relationship between medical concepts and legal or moral constructs, such as free will.

While many philosophical and legal scholars assume that individuals are always exercising their free will, many of our decisions may actually be caused by events that are not within our control. In order to exercise one's free will, one must be able to behave differently given the same circumstances. To have freedom of choice thus means that the behavior is neither somehow predetermined or a simple reflex response. Numerous neuroscientists have challenged the assumption of free will with arguments made about control and voluntary behavior (see, e.g., Carson, Milne, Pakes, Shaley, & Shawyer, 2007). To be more precise, determinists have incorporated neuroscience into the free-will debate by contending that the brain determines and enables the mind, and, since the brain is a physical thing, it is subject to the rules of the physical world, and since the physical world is determined, the brain, therefore, must also be determined (Gazzangia & Steven, 2004). If the brain is determined and the brain enables the mind, all thoughts and actions arising from the mind must also be determined events rather than voluntary expressions of free will. In other words, since all human acts are events and every event has an antecedent cause, all human acts are therefore caused by antecedent events (Gazzangia & Steven, 2004). Since the antecedents of acts include neural events, the agents of the acts have no control (Siegela & Douard, 2011). In contrast, critics of the deterministic view of free will highlight that, in particular, neuroimages do not demonstrate the brain's intentionality during the illegal act. Functional neuroimaging was not intended to assess volition, and while it may offer insights into the processes that result in a particular behavior, whether or not the images can objectively assess human reason is still open to debate (Aggarwal, 2009).

Although neuroscience is increasingly revealing the neural correlates of philosophical concepts, such as the self and free will (Wagner & Reinecker, 2003; Gillihan & Farah, 2005), not all neuropsychiatric, neurological, and neuropsychological disorders and diseases result in loss of free will. However, certain disorders and diseases, including drug addiction and schizophrenia, may impair an individual's ability to act freely. This possibility is clearly articulated in the M'Naghten rule that provides that a defendant is not responsible for criminal acts if a mental disorder prevented the person from knowing what he or she was doing or, if the person was aware of his or her act, he or she nonetheless did not know that it was wrong. The formulations of the legal tests for insanity have varied over the years; however, the basic principle underlying all of the formulations has remained.[3] That basic principle reflects the "central thought that wrongdoing must be conscious to be criminal" and that the moral basis for criminal punishment rests on the "belief in freedom of the human will and a consequent ability and duty of the normal individual to choose between good and evil" (*Morissette v. United States*, 1952, p. 252). Consider the following.

In 2001, Andrea Yates drowned her five children in a bathtub because she "believed she was saving her children from Satan by killing them" and that this was the "morally right" thing to do (Ewing & McCann, 2006, p. 234). At trial, the defense expert testified that "Mrs. Yates had a choice to make: to allow her children to end up burning in hell for eternity or to take their lives on earth," suggesting that Yates knew killing her children was "legally wrong" but "morally right" (Ewing & McCann, 2006, p. 235). During trial, the prosecution's expert witness testified that he was a consultant for the TV show *Law & Order* and that a show had recently aired in which a woman with postpartum depression, who had drowned her children in the bathtub, was found not guilty by reasons of insanity (Williams, 2005). After discovering that this episode never aired, defense counsel moved for a mistrial, arguing that this testimony may have mislead jurors into believing that Yates had planned the murders by watching this show. However, the judge denied the motion and over defense counsel's argument that Yates fit the definition of legal insanity, the jurors found her guilty and sentenced her to life in prison. On appeal, Yates's conviction was reversed and she was, subsequently, found not guilty by reason of insanity (Williams, 2005).

This case clearly illustrates the problems associated with assessing abstract concepts, such as free will, and using our as of yet limited understanding about the relationship between the brain and behavior to answer a legal question that reduces diverse mental states to two categories: sane or insane. The notion that that there is something more to an individual than his or her physical manifestation runs deep in the human psyche and is a major element in many religions (Farah, 2005). However, neuroscience has begun to challenge this view by suggesting that not only motor control and perception but also free will may all merely be features of an automaton.

The problem of free will versus determinism continues to puzzle many scientists and philosophers. While some scholars hold steadfast to the idea that human beings have, indeed, free will, others have argued that with the current advances made in the neurosciences, the notion of free will is but an illusion. As long ago as the early Greek civilization, individuals have debated whether or not the laws of nature and the perceived ability of humankind to make conscious decisions that are not merely a reflection of genetics, or a particular environment, are compatible (Cashmore, 2010). "If all movement is always interconnected, the new arising from the old in a determinate order—if the atoms never swerve so as to originate some new movement that will snap the bonds of fate, the everlasting sequence of cause and effect— what is the source of the free will possessed by living things throughout the earth" (Lucretius, 1951, p. 67)? If it is true that the brain generates all of our behaviors and the effects all result from the inorganic laws of physics, over which we have no control, all of our choices are predetermined and, thus, free will is nothing more than an illusion.

Many scholars have noted that our brain is governed and controlled by impulses, neurochemicals, hormones, and genetics—in short, by biochemistry. Biochemistry, in turn, is merely a type of chemistry, and all the atoms and molecules that make up our chemistry obey the laws of physics (Crabtree, 1999). Thus it may be argued that all our actions are the unavoidable consequences of uncontrollable forces; neurons don't fire at random—they fire in accordance with the laws of physics, which are firmly beyond human control (Cooper, Bloom, & Roth, 1996). Until recently, almost all attempts to understand the functional activity of the brain have been based, at least implicitly, on some principles of classic physics. Classical physics, which is dominated by the principle of complete determinism, assumes that everything is predetermined. Every event is the inevitable consequence of a preceding event, including future events, which are completely predictable because they are causally determined by a combination of physical laws and of past and present events. Therefore all our behaviors, thoughts, and emotions are caused by past external and internal physiological events, and free will and consciousness are mere epiphenomenon of matter—nothing more than the complex functions of the material brain, governed by physical laws (McFarlane, 2000). The issue of determinism versus free will has also been addressed in case law. For example, in *United States v. Torniero* (1983), the court noted that while the notion that the behavior of the insane person is caused by forces other than that person's will is pervasive in the legal literature, courts should abandon this idea because it is laden with difficulties. The court, specifically, worried that the deterministic understanding of an insane defendant's behavior could logically apply to any and all defendants, based on the scientific view that all human behaviors are caused by prior events.

Many scholars have argued that the classical theory of physics is, in fact, the proper theory to apply for understanding the relationship between brain and behavior, even though it is known to be fundamentally false and empirically incorrect in "domains of phenomena that depend sensitively, as the brain appears to do, on the motions of ions, or on the effects of intentional choices (Crick & Koch, 2003, p. 124). If, as argued by classical physics, all behavior is predetermined, then the criminal law's requirement of free will is not applicable, and empirical research on the exact relationship between violent behavior and brain function, for the purpose of assessing legal concepts, such as culpability, is unnecessary.

As noted, in the past the dominant paradigm in philosophy and neuroscience was based on classical physics, which attempted to explain away the notion of free will; however, advances made in the neurosciences, in particular the introduction of functional brain imaging technology, do not readily lend themselves to explanations that assume that all behavior is predetermined (Stapp, 1999). In recent years, the Newtonian mechanistic and the Einsteinian deterministic theory of relativity have been refuted by modern physics, more specifically, quantum physics. According to quantum physics, the behavior of particles at the subatomic level can only be expressed in probabilistic terms, as opposed to deterministic terms. In other words, quantum physics assumes uncertainty at the microscopic level. This view was further expanded by the principle of complementarity. According to Niels Bohr (1958), who extended this principle from physics to biology and even mental phenomena,

> the impossibility in psychical (i.e. psychological) experience
> to distinguish between the phenomena themselves and their
> conscious perception clearly demands a renunciation of a simple
> causal description on the models of classical physics, and the very
> way in which words like '"thoughts" and "feelings" are used to
> describe such experience reminds one most suggestively of the
> complementarity encountered in atomic physics. (p. 21)

In other words, the reality of particles requires complementary descriptions—more than one point of view. As applied to the issue of brain dysfunction in the context of violent behavior, the theory of complimentary can, thus, be restated as follows: to reliably assess the effect of brain dysfunction on behavior requires a multimodal and multidisciplinary approach.[4]

1.3 The Doctrine of Mens Rea

One of the problems confronting the philosophy of law, influenced by neuroscience, is the ever-expanding interpretation of what influences free will and responsibility. As noted by Blackstone (1893), "no temporal tribunal can search the heart, or fathom the intentions of the mind, otherwise than as they are demonstrated by outward actions." However, our laws require for a guilty verdict not merely the commission of an act that is objectively wrong, such as killing someone, but also subjective fault. This is clearly expressed in the legal axiom, "*actus non facit reum nisi mens sit rea*" (the act is not culpable unless the mind is guilty; Glancy, Bradford, & Fedak, 2002). The leading US Supreme Court opinion on the matter observes

> A relation between some mental element and punishment for
> a harmful act is almost as instinctive as the child's familiar
> exculpatory "But I didn't mean to," and has afforded the rational
> basis for a tardy and unfinished substitution of deterrence and
> reformation in place of retaliation and vengeance as the motivation
> for public prosecution. Unqualified acceptance of this doctrine by
> English common law in the Eighteenth Century was indicated by
> Blackstone's sweeping statement that to constitute any crime there
> must first be a "vicious will." (*Morissette*, 1952, pp. 250–251)

The will of the actor has long been regarded as and remains the measure of criminal responsibility. To that end, the Model Penal Code, which has been adopted in one form or another by a majority of jurisdictions, sets forth the following four types of culpable mental states for purposes of *mens rea* analysis: (a) purposefulness (acting with the conscious purpose to engage in specific conduct or to cause a specific result), (b) knowledge (awareness that one's conduct is of a particular nature, or the practical certainty that one's conduct will cause a specific result), (c) recklessness (conscious disregard for a substantial and unjustifiable risk), and (d) negligence (the creation of a substantial or known risk of which one ought to have been aware).[5] Assigning relative moral judgments based on distinctions between purposeful, knowledgeable, reckless, and negligent conduct reflects common and widely shared moral intuitions, not merely amoral classification (Dressler, 2000). Employing the mental states of contemporary *mens rea* "is the mechanism through which the moral quality of a defendant's behavior becomes an integral concern of a criminal proceeding" (Sendor, 1986, p. 1374). To be more precise, "*mens rea* is central to the criminal law, and the moral evaluation of the will is central to *mens rea*" (Stern, 2012, p. 31).

As noted earlier, according to classical physics, everything is completely determined by mechanical conditions alone, without any reference to thoughts or intentions. The context in which research on the neuronal aspects of behavior is generally conducted assumes that brain functions alone are sufficient to explain all behaviors. This assumption is particularly apparent in the field of functional neuroimaging, in which patterns of changes in brain activation are used to explain, for example, cognitive functioning. However, opponents of determinism may quickly point out that determinism cannot be proven and that any attempt to base brain theory on classical physics is undermined by the fact that the classical theory cannot account for behavioral properties, such as brain plasticity (Schwartz, Stapp, & Beauregard, 2005). Finally, quantum theory is based on the notion that individuals act intentionally. Therefore, "as long as we maintain the current conception of ourselves as intentional and potentially rational creatures, as people and not simply as machines, the *mens rea* requirement in criminal law is both inevitable and desirable" (Morse, 2003, p. 51). However, it may be argued that there is nothing illusory in the concept of free will. There is no contradiction between the use of this concept and the fact that behavior arises from the movement of molecules within our bodies that, at the molecular level, can be perfectly deterministic (Rovelli, 2013).

1.4 Conclusion

Quantum theory is based on the notion that individuals act intentionally and that each such action is intended to produce an observable response. Classical physics, in contrast, rejects the notion of free will and assumes that all behavior is determined and, thus, free will is an illusion. There is no doubt that cognitive functions and mental phenomena can be explained to a great extent in terms of neuronal structures and functions. However, there is no philosophical or scientific consensus on the definition of mental impairments, dysfunction, or disorders. *Order* and *disorder* and *normal* and *abnormal* are normative terms applied to behavior that science in general and cognitive neuroscience in particular cannot independently define (Morse & Hoffman, 2007). Our present knowledge and understanding about how structural and/or functional impairment may affect violent behavior does not allow us to assume that we lack the ability to form and intentionally execute various actions. Future neuroscientific findings may well call into question the notion of free will; however, even if this happens, what will probably always remain unclear is how normative judgments of legal responsibility can be affected by cognitive impairments. Further, how brain functions mediate the cognitive capacity for decision making is described entirely in objective terms, but, according to Glannon (2009), there is an essential subjective aspect of the will. Indeed, a description of cognitive-motor circuits alone cannot capture the first-person experience of deliberating and/or choosing and behaving in a particular way, or how this experience is influenced by the world around us. As noted by Bohr (1963), "in the great drama of existence[,] we ourselves are both actors and spectators" (p. 15).

Regardless of whether or not free will is an illusion, it is clear that the legal system can no longer ignore neuroscientific findings about the relationship between brain functions and violent behavior. Even if brain functions underlying all behaviors are causally determined, reliance on neuroscientific tests and/or neuroimaging techniques, in particular to assess complex legal concepts, is problematic, since neuroimaging techniques are bound to momentary states and can only demonstrate possible correlations between brain function and behavior. However, within the context of violent behavior, "the purpose is not to disclose the real essence of phenomena but only to track down as far as possible relations between the multifold aspects of our experience" (Bohr, 1934, p.18).

2

The Human Brain and Cognition

Men ought to know that from nothing else but the
brain come joys, delight, laughter and sorrows, griefs,
despondency . . . And by the same organ we become mad
and delirious, and fears and terrors assail us . . . All these
things we endure from the brain, when it is not healthy.

(Hippocrates, 400 BC)

2.1 Introduction

In April of 2013, President Barack Obama unveiled a bold new research program designed to revolutionize our understanding of the human brain, the Brain Research Through Advancing Innovative Neurotechnologies (BRAIN) initiative. This initiative's ultimate goals are to help scientists find new ways to treat, cure, and even prevent brain disorders, ranging from dementia of the Alzheimer's type to schizophrenia. The specific aims are to accelerate the development and application of new technologies that will allow researchers to produce dynamic pictures of the brain depicting how individual brain cells and complex neural circuits interact at the speed of thought. According to President Obama, these technologies will open new doors to explore, for example, how the brain processes and retrieves massive quantities of information and shed light on the complex relationships between brain functioning and behavior.

Throughout history, scientists have sought to understand the molecular and genetic make-up of the human brain, from Gall's phrenology in the nineteenth century to current concepts of the brain as a quantum computer. Indeed, understanding how the brain works presents one of the greatest scientific challenges of our time.

While there have been efforts to explain how various brain regions operate, to date, no general theory of brain function is universally accepted (Alivisatos et al., 2012) and much of how the brain works remains a tantalizing mystery. Remote from the rest of the human body, encased in skull bone, without any intrinsic moving parts and weighing approximately three pounds, the brain is undoubtedly the most complex biological structure in the known universe (Greenfield, 1998).

The brain does not simply grow, but rather develops in an intricately orchestrated sequence of stages (Purves & Lichtman, 1985). Major milestones of neural development include (a) the birth and differentiation of neurons from stem cell precursors, (b) the migration of immature neurons from their birthplaces in the embryo to their final location, (c) the outgrowth of axons and dendrites from neurons, (d) the generation of synapses between axons and their postsynaptic partners, and finally (e) the lifelong changes in synapses, which are presumed to underlie learning, and memory. Ranging in functions from the simple reflexes to complex cognitive processes, neural circuits have many diverse functions, such as memory, attention, and cognitive control, that depend on the development of distinct yet interconnected circuits of anatomically distributed cortical, and subcortical regions (Tau & Peterson, 2010). The developmental organization of these circuits is an extraordinary complex process that is influenced by many factors, such as genetic predispositions and neuroplastic responses to experiential demands, which moderate communications and connectivity between neurons, within individual brain circuits and regions, and across neuronal pathways (Tau & Peterson, 2010). Defects in neuronal development can lead to cognitive, motor, and intellectual disability, as well as neurological disorders, such as autism and mental retardation (e.g., Newschaffer et al., 2007).

In order to fully understand the relationship between the brain and behavior, converging data from a variety of sources, such as cognitive science, basic neuroscience, neuropsychology, and neuroimaging, are needed. First, however, a basic understanding of the brain and its functions is required. Consequently, what follows is a description of various brain structures and functions, focusing in particular on those brain regions that have been implicated in the etiology of violent behavior.

2.2 The Nervous System

The nervous system is traditionally divided into central and peripheral components. The central nervous system (CNS) comprises the brain and spinal cord (see Figure 2.1), while the peripheral nervous system includes peripheral ganglia, or clusters of nerve cells, sensory neurons, and motor neurons, which reciprocally connect the CNS to sensory receptors and effector systems, such as receptors that cause muscle contraction and glands that cause the release of hormones. Together these two systems control most every part of a human being's daily life, from breathing to thinking to cognition. Sensory nerves gather information from the environment and send most of that information to the spinal cord, which then sends the message to the brain. The brain then interprets that message and fires off a response, following which the effector neurons deliver the instructions from the brain to the rest of the body (Nolte, 2009).

The cells of the nervous system can be divided into two broad categories: (a) nerve cells or neurons (see Figure 2.2) and (b) a variety of supporting cells, which consist mostly of neuroglial cells, referred to simply as glial cells or glia. These supporting nerve cells are located between and around neurons to insulate, protect, and nourish them. Neurons are highly specialized to transmit messages from one part of the body to another. The structure of neurons, in many respects, resembles that of most other cells in the body. As shown in Figure 2.2, a typical neuron has a cell body, often called the soma, and specialized extensions for intercellular communication and signaling, known as dendrites and axon (Nolte, 2009). Dendritic branches or processes are specialized for receiving information from other cells, while the axon is designed for sending information to other cells. The basic purpose of neurons is to integrate information from other neurons and the number of inputs received by each neuron in the human nervous system can range from 1 to approximately 100,000. Some neurons transmit

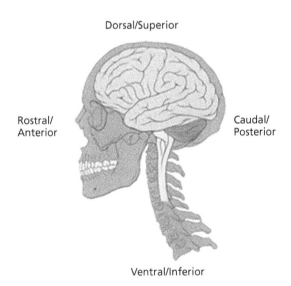

Figure 2.1 The Human Skull and Brain

Image courtesy of Wikimedia Commons, available at http://en.wikipedia.org/wiki/File:Skull_and_brain_normal_human.svg#file).

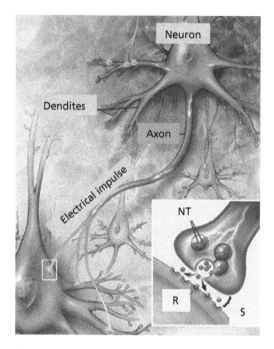

Figure 2.2 The Neuron and Synapse

Figure modified from http://en.wikipedia.org/wiki/Neuron and http://www.nia.nih.gov/Policies. htm.

messages locally, while others, such as the motor neurons in the spinal cord that control movement in the toes, may carry signals several feet away from the cell body.

There are a number of different types of glia in the brain. Broad categories include oligodendrocytes, microglia, and astrocytes, each of which is needed to optimize brain functions (Nolte, 2009).

- Oligodendrocytes are specialized cells that form the myelin sheaths around axons. The job of these cells is to speed up the electrical signal (action potential) that travels down an axon.
- Microglia are special immune cells that can detect damaged or unhealthy neurons and play an important role in neuroinflammation.
- Astrocytes are star-shaped glia that hold neurons in place, get nutrients to them, digest parts of dead neurons, communicate with neurons, and modify the signals they send or receive. Astrocytes generate signals that are chemical rather than electrical and release, typically by exocytosis, gliotransmitters. These small molecules travel to neighboring cells and deliver their message in a process very similar to that used by neurotransmitters.

2.3 The Human Brain

The living brain is soft and has a consistency similar to gelatin. Current esti-mates suggest that the adult human brain consists of about 10,000 different types of neurons and a total of 100 billion neurons and weighs on average 3 lbs (1.5 kg) with a volume of approximately 1,130 cubic centimeters (cm^3) in women and 1,260 cm^3 in men. Although men's brains are on average 100 g heavier than women's brains, this increased brain mass does not correlate with IQ or any other measures of cognitive functioning (Gur et al., 1999).

The cerebral cortex is nearly symmetrical, with left and right hemi-spheres that are approximate mirror images of each other. In most individu-als, the left hemisphere mediates language while the right hemisphere has no intrinsic capacity for language per se. The right hemisphere contributes to the emotional content of language but is thought to mediate synthetic functions, such as spatial relationships, forming whole concepts from many parts, and the like. Language processing is a "higher" brain function that takes place in the neocortex. In contrast, emotions and instincts are "lower" brain functions, which are mediated by evolutionarily older parts of the brain. However, recent research has suggested that both hemispheres can be involved in functions we thought were very lateralized, depending on the modality and how the information is processed (see, e.g., Ethofer et al., 2009; Martin, 1999). Indeed, neither hemisphere has total control over the func-tions associated with it. Brain function lateralization is particularly evident in the phenomena of right- or left-handedness, but a person's preferred hand is not a clear indication of the location of brain function.

2.3.1 Regions of the Brain

The human brain is subdivided into three main regions: forebrain, midbrain, and hind brain. Collectively, the midbrain and the hindbrain are called the brain stem. The hindbrain has three principal subdivisions: the medulla oblongata, the cerebellum, and the pons. The hindbrain tends to pass infor-mation to and receives controlling signals from the midbrain, which is itself controlled by the forebrain. The midbrain receives and processes sensory information and distributes it to different parts of forebrain for further pro-cessing. The forebrain then integrates sensory information of various kinds and formulates response, such as motor commands, that are executed by other parts of the CNS (Bear, Connors, & Paradiso, 2006).

The forebrain is subdivided into diencephalon (thalamus and hypothal-amus) and telencephalon (the cerebrum and basal ganglia). The thalamus is a sensory relay station that distributes sensory information to appropriate regions in the cerebral cortex, while the hypothalamus participates in the maintenance of homeostasis. The cerebral cortex is the largest part of the brain and is the area that is responsible for all our thinking activities. Indeed, the cerebral cortex is involved in complex processing of sensory information to form perceptions, in the planning and initiation of movements, and in associative learning and higher cognition. It is divided into two connected halves, the left and right cerebral hemispheres (Baer et al., 2006).

The left hemisphere controls the right side of the body, and the right hemisphere controls the left. More specifically, in most people, the left hemisphere primarily controls verbal functions such as speech and language while the right hemisphere primarily controls visual spatial (nonverbal) functions, such as those involved in drawing or finding one's way in unfamiliar surroundings. These two hemispheres are known to process material in different ways with the left cerebral hemisphere specializing in processing material in a sequential and logical way while the right cerebral hemisphere processes information in an intuitive and holistic manner (Baer et al., 2006). Furthermore, each cerebral hemisphere is divided into four lobes by sulci and gyri[1] (see Figure 2.3).

Most of the human cerebral cortex is made up of six layers and is referred to as neocortex. The term "gray matter" refers to the neurons in the brain, whether cerebral, cerebellar, or hippocampal, and is mainly made up of neuronal cell bodies and glia. "White matter" refers to the large part of subcortical tissue consisting mostly of axons that enter and leave the cortex (Nolte, 2009) (see Figure 2.3).

Among the internal structures, the basal ganglia play a major role in the organization and guidance of complex motor functions. The basal ganglia include the striatum (the caudate and the putamen) and the globus pallidus. Another important nucleus is the amygdala, which plays a role in emotional behavior. The different parts of the cerebral hemispheres are interconnected by large bundles of axons, the most prominent of which are the corpus callosum, the anterior commissure, and the fornix (Nolte, 2009). The ventricular system in the CNS is a series of interconnected, fluid-filled spaces in the core

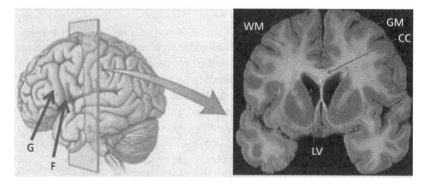

Figure 2.3 Cerebrum on the left shows valleys called sulci or fissures (F) that lie between the raised folds or ridges called gyri (G). A coronal slice on the right shows, gray matter (GM), white matter (WM), and lateral ventricle (LV).

of the forebrain and brain stem. The cerebrospinal fluid permeates through the ventricular system into the subarachnoid space. The primary function of the cerebrospinal fluid is to cushion the brain within the skull and serve as a shock absorber for the CNS; however, it also circulates chemicals and nutrients filtered from the blood and removes waste products from the brain (Baer et al., 2006).

2.3.2 The Lobes of the Brain and Their Functions

The brain lobes were originally a purely anatomical classification but have been shown to be related to different brain functions. Traditionally, each cerebral hemisphere was conventionally divided into four lobes; however, the Terminologia Anatomica (1998) divides the cerebrum into the frontal, parietal, temporal, and occipital lobes,[2] the limbic system, and the insular cortex (Ribas, 2010; see Figure 2.4). Although somewhat simplistic, useful models attribute characteristic cognitive functions to each of the lobes (see Table 2.1).[3]

2.3.2.1 The Frontal Lobes

The frontal lobes are located at the front of each cerebral hemisphere and contain most of the dopamine-sensitive neurons in the cerebral cortex, which are associated with reward, attention, short-term memory tasks, planning, and motivation (see Figure 2.4). In human beings, the frontal lobes

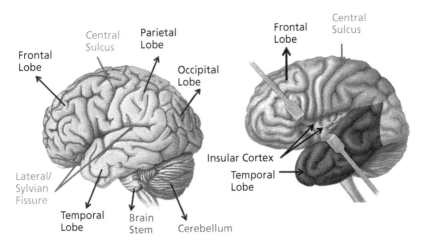

Figure 2.4 The Major Lobes of the Cerebrum and Insular Cortex. Frontal, parietal, temporal, and occipital lobes (left) and insular cortex, which is located behind the temporal lobes (right).

Table 2.1 Brain Areas and Their Specific Functions

Brain Lobes	Functions	Effects of Dysfunction
Frontal	Conscious thought, planning, organizing, problem solving, decision making, impulse control, memory, selective attention, and controlling emotions and behavior	Emotions, impulse control, language, executive functions, mood, memory, social, and sexual behaviour
Temporal	Recognition, processing, understanding, and production of sound, various aspects of memory, face recognition	Hearing, language, sensory problems, such as inability to recognize familiar faces
Occipital	Receiving and processing visual information, perceiving shapes and colors	Visual field (e.g., distorted perceptions of size, color, and shape)
Parietal	Integration of sensory information from different senses and parts of the body	Inability to recognize and locate parts of the body
Limbic system	Emotion, memory, long-term memory, motivation, and olfaction	Disturbances in emotion, such as increased anxiety
Insular cortex	Pain and other senses	

attain maturity at approximately age 25. The frontal lobes are made up of the anterior portion (prefrontal cortex) and the posterior portion and are divided from the parietal lobe by the central sulcus. The anterior portion is responsible for higher cognitive functions (e.g., executive functions) while the posterior portion consists of the premotor and motor areas, which govern voluntary movements. Functions of the frontal lobes include reasoning, planning, organization, judgment, attention/concentration, mental flexibility, initiation, inhibition, self-monitoring, problem solving, expressive language, and motor skills (movement). The frontal lobes are vulnerable to traumatic injury due to their location, and damage to these lobes can lead to changes in sexual habits, socialization, attention, and increased risk-taking (Squire et al., 2012).

The frontal lobes executive functions are responsible for the ability to (a) recognize future consequences, resulting from current actions; (b) choose between good and bad actions (or better and best); (c) override and suppress socially unacceptable responses; and (d) determine similarities and differences between things or events. The frontal lobes also play an important part in retaining long-term memories that are not task based. These are often memories associated with emotions derived from input from the brain's limbic system. The frontal lobes modify those emotions to generally fit socially acceptable norms (Nolte, 2009).

2.3.2.2 The Parietal Lobes

These lobes are located in the middle section of the brain, behind the central sulcus above the occipital lobes, and are associated with processing tactile sensory information, such as pressure, touch, and pain (see Figure 2.4). The somatosensory cortex, which is located in the parietal lobes, is essential for the processing of the body's senses and the integration of sensory information from various parts of the body. Functions of the parietal lobes include information processing, spatial orientation, reading, and voluntary motion. Damage to the parietal lobes can result in problems with verbal memory and language and can impair the ability to control eye movement. Damage to the left parietal lobe can cause Gerstmann's syndrome, aphasia (language disorder), and agnosia (abnormal perception of objects), while damage to the right parietal lobe can result in impaired personal care skills and impaired drawing ability. Bilateral parietal lobe damage causes Balint's syndrome, which is characterized by impaired visual attention and motor activities (Nolte, 2009).

2.3.2.3 The Temporal Lobes

The temporal lobes are situated on either sides of the brain, just above the ears and contain the primary auditory cortex, which is responsible for all auditory processing, as well as the hippocampus, which is responsible for the formation of long-term memory and sorting new information (see Figure 2.5). Functions of both the left and right temporal lobes include distinguishing and discrimination smells and sounds and controlling visual memory (right lobe) and verbal memory (left lobe). Damage to the temporal lobes can lead to problems with memory, speech perception, hearing, and language skills (receptive language, i.e., understanding language). Left temporal lobe damage leads to decreased ability to recall audio and visual content, difficulty in recognizing words, and remembering verbal material. Right temporal lobe damage may result in a number of difficulties, such as problems with recognizing visual content and tonal sequences and recalling previously encountered music (Baer et al., 2006).

2.3.2.4 The Occipital Lobes

Located in the rearmost portion of the skull, the occipital lobes are part of the forebrain (see Figure 2.4). These lobes are the visual processing center of the brain and contain most of the anatomical region of the visual cortex. Functions of the occipital lobe include visual reception, visual-spatial processing, and color and motion recognition. Damage to these lobes can cause visual problems, such as difficulty recognizing objects and with depth and color perception, and can lead to an inability to recognize words or associate meaning to visual input (Nolte, 2009).

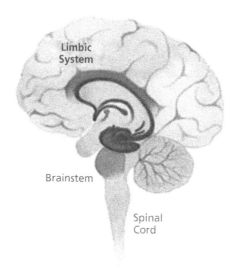

Figure 2.5 The Limbic System

Image courtesy of Wikimedia Commons, available at http://en.wikipedia.org/wiki/File:Brain_limbicsystem.jpg

2.3.2.5 The Limbic System

The limbic system comprises a set of evolutionarily primitive brain structures located on top of the brain stem and buried under the cortex (see Figure 2.5). The main components of the limbic system, often referred to as the "emotional brain," include the thalamus, hypothalamus, amygdala, and hippocampus. Limbic system structures are involved in many of our emotions and motivations, particularly those that are related to survival, and play an important role in controlling behavior, such as affection, fear, and anger. The limbic system is also involved in feelings of pleasure that are related to our survival, such as those experienced from eating (Nolte, 2009).

2.3.2.5.1 The Hypothalamus

About the size of a pearl, the hypothalamus directs a number of important functions in the body (see Figure 2.5). More specifically, it is responsible for certain metabolic processes and other activities of the autonomic nervous system, and it synthesizes and secretes neuro-hormones, which in turn inhibit or stimulate the secretion of pituitary hormones. These functions participate in the control of body temperature, hunger, aspects of parenting and attachment behaviors, thirst, fatigue, sleep, and circadian cycles. In addition, connections with structures of the nervous and endocrine systems enable the hypothalamus to play a vital role in maintaining homeostasis[4] (Baer et al., 2006).

2.3.2.5.2 The Amygdala

The amygdala plays a key role in the processing of emotions and is linked to both fear responses and pleasure (see Figure 2.5). The amygdala has also been shown to play an important role in mental states and has been related to many psychological disorders. For example, the amygdala has been linked to obsessive-compulsive disorder, posttraumatic stress disorder, borderline personality disorder, and bipolar disorder (Donegan et al., 2003; Rauch et al., 2000). More specifically, subjects with borderline personality disorder showed significantly greater left amygdala activity than normal control subjects (Donegan et al., 2003), while adult and adolescent bipolar patients were found to have considerably smaller amygdala volumes and somewhat smaller hippocampal volumes (Blumberg et al., 2003). In addition, individuals with psychopathy have been found to have reduced autonomic responses, relative to control subjects, to instructed fear cues (Blair, 2008). Further, research studies have suggested that this part of the brain plays an important role in the display and modulation of aggression (Davidson, Putnam, & Larson, 2000).

2.3.2.5.3 The Cingulate Cortex

The cingulate cortex is usually considered to be a part of the limbic system. The cingulate gyrus is superior to the corpus callosum, located between the cingulate sulcus and the sulcus of the corpus callosum (see Figure 2.5). The cingulate cortex is believed to be involved in consciousness and plays a role in various functions linked to the regulation of the body's homeostasis and emotions. These functions include perception, motor control, self-awareness, cognitive functioning, and interpersonal experience, and, in relation to these, it is involved in psychopathology (Nolte, 2009). Research studies have also indicated that the cingulate cortex plays a role in (a) anxiety disorders (Paulus & Stein, 2006), (b) emotion dysregulation (Thayer & Lane, 2000), and (c) behaviors, ranging from error prediction to pain perception and from political persuasion to one's feeling of optimism (Gage, Parikh, & Marzullo, 2008). Further, this network is presumed to play a pivotal role in executive functioning.

2.3.2.5.4 The Insular Cortex

The insular cortex, or insula, is part of the cerebral cortex folded deep within the lateral sulcus separating the temporal lobe from the parietal and frontal lobes (see, Figure 2.3). The insular cortex is integral to the experience of emotions, the processing of tastes, the memory of procedures, the control of motor responses, and interpersonal behavior (Nolte, 2009). Research studies have also suggested that this cortex is intimately involved in decision making, especially when the outcomes are uncertain (e.g., Preuschoff, Quartz, & Bossaerts, 2008). Further, neuroimaging studies have shown that when individuals anticipate the possibility of potential adversities, the insular cortex becomes especially activated (Smith et al., 2009). In fact, anticipation of negative stimuli has been regarded as one of the key functions of the insular cortex (Seymour, Singer, & Dolan, 2007). Activation of the insula has also been correlated with risk aversion (Kuhnen & Knutzon, 2005; Paulus, Rogalsky, Simmons, Feinstein, & Stein, 2003). More specifically, individuals with lesions in the insular cortex were found to prefer more risky options on gambling tasks, that is, options in which the outcomes are less certain (Clark et al., 2008).

2.3.3 Neuronal Signaling

The purpose of the nervous system is to transfer information from the internal and external environment to the peripheral nervous system to the CNS, process the information in the CNS, and send the information on how to respond back to the effector organs of the body. This transfer of information from the environment through neurons and back to the external environment is known as neuronal signaling. Neurons have unique capabilities for communicating within the cell (intracellular signaling) and communicating between cells (intercellular signaling). More specifically, the neuronal surface membrane contains an abundance of proteins, known as ion channels, which allow small charged atoms to pass through from one side of the membrane to the other. This mechanism is how the cell body of a neuron communicates with its own terminals via the axon, while communication between neurons is achieved at synapses by the process of neurotransmission (Squire et al., 2012).

2.3.4 Synaptic Transmission

The point at which a signal or activity is transmitted from one nerve cell to another or, for example, from a motor neuron to a muscle cell, is called a synapse. Synapses are classified into two general groups: electrical synapses and chemical synapses. In both types, the input cell, called the presynaptic cell, comes nearly into contact with the output cell, called the postsynaptic cell. More specifically, at the electrical synapse, two neurons are physically connected to one another through gap junctions,[5] which contain precisely aligned paired channels in the membrane of each neuron (Nolte, 2009). The pores of the channels connect to one another allowing the exchange of ions and small molecules, such as adenosine triphosphate (ATP) and second messengers, while the gap junction permits the current to flow from the presynaptic neuron and initiates or inhibits the generation of a postsynaptic membrane potential. The separation between the presynaptic and postsynaptic neurons is called the synaptic cleft, and transmission between the two neurons is based on special molecules called neurotransmitters (Nolte, 2009). The sequence of events involved in the chemical neurotransmission at a synapse are as follows:

- In the presynaptic neuron, the neurotransmitter molecules are synthesized and stored in vesicles.
- An electrical impulse, or action potential, reaching the presynaptic neuron terminal triggers a series of events that causes neurotransmitter molecules to be released into the synaptic cleft.
- Neurotransmitters binds to specific receptors on the membrane of postsynaptic neuron leading to (a) a change in ionic permeability of postsynaptic neuron or (b) an intracellular release or production of a second messenger, which in turn interacts directly or indirectly with an ion channel, causing it to open or close. The postsynaptic currents generated by the change in permeability of ions changes the membrane potential.
- Postsynaptic conductance changes and the potential changes that accompany them change the probability that an action potential will be produced in the postsynaptic cell (Squire et al., 2012).

Postsynaptic potentials are called excitatory if they increase the likelihood of a postsynaptic action potential occurring and inhibitory if they decrease this likelihood (Purves et al., 2001).

2.4 Neurotransmitters and Neuroreceptors

Neurotransmitters are chemical signaling molecules that are released into the synaptic cleft from the presynaptic nerve terminal and then bind to specific receptors on the postsynaptic nerve terminal. A neurotransmitter fits into this receptor region in much the same way as a key fits into a lock. When the transmitter is in place this alters the neuron's outer membrane potential (or excitability) by opening or closing the ion channels and triggers a change, such as the contraction of a muscle or increased activity of an enzyme in the cell (Nolte, 2009).

In general, neurotransmitters can be classified into two broad categories: small molecule neurotransmitters and neuropeptides. The small molecule neurotransmitters include acetylcholine, the amino acids (glutamate, aspartate, gamma-aminobutyric acid (GABA), glycine) and the biogenic amines (dopamine, norepinephrine, epinephrine, serotonin, histamine). Glutamate receptors are synaptic receptors located primarily on the membranes of neuronal cells and astrocytes. Glutamate is especially prominent in the human brain where it is the body's most abundant neurotransmitter, the brain's main excitatory neurotransmitter, and the precursor for GABA, one of the brain's main inhibitory neurotransmitters (Petroff, 2002).

Neuroreceptors are protein molecules embedded in the plasma membrane of the pre- and postsynaptic neuron. Each receptor has a distinctly shaped part that selectively recognizes a particular chemical messenger. The two main families of receptors involved in neurotransmitter–receptor interaction are (a) the ligand-gated ion channels, which combine the receptor site and ion channel into one molecular entity and give rise to rapid postsynaptic changes in the membrane potential, and (b) metabotropic receptors, which regulate the activity of ion channels indirectly via G-proteins and induce slower, long-lasting electrical response. For each neurotransmitter, there may be more than one structurally and pharmacologically distinct receptor subtype that could be expressed on the membrane of a pre- or postsynaptic neuron depending on its exact location in the specific area of brain (Squire et al., 2012). For example, dopamine has five receptor subtypes, while serotonin or

Table 2.2 Neuroreceptors, Neurotransmitters, and Their Role in Brain Function

Neuroreceptor	Neurotransmitter	Role
Adrenergic	Adrenaline and noradrenaline	Stimulate the sympathetic nervous system, responsible for fight-or-flight responses
Dopaminergic	Dopamine	Inhibit the transmission of nerve impulses in the substantia nigra, basal ganglia, and corpus striatum. Abnormal receptor signaling and dopaminergic nerve function is implicated in several neuropsychiatric disorders
Serotonergic	Serotonin or 5-Hydroxytryptamine (5-HT)	Influence biological and neurological processes, such as aggression, anxiety, cognition, learning, and memory
Cholinergic	Acetylcholine	Transmit nerve impulses that contract or dilate muscles and increase stomach peristalsis, urinary tract contractions, and voluntary voiding pressure on the bladder
GABAergic	GABA	Chief inhibitory neurotransmitter in the CNS; plays a role in regulating neuronal excitability throughout the nervous system
Glutaminergic	Glutamate (glutamic acid)	Responsible for postsynaptic excitation of neural cells and important for neural communication, memory formation, learning, and regulation
Opioid receptors	Natural opioids such as endorphins	Endorphins reduce the sensation of pain and affect emotions. Opioid receptors are implicated in analgesia, convulsant, anticonvulsant, sedation, and antidepressant effects.

Note: CNS = central nervous system; GABA = gamma-aminobutyric acid.

YBP Library Services

VALLABHAJOSULA, BRIGITTE.

MURDER IN THE COURTROOM: THE COGNITIVE
NEUROSCIENCE OF VIOLENCE.
                 Paper   330 P.
NEW YORK: OXFORD UNIVERSITY PRESS, 2015
SER: AMERICAN PSYCHOLOGY-LAW SOCIETY SERIES.

DISCUSSES CHALLENGES COURTS FACE IN DETERMINING
RELIABILITY OF NEUROSCIENTIFIC EVIDENCE.
LCCN 2014024193
  ISBN 0199995729   **Library PO#** SLIP ORDERS

	List	75.00 USD
6207 UNIV OF TEXAS/SAN ANTONIO	**Disc**	17.0%
App. Date 5/06/15 CRJ.APR 6108-09	**Net**	62.25 USD

SUBJ: 1. VIOLENCE--PSYCH. ASPECTS. 2.
NEUROPSYCHOLOGY.

CLASS RC569.5   DEWEY# 616.8582   LEVEL ADV-AC

YBP Library Services

VALLABHAJOSULA, BRIGITTE.

MURDER IN THE COURTROOM: THE COGNITIVE
NEUROSCIENCE OF VIOLENCE.
                 Paper   330 P.
NEW YORK: OXFORD UNIVERSITY PRESS, 2015
SER: AMERICAN PSYCHOLOGY-LAW SOCIETY SERIES.

DISCUSSES CHALLENGES COURTS FACE IN DETERMINING
RELIABILITY OF NEUROSCIENTIFIC EVIDENCE.
LCCN 2014024193
  ISBN 0199995729   **Library PO#** SLIP ORDERS

	List	75.00 USD
6207 UNIV OF TEXAS/SAN ANTONIO	**Disc**	17.0%
App. Date 5/06/15 CRJ.APR 6108-09	**Net**	62.25 USD

SUBJ: 1. VIOLENCE--PSYCH. ASPECTS. 2.
NEUROPSYCHOLOGY.

CLASS RC569.5   DEWEY# 616.8582   LEVEL ADV-AC

5-hydroxytryptamine (5-HT) has at least fourteen receptor subtypes (Barnes & Sharp, 1999).

Increasing our knowledge about the neurotransmitters in the brain and the action of drugs on receptor molecules is one of the most important endeavors in neuroscience research. Armed with this information, scientists hope to find the circuits implicated in disorders, such as dementia of the Alzheimer's type, depression, schizophrenia, and drug addiction (see Table 2.2). Sorting out the various chemical circuits is vital to understanding how the brain functions under normal physiological conditions and in neuropsychiatric and neurologic diseases.

2.5 Human Brain Pathology

Although the human brain is protected by the skull and meninges, surrounded by cerebrospinal fluid, and isolated from the bloodstream by the blood–brain barrier,[6] the delicate nature of the brain makes it particularly vulnerable to diseases and injuries. Neurodegenerative diseases, including dementia of the Alzheimer's type, Parkinson's disease, and Huntington's disease, which are caused by the gradual death of individual neurons, can lead to decreased movement control and cognitive impairment (e.g., memory). For example, dementia of the Alzheimer's type is characterized by loss of synapses and neurons in the cerebral cortex and certain subcortical areas. This loss results in gross atrophy of the affected regions, including degeneration in the parietal and temporal lobes and parts of the frontal cortex and cingulate gyrus (Jagust, 2006; Wenk, 2003; see Figure 2.6).

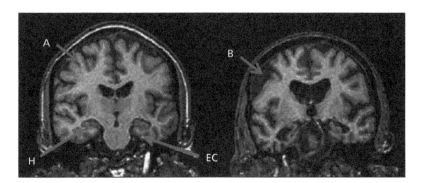

Figure 2.6 Coronal MRI Images of Normal Subject (A) and Patient with AD (B). Hippocampus (H) and entorhinal cortex (EC) are labeled on normal subject and show severe atrophy in the AD patient. The AD subject also shows significant cortical atrophy.

Reproduced with permission of Elsevier from Jagust, 2006. Positron emission tomography and magnetic resonance imaging in the diagnosis and prediction of dementia. *Alzheimer's & Dementia*, 2(1), 36–42.

The causes of mental disorders, such as clinical depression, schizophrenia, bipolar disorder, and posttraumatic stress disorder, are varied and in some cases unclear, and theories may incorporate findings from a range of fields, such as neuropsychology, molecular imaging, and neurochemistry. For example, individuals diagnosed with schizophrenia have been found to have changes in both brain structure and brain chemistry, including decreased dopamine levels (van Os & Kapur, 2009). Further, studies using neuropsychological tests and brain imaging technologies, such as fMRI and PET, to examine functional differences in brain activity, have shown that differences between schizophrenic and control subjects seem to most

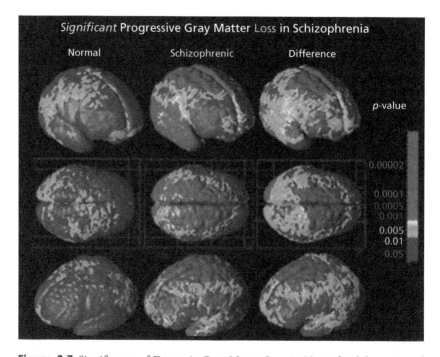

Figure 2.7 Significance of Dynamic Gray Matter Loss in Normal Adolescents and Schizophrenia. Highly significant progressive loss occurs in schizophrenia in the parietal, motor, supplementary motor, and superior frontal cortices. Broad regions of the temporal cortex, including the superior temporal gyrus, experience severe gray matter attrition. By comparison of the average rates of loss in disease (middle column) with the loss pattern in normal adolescents (first column), the normal variability in these changes can also be taken into account, and the significance of disease-specific change can be established (last column). See Color Plate 1 in insert.

Reproduced with permission from Thompson et al., 2001. Mapping adolescent brain change reveals dynamic wave of accelerated gray matter loss in very early-onset schizophrenia. *Proceedings of the National Academy of Science*, 98(20), 11650–11655. Copyright (2001) National Academy of Sciences, U.S.A.

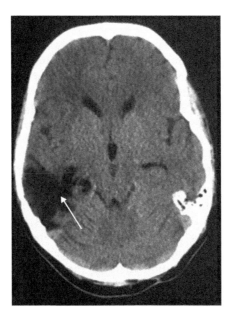

Figure 2.8 Brain CT Scan of Traumatic Brain Injury. Years after a traumatic brain injury the scan shows an empty space where the damage occurred.

Image courtesy of Wikimedia Commons, http://en.wikipedia.org/wiki/File: Traumaticbrain injury2010.jpg

commonly occur in the frontal lobes, the hippocampus and temporal lobes (Thompson et.al., 2001; Goghari, Macdonald, & Sponheim, 2014; Guo et al., 2014; Honea, Crow, Passingham, & Mackay, 2005; Kircher & Thienel, 2006; see also Figure 2.7).

Injuries to the brain can also vary but, in general, when symptomatic tend to affect large areas of the organ (temporal and frontal lobes are particularly vulnerable), sometimes causing major deficits in intelligence, memory, and personality.[7] Indeed, traumatic brain injuries often result in persistent disability, due particularly to cognitive impairments (Mendez, Hurley, Lassonde, Zhang, & Taber, 2005, Whitnall, McMillan, Murray, & Teasdale, 2006) with the cognitive domains of executive functioning, processing speed, and memory being most frequently affected (Draper & Ponsford, 2008; Spitz, Maller, O'Sullivan, & Ponsford, 2013; see Figure 2.8). Further, a cerebrovascular accident, such as a stroke, caused by the blockage or rupturing of blood vessels in the brain, can cause permanent neurological damage and even death. Although strokes can strike any region of the brain, studies have indicated that many patients reported cognitive complaints following a stroke (Lamb, Anderson, Saling, & Dewey, 2013) and attentional and executive impairments in particular have frequently been found in stroke patients (Stephens et al., 2004).

2.6 Conclusion

In September 2013, the National Institutes of Health released a 58-page report on the future of neuroscience, the first significant step in developing President Obama's BRAIN Initiative, which attempts to revolutionize our understanding of the human brain and uncover new ways to prevent, treat, and cure disorders, such as schizophrenia and traumatic brain injury. More specifically, the report outlines nine goals for the initiative, including linking human behavior with the activity of neurons.

While the universe is full of complex systems, one of the most intricate known is the human brain, which Isaac Asimov (1970) once described as "the most complex and orderly organization of matter in the universe" (p. 10). Deciphering the neural code is the ultimate goal of many scientists; however, despite many technological advances in brain research over the past few decades, neuroscientists have yet to master the syntax that converts action potentials into, for example, emotions and behaviors (Horgan, 2004). The problem is that the brain is more than just the sum of its parts; the brain's components do not operate in isolation from one another.

Although techniques for assessing brain functions are developing rapidly and clearly help to advance our understanding of the relationship between brain function and behavior, prudence and restraint in their applications is, nevertheless, advisable. We still do not know exactly how the various systems of the brain interact or what particular brain dysfunction may result in future psychopathology. Indeed, while researchers have been able to describe mental processes that relate, for example, neural circuits to the behavior of an individual, the mappings from brain activity to mental process and from mental process to behavior still remain complex and not well understood (The Royal Society, 2011).

The growing body of literature on the relationship between brain functioning and behavior over the past few decades has not only dramatically increased our understanding of how cognitive functions affect behavior but has also had a profound influence on the law. Indeed, in a dramatic expression of faith in neuroscience technology, the British Home Secretary stated in 2007 that convicted pedophiles would be required to undergo brain MRI scans to aid in assessing the likelihood of reoffending (Looney, 2010). Clearly, neuroscientific advances have implications for the legal system where they raise issues for the law, from matters relating to the admissibility of scientific evidence to decisions about criminal culpability, competency, and future dangerousness. However, as noted by many scholars, brain scan images are not what they appear to be. As discussed in chapter 8, there are, in fact, many inherent limitations and problems associated with neuroscience-based evidence, including questions of causation. Resolution of the issues and problems associated with the forensic use of brain imaging techniques in particular require and interdisciplinary collaboration. More specifically, resolution requires knowledge not only from the fields of forensic mental health, neuroscience, and the law but also from the fields of radiology, biology, molecular chemistry, physics, and neuropsychology.

3

The Basics of Neuroimaging

A science of the mind must reduce complexities (of behavior) to their elements. A science of the brain must point out the functions of its elements. A science of the relations of the mind and brain must show how the elementary ingredients of the former correspond to the elementary functions of the latter.

(Williams James, 1890)

3.1 Introduction

For centuries, criminologists and philosophers have speculated about the possible biological causes of violence. For example, in 360 BC, Plato wrote: "For no man is voluntarily bad; but the bad becomes bad by reason of an ill disposition of the body . . . [which] happens to him against his will" (Kirchmeier, 2004, p. 631). Although aggressive and violent behavior is seldom due to a single sociological, biological, or psychological cause, we are closer than ever before in identifying the biological basis of violent behavior. Indeed, many neuroscientists now refer to crime as a disease, or psychopathology, and a biological brain-proneness toward violence is now widely accepted by some neuroscientists (Kirchmeier, 2004; Raine, 1993).

That neuroimaging can be used to assess an individual's criminal responsibility or culpability is no longer a novel idea, even if it remains controversial. As has been noted, functional magnetic resonance imaging (fMRI) can display the structure and function of the brain regions that regulate our capacity for impulse control. Furthermore, "significantly reduced metabolic activity in . . . this part of the brain, could excuse [a person] from [a] charge of responsibility [o]n the basis . . . that she lacked [a relevant] capacity" (Glannon, 2005, pp. 68, 75). To date, numerous neuroimaging and neuropsychological studies have suggested that the prevalence rates of brain dysfunction and mental disorders among criminal populations and individuals within the criminal justice system are extremely high. It is, therefore, not surprising that the number of defendants seeking to admit evidence of brain dysfunction or mental illness, especially in the form of neuroimaging scans, has steadily increased as this technology has become more widely available.

The important role neuroimaging evidence can play in criminal cases was clearly illustrated in *Roper v. Simmons* (2005). In *Roper*, the US Supreme Court entertained a challenge, under the Eighth Amendment's injunction against cruel and unusual punishment, to a state law permitting the execution of juveniles who were under the age of 18 at the time they committed a capital offense. Among the numerous amicus briefs submitted, the arguments by the American Psychological Association and the American Medical Association were cited in the final ruling. Both briefs made novel use of neuroimaging-based evidence to argue that adolescents are categorically less blameworthy than adults and, as a result, should not be sentenced to death. More specifically, these briefs cited structural and functional neuroimaging studies showing that the neocortical regions of the brain, which are believed to be responsible for risk assessment, impulse control, and high-level cognition, are not yet fully developed in adolescents (*Roper v. Simmons,* 2005).

The neurobiological theory of violence set forth by the *Roper* amici, with its focus on frontal lobe dysfunction, represents one of the major mitigation arguments used by neuroscientists in forensic settings. Indeed, those who represent criminal defendants often "are looking for that one pixel in their client's brain scan that shows . . . a malfunction in the normal inhibitory networks," which would allow them to claim a right to leniency arguing that their client could not control his or her actions (Thompson, 2006, p. 52). Other experts have argued that neither positron emission tomography (PET) nor single photon emission tomography (SPECT) scans have any scientifically supportable exculpatory role in determining or predicting an individual's responsibility for committing a crime and may, in fact, mislead a judge and jury (Mayberg, 1996; Reeves, Mills, Billick, & Brodie, 2003).

Although the extent to which neuroimaging findings can be used as mitigating evidence remains debatable, many defendants now present evidence of brain dysfunction based on such scans. However, while there are many exciting possibilities for how neuroscience and the law may collaborate, a number of major issues and limitations associated with neuroimaging evidence must be considered, including

- Neuroimages can only provide post hoc explanations (Raine, 1993).
- "No pixel in a brain will ever be able to show culpability or non-culpability" (Gazzaniga, 2005, p. 100).
- Neuroimages provide only one explanation of many for the expression of violent behavior, and even if brain abnormalities are found,

individual differences in the extent and location of the injury present major problems for the interpretation of brain images in the legal setting (Mobbs, Lau, Jones, & Frith, 2007).
• Correlations between violent behavior and brain function are, at best, imperfect, calling into question both the diagnostic and predictive accuracy of neuroimaging evidence.

3.2 The Basics of Neuroimaging

3.2.1 Biochemical and Molecular Basis

The scientific study of the relationships between brain function and behavior has steadily increased over the last few decades, in part due to the many scientific advances made in the fields of imaging instrumentation, molecular biology, and electrophysiology. However, while we now much better understand the complex processes that occur within a single neuron, exactly how networks of neurons produce violent behavior is still not as well understood. As Kandel and colleagues (2000) noted:

> The task of neural science is to explain behavior in terms of the activities of the brain. How does the brain marshal its millions of individual nerve cells to produce behavior, and how are these cells influenced by the environment? (p. 5)

The emergence of powerful new techniques, such as neuroimaging, allows researchers to address abstract questions, such as how human cognition is mapped to specific neural circuits and how dysfunctions in any one component of these circuits may affect cognition and behavior. As discussed in chapter 2, brain function is directly related to neural signaling and transmission of electrical activity via the chemical and electrical synapses. In addition, neuronal activity depends on the continuous supply of oxygen and glucose[1], which are provided by cerebral blood flow (CBF; Miller & Bell, 1987).[2] This dependency makes the human brain sensitive and vulnerable to CBF variations. Indeed, since the brain has no internal energy stores, all its metabolic needs must be met through the continuous flow of blood. Normally, CBF is tightly regulated to meet the brain's metabolic demands and must be maintained at a flow of approximately 50 milliliters of blood per 100 grams of brain tissue per minute in adult humans (Cipolla, 2009). In fact, a lack of blood supply for only a few seconds can lead to observable metabolic derangement, while a lack of blood supply for more than five minutes can lead to irreversible neuronal damage. Changes in the electrical activity of neurons, which can be excitatory or inhibitory, have been indirectly attributed to the alterations in regional cerebral blood flow (rCBF) or the regional cerebral metabolic rate of glucose (rCMRglc; Goldberg, 2001). In other words, changes in regional brain activity are accompanied by changes in glucose metabolism and, as a consequence of autoregulation, changes in rCBF (Malonek & Grinvald, 1996). This relationship between neuronal activity, glucose metabolism, and rCBF constitutes the basis for several PET and SPECT imaging techniques[3] (see Sokoloff, 2008). In addition, fMRI is based on the observation that changes in blood flow related to changes in neuronal function are accompanied by corresponding changes in oxyhemoglobin concentration in a particular area of the brain (Amaro & Barker, 2006).

3.2.2 Neuroimaging Techniques

The term "neuroimaging" includes the use of various technologies to either directly or indirectly image the structure or function of the brain and its response to normal and abnormal processes, which range from changes induced by ordinary experiences, such as smelling roses, to changes produced by extraordinary insults, such as gunshot wounds. Neuroimaging can be classified into two broad categories: (a) structural (anatomic) neuroimaging and (b) functional neuroimaging. These imaging techniques and some of their applications are listed in Table 3.1.

Structural neuroimaging attempts to noninvasively visualize gross pathology in the brain of the type that could be seen with the eye if the brain were removed from the head and sliced into thin sections. Structural imaging can be used for the diagnosis of gross (large-scale) intracranial diseases, such as stroke, tumors, and traumatic brain injury. The most common structural imaging techniques are X-ray computed tomography (CT) and magnetic resonance imaging (MRI). CT scanning generates images that represent the degree to which different types of brain tissue absorb and deflect X-ray beams (see Figure 3.1). In MRI, images are constructed from the electromagnetic signals that are emitted by the nucleus (proton) of hydrogen atoms, which are found predominantly in tissue water (Brenner & Hall, 2007; see Figure 3.2)

One of the specialized MRI scan sequences, known as diffusion tensor imaging (DTI), can be used to characterize and map the three-dimensional anisotropic diffusion of water molecules as a function of spatial location and to examine the connectivity of different regions in the brain (Alexander, Lee, Lazar, & Field, 2007; see Figure 3.3). More specifically, the fact that water diffusion is sensitive to the underlying tissue microstructure provides a unique method of assessing the integrity and orientation of neural fibers, such as whiter matter in the brain, which may be useful in assessing a number of neurological disorders (Beaulieu, 2002).

Functional neuroimaging techniques are primarily based on rCBF, rCMRglc, or neuroreceptor signaling. They are most commonly used to quantify neuroreceptor status, diagnose diseases that cause metabolic derangement, and study the neurobiology and cognitive psychology associated with various neurological and neuropsychiatric disorders, such as major depression and schizophrenia. Some of the most common neuroimaging techniques used to measure neuronal function are fMRI (see Figure 3.4),

Table 3.1 Imaging Techniques and Their Applications

Imaging Technique	Used To
Structural Imaging Techniques	Assess brain structure and diagnose gross (large-scale) intracranial disease, such as tumor and injury
CT	Assess tissue composition and brain morphology
MRI Gradient Echo or Spin Echo Echoplanar MRI Diffusion-weighted MRI Perfusion-weighted MRI DTI	Assess tissue composition and brain morphology
Functional Imaging Techniques	Image cerebral blood flow, metabolism, metabolite concentration, neuroreceptor function, and detect abnormal foci (lesions)
fMRI	Generate images of changing blood flow in the brain associated with neural activity
ASL	Generate images of changing blood flow in the brain associated with neural activity
MRS	Characterize brain tissue and determine the concentration of brain metabolites, such as N-acetyl aspartate, choline, and creatine
PET	Image normal and abnormal functional regional abnormalities (cerebral blood flow, metabolism, neuroreceptor) following administration of specific positron emitting radiotracers, or radiopharmaceuticals
SPECT	Image normal and abnormal functional regional abnormalities (cerebral blood flow and neuroreceptor) following administration of specific single photon emitting radiotracers or radiopharmaceuticals

Note. CT = computed tomography; MRI = magnetic resonance imaging; DTI = diffusion tensor imaging; fMRI = functional MRI; ASL = arterial spin labelling; MRS = magnetic resonance spectroscopy; PET = positron emission tomography; SPECT = single photon emission computed tomograph.

magnetic resonance spectroscopy (MRS; see Figure 3.5), and nuclear medicine techniques based on the administration of a radiotracer or a radiopharmaceutical for detection with PET (see Figure 3.6) or SPECT (see Figure 3.7).

MRI can identify the anatomical location of a tumor, while MRS can compare the chemical composition of normal brain tissue with abnormal tumor tissue without removing tissue samples or using radioactive or contrast agents. Further, PET and SPECT allow in vivo quantification

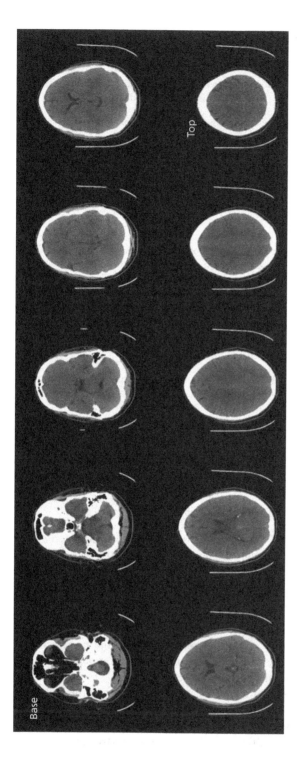

Figure 3.1 CT Scans of Normal Human Brain. Scans show normal anatomy at different levels from the base to the top of head. Images courtesy of Weill Medical College, Cornell University.

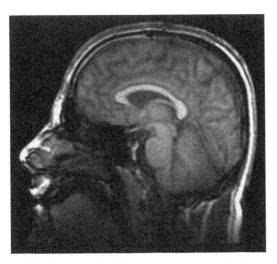

Figure 3.2 MRI Scan of Normal Human Brain (Sagittal Section).

Image courtesy of Wikimedia Commons (O. Stollmann), available at http://commons.wikimedia.org/wiki/File:Mri_brain_side_view.jpg.

of biochemical processes by measuring the concentration of radiotracers that reflect the activity of rCBF, rCMRglc, or neuroreceptor concentration (Phelps, 2000). PET, SPECT, and fMRI all can measure surrogates of rCBF; however, only PET is ideally suited to quantitatively assess neuronal function based on rCMRglc or neuroreceptor interaction (Herholz, Herscovitch, & Heiss, 2004).

Each neuroimaging technique is designed to convey distinctly different types of information. Whether structural or functional, brain imaging can involve a variety of methods, each of which is designed to detect and measure specific signals of some property related to the brain, with a detection device that is usually outside of the brain. These signals vary widely in parameters, including specificity, sensitivity,[4] temporal and spatial resolution,[5] and fidelity toward reflecting the physiological process being studied (Reeves et al., 2003). More specifically, as shown in Table 3.2, the spatial resolution can vary from 0.1 to 10 mm, while the temporal resolution can vary from a few seconds to several minutes or longer.

Regardless of the source, signals result in distinctive patterns that allow for comparisons among individuals. These signals can, as in the case of PET, SPECT, MRI, and fMRI, be fed into a computer that stores the data and uses the information to reconstruct an image of the brain. In order to enhance the visual impact, these images are often color-coded along a spectrum from blue and green to red and yellow to reflect the varying degrees of activity in specific regions of the brain (Brown & Eyler, 2006).

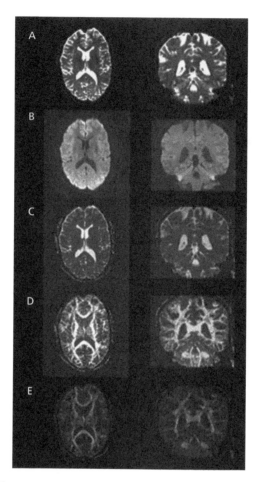

Figure 3.3 Diffusion Tensor Based Images. T2-weighted MRI (A), diffusion-weighted images (B), apparent diffusion coefficient maps (C), fractional anisotropy maps (D), and direction-coded fractional anisotropy maps (E) in axial (left column) and coronal (right column) views. In the direction-coded fractional anisotropy maps, red represents fibers crossing from left to right, green crossing in the posterior anterior direction, and blue crossing in the inferior–superior direction in a normal head coordinate system. See Color Plate 2 in insert.

Images courtesy of H. U. Voss and N. D. Schiff, Weill Medical College of Cornell University.

3.2.3 Displaying Neuroimages

All neuroimaging techniques generate a number of slices, or sections, of the brain based on tomography.[6] These representations are then used to identify the specific cortical and subcortical structures in the brain that may be associated with a disorder, disease, or dysfunction. Three directional planes exist in the brain: rostral/caudal, dorsal/ventral, and medial/lateral

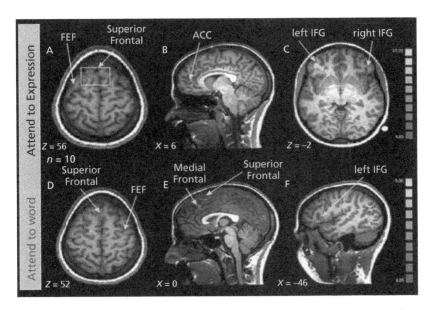

Figure 3.4 fMRI BOLD Activation in an Emotional Stroop Task. Activation from incongruent blocks compared with congruent blocks in the expression (A-C) and word instruction conditions (D-F). See Color Plate 3 in insert.

Courtesy of Wikimedia Commons, available at http://en.wikipedia.org/wiki/File:FMRI_BOLD_activation_in_an_emotional_Stroop_task.jpg

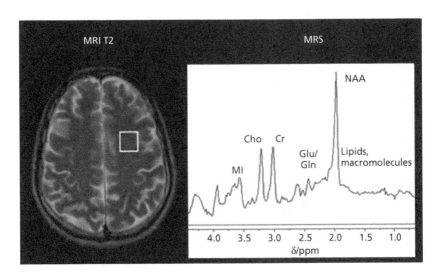

Figure 3.5 Magnetic Resonance Spectroscopy Scan of a Normal Human Brain at 3T.
The concentrations of various metabolites such as N-acetyl aspartate, choline, and creatine are measured in a given region of interest (box) in the MR1 T2 scan.

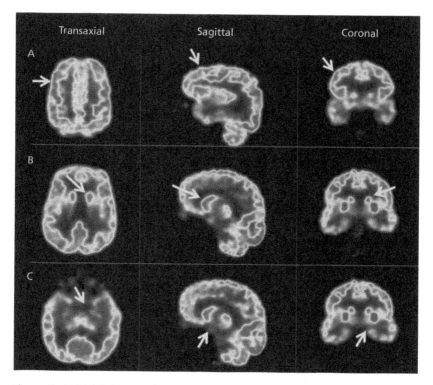

Figure 3.6 FDG-PET scan of Normal Human Brain. Scan shows the brain at the level of mid frontal gyrus (A), caudate head (B), and amygdala (C). See Color Plate 4 in insert.

Adapted from images available from the Whole Brain Atlas at http://www.med. harvard.edu/AANLiB/cases/.caseNA/pb9.htm.

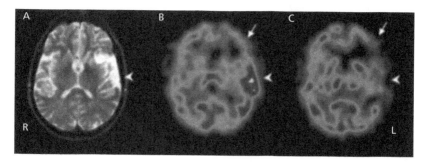

Figure 3.7 Comparison of Brain SPECT with MRI Scan. Left temporal lobe infarction (arrowhead) in MRI-T2 scan (A). 99mTc-HMPA SPECT obtained 1 week after stroke shows luxury perfusion (B) but hypoperfusion 1 month after stroke (C). Perfusion changes (arrow) also seen in frontal right lobe (B and C). See Color Plate 5 in insert.

Reprinted by permission of SNMMI from Catafau, A. M. (2001). Brain SPECT in clinical practice. Part I: Perfusion. *Journal of Nuclear Medicine, 42*(2), 259–271, Figure 5.

Table 3.2 Comparison of Neuroimaging Techniques

Imaging Modality	Form of Energy Used	Spatial Resolution (mm)	Temporal Resolution (msec/frame)
CT	X- rays	0.5–1.0	1,000–2,000
MRI	Radio frequency waves	0.2–1.0	5,000–10,000
fMRI	Radio frequency waves	2.0–4.0	500–3,000
PET	Annihilation photons	4.0–6.0	200–300
SPECT	γ-photons	6.0–10.0	10,000–15,000

Note: CT = computed tomography; MRI = magnetic resonance imaging; fMRI = functional magnetic resonance imaging; PET = positron emission tomography; SPECT = single photon emission computed tomography.

(Bergman & Afifi, 2005). When sectioning or cutting the brain, the planes that are visible depends on the type of section obtained (see Figure 3.8). A sagittal (median) plane is perpendicular to the ground and separates left from right. A transverse (axial) plane is parallel to the ground and separates the dorsal or front from the ventral or back planes. A coronal (frontal) plane is also perpendicular to the ground and separates the rostral from the caudal and the ventral from the dorsal planes (Bergman & Afifi, 2005). All modern imaging modalities can provide tomographic slices in all three planes.

3.3 The Specifics of Structural Neuroimaging

3.3.1 Computed Tomography

CT or X-ray computed axial tomography is an X-ray procedure that is generally used to define normal and abnormal structures in the brain. A CT scanner is a large, donut-shaped X-ray machine that takes X-ray images at many different angles around the body. These X-ray images are processed by a computer that produces cross-sectional pictures, or slices of the brain.[7] When all the slices

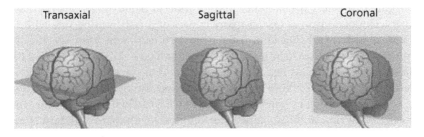

Figure 3.8 Illustration of Transaxial, Sagittal, and Coronal Planes

are added together, a three-dimensional picture of the body or brain can be obtained. This recorded image is called a tomogram (Brenner & Hall, 2007).

In the original CT scanners, the X-ray source and the detectors would rotate around an object. After a complete rotation, the object (patient) would be moved forward, and the next rotation would be started. In spiral or helical CT scanners,[8] the X-ray source and the detectors move continuously. Modern CT scanners have many detectors, with 64 being typical, although multiples are sold for special applications to high-end users. Modern scanners significantly shorten the examination time, substantially increase resolution, and often decrease radiation exposure when compared to earlier generations of machines (Bushberg, Seibert, Leidholdt, & Boone, 2002). Further, because the image acquisition takes place over a shorter period of time, the potential for distortions caused by movement as a patient breathes, which is inevitable during longer scans, is reduced. In addition, this technique's high level of sensitivity makes it a particularly useful tool in diagnosing small blood clots and cancerous tumors (Grossman & Yousem, 2003). CT scans can provide more detailed information about brain tissue and brain structures than standard X-rays of the head, thus providing more information related to injuries and/or diseases of the brain. However, CT struggles to distinguish gray matter from white matter and the boundaries of complex cortical structures, such as the hippocampus. Nevertheless, CT is useful for the assessment of brain tumors and other lesions, injuries, intracranial bleeding, and structural anomalies, such as hydrocephalus. CT scans can also be used to detect clots in the brain that may be responsible for strokes and can provide guidance for brain surgery or biopsies of brain tissue (Grossman & Yousem 2003).

In order to improve image contrast, CT contrast agents or dyes can be used to increase the conspicuity of specific areas so that the organs, blood vessels, or tissues are more clearly demarcated. The most common type of contrast materials used for brain CT contains iodine that is usually injected by means of an intravenous line. Increasing the visibility of all surfaces of the organ or tissue being studied helps the clinician to determine the presence and extent of a disease or injury (Grossman & Yousem, 2003). As shown in Figure 3.9, the blood vessels and tissues containing the dye appear as white on the CT scan similar to bone. A newer specialized CT technique called CT perfusion imaging can detect the presence and location of blood vessel obstructions. This technique involves taking many images at a fast framing rate while a contrast medium is being administered into a patient's vein. More specifically, contrast agents help to identify blood volume and flow in different parts of the brain, as well as the average time it takes blood to travel through the blood vessels. Perfusion CT allows rapid qualitative and semiquantitative evaluation of cerebral perfusion by generating maps of CBF, cerebral blood volume, and mean transit time and can be performed quickly with many standard spiral or multidetector CT scanners (Hoeffner et al., 2004). This is accomplished by scanning the patient several times every few seconds before, during, and after

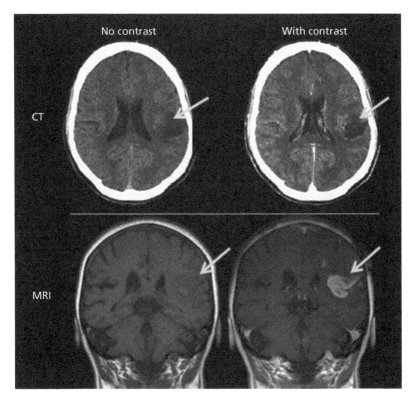

Figure 3.9 CT and MRI With and Without Contrast Enhancement. CT scan with and without contrast enhancement (top) shows glioma of the left parietal lobe. Defect of the blood–brain barrier after stroke shown in MRI (bottom). T1-weighted images (bottom), left image without contrast and right image with contrast medium administration.

Images courtesy of Wikimedia Commons.

the intravenous delivery of an iodine-containing contrast agent that absorbs the X-rays. Further, CT perfusion data can (a) positively identify patients with nonhaemorrhagic stroke in the presence of a normal conventional CT (Miles & Griffiths, 2003), (b) be used to assess patients with other cerebrovascular diseases, and (c) may be helpful in the diagnosis and assessment of treatment response in patients with various types of tumors (Hoeffner et al., 2004).

3.3.2 Magnetic Resonance Imaging

MRI is a medical imaging technique most commonly used to visualize body structure. Unlike CT, MRI provides detailed images of the body with much greater contrast between the different soft tissues, making it especially useful in brain imaging. MRI is based on a physical phenomenon called nuclear magnetic resonance, which was first described in 1931 by Isidor Rabi[9] and his colleagues. The nuclear magnetic resonance phenomenon is observed when a substance with nuclei containing an odd number of protons and neutrons is placed in a strong magnetic field and radiofrequency pulses are applied at the Larmor frequency[10] to rotate the nuclei away from the main magnetic field (Westbrook, 2011). As the precessing nuclei relax and realign with the main magnetic field, a changing magnetic field is produced, resulting in a detectable voltage in the coil (Edwards, 2009).

Variations in the relaxation times of hydrogen atoms in different brain structures and tissue types create the contrast differences that MRI uses to visualize and measure gross brain neuroanatomy (Rosenbloom, Sullivan, & Pfefferbaum, 2003). More specifically, MRI relies on signals derived from water molecules, which comprise between 70% and 80% of the average human brain. Each water molecule has two protons, which by virtue of their positive charge act as small magnets on a subatomic scale (Bushberg et al., 2002). Positioned within the large magnetic field of an MRI scanner, typically 30,000 to 60,000 times stronger than the magnetic field of the earth, these microscopic magnets collectively produce a tiny net magnetization that can be measured outside of the body and used to generate very high-resolution images that reveal information about water molecules in the brain and their local environment (Pooley, 2005).

During the procedure, the patient is placed on a moveable bed, which is inserted into the cylinder of the MRI scanner (see Figure 3.10). The scanner

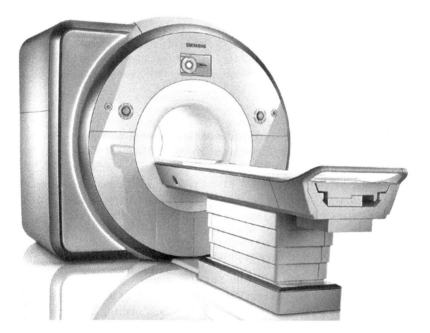

Figure 3.10 MRI Scanner (Siemens)

creates a very strong magnetic field, exposing hydrogen atoms in water molecules and other molecules in the body to radio waves, causing them to move away from the main magnetic field. As the hydrogen atoms precess and then move back into their original position, they produce a changing magnetic field, resulting in a detectable voltage in the radiofrequency coil that provides information about tissue in the area of the body that has been scanned. A computer processes information about how the molecules move and creates a detailed image of internal body structures. Different pulse timing parameters in the MRI sequence allow weighting of various tissues to have differing intensities based on their inherent relaxation properties. This relaxation emits energy that is detected by the scanner and is then mathematically converted into an image (Bushberg et al., 2002). The image and resolution produced by MRI is very detailed, and this technique can be used to detect small structural changes in the body. Further, while CT provides good spatial resolution, MRI provides comparable resolution with far better soft-tissue contrast.[11] More specifically, high-contrast resolution is important to facilitate a more precise visualization of structures and their pathology under investigation (Yoshioka & Burns, 2012).

MRI sequences can be designed to provide different image contrasts in order to highlight specific brain tissues of interest or a specific structural lesion (Pooley, 2005). An MRI sequence is an ordered combination of radiofrequency and gradient pulses designed to acquire the data to form the image. Several different types of sequences, such as T1-weighted[12] and T2-weighted[13] can be used to enhance tissues with short (lipids) or long relaxation times as well as those inbetween, such as gray and white matter (see Figure 3.2). In some cases, contrast agents (also called paramagnetic agents) are administered prior to scanning to increase the image contrast and accuracy of the images (see Figure 3.9). More precisely, contrast agents are chemical substances introduced to the anatomical or functional region being imaged to increase the differences between different types of tissue, with varying degrees of angiogenesis,[14] or between normal and abnormal tissue by altering the relaxation times.

Using MRI scientists can image both surface and deep brain structures with a high degree of anatomical detail and detect minute changes in these structures that may occur over time. For this reason, MRI is particularly useful in evaluating tumors, tissue damage, and blood flow in the brain. In fact, MRI is considered the most sophisticated type of imaging procedure to show brain structure. Further, while MRI cannot confirm a diagnosis of dementia of the Alzheimer's type (DAT), it can be used to detect some changes in the brain structure that are common in people with dementias. For example, MRI can be used to check for atrophy in key memory centers of the brain and can detect multi-infarcts, or small strokes that are common in people with vascular dementia (Grossman & Yousem, 2003). MRI has also been used to assess the brain structures of violent offenders and participants labeled as "psychopathic," and research studies have predominantly linked violent behavior and/or high psychopathy checklist scores to reduced gray matter volume in the prefrontal cortex and the temporolimbic structures (Barkataki, Kumari, Das, Taylor, & Sharma, 2006; de Oliveira-Souza et al., 2008; Müller et al., 2008). However, more recently it has been suggested that the changes in gray matter volume that have been reported to correlate with violent behavior and/or psychopathy may instead be related to lifelong substance use disorders (Schiffer et al., 2011).

3.3.3 Diffusion Tensor Imaging

DTI is a relatively new MRI technique that is used to assess water diffusion in biological tissues at a microstructural level. To be more precise, while conventional MRI shows the shape, size, and tissue composition (gray matter vs. white matter) of the brain and its basic parts, DTI shows the integrity of white-matter tracts that link regions of the brain to each other (Rosenbloom et al., 2003). DTI is based on the observation that the water molecules in the brain are always moving; that is, they are in Brownian motion.[15] DTI is able to detect the Brownian movement, or diffusion of water protons between and within individual cells, and produces measures of the orientation and magnitude of this movement (Rosenbloom et al., 2003). At the time of image

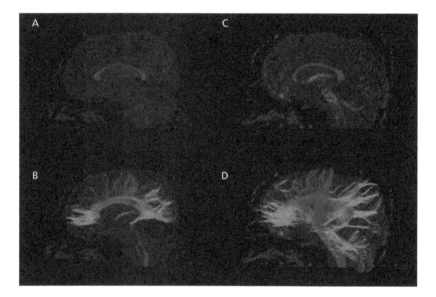

Figure 3.11 DTI Brain Tractography. DTI direction-coded fractional anisotropy map and tractography of a female patient with history of idiopathic basilar artery occlusion producing multifocal brain lesions (A and B) and a healthy volunteer (C and D). Fiber tracts are originating from the shown direction-coded fractional anisotropy slice centered on the midline of the brain only and do not reflect all fiber tracts of the brain. See Color Plate 6 in insert.

Images courtesy of H. U. Voss and N. D. Schiff, Weill Medical College of Cornell University.

acquisition a minimum of seven images are acquired for each brain section, and, from this set of images, a matrix (diffusion tensor) that describes the maximum direction of diffusion is calculated for every voxel[16] in the image (Dong et al., 2004).

DTI may be useful in the early recognition of cerebral ischemia[17] and may show tissue injury before conventional T1- or T2-weighted MRI sequences show pathology (Huisman, 2010; see Figure 3.11). It has also been suggested that DTI is able to differentiate between injuries that cause permanent damage and those that cause transitory loss of function as a result of temporary inflammation, edema, and/or shock (Jones et al., 2000). In addition, DTI has been used to test the theory that schizophrenia occurs as a result of frontal disconnection (Foong et al., 2001) and to show widespread abnormalities in tissue organization as a result of cortical maldevelopment (Eriksson, Rugg-Gunn, Symms, Barker, & Duncan, 2001). Investigations of white matter across a broad spectrum of neuropsychiatric conditions using DTI have also indicated that nonspecific alterations of white matter integrity are the rule and that the locations of these alterations are shared by various conditions (Wortzel, Kraus, Filley, Anderson, & Arciniegas, 2011).

3.3.4 Relative Advantages and Disadvantages of Computed Tomography, Magnetic Resonance Imaging, and Diffusion Tensor Imaging

As with all currently available tests, measures, and techniques, there are a number of advantages and disadvantages of using CT, MRI, and DTI. More specifically, it is widely believed that CT is more reliable than MRI in the detection of acute bleeding, but studies have shown that MRI is at least as sensitive as CT (Kidwell & Wintermark, 2008). CT is also preferred to MRI in cases of acute head injury when it is necessary to rapidly triage patients who require emergency surgery; however, in the weeks to months following head trauma, MRI is a more sensitive tool to evaluate for the presence of chronic hemorrhage and subacute shear injury (Provenzale, 2007). In addition, since most first-time seizures are caused by metabolic abnormalities or medications, CT is useful in these cases to exclude rare secondary causes for acute seizures, such as brain tumor, brain infection, or stroke. When seizures are longstanding, however, MRI is more sensitive in the assessment for structural sources of the seizures (Bernal & Altman, 2003).

It must be noted that while modern CT scanners produce fine-grained resolution, permitting some differentiation between white and gray matter,[18] even with high-resolution scanners a CT tends to provide information only about attenuation. CT also may not show the precise details of brain tissue damage that is common in people with dementia due to the inferior quality of the images and obstructed views of tissue that result from overlying bone. Finally, CT is not the preferred tool for diagnosing dementia since many people will have normal CT scans, at least in the early stages of this disease (Bernal & Altman, 2003).

There are also a number of advantages to using MRI instead of CT: (a) because MRI does not use ionizing radiation,[19] it is preferred over CT in patients requiring multiple imaging examinations; (b) MRI has a much greater range of available soft tissue contrast, depicts anatomy in greater detail, and is more sensitive and specific for assessing abnormalities within the brain itself; and (c) MRI allows for the evaluation of structures that may be obscured by artifacts from bone in CT images. Research studies have also shown MRI to be more sensitive for identifying early strokes (Chalela et al., 2007). MRI is also the modality of choice in evaluating known primary brain tumors and metastases, since it allows more accurate delineation of tumor margins, provides more information with which to differentiate between various tumor types (Cha, 2006), and is superior in detecting diseased or damaged tissue in people with dementia. The disadvantages of MRI include the amount of time it takes to acquire the scan and, as a consequence, its vulnerability to subject movement. However, the main limitation of CT and MRI techniques is that they are not as sensitive as some of the nuclear techniques for detecting functional abnormalities that matter in the context of forensic neuropsychology (Grossman & Yousem, 2003; see Figure 3.12).

DTI also has several limitations that, if not considered, can affect the interpretation of the information derived from this technique. For example, the voxel size used in DTI is usually 1 to 15 mm; however, because the axon is in the order of 0.01 mm, the signal from one voxel could represent thousands of axons, which may have different directions. In addition, artifacts due to, for example, image

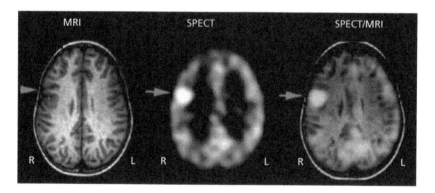

Figure 3.12 MRI vs. [99mTc]-HMPAO Brain Perfusion SPECT. MRI scan (left) is normal, while SPECT shows hyperemia (increased rCBF) at the time of the epileptogenic seizure. ASPECT/MRI fusion image (right) identifies the location of the focus. See Color Plate 7 in insert.

Reprinted with permission of Anderson Publishing from Mountz, J. M. (2007). PET/CT neuroimaging applications for epilepsy and cerebral neoplasm. *Applied Radiology*, *36*(11), 44–52. © Anderson Publishing Ltd.

noise or subject motion can lead to a changed or degraded signal or geometric image distortions of the DTI data (Basser & Jones, 2002). The major advantage of DTI is that it can provide details on organization and tissue microstructure better than any other currently available structural imaging modality.

3.4 The Specifics of Functional Neuroimaging

In contrast to structural imaging techniques, functional brain imaging plays an important role in our understanding of the relationships between various behaviors and brain functions. More specifically, this technique offers the possibility of coupling an image with neurocognitive functions and, in the case of PET and fMRI, to further integrate brain function with features of molecular and neural circuitry information. In other words, functional imaging can be used in one of two ways: (a) to look at baseline levels of brain activity and (b) to define regions that become active during specific behaviors and cognitive tasks (Crosson et al., 2010). Functional imaging can be achieved through a variety of methods, such as fMRI, MRS, PET, and SPECT, each of which measures a different physical property of the brain or the contrast media that is administered to enhance the image. However, among these different imaging technologies, fMRI and PET have been the most technologically advanced and have had the broadest application in the courtroom (Weiller, May, Sach, Buhmann, & Rijntjes, 2006).

3.4.1 Functional Magnetic Resonance Imaging

Functional MRI is a form of specialized MRI that works by detecting the changes in blood oxygen concentration and blood flow that occur in response to neural activity. It operates under the principle that changes in the brain's hemodynamics,[20] which relate to mental operations, can be detected and mapped using basic MRI instrumentation. Functional MRI is based on the observation that the properties of hemoglobin[21] in a strong magnetic field are dependent on its state of oxygen saturation. More specifically, increased neural activity in a particular brain region results in more consumption of oxygen from the blood near these neurons. Accompanying the increased oxygen consumption are increases in blood flow and blood volume of the local vasculature of the activated regions of the brain. The consequence is that the blood near a region of local neuronal activity has a higher concentration of oxygenated hemoglobin than blood in locally inactive regions (Cacioppo et al., 2003). Thus this form of MRI, known as blood-oxygen-level-dependent (BOLD) imaging, is the result of a complex interplay between changes in regional cerebral oxygen extraction, blood flow, and blood volume (Detre, 2006).

Almost all fMRI research studies use BOLD to determine where in the brain the activity occurs as the result of various experiences.[22] However, because the signals are relative and not individually quantitative, some researchers have questioned the use of BOLD. One of the main issues in investigating brain function using fMRI rests on the fact that specific brain functions are localized at various sites. This functional specialization can be identified with fMRI and mapped at high spatial resolution (Ogawa & Sung, 2007). Functional MRI is similar to PET in that it accurately localizes signal sources, thereby more closely identifying brain regions of the brain in terms of anatomy and function. In fact, its most important application is to map the hemodynamic responses of cognitive and affective stimuli to determine the anatomical locations that carry out specific cognitive and behavioral brain functions. For example, by using BOLD images, one can indirectly detect the increase in neuronal activity at the moment that a subject performs a specific cognitive task (Amaro & Barker, 2006). The underlying assumption is that cognitive functions are basically located in focal brain regions; however, evidence from brain studies suggests that most complicated behavioral and psychological processes are not located in a single brain center (Sarter, Berntson, & Cacioppo, 1996).

Arterial spin labeling is another fMRI technique based on weighting the MRI signal by CBF and cerebral blood volume. It utilizes magnetically labeled blood water as an endogenous tracer for quantification of brain perfusion. After a region of flowing blood is magnetized, the resulting tissue perfusion produces local change to tissue magnetization, which can be measured with a standard MRI imaging sequence and compared to an unlabeled control image (Detre, Rao, Wang, Chen & Wang, 2012). The cerebral blood volume method, however, requires injection of MRI contrast agents that are currently still under investigation.

Functional MRI is accepted as a technique for making major management decisions about brain surgery in patients with intractable temporal lobe epilepsy, but fMRI is not yet accepted for any other medical purpose despite more than 20 years of research. However, research has suggested that fMRI may be useful in the assessment of various neurological, psychiatric, and psychological disorders on a population level. For example, one study measuring brain activation in psychotic patients while they experienced auditory and verbal hallucinations found predominant engagement of the right inferior frontal region (Sommer et al., 2008). It has also been suggested that reduced functional response in the frontal and inferior parietal regions, as assessed with fMRI, may lead to serious violence in schizophrenia via impaired executive functioning (Kumari et al., 2006). Further, bipolar depression was found to be associated with increased bilateral orbitofrontal activation, increased right dorsolateral prefrontal cortex activation, and heightened left orbitofrontal activation (Altshuler et al., 2008). Functional MRI may also be useful in evaluating the effects of various types of drug addiction such as alcohol, cocaine, and methamphetamine (Fowler, Volkow, Kassed, & Chang, 2007; see Figure 3.13). While fMRI studies are powerful tools for driving the understanding of these disorders on a population-based level, less attention has been focused on their sensitivity and specificity in any single member of the group. Because these studies occur in the context of scientific research

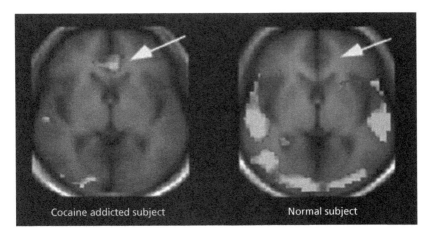

Figure 3.13 The Brain's Response to Cocaine Cues Imaged by fMRI. Arrows point to the activation of the anterior cingulate cortex, a region associated with emotional processing, while cocaine-addicted subjects watched videotapes containing cocaine-associated cues, even if they did not experience craving. See Color Plate 8 in insert.

Reproduced from National Institute of Health: Fowler, J. S., Volkow, N. D., Kassed, C. A., & Chang, L. (2007). Imaging the addicted human brain. *Science and Practice Perspectives*, 3(2), 4–16.

that places a premium on novelty, the extent to which the findings are reproducible by independent investigators has not always been well characterized, in part because competitive funding agencies and university promotion committees are not always structured to adequately incentivize proposals to repeat studies simply for the sake of establishing reproducibility.

3.4.2 Magnetic Resonance Spectroscopy

Based on the principles of MRI, MRS extracts metabolic and chemical information and, in fact, allows chemical sampling of the brain. MRS is noninvasive and permits the relative quantification of metabolites across a slice of the whole brain and in specific brain regions (Malhi & Lagopoulos, 2008). More specifically, MRS enables tissue characterization on a biochemical level, which cannot be achieved with traditional MRI. While MRS can be performed using a number of different nuclei, only the most clinically established method, ^{1}H spectroscopy (also referred to as proton spectroscopy), is discussed in detail.

MRS is increasingly used for brain research since it is the only method that allows for the observation of various neurometabolites, such as glutamate and lactate (Hoerst et al., 2010). In healthy tissue, metabolites are present in steady-state concentrations typical for that specific tissue. This concentration may change due to illnesses or functional disturbances, and these changes in concentration can be detected with MRS. In fact, metabolite changes often precede structural abnormalities, and MRS is able to show these abnormalities before MRI does (Fayed, Olmos, Morales, & Modrego, 2006). MRS has been used across a wide variety of neuropathological conditions, such as traumatic brain injury; however, the condition for which it has shown its greatest clinical potential is brain tumors.

Static or dynamic MRS measures of metabolite concentrations can reflect functional brain changes. For example, Hoerst and colleagues (2010) used MRS to study brain functioning in women with borderline personality disorder and found them to have significantly higher levels of glutamate in the anterior cingular cortex than controls, and higher levels of glutamate in the anterior cingular cortex were found to predict impulsivity and self-reported borderline personality symptoms. Many studies in adults and children have also shown a relationship between neurometabolite values and extent of cognitive dysfunction in various neurological and neuropsychiatric disorders (Ross & Sachdev, 2004).

3.4.3 Positron Emission Tomography

PET is a nuclear medicine[23] imaging technique, which produces three-dimensional images of functional processes in the brain. After injection of a tracer compound labeled with a positron-emitting radionuclide

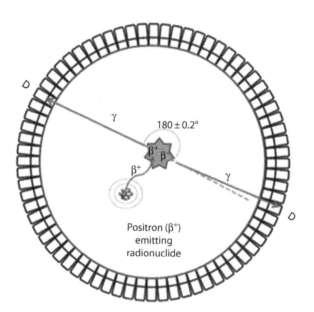

Figure 3.14 The Basics of PET Imaging. A positron (β^+) from a positron emitting radionuclide, such as F-18, travels several millimeters and interacts with an electron. Both particles annihilate and produce two 511 KeV photons (γ), which travel in opposite directions and are then detected simultaneously by a ring of detectors (D).

(radioisotope), the subject is placed within the field of view of a ring of detectors that are capable of registering the photons that result from the annihilation of positron/electrons pairs. More specifically, the radionuclide in the radiotracer decays and the resulting positively charged electrons subsequently annihilate on contact with negatively charged electrons after travelling a short distance (2–10 mm) within the body (see Figure 3.14). Every annihilation event produces two 511keV photons travelling in opposite directions, which are detected simultaneously by the detectors surrounding the subject (Phelps, Hoffman, Mullani, & Ter-Pogossian, 1975). Since about 2002, most commercial PET scanners are dual modality scanners; both PET and CT scanners are combined into one system in order to provide structural and functional imaging capability in one machine (see Figure 3.15). After the PET and CT scans have been acquired, the data is then mathematically reconstructed or processed to obtain tomographic images of PET, CT, and fused PET/CT.

The advantage of PET in imaging functional activity of the brain is based on the fact that a number of biological molecules in the body can be easily radiolabeled with positron-emitting radioisotopes. Radioisotopes, such as carbon-11, oxygen-15, and fluorine-18 make it possible, at least in theory, to

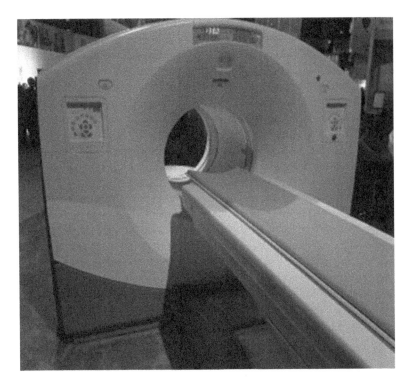

Figure 3.15 PET/CT Scanner (GE Healthcare)

Table 3.3 PET and SPECT Radiotracers for Brain Imaging Studies

Clinical Indication	PET			SPECT		
	Radio nuclide	Half-life (m)	Radio tracer	Radio nuclide	Half-life (m)	Radio tracer
Cerebral blood flow	O-15	2.033	[^{15}O]Water	Tc-99m	360	^{99m}Tc-HMPAO ^{99m}Tc-ECD
				I-123	793.2	^{123}I-IMP
Glucose Metabolism	F-18	109.771	2-deoxy-2-[^{18}F] fluoro- D-glucose (FDG)			
Dopamine D$_2$ Receptor	C-11	20.334	[^{11}C]Raclopride	I-123	793.2	^{123}I-IBZM

Note. PET = positron emission tomography; SPECT = single photon emission computed tomograph.

produce a radioactive version of almost any organic molecule (Herholz & Heiss, 2004).[24] This technology is also well established for linking inorganic positron emitting isotopes to small and large biological molecules so that their behavior in the brain can be followed on a moment-by-moment basis to characterize many different biological processes. In the last three decades, hundreds of PET radiotracers have been developed to study various diseases. Some of the most important radiotracers used in forensic brain imaging are listed in Table 3.3.

Using different radiotracers, PET can image CBF with radioactive water, oxygen metabolism with radioactive O_2, and glucose metabolism with radioactive glucose or an analog, fluorodeoxyglucose (FDG) in different areas of the working brain. Since PET can measure the differences in metabolism of oxygen and glucose used by various tissues in the body, PET is often regarded as a "metabolic imaging" technique. PET is a quantitative imaging technique that can estimate metabolic rates and neuroreceptor concentrations in absolute numbers, rather than only relative amounts (Herholz & Heiss, 2004). Further, in brain research PET is frequently used to identify the brain sites where drugs and naturally occurring neurotransmitters act and to show how quickly drugs reach and activate a neuroreceptor system, such as the dopamine or serotonin receptor systems. PET is also frequently used to assess brain changes following chronic drug abuse, during withdrawal from drugs, and while the subject is experiencing drug craving (Herholz & Heiss, 2004).

3.4.3.1 Positron Emission Tomography—Blood Flow

Quantification of rCBF is key to understanding pathological and normal brain physiology. While several imaging techniques for measuring rCBF are

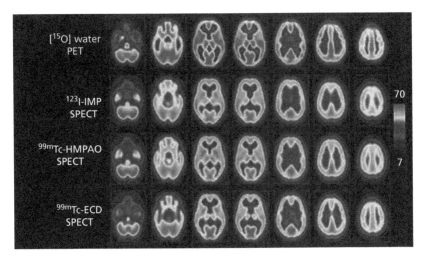

Figure 3.16 Estimation of rCBF Based on [¹⁵O]water-PET. Comparison of rCBF measured with three different SPECT tracers. Anatomically standardized averaged CBF images are transaxial sections. Scale maximum and minimum values for all images are 70 and 7 ml/100 ml/min, respectively. See Color Plate 9 in insert.

Reproduced from Fro, H., Inoue, K., Goto, R., Kinomura, S., Taki, Y., Okada, K., . . . Fukuda, H. (2006). Database of normal human cerebral blood flow measured by SPECT: I. Comparison between I-123-IMP, Tc-99m-HMPAO, and Tc-99m-ECD as referred with O-15 labeled water PET and voxel-based morphometry. *Annals of Nuclear Medicine*, *20*(2), 131–138, Figure 2, with permission from Springer Science and Business Media.

available, PET with [¹⁵O]H₂O (water) as a radiotracer is often thought of as the gold standard, especially when absolute measures of rCBF are of interest (Chen, Wieckowska, Meyer, & Pike, 2008). Figure 3.16 shows a comparison of rCBF in normal subjects measured with [¹⁵O]water-PET with three different radiotracers (Ito et al., 2006).

Since rCBF depends on neuronal function, the measurement of rCBF during various tasks, including cognitive tasks, has become a main method for studying brain functions. For example, the PET scan shown in Figure 3.16 clearly identifies the decreased rCBF in the frontal lobes (white arrows) and following treatment shows significant increase in rCBF (Wintermark et al., 2005). PET rCBF studies have also been extensively used to study a number of neuropsychiatric diseases, such as dementias, depression, and schizophrenia. These studies are often performed at rest, although PET blood flow can also be employed in activation studies where the brain area of interest is activated by having the subject perform a cognitive task. Further, the relatively short physical half-life of ¹⁵O, which is 123 seconds, allows for multiple administrations (or doses) of [¹⁵O]water, and thus the sequential PET scans can be used to assess differences in rCBF between images collected during different cognitive states.

3.4.3.2 Positron Emission Tomography—glucose metabolism

PET using [^{18}F]-2-fluoro-2-deoxy-D-glucose (FDG) allows for the quantitative assessment of the cerebral metabolic rate of glucose utilization (Huisman et al., 2012). In fact, the most frequently studied biological process has been glucose metabolism because energy metabolism is closely linked to brain function, although in a very complex way (Brodie, 1996). The assessment of glucose metabolism begins with an injection of FDG. Since FDG is similar to glucose, it is used as a tracer to study glucose metabolism. Unlike glucose, however, FDG once transported into the cells is not metabolized completely and so gets trapped in the cells. The amount of FDG accumulated in the cells reflects the metabolic rate of the cells (Herholz & Heiss, 2004).

The power of FDG-PET lies in its ability to measure the rate of glucose metabolism in absolute units, and, to date, it is the only radiotracer approved by the Food and Drug Administration for diagnosing brain tumors, epilepsy, DAT, and other forms of dementia (Silverman, 2004). Indeed, a study, comparing FDG-PET with histopathology has reported relatively high predictive accuracy (84% sensitivity, 74% specificity, 81% positive predictive power, and 78% negative predictive power) for the assessment of DAT (see Figure 3.17; Jagust, Reed, Mungas, Ellis, & Decarli, 2007). Further, in patients with temporal lobe epilepsy, who had surgically and pathologically confirmed lesions, the reported specificity and sensitivity of FDG-PET for localizing the seizure was found to be 89% and 91%, respectively (Herholz et al., 2004; Kim et al., 2003). FDG-PET has also been used in the assessment of brain tumors, although the current clinical gold standard for the diagnosis of brain tumors is MRI.

Although FDG-PET is not yet an integral part of clinical practice in psychiatry, the potential value of FDG-PET in neuropsychiatric diseases has been extensively evaluated. In fact, the core of neuroimaging research in psychiatry consists of functional imaging studies of the prefrontal cortex and the limbic system with a lot of attention on schizophrenia, major depression, and drug abuse (Zipursky, Meyer, & Verhoeff, 2007). For example, several investigators have reported that patients with schizophrenia have hypometabolism in the prefrontal cortex at rest or during a simple attention task (Herholz et al., 2004; Potkin et al., 2002) and this classical hypofrontality has been confirmed by frontal lobe tests, such as the Wisconsin Card Sort Test (Riehemann et al., 2001). However, in studies of nonmedicated patients with schizophrenia, hypermetabolic pattern in the frontal cortex and other brain regions has also been reported (Soyka, Koch, Möller, Rüther & Tatsch, 2005). In general, conflicting findings and the failure to replicate have been one of the factors that has tended to limit the use of FDG-PET in the clinical practice of neuropsychiatry. The other problem is that even strong results tend to describe populations of patients versus controls. The sensitivity and specificity for any *single* member of these groups is not as well characterized, as some patients will have findings that are more typical of healthy volunteers, while some controls will have findings that are more typical of the patient group.

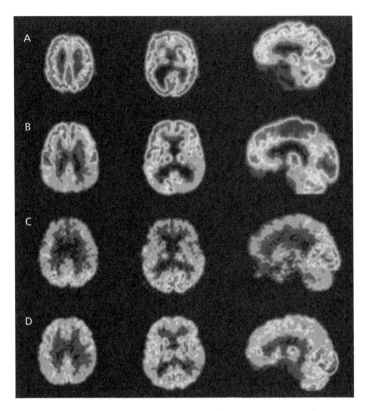

Figure 3.17 FDG-PET of Normal Subject and Subjects with AD and FTLD. Normal subject (A), patient with AD (B and D), and patient with frontotemporal lobar degeneration (FTLD) (C). See Color Plate 10 in insert.

Reproduced with permission from Jagust, W., Reed, B., Mungas, D., Ellis, W., & Decarli, C. (2007). What does fluorodeoxyglucose PET imaging add to a clinical diagnosis of dementia? *Neurology*, 69(9), 871–877. Copyright © 2007, Wolters Kluwer Health

3.4.4 Single Photon Emission Computed Tomography

SPECT is based on the emission of gamma ray photons, by a variety of radiotracers, and the detection of the photons by a device known as "gamma camera." A SPECT instrument may consist of a single-head, dual-head, or triple-head gamma camera, but the most common SPECT camera, at present, is dual-headed (see Figure 3.18). SPECT scans allows physicians to visualize brain function, such as brain perfusion or rCBF, by first intravenously injecting a radiotracer into a patient. In the last three decades, a number of commercially available and experimental radiotracers have been used for SPECT imaging studies to assess rCBF; however, the most commonly used radiotracers are ^{99m}Tc-HMPAO (Ceretec™) and ^{99m}Tc-ECD (Neurolite™). Following the intravenous injection, these radiotracers are transported into the brain tissue,

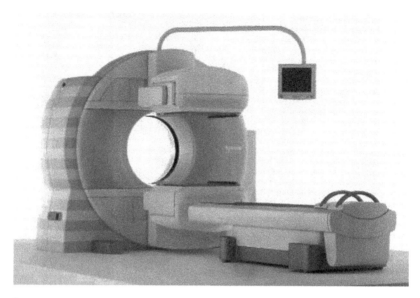

Figure 3.18 SPECT Dual-Headed Gamma Camera (Siemens)

usually within 2 to 3 minutes, and as the blood flows through the brain the amount of radiotracer taken up by different areas in the brain reflects their relative rCBF (see Figure 3.16). More specifically, after the background activity has been cleared (which takes about 15 to 60 minutes), the gamma camera detectors rotate around the subject's head and obtain many images at different angles to monitor the radiotracer uptake in different areas of brain. The cameras detect the gamma rays emitted by the radiotracer and record the distribution and the amount of uptake in different areas of brain. A computer collects the information and translates it into multidimensional cross-sections that can be manipulated to form a three-dimensional image of the brain. In general, brain areas with structural and functional abnormalities show decreased radiotracer levels compared to healthy brain tissue (O'Connor & Kemp, 2006), although some diseases are characterized by increased blood flow.

As noted, brain SPECT provides three-dimensional information on the perfusion status of brain tissue. While this information is often complementary to the anatomic details provided by structural neuroimaging techniques, brain perfusion SPECT has clinical value by itself since functional impairment in cerebral diseases often precedes structural changes. Consequently, SPECT can be used to define a patient's pathologic status when neurological or psychiatric symptoms cannot be explained by structural neuroimaging findings (Catafeu, 2001). More specifically, SPECT is sometimes more sensitive to brain injury than either CT or MRI because it can detect reduced blood flow to injured sites or distant areas of the brain that have not been injured themselves but are reciprocally innervated by neurons that have been injured. Similarly, in the early phase of frontal lobe dementia, CT or MRI may show normal findings or only mild frontal cerebral atrophy, while SPECT usually shows more conspicuous hypoperfusion of the frontal lobes (Miller et al., 1991). Further, since blood flow is usually coupled to local brain metabolism and energy use, the ^{99m}Tc-HMPAO and ^{99m}Tc-ECD radiotracers are often used to infer changes about underlying regional cerebral metabolism in an attempt to diagnose and differentiate the different causal pathologies of various types of dementia. In fact, the accuracy of SPECT in diagnosing DAT was found to be as high as 88% (Bonte, Harris, Hynan, Bigio, & White, 2006). In addition, some investigators have reported that SPECT is valuable in assessing psychiatric, mood, anxiety, substance abuse, psychotic, and behavioral disorders. For example, Soderstrom and colleagues (2002) in studying subjects convicted of impulsive violent crimes, by comparing their SPECT and MRI scans to those of healthy control subjects, found abnormalities in all but five of the criminal subjects. These abnormalities included decreased blood flow to the hippocampus, the left white frontal matter, the right angular gyrus, and the medial temporal gyrus and a significant increase in blood flow to both sides of the parietal association cortex (Soderstrom et al., 2002).

3.4.5 Relative Advantages and Disadvantages of Functional Imaging Techniques

As is the case with structural imaging techniques, each of the functional imaging modalities has its advantages and disadvantages. More specifically, fMRI has better temporal resolution than PET and SPECT and, because it can produce images of brain activity as fast as every second, scientists can determine with greater precision when brain regions become active and how long they remain active. In contrast, both PET and SPECT currently take 30 seconds to several minutes or longer to obtain a single image. In addition, fMRI can be coupled with contemporaneously acquired structural MRI sequences to produce an image that distinguishes structures less than a millimeter apart, whereas the latest commercial PET scanners can resolve images of structures only within 4 to 5 mm of each other. In summary, fMRI provides superior image clarity along with the ability to assess blood flow and brain function within seconds (Matthews, Honey, & Bullmore, 2006). However, FDG-PET can (a) detect disease, such as DAT, prior to changes in structure; (b) reveal metabolic changes in the brain, such as changes due to drug use; and (c) show the extent of disease in distant brain structures that have not been directly affected by local insults but have become dysfunctional because their wiring has been cut. Further, PET may detect changes in brain chemistry or functioning before symptoms appear (Herholz & Heiss, 2004). To date, PET also retains the significant advantage of being able to identify which brain receptors are being activated by neurotransmitters, drug abuse, and potential treatment compounds. Since it is a tracer method, PET has the distinct advantage of being, thus far, the best modality for the detection of a wide variety of biochemical processes. For example, PET has been used to measure the regional distributions of dopamine and serotonin transporters and receptors and binding of various pharmacological agents and cellular processes (Klunk et al. 2003; Rapoport, 2005). Another advantage of PET is that it has a high degree of quantification accuracy regarding pre- and postintervention changes in brain regions with altered brain perfusion or metabolism (Wintermark et al., 2006). In addition, because [^{15}O]water-PET is quantitative and usually considered to be the gold standard for the measurement of rCBF, assessment of brain regional activations under different cognitive tasks provides physiologically relevant information (Raichle & Snyder, 2007).

Although SPECT is widely available, it has the lowest spatial and temporal resolution of all modern neuroimaging techniques. In addition, SPECT is not a quantitative technique, although its images can be processed to provide a semiquantitative estimation of brain activity. However, SPECT can compete with PET in providing information about local brain damage from many processes, such as tumors and strokes (Catafau, 2001). Generally, SPECT tracers are more limited than PET tracers in the types of brain activity they can monitor and decay more slowly than many PET tracers. SPECT studies often require longer test and retest periods than PET studies do. Further, the quality of the pictures generated by SPECT is not as good as that generated by more advanced functional scans, such as PET scans.

Accurate anatomical localization of functional abnormalities obtained with PET or SPECT is known to be problematic. More specifically, while these techniques can visualize certain normal anatomical structures, the spatial resolution is generally inadequate for accurate anatomic localization of pathology. Combining PET or SPECT with a high-resolution anatomical imaging modality, such as CT or MRI, can resolve the localization issue as long as the images from the two modalities are accurately coregistered (Cherry, Louie, Jacobs, & Townsend, 2008). Although current software algorithms permit highly accurate coregistration of anatomic and functional datasets, motion artifacts can adversely affect image fusion and the overall quality of the images (Forster et al., 2003).

3.5 Functional Neuroimaging and Brain Activation

An emerging practice is to conduct functional imaging while the subject is challenged with various neuropsychological tests and neurobehavioral probes that are known to activate the brain area of interest. Although the roots for noninvasive functional neuroimaging can be traced back to the 1940s, the field accelerated in the 1980s with PET blood flow studies using the brain's responses to carefully controlled sensory, cognitive, and motor events. The problem, however, is that one must have a "baseline state" against which to measure stimulus or task-induced changes in brain regional activities. When functional images or scans acquired during the baseline (resting state)[25] or control state[26] are subtracted from those acquired in a "task state," the vast majority of changes observed are activity increases or "activations".[27] While the term "physiologic baseline" or "rest state" is applicable only to PET studies, the terms "control state" and "control condition" may be applied equally to PET and fMRI imaging techniques.

Baseline is an important issue in cognitive neuroscience, especially when functional brain imaging techniques are used to measure changes in brain activity that are presumed to be associated with specific mental operations, such as executive functions. In fact, it has been contended that left unconstrained the baseline activity would vary unpredictably and consequently affect the specificity of a functional activation scan (Gusnard & Raichle, 2001). Further, both PET and SPECT at the resting (baseline) state are clinically useful for the detection of both structural and functional abnormalities in a number of neuropsychiatric disorders, such as dementia and schizophrenia. The major limitation with resting state studies, however, is that the processes involved in cognitive tasks cannot be linked to specific brain regions. The resting state is also of limited use due to its variability across individual subjects (Weinberger, Berman, & Zec, 1986). Variations in rCBF may therefore simply reflect the subjective experience of the procedure itself rather than indicate an underlying pathology. It has also been contended that the "resting state" is a misnomer:

> The brain does not become inactive or empty of thought in the
> absence of specific experimental tasks or instructions; on the
> contrary, patients report after scans that when at "rest" they typically
> recalled past experiences, or made future plans.
> (Andreasen et al., 1997, p. 1732)

In addition, because resting-state studies are usually associated with single measurements, they provide no clues about how a brain region may respond to the challenge posed by a cognitive task, such as the Wisconsin Card Sort Test (Frith et al., 1995). Nevertheless, obtaining a baseline is often crucial since it can provide information regarding, for example, frontal lobe dysfunction due to major structural and functional abnormalities.

As previously discussed, many neuropsychiatric disorders are associated with functional brain abnormalities. The metabolism and blood flow in specific impaired brain areas can be activated by carefully designed "activation" tasks, such as a cognitive task. More specifically, in functional neuroimaging techniques that employ a cognitive task, cognitive "activation" refers to a specific psychological state or occurrence that is deemed to be active in specific areas in the brain relative to the baseline state (Wager, Hernandez, Jonides, & Lindquist, 2007). In the interpretation of neuroimaging data it is important to remember that activation in a given brain region means that this region is associated with the performance of that particular activation task.

In other words, a cognitive brain activation study is a cortical stress test in that it imposes a selective physiological load on a specific brain area (Wager et al., 2007). This analogy is particularly important in light of research findings, which have shown that functional abnormalities evident during the performance of cognitive tasks are not found during resting baseline rCBF (Zemishlany et al., 1996). Consequently, many studies attempt to assess brain activity while the subject is engaged in a specific mental task. For example, in the case of frontal lobe dysfunction in the context of aggressive behavior, one would want to use a neuropsychological test known to activate the prefrontal cortex. Despite its usefulness, a major limitation of FDG-PET is the relatively long uptake period ($\geq$20 minutes) required to record the glucose metabolism rate related to functional activity. Therefore, this excludes the use of activation tasks that cannot be maintained over that period of time. With [^{15}O] water PET studies of rCBF, multiple replications of conditions in the same subject can be performed sequentially in a short period of time (about one new task every 10 minutes), and, as a result, PET blood flow studies can be used for activation studies. SPECT can also be used in activation protocols to identify brain abnormalities or dysfunctions. However, SPECT tracers are more limited than PET tracers in the type of brain activity they can detect. Further, because SPECT tracers are longer lasting than PET tracers, most baseline and activation studies of the brain must be performed on different days. In addition, the spatial resolution of SPECT is low (8 to 10 mm) compared to PET, which is 4 to 6 mm (Levin, 2005). In recent years, fMRI has become the dominant imaging technique because it does not involve ionizing radiation and allows more rapid signal acquisition; however, there are practical considerations limiting the routine use of fMRI as a clinical tool (Matthews et al., 2006).

Neuroimaging activation procedures are frequently employed for the assessment of frontal lobe dysfunction. Hypofrontality has been observed in patients with neuropsychiatric disorders not only at rest but also during activation of the frontal cortex. For example, better performance on the Wisconsin Card Sort Test was found to correlate with rCBF increase in the prefrontal cortex of control subjects and in the parahippocampal gyrus of schizophrenic patients (Ragland et al., 1998). Patients with depression were also found to show less activation in prefrontal brain regions similar to the schizophrenic patients, suggesting that impairment of executive functions is not unique to schizophrenic subjects (Hugdahl et al., 2004). Also, Kirsch and colleagues (2006) have suggested that using PET with fMRI is a suitable method to quantify prefrontal cortex dysfunction in patients suffering from schizophrenia and other neuropsychiatric disorders. However, because fMRI BOLD signals, for reasons currently not well understood, do not remain constant, some researchers have concluded that the fMRI baseline cannot be defined (Raichle & Snyder, 2007). Unlike PET activation studies, fMRI, as it is conventionally practiced, using BOLD imaging, does not offer a similar absolute reference and is not a true measure of blood flow. Therefore, estimated changes in parameters, such as oxygen consumption, must be viewed with caution until further work is done to determine their validity (Raichle & Snyder, 2007).

3.6 Functional Neuroimaging and Data Analysis

It has been suggested that the brain adheres to two fundamental principles of functional organization: (a) functional integration and (b) functional specialization, where the integration within and among specialized areas is mediated by effective connectivity (Friston, 2011). More specifically, while functional localization implies that a function can be localized in a cortical area, functional specialization suggests that a cortical area is specialized for some aspects of motor or perceptual processing, and that this specialization is anatomically separated within the cortex (Friston, Ashburner, Kiebel, Nichols & Penny, 2007). After the data has been obtained from the scanner, image processing is required to extract the quantitative information from the images as requested by the clinician. This information may include brain volume, blood flow, size and shape of brain structures, thickness of cortex, or functional activation. The major steps of data analysis include (1) data acquisition, (2) preprocessing, (3) model estimation, and (4) analysis of results. Although these steps are not standardized from one technology, machine, or laboratory to the next, there are two major methodological approaches for analyzing functional imaging data, which address the long-standing debate about functional specialization versus functional integration in the brain (Cohen & Tong, 2001).

The first approach, brain mapping, produces three-dimensional images of neuronal activation, showing which areas of the brain respond to a cognitive challenge. This method is also known as the study of functional specialization and generally proceeds using some form of statistical parametric mapping (SPM). SPM is a voxel-based approach that employs topological inference and classical statistics to explain regionally specific responses to experimental factors (Ashburner & Friston, 2000). Using SPM, functional neuroimaging data is spatially processed so that it conforms to an established anatomical space in which responses are characterized, typically using the general linear model. To accommodate the spatial nature of the imaging data, and also to account for the multiple statistical comparisons made, the SPM technique makes use of random field theory and/or other statistical procedures. The SPM technique can also be employed with structural data to find brain regions containing a higher gray matter density. This statistical method is known as voxel-based morphometry (Ashburner & Friston, 2000).

The second approach is known as functional integration, where models are used to describe how different brain regions interact. In fact, investigation of effective connectivity in brain networks, such as the direct causal influence that one brain region exerts over another region, has been increasingly recognized as an important tool for understanding brain function in neuroimaging studies (Roelstraete & Rosseel, 2011). The three most widely used methods to study functional integration are (a) dynamic causal modeling, (b) structural equation modeling, and (c) Granger causality. Dynamic causal modeling has been specifically designed for the analysis of functional imaging data and has become the gold standard for studying effective connectivity between brain regions, including the direct influence one brain region has over another (Friston, 2011).

3.7 Hybrid Neuroimaging Techniques

Hybrid imaging techniques allow for the direct fusion of structural and functional information and have become an attractive strategy due to their ability of providing accurate anatomical and functional information simultaneously (Cherry, Louie, Jacobs, & Townsend, 2008). The combination of PET and CT was first introduced commercially in 2001, followed by SPECT/CT in 2004. PET/CT and SPECT/CT are in routine clinical use and can provide physicians with a more complete picture of what is occurring in the brain, both anatomically and metabolically, at the same time (see Figure 3.19). Since functional brain images obtained by PET/CT or SPECT/CT can be more precisely aligned or correlated with anatomic imaging obtained by CT scanning, these systems are more accurate and have higher sensitivity and diagnostic accuracy than PET, SPECT, or CT alone (Branstetter et al., 2005; Townsend, 2008). At this time, PET/CT hybrid systems are routinely used in the clinic while PET/MRI hybrid systems are still under extensive evaluation.

PET and MRI provide complementary information in the study of the human brain. The feasibility of simultaneous PET and MRI data acquisition for human studies was first demonstrated in 2007. In 2010, a fully integrated PET/MRI commercial scanner became available for human whole-body imaging (Biograph mMR; Siemens; Catana Drzezga, Heiss, & Rosen, 2012). The features of this new technology may be particularly appealing to applications in neuroscience and translational neurologic and psychiatric research, considering that MRI represents the first-line diagnostic imaging modality for numerous indications and that a great number of specific PET tracers are available today to assess functional and molecular processes in the brain (Catana et al., 2012). A simultaneous PET/MRI scan of a patient with DAT is shown in Figure 3.20.

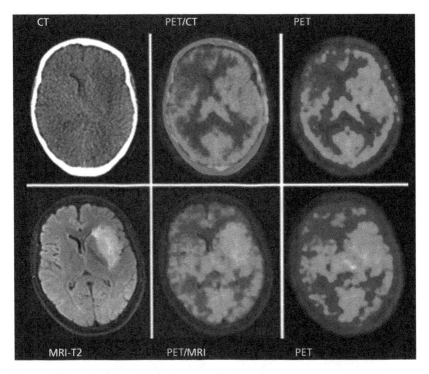

Figure 3.19 Hybrid PET/MRI of Intracranial Masses. PET/MR and PET/CT images of patient with low-grade glioma extending on left side from insular cortex to temporal lobe and frontal operculum. Top row: PET/CT data: low-dose noncontrast-enhanced CT image (left), fusion image (center), and PET image (right). Bottom row: PET/MRI data: T2-weighted FLAIR image (left), fusion image (center), and 11C-methionine PET image (right). See Color Plate 11 in insert.

Reprinted by permission of SNMMI from Boss, A., Bisdas, S., Kolb, A., Hofmann, M., . . . Stegger, L. (2010). Hybrid PET/MRI of intracranial masses: Initial experiences and comparison to PET/ CT. *Journal of NuclearMedicine, 51*(8), 1198–1205, Figure 4.

3.8 Neuroreceptor and Neurotransmitter Imaging

Neuroreceptor and neurotransmitter imaging is predominantly used to investigate various neurodegenerative and neuropsychiatric disorders. The potential value of neuroreceptor imaging based on PET was first demonstrated in 1983 using dopamine D_2 receptor ligand $[^{11}C]N$-methylspiperone in patients with schizophrenia (Wagner et al., 1983). Since then, a number of PET and SPECT radiotracers have been developed to image neurotransmitter synthesis, neuroreceptor binding on the postsynaptic neuron, and specific transporters on the presynaptic neuron (Heiss & Herholz, 2006; Zimmer & Luxen, 2012).

In preparation for imaging, radioligands[28] are usually administered intravenously into the human body and are subsequently taken up by the organ of interest. The distribution, density, and activity of receptors in the brain can be visualized using radioligands labeled for PET and SPECT. In vivo receptor function, estimated by an outcome measure obtained through the data analyses, is usually represented by the binding potential, which reflects the densities of transporters or receptors in a brain region of interest (Heiss & Herholz, 2006).

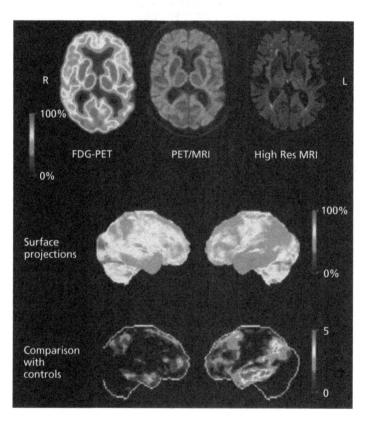

Figure 3.20 Simultaneous PET/MRI Study in Patient with Alzheimer's Disease. Areas with reduced metabolism representing impaired neuronal function are visible in the left temporoparietal cortex (green). Surface projections of cerebral metabolism and of z score images (comparison with controls) are shown in middle and bottom rows. See Color Plate 12 in insert.

Reprinted by permission of SNMMI from: Catana, C., Drzezga, A., Heiss, W. -D., & Rosen, B. (2012). R.PET/MRI for neurologic applications. *Journal of Nuclear Medicine* 53(12), 1916–1925. Figure 5.

3.8.1. Serotonin receptor and transporter imaging

Serotonin (5-hydroxytryptamine) is formed in the body from the essential amino acid tryptophan and released into the synapse during neurotransmission. Serotonergic action is terminated primarily via uptake of serotonin through the specific serotonin transporter (SERT) on the presynaptic neuron. Various agents can inhibit serotonin reuptake, such as Prozac, Lexapro, and Zoloft. Serotonin mediates its numerous effects by binding to a large family of receptors categorized according to their structural diversity, mode of action, and pharmacologic specifications (see Table 3.4). Serotonin is a modulatory neurotransmitter in the brain that regulates various emotions and behaviors and plays a central role in brain development (Holmes, Murphy, & Crawley, 2003). In fact, research studies have indicated that serotonin has an inhibitory action in the brain (Daw, Kakade, & Dayan, 2002; Siever, 2008) and is deeply involved in the inhibition of aggression (Davidson, Putnam, & Larson, 2000). The serotonergic system has also been implicated in a number of neurological and psychiatric disorders, such as depression and schizophrenia.

Although serotonin imaging has many potential clinical uses, there are currently no psychiatric or neurologic diseases in which serotonin imaging is used for routine clincial diagnosis (Parsey, 2010). However, the relative clinical efficacy of various antidepressant drugs, such as Prozac, which belongs to the pharmacologic class of SERT reuptake inhibitors, has been evaluated using various radiotracers (Belmaker & Agam, 2008; see Table 3.4).

Further, SERT neuroimaging studies, performed in patients with aggressive personality disorders using PET radiotracers, have found reduced SERT activity in the cingulate and orbitofrontal cortices in patients with aggressive personality disorders relative to normal control subjects (Siever, 2008). A recent study, however, has suggested that SERT availability is related only to a trait of the disorder and not to the full clinical diagnosis of impulsive aggressive disorder (Giessen et al., 2013). 5-hydroxytryptamine$_{2A}$ receptor binding studies have also reported a significant increase in receptors in physically aggressive patients with personality disorders and in female borderline personality disorder patients (Siever, 2008).

3.8.2 Dopamine Receptor and Transporter Imaging

Dopamine is a small organic chemical that functions as a neurotransmitter in the brain. Dopaminergic systems play a major role in (a) reward-motivated behavior, (b) motor control, (c) controlling the release of several important hormones, and (d) the regulation of various brain functions, including learning and behavior (Varrone & Halldin, 2010). Dopamine activates five known types of dopamine receptors that are found throughout the body and brain. D_1 receptors are the most abundant dopamine receptor in the central nervous system and are found in the cortex, striatum, limbic system, and cardiovascular system. These receptors regulate the growth and

Table 3.4 Receptor Binding Radiotracers for PET and SPECT

Neuroreceptors	Radiotracers for		Binding Site
	PET	SPECT	
Serotonergic system	[^{11}C](+)McN-5652 [^{11}C]DASB	^{123}I-ADAM ^{123}I-βCIT	Serotonin transporter
	[^{11}C]WAY 100635 [^{11}C]DWAY [^{18}F]MPPF		Serotonin receptor, 5-HT$_{1A}$
	[^{18}F]Altanserin [^{11}C]MDL100,907		Serotonin receptor, 5-HT$_{2B}$
Dopaminergic system	[^{18}F]FDOPA		Aromatic L-amino acid decarboxylase
	[^{11}C]β-CFT [^{11}C]PE2i [^{18}F]FP-CIT	^{123}I-FP-CIT (DaTSCAN™) ^{123}I-Altropane	Dopamine transporter
	[^{18}F]FP-DTBZ (AV-133)		Vesicular monoamine transporter
	[^{11}C]Raclopride [^{11}C]FLB 457 [^{18}F]Fallypride	^{123}I-IBZM	Dopamine D$_2$ receptor
Cholinergic system	[^{11}C]MP4A [^{11}C]AMP		Acetylcholinesterase
	[^{11}C]Nicotine [^{18}F]FA [^{18}F]AZAN [^{18}]Nifene		α$_4$β$_2$ Nicotinic acetylcholine receptor

Note. PET = positron emission tomography; SPECT = single photon emission computed tomograph; 5-HT = 5-hydroxytryptamine.

development of neurons in the brain, play a role in behavioral responses, and modulate the actions of D$_2$ dopamine receptors. Dopamine is also involved in the initiation and performance of aggressive behavior, and decreased D$_1$ receptors have been implicated in depressed patients with anger attacks (Siever, 2008).

Some of the most commonly used PET and SPECT radiotracers used to image dopaminergic system are listed in Table 3.4. In 2011, the Food and Drug Administration officially approved striatal dopamine transporter imaging (DaTscan™) to assist in the evaluation of adult patients with suspected Parkinsonian syndromes. PET studies using D$_2$ receptor radioligands can provide valuable information on the impact of DA receptor density on the pathogenesis and development of neuropsychiatric and neurological diseases (Prante et al., 2013). In fact, numerous SPECT and PET studies have linked the dysregulation of the dopaminergic system to the pathophysiology of many diseases, including DAT, schizophrenia, attention deficit hyperactivity disorder, depression, and drug addiction (Neve, Seamans, & Trantham-Davidson, 2004; Pivonello et al., 2007).

3.8.3 Acetylcholine Receptor and Transporter Imaging

Acetylcholine (ACh) is a neurotransmitter involved in cognitive behaviors, such as attention, memory, motivation, and reward (Naqvi & Bechara, 2005). The primary role of ACh is to modulate the release of various neurotransmitters, including dopamine (Lotfipour, Mandelkern, & Brody, 2011). Radiotracers used to image the expression of acetylcholinesterase (AChE), which is an enzyme that inactivates ACh and terminates the cholinergic transmission, are listed in Table 3.4. PET brain neuroimaging of AChE is a particularly valuable tool for studying patients with dementia. Reduction in AChE activity has also been reported in patients with mild cognitive impairment, especially in those patients who later converted to DAT, suggesting that AChE changes might precede the development of clinical DAT (Heiss & Herholz, 2006).

3.9 Electroencephalography and Quantitative Electroencephalography

Electroencephalography (EEG) records the electrical activity of the brain via electrodes that are placed on the scalp. Rather than measuring electrical currents directly, it works by recognizing changes and measuring differences in voltage between different areas of the brain and looks for abnormalities in the patterns of brain activity. The resulting images are depicted as a series of wavy lines drawn by a row of pens on a moving piece of paper or as an image on a computer screen. In fact, due to its extremely high temporal resolution, EEG was the first neuroimaging modality to depict the working of the human brain in near real time (Illes & Racine, 2005). Although not a true neuroimaging technique in some sense, EEG can be used to assess global brain function. The main diagnostic application of EEG is in the case of epilepsy, as epileptic activity can create clear abnormalities on a standard EEG. In addition, EEG can detect strokes, tumors, and other focal brain disorders, although it is not considered a modality of choice when these conditions are suspected.

Quantitative EEG (QEEG) is used to aid in identifying mental health conditions by means of statistical evaluations of the EEG. QEEG is useful as an adjunct to traditional clinical assessment, because it provides a sensitive and specific method to detect subtle variations in the activity of the brain that might otherwise go unnoticed by the clinician. Unlike EEG, QEEG does not assess the structure of the brain but rather evaluates the manner in which a particular person's brain functions (Thornton & Carmody, 2009). QEEG is not designed to diagnose epilepsy, for example, or other structural impairments such as brain tumors. However, QEEG can help to identify mild dementia and mild cognitive impairment and can increase diagnostic accuracy when used with other imaging techniques. It has also been suggested that QEEG is useful in assessing frontal lobe dysfunction in patients with obsessive-compulsive disorder (Tot, Özge, Çömelekoglu, Yazici, & Bal, 2002). Further, research studies have suggested that QEEG may be useful to assess differences in brain electrical activity among offenders diagnosed with antisocial personality disorder and psychopathy (Calzada-Reyes, Alvarez-Amador, Galan-Garcia, & Valdés-Sosa, 2012, 2013; Calzada-Reyes, Alvarez-Amador, Galan-Garcia, et al., 2012). Although readily available and easily administered, EEG and QEEG, however, are not suitable for the assessment of subcortical structures, such as the anterior cingular cortex, and due to poor spatial resolution provide little detailed information.

3.10 Conclusion

The desire to understand the brain structure and its functions has led to the development of a number of very sophisticated imaging modalities that make it possible to see the brain in action. In addition to increasing our understanding of the architecture of the brain and its changes through neurodevelopment and neurodegeneration, these imaging techniques have suggested close relationships between brain structures and functions and, as a consequence, human behavior, both in health and disease. However, as previously noted, brain imaging is not yet a fully mature science, and, therefore, the interpretation of brain scans, just as the interpretation of neuropsychological test data is, in fact, often somewhat subjective. Given the tremendous obstacles to isolating cognitive processes, compounded by the brain's plasticity and ability to perform a given task in multiple ways, it is difficult to establish a clear relationship between a brain region's functions and any associated cognitive processes. Further, because most neuroimaging modalities depend on proxies, such as blood flow, to serve as indirect measures of regional brain functioning, any measurement derived from one of these techniques is necessarily attenuated from the ultimate object of interest, namely, cognitive functioning (Snead, 2008). In addition, variations in scan processing and display, nonstandardized definitions of normal and abnormal, and lack of published results on the specificity and sensitivity for scans used to identify specific disorders and diseases call into question the validity of conclusions and opinions derived from neuroimaging data. Some of these issues where highlighted in *Entertainment Software Association v. Blagojevich* (2005). In this case, the plaintiff sued the state (represented by the defendant, Blagojevich, governor of the state of Illinois) in an attempt to enjoin the enforcement of a state law designed to prohibit the promotion of violent or explicit video games to minors without parental consent. More specifically, the state sought to regulate the distribution of games because it believed that exposure to violent media causes a lack of behavioral inhibition in minors. In support of its claim, the defendant relied on an fMRI study that found (a) reduced frontal lobe activity in subjects with disruptive behavior disorder and (b) a relationship between violent media exposure and changes in brain functioning in both the experimental and control groups (Kronenberger et al., 2005). This study, however, had a number of methodological flaws that clearly called into question the validity of the findings; for example, (a) study participants were only simulating playing video games while being scanned, therefore changes in brain wave activity could not be directly associated with the actual playing of violent games; (b) reduced frontal activity does not necessarily imply susceptibility to violent behavior since other brain regions are also involved in violence; and (c) testimony that reduced frontal lobe activity suggests lack of impulse control can be misleading because a reduction in frontal activity can be attributed to other mental and physical processes aside from exposure to violent media (Shafi, 2009). The court subsequently found this study to be invalid and therefore could not support the defendant's claim that violent media exposure causes violent behavior. Clearly, "data from fMRI, SPECT, and PET scans can be referenced and presented in dazzling multimedia displays that may inflate the scientific credibility of the information presented" (Baskin, Edersheim, & Price, 2007, p. 268).

4

Neuropsychological Assessment

> Your joys and your sorrows, your memories and your
> ambitions, your sense of personal identity and free will, are
> in fact no more than the behavior of a vast assembly of nerve
> cells and their associated molecules.
>
> (Crick, 1994, p. 3)

4.1 Introduction

Within the forensic setting, mental health experts can make valuable contributions to issues of, for example, competency to stand trial, sanity, and mitigation regarding eligibility for the death penalty (Marcopulos, Morgan, & Denney, 2008; Yates & Denney, 2008). In fact, the expert witness may be required to provide answers to a variety of questions, including does the defendant have a cognitive impairment and, if so, what functional deficits are related to the impairment? Neuropsychologists attempt to answer these questions by a variety of means, including the administration of neuropsychological tests and measures. To that end, the analysis of the pattern of performance among a large number of tests is a key factor in the assessment of cognitive functioning and the choice of tests used should sample a wide range of functional domains (Spreen & Strauss, 1997). It is the combination of objective scores, behavioral observations, and consistency in emerging pattern of results, along with a comprehensive clinical history, that constitute the art and science of the neuropsychological assessment (Spreen & Strauss, 1997).

Over the years, courts have become increasingly distrustful of measures and techniques used to form expert opinions and, consequently, have imposed more rigorous guidelines for the admissibility of expert testimony at trial. As discussed in detail in chapter 7, under *Daubert v. Merrell Dow*

Pharmaceuticals, Inc. (1993) courts are asked to examine the validity and reliability of the instruments used to collect the data and to analyze the validity and reliability of the inferential methods used by clinicians to generate opinions and diagnoses. *State v. Cavalieri* (1995) clearly illustrates these points.

In *Cavalieri*, the New Hampshire Supreme Court, focusing directly on the admissibility of the Millon Clinical Multiaxial Inventory-II and the Minnesota Multiphasic Personality Inventory-2 (MMPI-2) in addressing sex offender profiles, held that the heterogeneity of test data for sex offenders precluded its admissibility. More specifically, the court questioned whether studies of sex offenders admitting to their offenses also applied to those denying them, requiring that accurate classifications be rendered based on scientifically acceptable and reliable methodology. Thus, under the *Daubert* standard, a conclusion will not be admissible simply because a part of the methodology is scientifically valid; "the entire reasoning process must be valid" (*Daubert*, 1993, p. 2796).

As previously noted, numerous disorders and diseases have aggressive behavior and/or cognitive/executive dysfunction as part of their symptomatology. For example, compared to impulsive murderers, premeditated murderers are almost twice as likely to have a history of mood or psychotic disorders (61% vs. 34%), while impulsive murderers are more likely to be developmentally disabled and have cognitive and intellectual impairments compared to premeditated murderers (59% vs. 36%; Hanlon et al., 2013). Deficits in executive functioning, in particular, have long been presumed to be central to the onset and persistence of severe antisocial and aggressive behavior and have been the focus of most of the studies on the etiology of violence undertaken to date (Ogilvie, Stewart, Chan, & Shum, 2011).

Assessing cognitive functioning in the context of violent behavior is particularly problematic because personality disorders are highly comorbid conditions, frequently occurring in combination with mental illnesses and/or substance abuse disorders, and because many individuals have intellectual disabilities, or severe mental illness (Coid, Yang, Tyrer, Roberts, &Ullrich, 2006; Mason, 2007). The assessment of general intellectual functioning is also complicated by the fact that research data has indicated that general intellectual ability may account for a large proportion of the shared variance between neuropsychological tests of frontal lobe function and measures of general intellectual ability (Obonsawin et al., 2002). These neuropsychological test findings have been supported by lesion mapping studies of patients with focal brain lesions by finding that impairment on measures of general intelligence, such as the Wechsler Adult Intelligence Scale (WAIS), is associated with selective damage to frontal and parietal regions, as well as white matter association tracts connecting these areas (Barbey et al., 2012; Gläscher et al., 2010).

Surveys focusing on the use of psychological tests in the forensic setting have confirmed the widespread use of objective tests and measures, including personality inventories (e.g., Archer, Buffington-Vollum, Stredny, & Handel, 2006; Bow, Flens, & Gould, 2010). However, while psychological testing is an important component of most forensic evaluations, the specific tests used tend to vary significantly (Archer et al., 2006). Since a review of all currently available tests, measures, and techniques to assess psychiatric and personality disorders and cognitive/executive functioning is beyond the scope of this chapter, what follows is a detailed review of the most frequently used psychometric tests and personality inventories used to assess *Diagnostic and Statistical Manual of Mental Disorders* (fourth edition, text revision [*DSM–IV–TR*]; American Psychiatric Association, 2000) Axis I and Axis II disorders and, frontal lobe/executive and intellectual functioning. In 2013, the American Psychiatric Association published the *DSM* (fifth edition [*DSM–5*]). However, since most studies reviewed for this book have relied on the *DSM–IV–TR*, for diagnostic purposes, only the *DSM–IV–TR* is discussed.

4.2 The Initial Assessment

Most clinical or forensic assessments usually begin with a clinical interview. The first structured and semi-structured interviews[1] were created in the late 1980s and while the exact format of currently used inventories and interviews varies, they all are based on questions that are keyed into the diagnostic criteria of the *DSM–IV–TR* published by the American Psychiatric Association.

Since under *Daubert* the entire methodology must be valid, any test, measure, and/or technique employed to reach a conclusion must be valid, including the interview process. Furthermore, since many Axis I and Axis II disorders have cognitive dysfunction, in particular frontal lobe dysfunction and/or aggressive and violent behavior, as part of their symptomatology, any assessment in the forensic context must also include a valid assessment of the presence or absence of any of these disorders.[2] To that end, there are a number of structured, semistructured, and self-report measures available designed to assess Axis I and Axis II disorders; however, the most frequently used diagnostic tools used for assessing these disorders are the (a) Structured Clinical Interview for the *DSM–IV–TR* (SCID), (b) Millon Clinical Multiaxial Inventory-III (MCMI-III), (c) MMPI-2, and (d) Personality Assessment Inventory (PAI).

4.2.1 Structured Clinical Interview for the *DSM–IV–TR*

The SCID is a semistructured interview for making Axis I and Axis II diagnoses using *DSM–IV–TR* criteria. The clinical syndromes found on Axis I of the *DSM* represent acutely disturbing, often fluctuating, and transient patterns of symptoms that are typically experienced by an individual as ego-dystonic.[3] In contrast, the personality disorders diagnosed on Axis II represent pervasive and stable patterns of attitudes, thoughts, and behaviors that are commonly experienced by a person as ego-syntonic[4] (Haddy, Strack, & Coca, 2005). The first scale of the SCID (SCID-I) consists of a present mental state interview that provides differential diagnosis for Axis I disorders (primarily mood and substance abuse disorders). The second scale of the SCID (SCID-II) closely follows the language of the *DSM–IV–TR* Axis II personality disorders criteria.

The SCID has undergone numerous revisions and has gained widespread use as a criterion measure in several studies to cross-validate other diagnostic instruments and clinical diagnoses (see, e.g., Messina, Wish, Hoffman, & Nemes, 2001). However, to date, only a few studies have sought to assess the reliability of the SCID, and those that have, have reported good to excellent test–retest reliability of the diagnosis of antisocial personality disorders generated by the SCID-II in psychiatric and substance-abusing populations with kappas ranging from 0.75 to 0.95 (Kranzler, Tennen, Babor, Tennen, & Rounsaville, 1997; Kranzler, Kadden, Babor, Tennen, & Rounsaville, 1996).[5] Further, the interrater reliability of personality disorders assessed by the SCID-II was found to be good to excellent for the presence of any personality disorder, for cluster B and cluster C personality disorders, for the combination of personality disorders from more than one cluster, and for dimensional rating of all personality disorders (Farmer & Chapman, 2002).[6] More recently, a study simultaneously assessing the interrater reliability of the SCID I and SCID-II found moderate to excellent interrater agreement of the Axis I disorders, while most Axis II disorders showed excellent interrater agreement (Lobbestael, Leurgans, & Arntz, 2011).

The validity of any diagnostic assessment test or technique is generally measured by determining the agreement between the diagnoses made by test or technique and some hypothetical "gold standard." Unfortunately, to date, a gold standard for psychiatric diagnoses remains elusive. However, a number of studies have used the SCID as the gold standard in determining the accuracy of clinical diagnoses (see, e.g., Shear et al., 2000). At present, development efforts are underway for the SCID for *DSM–5*.

4.2.2 Personality Inventories

Any neuropsychological evaluation would be incomplete without the assessment of an individual's personality, affect, interpersonal function, and response style. To that end, many neuropsychologists administer at least one personality inventory as part of a standard assessment battery and generally rely on the MMPI-2, MCMI-III, or PAI (Camara, Nathan, & Puente, 2003).

It is well established that for self-report measures, such as the MMPI-2, MCMI-III, and PAI, reliability measures include internal consistency[7] and test–retest reliability.[8] A high degree of internal consistency is of particular importance, because a high reliability coefficient indicates that all items on the test are variations of the same skill or knowledge base. Conversely, if the reliability coefficient is low, it may suggest that the items on the test measures diverse knowledge or skills. Consequently, it has been suggested that an acceptable alpha coefficient for an instrument ranges between .70 and .90 (Streiner & Norman, 2008). However, it has been noted that while acceptable alpha coefficients provide a minimum standard that indicates, but does not guarantee, that the scale items are internally consistent, since alpha is directly related to the number of items in a scale, an unacceptably low alpha clearly indicates a lack of internal consistency (Wise, Streiner, & Walfish, 2010).

4.2.2.1 Minnesota Multiphasic Personality Inventory-2

The MMPI-2 is one of the most widely used personality tests and was originally designed for clinical diagnosis.[9] The MMPI-2 is now commonly used in the forensic setting, and it is well accepted as a valuable tool for assessing a variety of factors in this context. More specifically, while the purpose of the MMPI-2 may vary, it is generally used to evaluate the nature and extent of emotional distress, acute as well as chronic psychopathology, potential effects of psychological variables such as depression on cognitive test performance, and evidence of exaggeration or malingering. The original MMPI-2 consists of 567 true/false questions and is composed of (a) 10 clinical scales (CS) addressing patterns of psychopathology, (b) 15 content scales describing common clinical issues that the subject has endorsed, (c) numerous validity scales for evaluating whether or not a subject is malingering, and (d) hundreds of specialized research scales that often have either focused or limited clinical applications (Lees-Haley, Iverson, Lange, Fox, & Allen, 2002). Although the MMPI-2 is frequently used within the clinical and forensic setting, most research on the MMPI-2 has focused on its utility as a measure of malingering. Indeed, few studies have investigated the predictive accuracy of the various clinical scales. However, it has been shown that in a sample of adult inpatients with a primary psychotic disorder (PPD) or a primary mood disorder without psychotic features (PMD) the MMPI-2 was able to correctly classify PPD and PMD patients 70% of the time (Dao, Prevatt, & Horne, 2008).

In addition, a meta-analysis assessing the predictive accuracy of the MMPI-2 Depression scale found that this scale has a positive predictive power (PPP) of .68 and a negative predictive power (NPP) of .58, with a sensitivity of .64 and a specificity of .62 (Gross, Keyes, & Greene, 2000).

The MMPI-2 clinical scales were subsequently restructured to address problems in the originals, including inclusion of questionable subtle items, and the lack of theoretical grounding (Tellegen et al., 2006). Research findings on the validity of the restructured clinical scales have been mixed. For example, Nichols (2006) asserted that the original clinical scales are better suited for the prediction of psychiatric diagnoses than the restructured clinical scales because of the original scales' "syndromal fidelity"; that is, the multidimensional makeup of the clinical scale is consistent with multifaceted diagnostic syndromes. However, this assertion has been contradicted by empirical findings showing that the restructured clinical scales outperform the clinical scales in predicting psychiatric diagnoses (e.g., Simms, Casillas, Clark, Watson, & Doebbeling, 2005; Tellegen et al., 2006). Further, in a study of substance abusers, the restructured clinical scales demonstrated equivalent or improved convergent and discriminant validity compared to their clinical scale counterparts (Forbey & Ben-Porath, 2007). It has also been contended that the clinical scales are better than the restructured clinical scales for assessing complex mental disorders, such as psychopathy (Caldwell, 2006). However, Bolinskey and Nichols (2011) have argued that the restructured clinical scales RC4, RC7, and RC9 measure traits and behaviors that are not necessarily equivalent to those assessed by the original scales.

The most recent version, the MMPI-2-RF, has retained only 338 of the original 567 items and added new scales designed to capture somatic complaints. According to the MMPI-2-RF developers, all of the MMPI-2-RF's scales have demonstrated either equivalent or better construct and criterion validity compared to their MMPI-2 counterparts (Ben-Porath, 2012; Tellegen and Ben-Porath, 2008). However, the clinical scales were found to have comparatively lower alpha coefficients than the Content, Supplementary, or Restructured scales, based on the .70 alpha level criterion, with the exceptions of the Type A scale for women and the Low Self-Esteem and Ideas of Persecution scales. Further three of the five PSY-5 scales reported internal consistency estimates < .70, while the test–retest reliability for the MMPI-2 scales, in a one-week interval, all exceeded the .70 level, with the exception of the Pa scale for males and the Pd, Pa, Pt, Sc, Ma, and RC4 (antisocial personality disorder) scales for women (Wise et al., 2010). In addition, the percentage of MMPI-2 scales that showed test–retest reliability greater than or equal to .80 were 37% and 41% for men and women, respectively, and the percentage of all MMPI-2 scales that reached an alpha level of .80 were 27% and 29% (women and men, respectively; Wise et al., 2010).

Although the MMPI-2 is considered to have high clinical utility, it has been suggested that its use in the forensic setting may be problematic for the following reasons: (a) the MMPI-2 is not likely to withstand a *Daubert* challenge if it is offered as evidence of brain injury because it does not measure neuropsychological impairment, and (b) claims that the MMPI-2 indicates causation are indefensible under *Daubert* because the MMPI-2 profile provides evidence related to a subject's condition but not the cause of that condition (Lees-Haley et al., 2002).

4.2.2.2 Millon Clinical Multiaxial Inventory-III

The MCMI-III consists of 175 true/false items designed to assess basic personality styles, severe personality disorders, and clinical syndromes. The MCMI-III was developed to make the pathologies of personality operational and has undergone several revisions to maximize the similarity between *DSM* criteria and the MCMI-III scales. The first 10 scales of the MCMI-III are designed to detect basic personality patterns, including schizoid, antisocial, compulsive, passive-aggressive, and aggressive/sadistic personality. The MCMI-III also includes three pathological personality patterns (schizotypal, borderline, and paranoid). In addition, there are nine clinical syndrome scales (anxiety, somatoform, hypomania, dysthymia, alcohol abuse, drug abuse, psychotic thinking, psychotic depression, and psychotic delusions) as well as a scale that measures subjects' response tendencies (the internal validity scale; Millon, Millon, Davis, & Grossman, 2009). It must be noted that, because the MCMI-III norms are based on clinical populations, there is disagreement about its use with only a clinical population in contrast to those who argue for its use within the forensic population (Dyer, 2005).[10]

The MCMI-III uses base rate (BR) scores (range, 0–115; median, 60) to examine the probability that an individual exhibits the presence of a trait (BR scores 75–84) or prominence (BR ≥85) of a syndrome or disorder (Bow et al., 2010). When queried about the cutoff score used for interpreting BR scores on the MCMI-III, a large percentage of forensic psychologists were found to incorrectly identify the significance BR cutoff score of 75[11] and the prominence BR cutoff score of 85 (69% answered 80 or less; Bow, Flens, & Gould, 2010).

Little is known about the reliability and validity of this MCMI-III. However, an early meta-analysis of the MCMI-III and Axis II disorders concluded that (a) the MCMI-III scales lack sufficient "construct validity" to be used in forensic settings, and (b) the MCMI-III scales cannot be used to diagnose *DSM–IV* personality disorders since the test may generate errors in about 80% of diagnosed cases (Rogers, Salekin, & Sewell, 1999). It has also been argued that while the MCMI-III can be used as a screening inventory for trait prevalence, diagnosing personality disorders should be done through a combination of as many different methods as possible to gain information from different sources and reduce inherent method variability (Rossi, Haube, van den Branden, & Sloore, 2003). Most recently it has been suggested that the MCMI-III clinical syndrome scales generally measure the constructs they were intended for (Hesse, Guldager, & Linneberg, 2012). The MCMI-III was also found to demonstrate consistently high alpha coefficients (>.70), with the exception of the Compulsive and Narcissistic scales, while the test–retest reliability exceeded the .80 level (Wise et al., 2010). In fact, 78% of the MCMI-III scales obtained alpha coefficients ≥.80, and the percentage of MCMI-III scales that showed test–retest reliability greater than or equal to .80 was found to be 100% (Wise et al., 2010).

Some researchers have cautioned that any forensic expert who uses the MCMI-III is likely to encounter vigorous opposition to the use of this instrument in their forensic assessment (McCann, 2002), while others view the MCMI-III as meeting the *Daubert* admissibility criteria. More specifically, in Bow and colleagues' (2010) study, 76% of the respondents thought that the

MCMI-III met the *Frye* test, 69% believed that it met the *Daubert* criteria, and 21% of respondents using the MCMI-III reported having experienced an admissibility challenge.

4.2.2.3 Personality Assessment Inventory

The PAI, authored by Morey (1996), is a 344-item multiscale self-report measure of psychological functioning that assesses constructs relevant to psychopathology and personality evaluations such as depression or aggression in various contexts, including forensic assessment. The PAI has 22 nonoverlapping scales providing a comprehensive overview of psychopathology in adults. More specifically, the PAI contains the following four types of scales: (a) validity scales, which measure the respondent's approach to the test, including faking good or bad, exaggeration, or defensiveness; (b) clinical scales, which correspond to psychiatric diagnostic categories; (c) treatment consideration scales, which assess factors that may relate to treatment of clinical disorders or other risk factors but that are not captured in psychiatric diagnoses (e.g., suicidal ideation); and (d) interpersonal scales, which provide indicators of interpersonal dimensions of personality functioning (Morey, 1996).

To date, few studies have systematically assessed the validity of the PAI; however, research has supported the validity of the Schizophrenia scale for identifying psychotic spectrum disorders and their associated features (Morey, 2007). Further, PPP, NPP, sensitivity, and specificity for the Depression scale were found to be .62, .62, .70, and .52, respectively, while the Drug Problem scale was found to have. 65 sensitivity and specificity and a PPP and NPP of .61 and .69, respectively (Edens & Ruiz, 2008). More recently, the PAI was found to consistently demonstrate high alpha coefficients for the full scales and a test–retest reliability level ≥.75, excluding the Inconsistency and Infrequency scales[12] (Wise et al., 2010). Further, the percentage of PAI scales that demonstrated a test–retest reliability greater than or equal to .80 was found to be 61%, while 63% of the PAI scales obtained an alpha coefficient level of .80 (Wise et al., 2010). Despite its psychometric superiority over the MMPI-2, it has been argued that the PAI should not be considered a diagnostic measure.

4.3 Assessment of Cognitive/Executive Functioning

Neuropsychologists frequently use scientifically validated tests to evaluate brain functions. While neurological examination and computed tomography or magnetic resonance imaging scans assess the physical, structural, and metabolic condition of the brain, the neuropsychological examination and positron emission tomography, single photon emission tomography, and functional magnetic resonance imaging scans are the only way to formally assess brain function. Neuropsychological tests cover a wide range of mental processes from complex reasoning to simple motor functioning, and almost all tests results are compared with some normative standard, such as data from groups of non-brain-injured persons. If the norms are based on age and educational achievement, valid comparisons can be made between an individual's performance and that of persons in known diagnostic categories, as well as persons who do not have a diagnosis of brain injury (Spreen & Strauss, 1997).

It has been suggested that a combination of objective scores, behavioral process observations, and consistency in emerging pattern of results, along with a comprehensive clinical history, constitute the art and science of neuropsychological assessment (Spreen & Strauss, 1997). Consequently, most neuropsychologists select a unique combination of tests that focus on the diagnostic and examination questions of interest for an individual. As described in chapter 5 in detail, executive function refers to the ability to plan and execute behavior while constantly updating representations and goals in an always-changing environment. Central to these control functions is the ability to appropriately select actions that are advantageous and suppress actions that are either inappropriate or because they interfere with completion of motor and/or cognitive goals.

The concept of executive functions, despite being frequently mentioned in the scientific literature, has yet to be clearly defined. Indeed, research studies aimed at exploring the various aspects of this construct have produced contradictory findings, resulting in a lack of clarity and even controversy regarding the true nature of executive functioning abilities (Jurado & Rosselli, 2007). As previously noted, a large amount of research has focused on executive functioning in assessing the etiology of violent and aggressive behavior, and most of the evidence for the neural structures involved in executive functions has come from laboratory tasks, such as the Stroop Color and Word Test (Stroop) or the Wisconsin Card Sort Test (WCST). For example, research findings have indicated that psychopathic individuals show no impairment on measures of executive function linked to the dorsolateral prefrontal cortex, such as the WCST, but do score in the impaired range on measures linked to the orbital frontal cortex, such as the Porteus Maze Test (PMT; Mitchell, Colledge, Leonard, & Blair, 2002; Roussy & Toupin, 2000). In addition, in a recent study impulsive murderers were found to perform significantly poorer than instrumental murderers across various neurocognitive domains, with the largest effect size observed on measures of executive functions, attention, memory, and intelligence (Hanlon et al., 2013). It has also been suggested that sensitivity to frontal lobe damage is established when the Category Test, Trail Making Test (TMT) Part B, and Stroop discriminate between subjects who have frontal lobe damage and those that do not, while specificity is established when Part A of the TMT and other Stroop measures do not discriminate between these groups (Demakis, 2013).

Clearly, functional neuroimaging techniques alone cannot prove that a given brain region is critical for a specific cognitive task; neuropsychological testing is also required. While results from neuroimaging techniques can provide another perspective of the relationship between cognitive impairment and violent behavior, all currently available neuroimaging modalities suffer from inherent limitations. Therefore, any evaluation of cognitive impairment in the context of violent behavior must also include the administration of a number of valid and reliable tests specifically designed to assess frontal lobe/executive functioning. Unfortunately, to date few studies have sought to determine the scientific validity or evidentiary reliability of executive functioning tests, and, those that have examined multiple measures of executive functioning have found weak or mixed results (e.g., Salthouse, 2005). Let us now look more closely at the most frequently used executive functioning tests, bearing in mind that results from studies employing these tests may be divergent due to variations in the experimental paradigms used, thereby making them difficult to interpret across studies.

4.3.1 Wisconsin Card Sort Test

In clinical practice, this test is widely used with patients who have acquired brain injury, neurodegenerative disease, or mental illness, such as schizophrenia. The WCST is considered a measure of executive function because of its reported sensitivity to frontal lobe functioning in general and dorsolateral prefrontal cortex dysfunction in particular. As such, this test allows the clinician to assess the following "frontal" lobe functions: strategic planning, organized searching, utilizing environmental feedback to shift cognitive sets, directing behavior toward achieving a goal, and modulating impulsive responding (Heaton, Chelune, Talley, Kay, & Curtiss, 1993).

Initially, a number of stimulus cards are presented to the subject. The subject is not told how to match the cards; however, he or she is told whether a particular match is right or wrong. The mistakes made during this learning process are analyzed to arrive at a score (see Figure 4.1 for an example of the WCST). The original WCST used paper cards and was carried out with the experimenter on one side of the desk facing the participant on the other. However, since the early 1990s, computerized versions of the task have been available (see Figure 4.1). The latter has the advantage of automatically scoring the test, which was quite complex in the manual version. The test takes approximately 12 to 20 minutes to complete and generates a number of psychometric scores, including numbers, percentages, and percentiles of categories achieved, trials, errors, and perseverative errors (Heaton et al., 1993).

Many clinical studies on WCST performance have suggested that left frontal damage affects WCST performance more than right frontal damage;

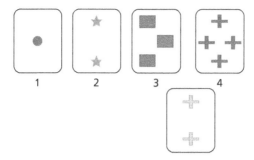

Figure 4.1 Illustration of Wisconsin Card Sort Test. This test uses stimulus and response cards that show various forms in various colors and numbers. Individually administered, it requires the subject to sort the cards according to different principles (i.e., by color or number). As the test progresses, there are unannounced shifts in the sorting principle that require the subject to change his or her approach. See Color Plate 13 in insert.

however, others have found no difference in laterality of damage in the frontal cortex (Goldstein, Obrzut, John, Ledakis, & Armstrong, 2004). Numerous neuroimaging studies on WCST performance have also reported a significant increase in metabolic or neural activity, and in a majority of the cases the increased activation was found in the dorsolateral prefrontal cortex and ventrolateral prefrontal cortex (e.g., Lie, Specht, Marshall, & Fink, 2006). Further, because research findings have indicated that WCST performance does not engage one specific brain area but involves a distributed neural network of both cortical and subcortical brain structures, the extent to which this test adequately assesses frontal lobe functioning has been questioned (Barcelo, 2001). It has also been established that the frontal lobes are, functionally, heterogeneous, suggesting that the WCST can only reveal specific aspects of frontal lobe processing, such as the shift from using an old rule to a new rule (Maes et al., 2006; Miller & Cummings, 2007).

Although the WCST is the most widely used test for the assessment of frontal lobe/executive functioning and has been described as "the gold standard of executive function tests" (Delis, Kaplan, & Kramer, 2001, p. 2), surprisingly, to date not a single study has attempted to systematically assess the sensitivity, specificity, PPP, and NPP of this test. However, a 2003 meta-analysis has concluded that the WCST is, indeed, sensitive to frontal lobe damage, although the effect size between frontally and nonfrontally damaged subjects was in the small to medium range (0.33).[13] The effect size increased to larger than 1.0 (i.e., greater than a standard deviation) when certain moderator variables, such as administration format or area damaged within the frontal lobes, were assessed (Demakis, 2004).

As discussed previously, the WCST is not specific to frontal lobe function; it does not engage one specific brain area but involves a widespread network of brain structures, each of which carries out distinct processes.

Therefore, in its present form the WCST cannot provide a valid description about the type and severity of executive dysfunctions or the anatomical regions in which these deficits occur (Nyhus & Barcelo, 2009). Based on these findings, the WCST should not be taken as a sole measure of prefrontal functioning. Nevertheless, one may still want to use the WCST scores as an index of the general status of a subject's executive functioning, regardless of its anatomical implications (Lezak, 1995).

4.3.2 Stroop Color and Word Test

This test consists of a word page with color words printed in black ink, a color page with Xs printed in color, and a color-word page with words from the first page printed in colors from the second page (the color and the word do not match; see Figure 4.2). The test-taker reads color words or names ink colors from different pages as quickly as possible within a specific time limit. The Stroop is based on the observation that individuals can read words much faster than they can identify and name colors. The Stroop yields three scores based on the number of items completed on each of the three stimulus sheets. In addition, an interference score, which is useful in determining an individual's creativity, cognitive flexibility, and reaction to cognitive pressures, can also be calculated (Golden, 1978).

A number of different test versions have been developed with variations in the color and number of the test items, the number of subtests, and the administration procedure. Despite these variations, the basic paradigm of the Stroop test has remained the same: an individual's performance on a basic task (e.g., reading names of colors) is compared with his or her performance on an analogous task in which a habitual response needs to be suppressed in support of an unusual one (i.e., naming the ink color that incongruously named color words are printed in). The increase in time taken to perform the latter task compared with the basic task is referred to as "the Stroop interference effect" and is considered to be a general measure of control

BLUE RED GREEN
PURPLE BLUE PURPLE
RED PURPLE RED

Figure 4.2 Illustration of the Stroop Color and Word Test. The subject is presented with names of colors written in the same color or in a different color. When the name of a color (e.g., "blue" or "red") is printed in a color not denoted by the name (e.g., the word "red" printed in blue ink instead of red ink), naming the color of the word takes longer and is more prone to errors than when the color of the ink matches the name of the color. See Color Plate 14 in insert.

and cognitive flexibility or executive functioning (e.g., Davidson, Zacks, & Williams, 2003).[14] This test was further developed by separating the task into four stages: (1) color fields, (2) congruent color words, (3) incongruent color words, and (4) combined. It has been argued that the additional strain put on the executive functions of the brain allows for a more precise diagnosis (Davidson et al., 2003).

Little is known about the validity and predictive accuracy of the Stroop; however, a meta-analysis has suggested that the Stroop alone would not be adequate to discriminate between frontal and nonfrontal subjects. More specifically, the amount of overlap between the distributions of these two groups, at effect sizes ranging from approximately 70% to 89%, indicated little separation of the groups and thus relatively poor sensitivity (true positives) and specificity (true negatives; Demakis, 2004). In addition, Stroop tasks associated with differential activation of the anterior cingulate cortex were found not to differentiate nonpsychopathic from psychopathic offenders (Dvorak-Bertsch, Sadeh, Glass, Thornton, & Newman, 2007). Finally, while the Stroop is commonly regarded as a test of prefrontal functioning, imaging studies have questioned this assumption (Alvarez & Emory, 2006; Gruber, Rogowska, Holcomb, Soraci, & Yurgelun-Todd, 2002).

4.3.3 Porteus Maze Test

This test was developed as a technique for measuring planning ability. Porteus believed that planning was fundamental to intelligent behavior and initially devised the procedure as a culture-free means of screening for mental deficiency (Riddle & Roberts, 1978). The PMT requires the subject to solve a series of mazes of increasing difficulty by drawing a continuous pencil line from a given start point to a goal point. There are currently three forms of the PMT: the Vineland Revision, the more difficult Extension series, and the most difficult Supplemental series. The three series of mazes are progressively more difficult in order to compensate for practice effects that have been observed on repeated administrations. Both quantitative and qualitative scoring can be derived. Qualitative aspects of performance on the PMT are evaluated by noting instances of careless, uncritical responding, such as entering blind alleys that occur very early or very late in the maze (Riddle & Roberts, 1978).

In the context of cognitive research, this test is often used to assess cognitive deficits or to evaluate treatment effects in schizophrenia, dementia, and alcoholism. Mazes have also been used to investigate personality traits such as impulsivity. Further, below-norm performance on maze tasks has been related to disturbed executive functions and therefore a dysfunction of the prefrontal cortex (Krikorian & Bartok, 1998). However, while mazes used in the context of spatial learning tasks have been applied in brain imaging studies, the literature lacks functional brain imaging studies on Porteus Maze-like tasks. The only functional neuroimaging study undertaken to date has suggested that the PMT activates a large network from visual to parietal regions, as well as the bilateral areas of the prefrontal cortex and subcortical and cortical motor areas. From these findings, Kirsch and colleagues (2006) concluded that the PMT is a suitable method to quantify prefrontal cortex dysfunction in patients suffering from schizophrenia and other neuropsychiatric disorders using functional magnetic resonance imaging. Indeed, mazes were found to activate the bilateral areas of the prefrontal cortex, demonstrating their unique role in decision-making processes (Kirsch et al., 2006).

4.3.4 Trail Making Test

The TMT has been widely used as a measure of scanning, visuomotor tracking, cognitive flexibility, and divided attention and is usually administered in two parts, Part A and Part B. Part A requires the subject to link in ascending order a series of 25 numbers (1-2-3 . . .) randomly distributed in space. Subjects are instructed to start their "trial" at the circle marked *Begin* and continue linking numbers until they reach the endpoint (circle marked *End*). Part B is similar, although instead of just linking numbers the subject must alternately switch between a set of numbers (1–13) and a set of letters (A–L), again linking in ascending order (1-A-2-B . . . ; see Figure 4.3; Lezak, Howieson, & Loring, 2004).

   The value of the TMT as a measure of frontal lobe functioning is questionable at best. For example, a study involving TBI patients found no correlation between lesion volume and location and scores on the WCST and the TMT. From these findings the authors concluded that (a) the TMT, if used in isolation, does not add anything unique about frontal lobe integrity and neuropsychological functioning in TBI patients, and (b) none of these measures can distinguish specific frontal lobe dysfunction (Anderson, Bigler, & Blatter, 1995). In contrast, Shibukya-Tayoshi and colleagues (2007) have noted that increase in prefrontal cortex activity during the TMT supports the use of

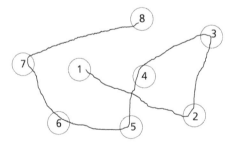

Figure 4.3 Illustration of Part A of the Trail Making Test. The subject is instructed to connect the set of dots as fast as possible while still maintaining accuracy. The time taken to complete the test is used as the primary performance metric.

this test. However, a study assessing the construct validity of this test concluded that Part A of the TMT primarily requires visuoperceptual abilities, Part B mostly reflects working memory and secondarily task-switching ability, while B–A minimizes visuoperceptual and working memory demands, thus providing a rather pure indicator of executive control functions (Sánchez-Cubillo et al., 2009). Finally, a recent meta-analysis has indicated that Part B of the TMT is unable to distinguish healthy control subjects from those with major depressive disorder (Lim et al., 2013).

4.3.5 Controlled Oral Word Association Test

The purpose of this test is to evaluate the spontaneous production of words within a limited amount of time. More specifically, the subject is asked to produce orally as many words as possible, beginning with a given letter of the alphabet. There are three trials administered, each employing a different letter (e.g., FAS, CFL), and subjects are allowed 60 seconds for each trial. During this task, subjects are prohibited from saying proper nouns (e.g., *Carl, California*) or saying the same word using a different ending (e.g., *cancel, canceled*; Loonstra, Tarlow, & Sellers, 2001). Test performance is measured by calculating the total number of acceptable words produced for all three letters. Errors and perseverations (word repetitions) are not included in this score. Errors include words that begin with the wrong letter, are proper nouns, or differ from a previous response by tense, plurality, or grammar usage. Changing a word ending to produce a new word that refers to a noun (e.g., *teach* and *teacher*) is considered acceptable, and such instances are scored as two separate words (Loonstra et al., 2001).

It has been noted that the Controlled Oral Word Association Test has excellent psychometric properties; the interrater reliability is 0.9, the test–retest reliability is similarly high, and correlations between letter sets range from 0.85 to 0.94 (Ross, Furr, Carter, & Weinberg, 2006; Troyer, 2000). It has also been concluded that the left anterior prefrontal cortex and anterior cingulate cortex dysfunction is associated with below-norm performance on this test (Audenaert et al., 2000). Further, according to Strauss and colleagues (2006), the Controlled Oral Word Association Test is a sensitive indicator of brain dysfunction; however, the scientific validity and evidentiary reliability of this test has yet to be systematically assessed.

4.3.6 California Verbal Learning Test-II

The California Verbal Learning Test-II (CVLT-II) tests levels of recall and recognition, semantic and serial learning strategies, serial position effects, learning rates, recall consistency, degree of vulnerability to proactive and retroactive interference, short-term and long-term retention of information, perseverations and intrusions in recall, and false positives in recognition. The test currently consists of two lists of four words from four categories (furniture, vegetables, ways of traveling, and animals) presented to the subject. The CVLT-II administration requires that a list of 16 words be presented to the individual for memorization, who is then instructed to recall those words over the course of five trials, again after a distracter list, and with cues to facilitate memory (Delis et al., 2001).

The CVLT-II was developed to enhance diagnostic accuracy in identifying and characterizing different memory disorders by evaluating the magnitude of learning and memory impairments and by evaluating the cognitive processes leading to impaired performance. The CVLT-II is well suited to measure subtle changes in verbal learning and memory ability and is presumed to be sensitive to temporo-hippocampal dysfunction (Osuji & Collum, 2005). Little is known about the predictive accuracy of this test; however, it has been contended that the recall discriminability index of the CVLT-II may be useful in improving the diagnostic accuracy of memory disorders across dementia populations (Delis et al., 2005). It has also been argued that, if a subject does well on this test, a clinician may reasonably conclude that the subject's verbal memory is intact. On the other hand, if a subject's performance on the CVLT-II is impaired, further testing may be warranted to more clearly determine the precise nature of the underlying cognitive deficit (McDowell, Bayless, Moser, Meyers, & Paulsen, 2004). Further, while the CVLT-II average scores are able to differentiate between controls and patients with various degrees of severity of traumatic brain injury, it should not be used in isolation to determine the presence or absence of acquired memory impairment (Jacobs & Donders, 2007).

4.3.7 Category Test

The Category subtest (CT) of the Halstead-Reitan Neuropsychological Test Battery is comprised of a total of 208 pictures consisting of geometric figures. For each picture, individuals are asked to decide whether they are reminded of the number 1, 2, 3, or 4, and then they press a key that corresponds to their number of choice. If they chose correctly a chime sounds, and if they chose incorrectly a buzzer sounds. The key to this test is that one principle, or common characteristic, underlies each subtest. The numbers 1, 2, 3, and 4 represent the possible principles. If individuals are able to recognize the correct principle in one picture, they will respond correctly for the remaining pictures in that subtest. The next subtest may have the same or a different underlying principle, and individuals must again try to determine that principle using the feedback of the chime and buzzer. The last subtest contains two underlying principles (Spreen & Strauss, 1997).

The CT is considered the battery's most effective test for detecting brain damage, but it cannot determine where in the brain the problem is. The test evaluates the ability to (a) draw specific conclusions from general information, (b) solve complex and unique problems, and (c) learn from experience (Spreen & Strauss, 1997). Surveys indicate that the CT, whether selectively administered or within the Halstead-Reitan Neuropsychological Test Battery, continues to be among the most widely utilized measures by neuropsychologists (Camara, Nathan, & Puente, 2000). Although the CT has been used for decades, little is known about its diagnostic efficiency. However, Lopez and colleagues (2000) found the CT Total Score reliability to be .9716 while the subtest reliabilities ranged from .4587 to .9590. Further, while this test may be sensitive to cerebral dysfunction, a false-positive rate of as high as 18% has been reported (Anderson, Bigler, & Blatter, 1995; Choca, Laatsch, Wetzel, & Agresti, 1997). More recently, subjects with frontal lobe damage were found to perform significantly worse than subjects with damage to posterior brain regions on all components of the Stroop and TMT Part A but not on the CT or the TMT Part B (Demakis, 2013).

4.3.8 Go/No-Go Task

The traditional GNG design involves only two stimuli: a Go stimulus and a No-go stimulus. Subjects are instructed to respond rapidly, generally with a button-press, to presentation of Go stimuli only, and response inhibition is measured by the ability to appropriately withhold responding to No-go stimuli. While some studies employ a more traditional GNG task design, with a single Go stimulus and a single No-go stimulus, other researchers use more complex designs involving multiple Go cues (Fassbender et al. 2004). For example, in one frequently used version of the task, Xs and Ys are alternately presented on the screen, and infrequently there is a two-letter repeat, which is the No-go signal; after presentation of an X, Y becomes the Go signal and X the No-go signal and vice versa (Hester et al., 2004).

Since there is no standardized version of the GNG, no reliability and validity data exist. Numerous neuroimaging studies, however, have suggested that a large number of structures, including the right lateralized parieto-frontal network and the presupplementary motor area, are involved in the performance of this task (Swick, Ashley, & Turken, 2011). Research findings have also suggested that increased response time variability, or inefficient performance, during a simple GNG is associated with activation of the right prefrontal cortex (Simmonds et al., 2007).

4.3.9 Conners' Continuous Performance Test II, Version 5.2

Continuous performance tasks (CPTs) are neuropsychological tests designed to measure an individual's selective and sustained attention and impulsivity and are frequently used as part of a battery of tests to assess individuals' executive functioning and/or their ability to sort and manage information. There are various types of CPTs, with the Conners' Continuous Performance Test II, Version 5.2 (CPT-II) being one of the most commonly used. In the

CPT-II, subjects are asked to click the space bar or press the mouse when they are presented with any letter except the letter X. In other words, the subject must refrain from clicking the space bar or pressing the mouse if the letter X is presented on the screen (Conners & MHS Staff, 2000).

According to the test developers, (a) the CPT-II test shows adequate consistency in terms of split-half reliability, (b) the standard error measurement values indicate that the CPT-II score is a reasonable match to the true performance of an individual, and (c) the CPT II has satisfactory accuracy in terms of both false positives and false negatives (Conners & MHS Staff, 2000). However, a 2007 study evaluating the validity and classification utility of the CPT-II in assessing inattentive and hyperactive-impulsive behaviors in children found no significant positive correlations between the CPT-II and parent and teacher ratings of inattentive and hyperactive-impulsive behaviors (Edwards et al., 2007). Similarly, results from a study assessing attention deficit hyperactivity disorder in adults indicated that the CTP-II is unable to differentiate between adults with this disorder and those with other psychiatric conditions (Solanto, Etefia, & Marks, 2004).

4.4 Assessment of Intellectual Functioning and Memory

In 1992 Daniel Burns was convicted of first-degree murder and cocaine trafficking and sentenced to death. On appeal, the Florida Supreme Court affirmed Burns's convictions but vacated his death sentence (*Burns v. State*, 1992). In 2002, after numerous appeals had been denied, Burns requested permission to file a supplemental brief concerning whether he met the statutory definition for mental retardation (e.g., *State v. Burns*, 2000). The Supreme Court of Florida granted that motion, and Burns and the State filed supplemental briefs. In his supplemental brief, Burns argued that when considering IQ scores, it is the Full-Scale IQ (FSIQ) score that provides the cutoff as to the subaverage intellectual functioning prong of the definition of mental retardation, as clearly stated in the administrative and scoring section of the Technical Manual for the third edition of the WAIS (WAIS-III) and as noted in *Atkins v. Virginia* (2002). Burns also contended that the FSIQ score merely represents a range (the statistical error of measurement must be considered in evaluating FSIQ scores) and that the use of rigid cutoff scores for determination of the intellectual functioning prong of a mental retardation is highly problematic. Indeed, as noted by the American Association on Mental Retardation, " the assessment of intellectual functioning through the primary reliance on intellectual tests is fraught with the potential for misuse if consideration is not given to possible errors in measurement" (Luckasson et al., 2002, p. 57). This process is facilitated by bearing in mind the concept of the standard error of measurement, which has been estimated to be 3 to 5 points for all well-standardized measures of general intellectual functioning (Luckasson et al., 2002). This means that, for example, an IQ score of 70 is best understood not as a precise score but as a range of confidence levels with parameters of at least one standard error of measurement (scores between 66 and 74; 66% probability) or two standard errors of measurement (scores between 62 and 78; 95% probability; Grossman, 1983).

On appeal, Burns further argued that the State's expert admitted ignorance of authoritative sources relied upon by *Atkins* (2002), which effectively disqualified his testimony as to the IQ component of the determination of mental retardation. Further, the expert's reliance on the 1993 WAIS was wrong and contrary to the directives contained in the WAIS Administrative and Technical Manual. Indeed, as noted in the WAIS-III Technical Manual, data indicates that an examinee's IQ score, in general, will be higher when outdated than when current norms are used. The State's expert subsequently admitted that only the most current version of the WAIS test should be administered, due to inflated results if an outdated test is used.[15] Indeed, a factor that can significantly impact an individual's FSIQ score is the Flynn effect, which is described as an increase in FSIQ of approximately 3 points per decade (Flynn, 2007).[16] The Flynn effect plays a particularly important role in *Atkins* cases, where individuals with FSIQ scores above 71 generally are not considered intellectually deficient[17] and therefore will not receive relief under the *Atkins* standard (Taub & Benson, 2013; see also *Keen v. State*, 2012).[18]

Currently, in the clinical and forensic setting, the WAIS tests, which include the WAIS (for adults and older adolescents), the Wechsler Intelligence Scale for Children (for children between the ages of 6 and 16), and the Wechsler Preschool and Primary Scale of Intelligence (for children between the ages of 2 years 6 months and 7 years 3 months) are the primary tests used to assess general intellectual functioning. The first version of the WAIS was published 1955 and subsequently revised numerous times. All of these tests are based on Wechsler's belief that intelligence is a complex ability that involves a variety of skills and, because intelligence is multifaceted, a test measuring intelligence must reflect this multitude of skills. After dividing intelligence into verbal and performance skills, Wechsler utilized the statistical technique of factor analysis to determine specific skills within these two major domains. These more specific factors formed the basis of the WAIS subtests (Kaplan & Saccuzzo, 2010).

4.4.1 Wechsler Adult Intelligence Scale, Third Edition

Research findings have indicated that the WAIS-III has excellent validity and reliability. According to the WAIS-III Technical Manual, the average reliability coefficients of the subtests, with the exception of the Picture Arrangement, Symbol Search, and Object Assembly subtests, range from .82 to .93, while the Symbol Search subtest had a coefficient of .77, the

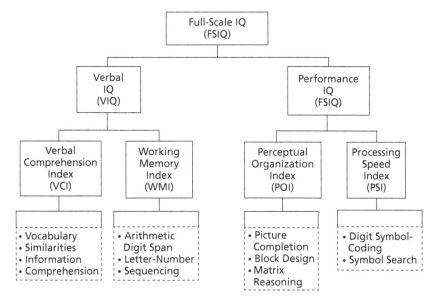

Figure 4.4 WAIS-III Scales and Indexes.

Image courtesy http://en.wikipedia.org/wiki/File:Wechsler_Adult_Intelligence_Scale

(Licensed under the Creative Commons Attribution-ShareAlike 3.0 License).

Picture Arrangement had .74, and the Object Assembly had .70 (Kaufman & Lichtenberger, 1999; see also Figure 4.4 for a description of the WAIS-III scales and indexes). In addition, interrater reliability is high with averages in the high .90s for most WAIS-III subtests, and the WAIS-III overall has higher reliability coefficients than the WAIS–Revised (Psychological Corporation, 1997). However, as argued by Coolican (2005):

> Note that psychologists have not discovered that intelligence has a normal distribution in the population. The tests were purposely created to fit a normal distribution, basically for research purposes and practical convenience in test comparisons. (p. 288)

Although the WAIS-III Technical Manual does not provide reliabilities for discrepancy scores, researcher have calculated the internal consistency reliability of the discrepancy scores for the WAIS-III IQ and Index and subtest scores from the data provided in the manual. The reliabilities for the IQ and Index discrepancy scores were found to range from .70 to .88 ($M = .83$, $SD = .04$), and the reliabilities for the subtest discrepancy scores were found to range from .44 to .85 ($M = .69$, $SD = .09$; Charter, 2001).

Despite its popularity, to date few studies have actually assessed the PPP, NPP, sensitivity, and specificity of the WAIS-III in general or its subtests in particular. However, researchers have questioned the clinical utility of using the Digit Span subtest as a measure of everyday attention. For example, Groth-Marnat and Baker (2004) found that while the Digit Span subtest was a weak but statistically significant predictor of attentional ability (accounting for 12.7% of the unique variance), the Picture Completion subtest was a better predictor (accounting for 19% of the unique variance). Further, both education and culture were found to significantly affect performance on the WAIS-III (Walker, Batchelor, & Shores, 2009). Consequently, special attention must be paid to neuropsychological assessments carried out in the cross-cultural context and in cultures where educational systems are more complex (Lam et al., 2013). Studies attempting to determine what exactly is measured by the Arithmetic subtest have also suggested that while this test may be considered a measure of concentration or working memory, results are influenced by other factors, such as verbal memory and, therefore, the test's specificity as a measure of concentration is limited (Karzmark, 2009).

4.4.2 Wechsler Adult Intelligence Scale, Fourth Edition

The latest version of the test, the WAIS-IV, was released in 2008, and, relative to the WAIS-III, 53% of the WAIS-IV items were changed. One of the most substantive changes made include the replacement of the Verbal IQ and Performance IQ with the Verbal Comprehension Index and Perceptual Reasoning Index, deletion of the Picture Arrangement and Object Assembly subtests, addition of the Visual Puzzles subtest (see Figure 4.4), and required administration of 10 subtests to obtain the FSIQ rather than 13 (Sattler & Ryan, 2009; Wechsler, 2008). The WAIS-IV includes 10 core subtests as well as 5 supplemental subtests and provides the following four index scores representing major components of intelligence: (a) Verbal Comprehension, (b) Perceptual Reasoning, (c) Working Memory, and (d) Processing Speed. In addition, the WAIS-IV provides two overall summary scores: the FSIQ and the General Ability Index. According to the test author, the average internal consistency estimates ranged from .78 to .94 for subtests, from .90 to .96 for factor index scores, and .98 for the FSIQ.

It has been suggested that a revised intelligence test should provide a better measure of intelligence when compared to the instrument it replaces. Thus it is may be assumed that the FSIQ score of the WAIS-IV represents an improved FSIQ score when compared to the WAIS-III's FSIQ score; however, to date, research supporting this assumption is sorely lacking (Taub & Benson, 2013). Results from a study employing structural equation modeling to empirically assess which instrument provides a more sound measure of intelligence have indicated that the WAIS-IV provides superior measurement, scoring, and structural models to measure the FSIQ when compared to the WAIS-III (Taub & Benson, 2013). In contrast, the Visual Puzzles subtest was found not to be a pure measure of visuoperceptual reasoning, at least in a mixed clinical sample, and thus other aspects of cognitive functioning should be considered when interpreting performance on this test (Fallows & Hilsabeck, 2012). Moreover, the results from tests of invariance have indicated that while the WAIS-IV and WAIS-III measure similar constructs, the same FSIQ score across these instruments are not equivalent and therefore should not be directly compared (Taub & Benson, 2013).

Finally, the following shortcomings related to the WAIS-IV have been noted:

- Crucial information on criterion validity is absent, and therefore important test characteristics, such as sensitivity and specificity, cannot be calculated (Loring & Bauer, 2010).
- Empirical evidence regarding the invariance of the WAIS-IV factor structure across ages is not provided. Without this evidence a clinician will not be able to assess whether composite and subtest scores actually reflect the same constructs across age groups (Benson, Hulac, & Kranzler, 2010).
- The theoretical underpinnings of the WAIS-IV are dubious because the WAIS-IV did not adopt an empirically supported theory of intelligence (Benson et al., 2010).
- The WAIS-IV structure has not been tested against a credible, alternative, theoretically based structural model; whether other methods of interpretation can better describe an individual's test performance has not been determined (Benson et al., 2010).

4.4.3 Wechsler Memory Scale, Third Edition

The Wechsler Memory Scale (WMS) is a battery of subtests frequently administered in a neuropsychological assessment and is designed to evaluate various aspects of learning and memory (Rabin, Barr, & Burton, 2005). More specifically, the third edition of the WMS (WMS-III) measures the following four different aspects of memory: (a) ability to remember information immediately after oral presentation, (b) ability to remember information immediately after visual presentation, (c) ability to remember both visual and auditory information immediately after it is presented, and (d) capacity to remember and manipulate both visually and orally presented information in short-term memory storage.

The WMS-III was published in 1997, and since its publication clinical experience has led many practitioners to raise questions about the clinical utility and validity of subtests and scores. To date, relatively few studies have evaluated the reliability and validity of the WAIS-III. However, Heaton, Taylor, and Manly (2003) have demonstrated that gender, ethnicity, and education, in addition to age, significantly affects false positive error rates when WAIS-III and WMS-III results are used to classify cognitive impairment.

It has also been pointed out that the normative data for the Verbal Paired Associates subtest provided in the WMS-III manual clearly show evidence of performance ceiling effects that limit the usefulness of the WAIS-III (Uttl, Graf, & Richter, 2002).

4.4.4 Wechsler Memory Scale, Fourth Edition

The most recent revision of the WMS, the WMS-IV, is made up of seven subtests: Spatial Addition, Symbol Span, Design Memory, General Cognitive Screener, Logical Memory, Verbal Paired Associates, and Visual Reproduction. A person's performance is reported as five Index Scores: Auditory Memory, Visual Memory, Visual Working Memory, Immediate Memory, and Delayed Memory (Wechsler, 2009). As noted in the Technical Manual, in the normative sample obtained internal consistency measures were: Immediate Total (.83–.90), Immediate Content (.66–.88), Immediate Spatial (.70–.83), Delayed Total (.80–.90), Delayed Content (.70–.84), and Delayed Spatial (.67–.82). Test–retest correlations for designs were Immediate Total (.73), Immediate Content (.64), Immediate Spatial (.50), Delayed Total (.72), Delayed Content (.64), and Delayed Spatial (.50). In addition, according to the test author, the new WMS-IV visual working memory Spatial Addition and Symbol Span subtests have good reliability and concurrent validity and are clinically sensitive, yielding large effect sizes in patients with known brain injury (Wechsler, 2009).

The WMS-IV was developed to improve on important shortcomings of the WMS-III, including issues contributing to less than optimal sensitivity to memory impairment, such as range restriction and verbally mediated visual memory tasks (Hoelzle, Nelson, & Smith, 2011). Aside from the information presented in the WMS-IV Technical Manual, however, little else is known about the validity and reliability of this test. Research findings have suggested that the WMS-IV may have greater utility than the WMS-III in identifying lateralized memory dysfunction and have supported the WMS-IV as an improved test instrument to evaluate auditory and visual memory (Hoelzle et al., 2011). However, according to Hoelzle and colleagues, more research is needed to assess the clinical utility of these dimensions and to identify how the Visual Memory and Visual Working Memory indices are diagnostically relevant and distinct from one another. In addition, it has been argued that the validity of the WMS-IV to specific diseases and prediction of clinical outcome is unknown[19] and test–retest data does not exist, which is problematic (Lohring & Bauer, 2010).

4.5 Conclusion

New drugs or medical devices and techniques cannot be approved without the appropriate research and are generally not available to clinicians and/or the public prior to approval. Unfortunately, no such expectation exists for psychological tests and measures. Although standards exist for test construction and internal psychometric characteristics, there are no uniform standards for establishing a test's utility in differential diagnosis or its performance in evaluating the target populations for which it will be used (Loring & Bauer, 2010). While there is no doubt that a conclusion regarding cognitive dysfunction can be validly made only through the use of a methodology that has been thoroughly validated in its ability to identify neurocognitive performances related to various brain–behavior conditions, the mere selection of standardized and psychometrically sound tests to identify cognitive deficits does not assure that the results will be forensically, or even neuropsychologically, relevant (Hom, 2003). Any expert testifying in a court of law must accept the fact that no single test or measure can infer a causal relationship between violent behavior and brain impairment since all testing instruments and technologies have their limitations that affect the ability to infer such a relationship (Tancredi & Brodie, 2007).

It has been suggested that neuropsychology must inform criminology (Fabian, 2010). Therefore, while it is important to integrate neuropsychological and neurological findings that are present in a particular case to the defendant's behavior at the time the crime was committed, the ultimate goal of the forensic neuropsychologist is to provide a thorough explanation to the trier of fact rather than an excuse (Reynolds, Price, & Niland, 2003). Further, since the content of any forensic assessment focuses on information related to the psycholegal question posed, knowledge of the psychometric properties, group norms, and idiosyncratic test interpretations is of particular importance (Kalmbach & Lyons, 2006). Given the current state of the literature in terms of the variations across studies in methodologies, however, caution must be exercised in interpreting any results. Indeed, even the results of earlier and present meta-analyses at best indicate that there is a robust association between violent behavior and cognitive impairment (Ogilvie et al., 2011).

5

The Etiology and Neurobiology of Violence

> Everything we do, every thought we've ever had, is produced
> by the human brain. But exactly how it operates remains one
> of the biggest unsolved mysteries, and it seems the more we
> probe its secrets, the more surprises we find.
>
> Neil deGrasse Tyson[1]

5.1 Introduction

Gaining insight into the brain is at the very core of understanding what it is
that makes us so human, but, as Watson (1996) has pointed out, "bridging
the gap between understanding the brain and understanding the mind and
behavior continues to elude us" (p. 544). Although violent behavior has been
and continues to be a significant social problem, the exact neuroanatomical
region responsible for violent behavior still remains somewhat elusive, despite
decades of research. However, with the development of new structural and
functional imaging techniques, it is now possible to ascertain regional brain
dysfunction with much higher accuracy than was previously possible.[2] In
fact, converging evidence from numerous studies of structure and function,
as well as from studies employing neuropsychological and neurological tests
and measures, have suggested that abnormal prefrontal circuitry in particular is likely to be involved in aggressive and antisocial behavior (e.g., Filley
et al., 2001).

While it may be argued that the tendency to behave violently across a
variety of situations is the result of brain dysfunction, violent behavior may
also simply be attributed to personality pathology. Clearly, evidence of a high
level of brain dysfunction in general and cognitive impairment in particular
among violent offenders does not prove a causal connection between brain
dysfunction and violence (Hawkins & Trobst, 2000). There are, however,

good reasons for assuming such a relationship. As previously noted, brain function and structure are under environmental and genetic controls, thus human behavior is determined by a combination of these influences. However, it may also be argued that violent behavior, like all other behavior, ultimately derives from normal or abnormal brain functioning (Hawkins & Trobst, 2000). In fact, aggressive and violent behavior has been associated with altered glucose metabolism and cerebral blood flow in neuroimaging studies of violent psychiatric patients and violent criminal offenders, abnormalities that may be independent of major mental disorders, current medication, or substance abuse. These findings have led to the assertion that evidence of brain-behavioral impairment may mitigate or excuse criminal conduct (Filley et al., 2001), and frontal lobe dysfunction in particular has been invoked to explain the behaviors of defendants charged with or convicted of violent crimes (Brower & Price, 2001). What follows is a discussion about the etiology of violence in general and the underlying relationships among various factors, such as neural circuits, neuromodulators, neurobiology, and neuropsychiatric diseases, in specific.

5.2 Phenomenology of Violent Behavior

Aggression, in its broadest sense, may be defined as forceful, hostile, injurious, or destructive behavior. Violence is a subset of aggression, characterized by the unwarrented infliction of injury, and is behavior that violates the legal code. The most widely utilized and perhaps most heuristically valuable bimodal classification of aggression is that of premeditated versus impulsive aggression (Siever, 2008). Premeditated violence, also termed predatory, instrumental, or proactive, is planned with clear goals in mind. In contrast, impulsive aggression, also referred to as reactive aggression, is affective (emotional) and hostile or retaliatory and is often precipitated by provocation associated with negative emotions, such as anger or fear (Meloy, 2006). Although violent behavior is heterogeneous in its origins and manifestations, most violent acts can be classified as impulsive or premeditated, and many perpetrators can be classified as committing predominantly impulsive or predominantly premeditated violent acts (Teten et al., 2011).

While all violent behavior is ultimately effected by the same upper motor neuron system located in several adjacent, highly interconnected regions of the frontal lobe and reciprocally connected with neurons in the basal ganglia, brainstem, cerebellum, and lower motor system in the spinal cord, the idea that impulsive and premeditated types of violence represent distinct psychological and neurological phenotypes has been supported in the literature (Declercq & Audenaert, 2011; Hanlon et al., 2013; Weinshenker & Siegel, 2002). Two areas of the brain in particular, the amygdala and the prefrontal cortex, significantly impact an individual's decision-making abilities and self-control. The amygdala mediates emotional states involved in contexts that require rapid action, such as fear and anger. The amygdala can be described as a "low-order" regulator of emotional reactions arising from autonomic processes (Siever, 2008). Once the lower order reactions have occurred, "higher order" emotional responses are elaborated by the ventromedial prefrontal cortex, which is driven by reflection and thoughts, requiring thinking, reasoning, and more conscious awareness. This diathesis can be conceptualized in terms of an imbalance between top-down control, which is provided by the orbital frontal cortex (OFC) and anterior cingulate cortex, and a bottom-up drive that is processed by the insula and amygdala (Siever, 2008; see Figure 5.1).

The susceptibility to violence can manifest differently depending on the broader context in which it occurs (Siever, 2008). More specifically, an imbalance between prefrontal control mechanisms and limbic drives is presumed to be responsible for a wide range of psychiatric disorders, such as the classical neuroses and their spectrums of mood disorders. In addition, the presence of both neurocognitive dysfunction and substance abuse disorders places an individual at greater risk for experiencing problems with reason,

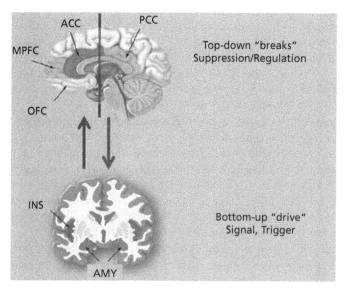

Figure 5.1 Modulation of Aggressive Behavior. Aggressive behavior can be viewed as an imbalance between top-down control, provided by the OFC and anterior cingulate cortex (ACC), and an excessive bottom-up drive that is triggered by the insula (INS) and amygdala (AMY). This diathesis model implies that the frontal lobes act as a circuit breaker for the reactive emotional responses generated by the amygdala. The two other areas involved in emotion regulation are the medial frontopolar cortex (MPFC) and the posterior cingulate cortex (PCC).

judgment, attention, planning, and other executive tasks that have been associated with aggression and impulsive behavior (Siever, 2008).

5.3 Neuroanatomy of Aggression and Violence

Aggressiveness, like all other emotions, is regulated by complex neural circuits, which involve several cortical and subcortical areas (see Figure 5.2). The frontal lobes, prefrontal cortex, temporal lobes, amygdala, and limbic system in particular have been linked to violent behavior (see, e.g., Bufkin & Luttrell, 2005; Siegel, 2005). Further, it has been hypothesized that the subcortical

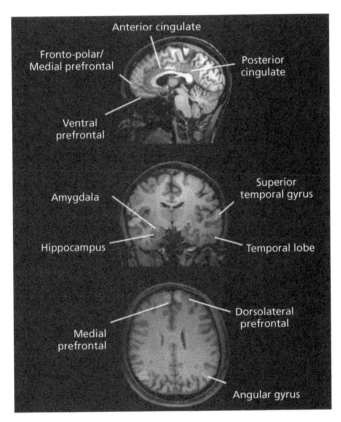

Figure 5.2 Brain regions that are presumed to be impaired in antisocial groups only (red), activated only in moral decision-making (green), and regions common to both antisocial behavior and moral decision-making (yellow). See Color Plate 15 in insert.

Reproduced from Raine, A., & Yang, Y. (2006). Neural foundations to moral reasoning and antisocial behavior. *Social Cognitive & Affective Neuroscience, 1*(3), 203–213, with permission from Oxford University Press.

structures that regulate emotions, such as the amygdala, are under the direct control of the prefrontal cortex (Seo, Patrick, & Kennealy, 2008).

5.3.1 The Frontal Lobes

The frontal lobes are the area of the brain that is most relevant to cognitive control processes (executive functions [EFs]) and violent and aggressive behavior. As previously discussed, the prefrontal cortex is associated with cognitive functions, including working memory, and selected and sustained attention. Frontal lobe responsibilities that can affect the outcome of criminal and violent behavior include controlling impulses, analyzing information, using past knowledge to regulate immediate behavior, and anticipating the future consequences of behavior.

It has been well established that the prefrontal cortex has several architectonically distinct regions; connections from the prefrontal cortex to other cortical and subcortical regions have been shown to involve at least two anatomically and functionally distinct systems (Petrides & Pandya, 2002). The first system, which mediates emotional tone, is ventrally located and involves the orbital surface of the frontal lobes, as well as paralimbic regions. The second system mediates the sequential processing of, for example, sensory information through a dorsolateral stream and involves the dorsolateral and medial areas of the frontal lobes, as well as interconnections with the cingulated gyrus and the posterior parietal lobe (Petrides & Pandya, 2002). In summary, the frontal lobes are the area where these systems are integrated and processed to modulate motivation and facilitate motor responses (Lichter & Cummings, 2001).

A pattern of anatomical and functional duality has also emerged from studies examining the connections between the prefrontal cortex and subcortical structures, in particular the basal ganglia. The basal ganglia, which consist of the striatum and globus pallidus, are reciprocally innervated by the substantia nigra and subthalamic nucleus to form a subcortical system that is important in coordinating and regulating cortically originating movement (Afifi & Bergman, 2005). The neurons originating from functionally related areas of the prefrontal cortex interact with topically discrete areas of the striatum, which are known to share functional properties (Lichter & Cummings, 2001). More specifically, the dorsolateral system of the frontal lobes connects to the dorsolateral caudate nucleus, while the ventral system maps onto the ventromedial portion of the caudate and adjacent portions of the nucleus accumbens. Information processed by the cortex, therefore, is received and processed by the basal ganglia in a way that maintains partial separation and specialization of functional domains (Lichter & Cummings, 2001).

Middleton and Strick (2002) have extended the neuroanatomy of frontostriatal circuits by describing seven categories of circuits based on research findings in primates; however, only four of these circuits are of relevance here. The four main circuits of interest are those that involve projections between the basal ganglia and the following regions of the prefrontal cortex: (a) dorsolateral, (b) lateral orbitofrontal, (c) medial orbitofrontal, and (d) and anterior cingulate (Middleton & Strick, 2002). As the foregoing suggests, the prefrontal cortex appears to be the site of convergence for information from different yet overlapping circuits that are involved in motivation, cognitive processes, emotion, and motor functions (Passingham & Wise, 2012).

5.3.2 Executive Functioning

EFs have historically been associated with activity in the frontal or prefrontal cortex. More specifically, the following two divisions of the frontal lobes are presumed to be responsible for different EFs: (a) the dorsolateral prefrontal cortex, which is associated with cognitive functions, such as language, working memory, and selective and sustained attention, and (b) the ventral and polar frontal cortex, which assists in the regulation of social and self-awareness, emotions, and decision-making. Consequently, it has been suggested that the frontal lobes are involved in "supervisory" or "executive" functions (Pennington & Ozonoff, 1996).

As previously noted, a diverse set of functional deficits has been attributed to impairment of EF. Indeed, individuals with executive dysfunction have been shown to have difficulties initiating appropriate actions, setting reasonable goals, regulating attentional resources, planning and organizing behavior, inhibiting inappropriate behavior, monitoring their own behavior, and shifting between activities (Blair, Mitchell, & Blair, 2005). While there remains an ongoing debate regarding the degree to which EFs are in fact regulated by the frontal lobes, it is almost impossible to find a discussion of EF that does not make reference to frontal lobe abnormalities, and in parallel fashion there is rarely a discussion of frontal lobe impairment without references to executive dysfunction (Alvarez & Emory, 2006).

5.3.3 The Frontal Lobes and Aggression

Society draws a clear legal distinction between the consequences of behaviors presumed to be under an individual's volitional control and those presumed to be outside such control (Goldberg, 2001). Volitional control, however, implies more than just conscious awareness; it infers the ability to (a) anticipate the consequences of one's actions, (b) decide whether or not a specific action should be taken, and (c) choose between inaction and action. At a cognitive level, the capacity for volitional behavior depends on the functional integrity of the frontal lobes, and the capacity for restraint depends, in particular, on the OFC (Goldberg, 2001).[3]

As previously noted, the frontal cortex is extensively connected to the limbic system, as well as to cortical association regions, thereby receiving both emotional and higher order information. More specifically, material from all sources (e.g., internal and external, conscious and unconscious) is integrated into ongoing activity so that behaviors can be modulated to satisfy drives within the constraints of the internal and external environments (Golden, Peterson-Rohne, & Gontkovsky, 1996). Based on a constant monitoring of internal needs and external demands and possibilities, the frontal lobes control the essential elements of intentions. Planning and programming of complex activity is required to enact these intentions and to provide continuity and coherence of behavior across time (Golden et al., 1996). Further, even the most simple of intentions requires translation into action, including simply starting or stopping specific behaviors, thus plans must be implemented and progress toward goals monitored so that adjustments can be made as needed (Golden et al., 1996).

Three distinct behavioral neurological syndromes have been observed following injury to certain areas of the prefrontal cortex:

- Damage to the dorsolateral region may result in a "frontal abulic" syndrome, which is characterized by loss of creativity and initiative, a tendency toward emotional apathy and flat affect, and reduced ability to concentrate (Mesulam, 2002). Cognitively, these symptoms manifest as the traditional "dysexecutive syndrome," which involves problems with working memory, verbal fluency, planning, perseveration, and temporal organization of behavior (Fuster, 1997).
- Damage to the orbitofrontal region may result in a "frontal disinhibition" syndrome, which is characterized by deficits in the "exclusionary" aspect of attention (Fuster, 1997, p. 174). More specifically, individuals with this disorder show impaired moral judgment and disregard social conventions, and their affect is generally euphoric, with irritability, paranoia, and contentiousness. Cognitively, individuals with frontal disinhibition syndrome have problems with focused attention (Fuster, 1997).
- The third syndrome, referred to as "akinetic mutism," may result from damage to the medial/cingulate cortex (Fuster, 1997; Pennington & Ozonoff, 1996). This disorder is poorly defined but is presumed to involve apathy and deficits in the ability to initiate speech and other spontaneous behaviors. Cognitively, the anterior cingulated cortex is important for motivation, initiation, and response selection (Fuster, 1997).

Many of the functional changes that are observed following frontal lobe damage also parallel the behavioral sequelea of a number of psychiatric disorders, thus providing a conceptual connection between psychopathology and frontal lobe circuits (Lichter & Cummings, 2001). Clinical parallels can, in fact, be drawn for each of the three neurological prefrontal syndromes. The dorsolateral-frontal abulic syndrome resembles the symptomatology of attention deficit hyperactivity disorder (ADHD), as well as depression to some degree. The orbitofrontal-disinhibition syndrome resembles antisocial personality disorder (APD) and mania. Finally, the cingulated-akinetic mutism syndrome resembles the symptoms of major depressive disorder, while excessive cingulate activity is analogous to symptoms of anxiety disorders[4] (Lichter & Cummings, 2001).

Damage to the frontal systems results in consequences that are diverse, multifaceted, and often catastrophic. For example, prefrontal lobe damage frequently produces deficits in motivation or "drive," resulting in inertia and apathy sometimes labeled "pseudodepression" (Kwentus, Hart, Peck, & Kornstein, 1985), while victims of prefrontal injury may behave in a childlike and selfish manner, resulting in features often labeled "pseudo-sociopathic" (Kwentus et al., 1985). Further, since the prefrontal cortex engages in temporally oriented programming to accomplish tasks, damage to it often results in impaired problem solving and an inability to anticipate consequences (Kandel & Freed, 1989). Indeed, impulsive homicide offenders have been found to have hypoactivation in brain areas presumed to underlie impulse control and other EFs, as well as decreased regional cerebral blood flow in the anterior cingulate and orbitofrontal cortices (Amen, Hanks, Prunella, & Green, 2007; Hanlon et al., 2013). However, while research has led to an association between frontal lobe impairment and violent behavior, there is also clear evidence that the problems associated with frontal lobe dysfunction are not solely restricted to damage to the frontal lobes. As Goldberg (2001) observed, "frontal lobe dysfunction does not always signify a frontal lobe lesion. In fact, in most instances it probably does not" (p. 116).

5.3.4 The Limbic System

The limbic system is a complex collection of brain structures that includes the amygdala, hippocampus, anterior thalamic nuclei, septum, habenula and limbic cortex. The hypothalamus is also a critical component of the limbic system because of its role in the autonomic and endocrine systems that participate in the expression of emotion (Afifi & Bergman, 2005). The limbic system supports a variety of functions, including emotions, motivation, long-term memory, and olfaction. Since the limbic system is intimately connected to the temporal lobe, the term "temporolimbic" has often been used to reflect this close neuroanatomical relationship.

Violent and aggressive behavior is presumed to arise from the operations of the limbic system under certain circumstances, with the amygdala being the structure most often implicated. More specifically, the critical abnormality implicated in impulsive aggression and violence is hyperactivity of the limbic system in response to negative or provocative stimuli, particularly anger-provoking stimuli (Siever, 2008). In fact, research has indicated that activation in the limbic system in the face of diminished top-down regulation can lead to disinhibited anger and aggression (Siever,

2008). Further, in patients with borderline personality disorder, hyperactivity of the amygdala has also been reported (Minzenberg, Fan, News, Tang, & Siever, 2007; Siever, 2008). In contrast, the predatory aggression characteristic of psychopathy and APD is presumed to be associated with reduced amygdala responsiveness, autonomic activity, and aversive conditioning (Anderson & Kiehl, 2012).

5.3.5 The Temporal Lobes

Structures of the limbic system, including the amygdala and hippocampus, are located within the temporal lobes, which are known to play an important role in organizing sensory input, auditory perception, language and speech production, as well as memory association and memory formation (Afifi & Bergman, 2005). Temporal lobe dysfunction is characterized by episodes of exaggerated and/or unprovoked anger, intellectual impairment, auditory and/or visual hallucinations, delusions, and receptive language impairment and is implicated in the susceptibility to aggression and violence (Siever, 2008). Research studies have supported the association between violent behavior and temporal lobe impairment. For example, Bufkin and Lutrell (2005) found temporal lobe dysfunction in 70% of aggressive and/or violent group studies, with reductions in left temporal lobe activity being present in six out of seven studies. Further, abnormal temporal lobe structure is common in murderers pleading not guilty by reason of insanity (Raine et al., 1998). In addition, patients with temporal lobe epilepsy experience recurrent epileptic seizures arising from one or both temporal lobes of the brain, which may be associated with subacute postictal aggressive behaviors (Ito et al., 2007).

5.4 Neurochemistry: Neurotransmitters and Neuromodulators

As previously discussed, neurotransmitters, including serotonin, norepinephrine, dopamine, acetylcholine, and gamma-aminobutyric acid are released into a synapse by the nerve ending of a presynaptic neuron that is used to communicate with the adjacent postsynaptic neuron. Neuromodulators,[5] such as endorphins, are released by the nerve endings and have their effect sometimes quite far from the neuron from which they were released (Kandel, Schwartz, & Jessell, 2000). Research studies have established that many neurotransmitters, such as serotonin and dopamine, and hormones, including steroids, and opioids, are involved in the modulation of aggressive behavior. More specifically, most of the current evidence strongly supports the roles of serotonin and norepinephrine, with serotonin playing a greater role in the etiology of aggressive behaviors (Clark & Grunstein, 2004).

5.4.1 Serotonin or 5-Hydroxytryptamine

In the central nervous system, serotonin exerts inhibitory control over impulsive aggression and is presumed to play an important role in the modulation of anger and aggression. However, serotonergic dysfunction will influence aggression differently, depending on the individual's impulse control, emotional regulation, and social abilities (Krakowski, 2003). Serotonin facilitates prefrontal cortical regions, such as the OFC and anterior cingulate cortex, which are involved in modulating and often suppressing the emergence of aggressive behaviors primarily by acting on serotonin 5-HT_2 receptors in these regions (Clark & Grunstein, 2004). Thus, deficiencies in serotonergic innervation of these regions or reduced levels of serotonin in the brain can be expected to result in disinhibited aggression upon provocation (Siever, 2008).

The first suggestion of a link between reduced serotonin function and impulsive aggression was advanced in 1983 by Linnoila and colleagues, who showed that the concentration of a primary metabolite of serotonin in the cerebrospinal fluid, 5-hydroxyindoleacetic acid, was lower in impulsive violent offenders than in nonimpulsive violent offenders. Subsequently, the idea of a low serotonin syndrome has been substantiated using various measures of serotonin function (Caspi et al., 2003). For example, PET imaging of serotonin transporter and receptor density studies with [11C]McNeil 5652, [11C] DASB, and [11C]MDL100907 have provided some objective evidence that pathological impulsive aggressive behavior is associated with decreased serotonin activity (Siever, 2008; Rylands et al., 2012).

5.4.2 Norepinephrine (Noradrenaline)

It is well known that norepinephrine mediates and is modulated by other neurochemicals, many of which affect behavior. More specifically, the noradrenergic system interacts with various neurotransmitters, including serotonin, and neurotropic factors, including somatostatin, which have been associated with aggressive behavior, anxiety, and depression, in nondemented populations (Herrmann, Lanctôt, & Khan, 2004). Further, norepinephrine and norepinephrine metabolite levels have been found to positively correlate with aggressive behavior in patients with personality disorders (see, e.g., Gerra et al., 1996).

Although aggressive behavior has been associated with an increase in noradrenergic activity, the evidence for a noradrenergic involvement in human aggression is indirect. More specifically, plasma levels of epinephrine and norepinephrine have been related to experimentally induced hostile behavior in normal subjects (Gerra et al., 1997), while other researchers have suggested a correlation between norepinephrine metabolite, 3-methoxy-4-hydroxyphenylglycol in the blood and aggression (Swann et al., 2013). In addition, it has been demonstrated that pharmacological noradrenergic stimulation by drugs, such as yohimbine, can increase plasma levels of norepinephrine and increase rapid-response impulsivity (Swann et al., 2013).

5.4.3 Dopamine

As a neurotransmitter, dopamine plays an important role in motor control, motivation, arousal, cognition, and reward. For example, dopaminergic hyperfunction or dysregulation has been linked to impulsivity and emotional dysregulation in patients with borderline personality disorder (Friedel, 2004) and to depressive disorders (Galani & Rana, 2011). Furthermore, dopamine is presumed to play a major role in reward-motivated behavior, and a variety of addictive drugs, such as cocaine and amphetamine, are known to amplify the effects of dopamine (Blum et al., 2012). Dopamine is also involved in the initiation and performance of aggressive behavior, and decreased D_1 receptors, in particular, have been implicated in depressed patients with anger attacks (Siever, 2008). In fact, a modified diathesis-stress model of impulsive aggression proposes that the dysfunctional interactions between the dopamine and serotonin systems in the prefrontal cortex may be an important mechanism underlying the relationship between impulsive aggression and its comorbid disorders (Seo, Patrick, & Kennealy, 2008). More specifically, serotonin hypofunction may represent a biochemical trait that predisposes an individual to impulsive aggression, with dopamine hyperfunction contributing in an additive fashion to the serotonergic deficit (Seo et al., 2008).

5.4.4 Testosterone

Increased testosterone levels have long been linked to aggression, antisocial behavior, and sensation seeking. However, while high concentrations of testosterone have been reported in populations characterized by high aggression, including criminals with personality disorders, alcoholic violent offenders, and spousal abusers (Coccaro, Beresford, Minar, Kaskow, & Geracioti, 2007), a direct correlation between plasma or cerebrospinal fluid testosterone concentration and aggression, has not yet been well established (Siever, 2008). In fact, some investigators have refuted the notion that testosterone causes aggressive, egocentric, and risky behavior (Eisenegger, Naef, Snozzi, Heinrichs, & Fehr, 2010).

5.5 Molecular Genetics and Genotypes

The possibility of a genetic contribution to violent behavior has received considerable attention; however, the extent to which genetics play a causal role in aggression and violence is unclear. Indeed, no gene for human violence has yet been discovered; available evidence from molecular genetics instead suggests that multiple genes may interact to predispose an individual to violent behavior.

A number of molecular genetic studies have focused on genetic variants (polymorphisms) of serotonin receptors, dopamine receptors, and neurotransmitter metabolizing enzymes. For example, studies of a mutation in the enzyme monoamine oxidase-A have shown to cause a syndrome that includes violence and impulsivity in humans (Tremblay, Hartup, & Archer, 2005). Further, individuals with low levels of the monoamine oxidase-A gene were found to display more aggression and exhibit significant volume reductions in the bilateral amygdala, anterior cingulate cortex, and subgenual anterior cingulate cortex (Meyer-Lindenberg et al., 2006). However, a 2013 meta-analysis that synthesized data on 12 polymorphisms, including monoamine oxidase- A, did not find any strong associations between these polymorphisms and aggression (Vassos, Collier, & Fazel, 2013). Based on these findings Vassos and colleagues concluded that the current evidence does not support the use of such genes to predict dangerousness.

As the previous discussion suggests, while genetic studies have shed some light on the etiology of violence, genetics operate at the population level, and thus it is not possible to make predictions about an individual's likelihood to commit a violent act. In addition, these studies typically provide only an estimate of the relative influence of genetic factors on a given behavior, which suggests that other factors may also contribute to violent behavior. Further, the precise extent to which genetics contribute to violent behavior is still largely unknown (Vassos et al., 2013).

5.6 Clinical Correlates of Violent Behavior: Cognitive Impairment

Our knowledge of aggression and violence in humans is largely derived from studies of individuals who have committed violent acts. As a consequence, the field starts with what might be a selection bias. As previously noted, a number of risk factors for aggression have been identified, including frontal and temporal lobe lesions, altered neurotransmitter levels, substance abuse, and mental illness. Many of these biological and biochemical abnormalities and cognitive dysfunctions are also the basis for many neurological, psychiatric, and psychological disorders. It must also be remembered that the contribution of brain dysfunction to violence may stem not only from structural damage in a certain brain region but also from neurochemical, neurophysiological, and functional disturbances and impairments that are not always detectable by conventional neurodiagnostic methods. Reliable neuropsychological tests and measures may, in fact, may be more sensitive to brain dysfunction at a microscopic level than other techniques and may provide unique insights regarding the cerebral mediation of violent behavior (Filley et al., 2001).

Neuropsychological dysfunction or neurological deficits can rarely be implicated as the sole or direct cause of violent behavior; however, cognitive dysfunction is one factor that has been shown to play a crucial role. Indeed, research into the neurocognitive functioning of aggressive and violent individuals has consistently shown that violent adults perform in the impaired range on tasks of executive functioning that may be linked to structural and functional brain abnormalities, particularly in the prefrontal regions (see, e.g., Ogilvie, Stewart, Chan, & Shum, 2011). Numerous studies have also pointed to a relationship between low IQ and memory impairment and violent and antisocial behavior (see e.g., Hanlon et al., 2013). However, it has been noted that the relationship between criminal offending and IQ is not linear, nor may it be as strong as once presumed (Herrero, Escorial, & Colom, 2010).

5.7 Clinical Correlates of Violent Behavior: Neurological Disorders

5.7.1 Epilepsy

Epilepsy is a disorder characterized by sudden surges of disorganized electrical impulses in the brain (seizures), and it is the most common chronic neuropsychological disease affecting the general population. Seizure attacks generally take place in phases. The ictal event of a seizure is the actual seizure itself, while the nonictal phases are usually classified as preictal, postictal, and interictal. Episodic violence associated with epilepsy can appear during one or more of the epileptic phases. The preictal, or prodromal, phase is a period of minutes, hours, or even days prior to the onset of a seizure, but aggression seems to be a relatively rare occurrence during this stage (Marsh & Krauss, 2000). Aggressive and violent behavior has been most frequently associated with the ictal phase of the disease, and characteristics of ictal violence include (a) the seizure episode is sudden, without provocation, and lasts at most a few minutes; (b) automatisms and other stereotypic phenomena of the patient's typical seizures accompany the aggressive act, and the act is associated with these phenomena from one seizure to the next; (c) the behavior is poorly directed and is unskilled; and (d) purpose and interpersonal interaction are absent (Marsh & Krauss, 2000).

The proposed relationship between epilepsy and aggression is presumed to be due to permanent changes in personality functioning produced by the seizure activity itself, but to date this has not been supported by the research. It has been shown that frontal lobe glucose metabolic values, assessed with $[^{18}F]$-2-fluoro-2-deoxy-D-glucose (FDG)-PET, are strong predictors of executive functioning in patients with epilepsy (McDonald et al., 2006; see Figure 5.3). However, a systematic review has cautioned against drawing

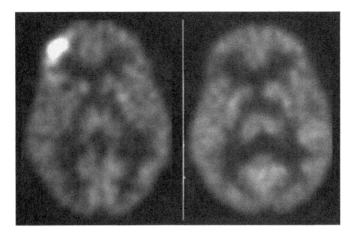

Figure 5.3 FDG-PET Scan of Epilepsy. FDG-PET scan of a 29-year-old subject with right frontal epilepsy, performed during an ictal phase, shows right frontal hypermetabolic focus (left). Seventy-two hours later, a follow-up interictal PET scan shows hypometabolism in the same region, confirming an interictal seizure focus with decreased glucose metabolism (right).

Reprinted from Leung, D. K., & Van Heertum, R. L. (2009). Interventional nuclear brain imaging. *Seminars in Nuclear Medicine*, *39*, 195–203, with permission from Elsevier.

any conclusions about the relationship between violence and epilepsy due to methodological shortcomings of the studies reviewed (Fazel, Philipson, Gardiner, Merritt, & Grann, 2009).

5.7.2 Dementias

5.7.2.1 Dementia of the Alzheimer's Type

Dementia of the Alzheimer's type (DAT), the most common form of dementia, is characterized by loss of neurons and synapses in the cerebral cortex and certain subcortical regions. This loss results in gross atrophy of the affected regions, including degeneration in the temporal lobes, parietal lobes, parts of the frontal cortex, and cingulate gyrus (Wenk, 2003). Evidence from longitudinal and neuroimaging studies converge to indicate that psychological functions other than episodic memory are affected very early in the course of DAT and may predate or influence the apparent memory deficits. In fact, changes in personality and difficulties in executive functioning are prominent (Storandt, 2008). Violent and aggressive behavior has also been linked to DAT and is presumed to be because individuals with DAT may be (a) misperceiving their environment believing that they are defending themselves, (b) disoriented and confused about where they are, and (c) experiencing delusions or hallucinations (Ballard & Corbett, 2013).

5.7.2.2 Frontotemporal Dementia

Another form of dementia, frontotemporal dementia (FTD) is a clinical syndrome caused by degeneration of the frontal lobes of the brain, which may extend back to the temporal lobes. In contrast to other forms of dementia, in FTD there is relative preservation of visuospatial skills and memory and early alterations in personality and behavior (Rosen, Hartikainen, et al., 2002). More specifically, the symptoms of FTD can be classified into two groups, which underlie the functions of the frontal lobes: (a) behavioral symptoms and/or personality change, including apathy and aspontaneity, and (b) symptoms related to problems with executive functioning (Neary, Snowden, & Mann, 2000). Structural MRI scans of FTD also often reveal frontal lobe and/or anterior temporal lobe atrophy; however, in the early stages of the disease the scan may seem normal. Further, FDG-PET scans typically show frontal and/or anterior temporal hypometabolism, which differentiates FTD from DAT (Figure 5.4), since PET scans in DAT classically show biparietal hypometabolism (Rosen et al., 2002). Research studies in FTD patients have also indicated that increased activity of dopaminergic neurotransmission and altered serotonergic modulation of dopaminergic neurotransmission is associated with agitated and aggressive behavior, respectively (Engelborghs et al., 2008). In addition, poor performance on neuropsychological tests of executive, language, and visuospatial function; less disinhibition; agitation/aggression; and smaller medial, lateral, and orbital frontal lobe volumes was shown to predict rates of decline in subjects with FTD (Josephs et al., 2011).

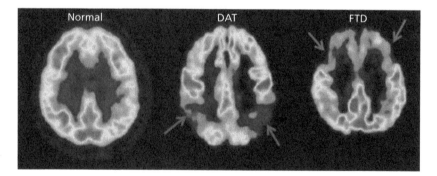

Figure 5.4 FDG-PET Scans in Normal and Dementia Subjects. In subject with DAT, significant hypometabolism is seen in the temporo-parietal areas (red arrows). In contrast, in the subject with FTD, hypometabolism is found in the frontal areas (blue arrows). See Color Plate 16 in insert.

Adapted from Jacobs, A. H., Winkler, A., Castro, M. G., & Lowenstein, P. (2005). Human gene therapy and imaging in neurological diseases. *European Journal of Nuclear Medicine and Molecular Imaging, 32*, S358–S383, with permission from Springer Science and Business Media.

5.7.3 Traumatic Brain Injury

Traumatic brain injury (TBI) occurs when an outside kinetic force mechanically injures the brain. TBI can be classified based on severity (mild, moderate, or severe), mechanism (closed or penetrating head injury), or other features (e.g., occurring in a specific location or over a widespread area). Research findings strongly indicate that TBI can cause deficits in the prefrontal cortex (see Figure 5.5), thus leading to a predisposition to violent behavior (see, e.g., Williams et al., 2010). It has also been demonstrated that TBI patients score more poorly than non-TBI patients on measures of IQ and executive functioning, such as the Wisconsin Card Sort Test (Marsh & Martinovich, 2006). Furthermore, it has been suggested that criminal behavior and violence may be the consequence of head injuries acquired during childhood and youth (León-Carrión & Ramos, 2003). In addition, a 2003 study found

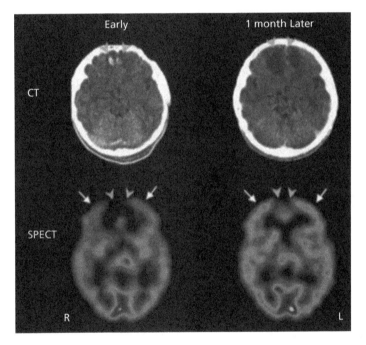

Figure 5.5 CT and SPECT Scans of Patient with TBI. At time of admission, a CT scan showed focal defects due to frontal lobe hemorrhage (orange arrows), while ^{99m}Tc-HMPAO SPECT showed markedly decreased regional cerebral blood flow in frontal lobes (orange and white arrows). One month later, CT showed resolution of the hematomas while SPECT still showed focal abnormalities (orange arrows). See Color Plate 17 in insert.

Reprinted from Catafau, A. M. (2001). Brain SPECT in clinical practice. Part I: Perfusion. *Journal of Nuclear Medicine*, *42*(2), 259–271, Figure 4, with permission from SNMMI.

that (a) 33.7% of the TBI patients demonstrated significant aggressive behavior during the first six months after their injury, (b) aggression was significantly more frequent among subjects with TBI than patients in a comparable group with traumatic injury that did not involve the brain, and (c) aggressive behavior was significantly associated with the presence of major depression, a history of drug or alcohol abuse, and frontal lobe lesions (Tateno, Jorge, & Robinson, 2003). Finally, homicides committed by returning veterans have been linked to posttraumatic stress disorder (PTSD) and/or TBI (Wortzel & Arciniegas, 2010).

5.7.4 Brain Tumors

Brain tumors can be malignant (cancerous) or benign (noncancerous). The threat level from brain tumors depends on a combination of factors, such as the type of tumor, its location, its size, and its state of development. Tumors can occur in different parts of the brain and may or may not be primary tumors. A primary tumor is one that has started in the brain, as opposed to a metastatic tumor, which is something that has spread to the brain from another part of the body (Herholz, Langen, Schiepers, & Mountz, 2012). Secondary tumors of the brain are metastatic tumors, and the most common types of cancers that bring about brain metastasis include lung cancer, breast cancer, and malignant melanoma (Herholz et al., 2012). It has been suggested that aggression and violence may in fact be associated with certain types of brain tumors (Villano, Mlinarevich, Watson, Engelhard, & Anderson-Shaw, 2009).

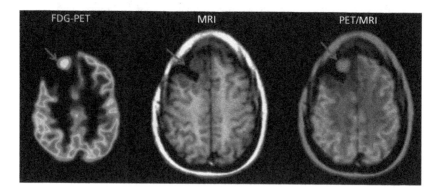

Figure 5.6 Brain Tumor Imaging. FDG-PET scan (left) shows focal metabolic abnormality involving the right frontal lobe. Contrast MRI scan (middle) shows enhancement in the right frontal lobe. PET/MRI fused image (right). See Color Plate 18 in insert.

Reprinted from Herholz, K., Langen K. J., Schiepers C., & Mountz J. M. (2012). Brain tumors. *Seminars in Nuclear Medicine, 42*, 356–370, with permission from Elsevier.

Neuroimaging techniques, in particular CT, MRI, and FDG-PET, play central roles in the diagnosis of brain tumors. However, a diagnosis of brain tumor can only be definitively confirmed by histological examination of tumor tissue samples obtained either by means of brain biopsy or surgery. The clinical utility of PET and MRI for identifying brain tumor recurrence is shown in Figure 5.6.

5.8. Clinical Correlates of Violent Behavior: Psychiatric Disorders

5.8.1. Psychotic Disorders

Schizophrenia is a mental disorder characterized by abnormalities in the expression or perception of reality and most commonly manifests as auditory hallucinations, bizarre or paranoid delusions, or disorganized speech and thinking with significant social or occupational dysfunction. Aggression and violence are sometimes found in schizophrenic patients, with theorists suggesting a pathophysiological role of certain areas of the brain, including the frontal cortex, the limbic system, and the basal ganglia. The limbic system, because of its role in the control of emotions, has proven to be the most fertile area for neuropathological studies of schizophrenia (Spaletta et al., 2001).

To date, numerous studies examining the association between aggression and psychiatric disorders have, in particular, attempted to identify the clinical parameters of violence. For example, reduced prefrontal cognitive activation, assessed with SPECT, was found to be associated with aggression in schizophrenia (Spaletta et al., 2001). It has also been established that schizophrenic patients show a remarkable number of characteristic abnormalities of executive circuitry, evident in vivo with functional neuroimaging techniques (Eisenberg & Berma, 2010); however, the association between aggression and schizophrenia is questionable. While individuals with schizophrenia may display agitation, as well as poor impulse control when ill, a schizophrenic patient is no more likely to commit homicide than is a member of the general population. Indeed, while negative symptoms have been associated with frontal lobe dysfunction and persecutory delusions and command hallucinations have been associated with violence in some schizophrenics, serious violent behavior such as homicide by such individuals is infrequent (Martino, Bucay, Butman, & Allegri, 2007).

A number of studies have also been successful in establishing differences in the cerebral metabolic patterns between individuals with schizophrenia and normal controls and between the different types of schizophrenia and different symptom profiles. Since schizophrenic patients with predominantly negative symptoms exhibit reduced prefrontal activation compared to patients without negative symptoms, hypofrontality (reduced metabolism

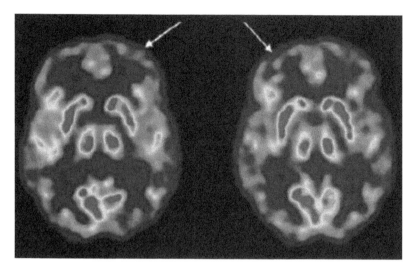

Figure 5.7 FDG-PET Scan of Patient with Schizophrenia. The scan shows mild global decrease, particularly in the frontal regions (arrows), consistent with some of the reported findings in the literature. See Color Plate 19 in insert.

Image Courtesy of Open Access Publications: Hayempour, B. J., Cohen, S., Newberg, A., & Alavi, A. (2013). Neuromolecular imaging instrumentation demonstrating dysfunctional brain function in schizophrenic patients. *Journal of Alzheimer's Disease and Parkinsonism*, 3, 114.

and blood flow) has been related to negative symptomatology in schizo-phrenia (Hayempour, Cohen, Newberg, & Alavi, 2013; Potkin et al., 2002; see Figure 5.7). Further, SPECT studies have suggested that, at rest, hypo-frontality is a common feature in subject with schizophrenia, suggesting that the OFC might play an important role in the development of severe negative symptoms (Kanahara et al., 2013). Seethalakshmi and colleagues (2007) also observed that chronicity and severity of illness do not influence cerebral glucose metabolism. More specifically, study participants with nega-tive schizophrenia had significantly decreased metabolism in all regions of the brain compared to the positive type. However, the positive syndrome of schizophrenia was associated with significantly increased glucose metabo-lism in the medial temporal regions, basal ganglia, and left thalamic regions (Seethalakshmi et al., 2006).

5.8.2. Mood Disorders

5.8.2.1 Major Depressive Disorder

Major depressive disorder, also known as clinical depression, major depression, unipolar depression, or unipolar disorder, is a mental disorder characterized by a pervasive low mood, low self-esteem, and loss of interest or pleasure in normally enjoyable activities. EF abnormalities have been consistently found in studies on depressive disorders, and these neuropsychological disturbances have been correlated with reduced blood flow in the mesial prefrontal cortex and structural changes in the cingulate gyrus and white matter of the orbitofrontal and prefrontal cortex (Bremner et al., 2002; Taylor et al., 2003). Further, Graz and colleagues (2009), who studied criminal behavior and violent crime in former in-patients with affective disorder, found that 49% of the study participants had bipolar disorder and 45% had major depression. However, while for some individuals depression exacerbated aggressive behaviors, for others it may actually function as a protective factor by increasing inaction and lethargy. Therefore, it is difficult to find a reliable link between depressed mood and aggression (Ferguson et al., 2005).

5.8.2.2 Bipolar Disorder

Bipolar disorder (BD) is a psychiatric diagnosis that describes a category of mood disorders defined by the presence of one or more episodes of abnormally elevated mood, clinically referred to as mania or, if milder, hypomania. Individuals who experience manic episodes also commonly experience depressive episodes or symptoms or mixed episodes in which features of both mania and depression are present at the same time. These episodes are usually separated by a period of normal mood, but in some individuals, depression and mania may rapidly alternate (Jones & Bentall, 2006). Individuals with BD are prone to agitation that may result in impulsive aggression during manic and mixed episodes. Impulsive aggression, as opposed to premeditated aggression in particular has been found to be most commonly associated with BD, and, as previously noted, impulsive aggression has been associated with low serotonin levels, high catecholamine levels, and a predominance of glutaminergic activity relative to γ-aminobutyric acid activity (Swann, 2003).

MRI studies have also reported ventricular enlargement, temporal lobe reduction, and volumetric abnormalities of the striatum in patients with BD (Bearden, Hoffman, & Cannon, 2001). Further, a PET study using a continuous performance task has shown that abnormalities in BD are not restricted to the frontal lobes, reporting metabolic disturbances of the anterior cingulate cortex, cerebellum, and posterior cortical areas, irrespective of mood state (Ketter et al., 2001). In addition, it has been established that BD patients are significantly impaired on tests of EF, such as the Wisconsin Card Sorting Test, Trail Making Test, and Stroop test (Pradhan, Chakrabarti, Nehra, & Mankotia, 2008; Roth et al., 2006). More recently, research findings have indicated that a large percentage of individuals with BD were in a manic or mixed phase of their illness at the time of the arrest (e.g., Christopher, McCabe, & Fisher, 2012).

5.9 Clinical Correlates of Violent Behavior: Personality Disorders

5.9.1 Obsessive-Compulsive Personality Disorder

Obsessive-compulsive personality disorder (OCD) is characterized by repetitive, intrusive thoughts and images and/or repetitive, ritualistic mental or physical acts performed to reduce anxiety. OCD is a clinically heterogeneous condition, such that two patients with clear OCD can display completely different symptom patterns (Kessler et al., 2005). Suggestions have been made that the primary dysfunction is in the OFC; however, neuroimaging studies have also found dysfunction in the anterior cingulate and dorsolateral regions (Aycicegi, Dinn, Harris, & Erkman, 2003; van den Heuvel et al., 2005). To date, few studies have examined the relationship between OCD and aggression; however, compulsive personality disordered patients were found to have significantly greater impulsive aggression scores than noncompulsive patients (Stein et al., 1996).

5.9.2 Antisocial Personality Disorder

The *Diagnostic and Statistical Manual of Mental Disorders* (fourth edition, text revision; American Psychiatric Association, 2000) defines APD (in Axis II Cluster B) as follows:

1. There is a pervasive pattern of disregard for and violation of the rights of others occurring since age 15 years, as indicated by three or more of the following:
   - failure to conform to social norms with respect to lawful behaviors as indicated by repeatedly performing acts that are grounds for arrest;
   - deception, as indicated by repeatedly lying, use of aliases, or conning others for personal profit or pleasure;
   - impulsivity or failure to plan ahead;
   - irritability and aggressiveness, as indicated by repeated physical fights or assaults;
   - reckless disregard for safety of self or others;
   - consistent irresponsibility, as indicated by repeated failure to sustain consistent work behavior or honor financial obligations;
   - lack of remorse, as indicated by being indifferent to or rationalizing having hurt, mistreated, or stolen from another.
2. The individual is at least age 18 years.
3. There is evidence of conduct disorder with onset before age 15 years.
4. The occurrence of antisocial behavior is not exclusively during the course of schizophrenia or a manic episode.[6]

Although the exact etiology of APD is uncertain, much has been made of the relationship between antisocial or psychopathic behavior and brain dysfunction, in particular frontal lobe dysfunction. For example, APD has been associated with impairment on tests designed to assess executive functioning (Morgan & Lilienfield, 2000), although not all studies have supported this association (see, e.g., Crowell, Kieffer, Kugeares, & Vanderploeg, 2003). Research studies have also indicated that individuals with APD often present with abnormal MRI and SPECT results (Goethals et al., 2005; Raine, Lencz, Bihrle, LaCasse, & Colletti, 2000). Evidence from behavioral genetics studies has also led to the conclusion that a significant amount of the variance in APD is due to genetic contributions (Ferguson, 2010).

Although not all violent criminals have APD, there is a higher rate of severe violence among subjects with APD compared to the general population (Narayan et al., 2007). In addition, it has been suggested that individuals with APD engage in reactive violence rather than instrumental violence (Blair et al., 2005). Research findings have also led to the conclusion that there is a correlation between violent behavior and executive functioning. For example, Barkataki and colleagues (2005) found that subjects with APD, compared to healthy men, committed more errors of commission on the Go/No-Go Task, indicating impaired response inhibition, while other researchers have reported a negative correlation between symptoms of APD and performance on the Wechsler Adult Intelligence Scale Similarity subtest and no association of symptoms with measures of EFs (Stevens, Kaplan, & Hesselbrock, 2003). Finally, it has been shown that brain areas associated with both antisocial behavior and moral reasoning overlap significantly (Raine & Yang, 2006).

5.9.3 Psychopathy

Psychopathy, which is characterized by a shallow, callous, and manipulative interpersonal style combined with antisocial and reckless behavior, has frequently been associated with violent behavior. More specifically, psychopaths not only show little concern about the effects of their actions on others but also appear to show little regard for the impact of actions on themselves. Unlike individuals with a diagnosis of APD, psychopathic individuals show no indications of impairment on measures of EF associated with dorsolateral prefrontal cortex, such as the Wisconsin Card Sorting Test, Trail Making Test, or Controlled Oral Word Association Test (De Brito & Hodgins, 2009). However, individuals with psychopathy do present with frontal lobe dysfunction, albeit a dysfunction that is selective to those EFs that are mediated by the OFC, rather than the dorsolateral prefrontal cortex, as indicated by their performance on the Stroop or Go/No-Go tests (De Brito & Hodgins, 2009). In addition, a study assessing the extent of EF deficits in populations of primarily instrumental versus primarily reactive offenders found that the primarily instrumental group was largely intact on EF measures (Broomhall, 2005).

Research studies investigating structural abnormalities associated with APD or psychopathy have reported inconsistent results. However, studies using whole brain analyses have identified localized gray matter volume reductions in the frontopolar, orbitofrontal, and anterior temporal regions (de Oliveira-Souza et al., 2008; Müller et al., 2008). A more recent study investigating structural abnormalities using MRI in individuals diagnosed with APD and a Hare Psychopathy Checklist–Revised scores of 25 or higher (APD+P), also found that offenders with APD+P had significantly reduced gray matter volumes bilaterally in the anterior rostral prefrontal cortex and temporal poles relative to offenders with APD-P and nonoffenders (Gregory et al., 2012). Research findings have also indicated a correlation between psychopathy scores and medial prefrontal cortex activation in a moral decision-making paradigm (Glenn, Raine, & Schug, 2009) and have suggested that psychopathy may be associated with reduced posterior hippocampal and amygdala volume (Cope et al., 2012). Further, a study of connectivity in psychopathy has emphasized decreased structural and functional connectivity between the ventromedial prefrontal cortex (vmPFC) and the amygdala, as well as reduced structural integrity in the right uncinate fasciculus[7] (Motzkin, Newman, Kiehl, & Koenigs, 2011). According to Motzkin and colleagues, the finding of reduced functional connectivity between these regions suggests that the socioaffective deficits characterizing psychopathy may reflect impaired communication between the vmPFC and amygdala. Finally, it has been noted that the odds that antisocial offenders with relatively low anterior cingulate cortex activity will be rearrested are approximately double that of an offender with high activity in this region (Aharoni et al., 2013).

5.9.4 Borderline Personality Disorder

Borderline personality disorder (BPD) is characterized by severe deficiencies in impulse control and emotion regulation, which can result in self-destructive and aggressive behaviors. Accordingly, structural imaging studies have focused on the temporal lobe and frontal cortex, areas that are known to be associated with affect, emotion regulation, cognition, and impulsivity (McCloskey, Phan, & Coccaro, 2005). To date, evidence for morphological (structural) abnormalities in the frontal cortex of BPD patients appears to be nondefinitive. For example, van Elst and colleagues (2003) initially found significant volume loss associated with BPD in the orbitofrontal cortex but later failed to replicate these findings using different MRI methodology. The evidence for altered frontal activity and/or function in BPD has also received support from PET studies, which have noted differences in frontal lobe metabolism between control subjects and patients with BPD (Soloff et al., 2003). Patients with BPD who exhibit impulsive behavior were also found to have reduced regional cerebral blood flow in areas of the temporal and right prefrontal cortex (Goethals et al., 2005). Further, a review of the literature has indicated an association between BPD and criminality, particularly among incarcerated female offenders, with the committed crimes being frequently impulsive and violent (Sansone & Sansone, 2009). In addition, impulsive aggressive behaviors that include physical aggression directed toward self or others, such as suicide attempts and domestic violence, are presumed to account for a substantial portion of the morbidity and mortality associated with personality disorders, in particular BPD (Goodman & New, 2000).

5.10 Other Correlates of Violent Behavior

5.10.1 Intermittent Explosive Disorder

Intermittent explosive disorder (IED) is characterized by recurrent acts of impulsive, affectively driven aggression that are disproportionate to any actual provocation. Individuals with IED have elevated levels of trait anger and hostility and typically have frequent (e.g., twice a week) acts of verbal and physical aggression (McCloskey, Berman, Noblett, & Coccaro, 2006). Furthermore, IED confers functional impairment equal to or greater than most other Axis I and Axis II disorders (Kessler et al., 2005). Despite the public health impact of IED, relatively little is known about the neurobiology of this disorder. At the neurochemical level, IED appears to be associated with the dysregulation of the serotonergic system; however, to date only one imaging study has attempted to identify the specific brain regions affected by IED. More specifically, Coccaro and colleagues (2007) have demonstrated a link between amygdala-OFC dysfunction and impulsive aggression in IED based on the following evidence: (a) exaggerated amygdala and diminished OFC reactivity to faces conveying direct threat (anger) in IED subjects relative to controls; (b) lack of amygdala-OFC functional connectivity during the face processing task in IED subjects but a significant reciprocal (inverse) interaction between amygdala and OFC in controls; and (c) direct, positive correlation between amygdala reactivity to angry faces and extent of prior aggressive behavior.

5.10.2 Delirium

Delirium is a complex neuropsychiatric syndrome that typically involves a number of cognitive and noncognitive symptoms resulting in a broad differential diagnosis dominated by mental disorders. Delirium represents a generalized state of brain impairment that is acute rather than chronic in nature. There are a number of organic causes for delirium, including alcohol abuse, illegal substance abuse (e.g., LSD, PCP, cocaine, heroin), use of legal medications in improper doses, and metabolic imbalances (Mendez &

Kremen 2012). The underlying pathophysiological mechanisms of delirium remain somewhat unclear; however, evidence suggests that disruption of neurotransmission, including disruption of dopamine, may contribute to the development of this disorder (Martins & Fernandes, 2012). It has also been suggested that patients with delirium have widespread disruption of higher cortical function, with evidence of dysfunction in several brain areas, including subcortical structures, brain stem and thalamus, prefrontal cortices, and primary motor cortex (Burns, Gallagley, & Byrne, 2004).

Although individual delirium symptoms are nonspecific, their pattern is highly characteristic: acute onset (sometimes abruptly but often over hours or days), course fluctuation (symptoms tend to wax and wane over a 24-hour period and typically worsen at night), and symptoms are transient in nature (in most cases, delirium resolves within days or weeks). Delirium also frequently involves a prodromal phase over two to three days of malaise, restlessness, poor concentration, anxiety, irritability, sleep disturbance, and nightmares. A consequence of this broad symptom profile is that delirium has many guises and, depending on prevailing pattern, is easily mistaken for dementia or functional psychiatric disorders (Meagher, 2001).

5.10.3 Attention Deficit Hyperactivity Disorder

Several studies have found that male children and adolescents with high ratings on both ADHD behaviors and conduct problems have higher levels of early adult criminality than youth with either elevated ADHD ratings or conduct problems alone (Fischer, Barkley, Smallish, & Fletcher, 2002). Other studies, however, have failed to find an association between a diagnosis of ADHD in childhood and adult criminality (Lahey, Loeber, Burke, & Applegate, 2005). In addition, it has been suggested that ADHD may be a risk factor for executive dysfunction that leads to aggressive behavior, even if the pathology associated with ADHD itself does not lead to aggressive behavior (Blair et al., 2005).

5.10.4 Posttraumatic Stress Disorder

PTSD is a severe condition that may develop after a person has been exposed to one or more traumatic events, such as sexual assault, serious injury, or threat of death. Neuroimaging studies of PTSD have identified several key brain regions whose functions seem to be altered in PTSD, including the hippocampus, the amygdala, and the vmPFC. More specifically, these studies have found reduced activity in the vmPFC and increased activity in the amygdala (Newton, 2009). Research studies have also reported brain volume decreases in the hippocampus, anterior cingulate, subcallosal cortex, amygdala, and prefrontal cortex (Karl et al., 2006; Schuff et al., 2008; Weniger, Lange, Sachsse, & Irle, 2008). Further, PTSD patients whose symptoms increased over time showed accelerated atrophy throughout the brain, which was associated with greater rates of decline in verbal memory and delayed facial recognition (Cardenas et al., 2011). In addition, PTSD has been associated with neuropsychological changes, such as decline in delayed facial recognition as indexed by performance on the Faces II subtest of the Wechsler Memory Scale (third edition) and changes on the California Verbal Learning Test (Samuelson et al., 2009; Yehuda et al., 2006). Finally, victims of urban violence who developed PTSD were found to have poorer performance on the Spatial Span Forward subtest of the Wechsler Memory Scale (third edition) and poorer execution time and accuracy on the Stroop test compared to healthy controls (Flaks et al., 2014).

5.10.5 Substance Abuse

5.10.5.1 Alcohol Abuse

Numerous researchers have found a relationship between aggression, brain damage, and alcohol abuse. In fact, alcohol is the most commonly investigated drug, and the main effect of alcohol intoxication is the depression of inhibitors that predispose individuals toward aggressive behavior. More specifically, alcohol abuse and brain damage may have a synergistic effect on the disinhibition of behavior, together predisposing to a greater extent individuals with developmental or acquired brain defects toward aggression (Elliot, 1992). Furthermore, Manning and colleagues (2008) found significant increases in performance scores post-detoxification in working memory, verbal fluency, and verbal inhibition, but not in nonverbal EF tasks (e.g., mental flexibility and planning ability). However, despite increased scores on tests of verbal and memory skills, complex executive abilities showed little change after three weeks of abstinence (Manning et al., 2008). Moderate doses of alcohol were also found to decrease glucose metabolism in the human brain (Volkow et al., 2006; see Figure 5.8). In addition, a study assessing the long-term effects of Korsakoff's syndrome[8] found that although general knowledge, visual long-term memory, verbal fluency, and EFs improved slightly after two years, they still remained within pathological range (Fujiwara, Brand, Borsutzky, Steingass, & Markowitsch, 2008).

5.10.5.2 Drug Abuse

Addiction is a complex disease process of the brain that results from recurring drug abuse and is modulated by genetic, developmental, experiential, and environmental factors. The neurobiological changes that accompany drug addiction are not yet well understood however; until recently it was believed that addiction predominantly involves reward processes that are mediated by limbic circuits. Results from neuroimaging studies have identified frontal lobe volume losses in cocaine-dependent and heroin-dependent subjects and have noted negative correlations between normalized prefrontal

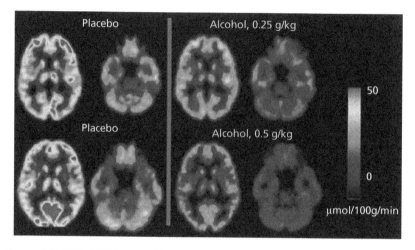

Figure 5.8 FDG-PET images of brain glucose metabolism for a subject tested at base-line (placebo) and after 0.25 g/kg alcohol consumption and for a subject tested at base-line and after 0.5 g/kg alcohol consumption. See Color Plate 20 in insert.

Reprinted from Volkow, N. D., Wang, G.-J., Franceschi, D., Fowler, J. S., Thanos, P. K., Maynard, L., . . . , Li, T. K. (2006). Low doses of alcohol substantially decrease glucose metabolism in the human brain. *NeuroImage, 29*, 295–301, with permission from Elsevier.

volumes and years of either cocaine or heroin use, implying a cumulative effect of substance abuse on frontal volumes (Franklin et al., 2002; Goldstein & Volkow, 2002).

Individuals with a history of long-term opiate abuse and dependence may also (a) suffer cognitive impairment, primarily within the domain of executive functioning (Verdejo-García & Pérez-García, 2007) and (b) have emotional disturbances associated with dysfunctions of limbic structures and the orbitofrontal cortex (e.g., Ersche et al., 2006). Brain-imaging studies of methamphetamine abusers have also reported frontal brain abnormalities, including impairment of neuropsychological function (Kalechstein, Newton, & Green, 2003). For example, Kim and colleagues (2006) have shown that decreased grey-matter density and glucose metabolism in the frontal region of the brain correlate with the impairment of frontal EFs in methamphet-amine abusers. It has also been established that the acute effects of canna-bis include interference with both visuo-spatial working memory and tasks loading heavily on EF (Grant, Grant, Contoreggi, & London, 2000). These cognitive deficits are detectable up to seven days following cannabis use and appear reversible. Indeed, evidence to support permanent persistent cog-nitive effects in heavy cannabis users is equivocal with some studies indi-cated long-term effects (after 24 hours to 28 days) on short-term memory and attention (Eldreth, Matochik, Cadet, & Bolla, 2004). In addition, chronic recreational cannabis use has been associated with diminished neuronal and

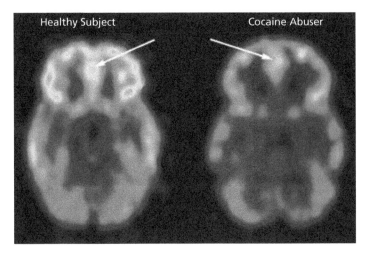

Figure 5.9 Cortical Metabolism in Cocaine Abusers. FDG-PET scan shows reduced brain glucose metabolism, especially in the OFC, compared to healthy control subjects. Red and yellow represent the highest level of metabolic activity, while blue and purple are the lowest level. See Color Plate 21 in insert.

Reproduced from National Institutes of Health: Fowler, J. S., Volkow, N. D., Kassed, C. A., & Chang, L. (2007). Imaging the addicted human brain. *Science & Practice Perspectives*, *3*(2), 4–16.

axonal integrity in the dorsolateral prefrontal cortex (Hermann et al., 2007). Finally, PET studies have established that cocaine and methamphetamine reduce glucose metabolic activity in the OFC, the brain area we rely on to make strategic rather than impulsive decisions (Fowler, Volkow, Kassed, & Chang, 2007; see Figure 5.9).

Empirically validating the unique impact of alcohol and substance abuse on violent behavior is difficult due to the complex nature of the phenomenon. Indeed, the effects cannot be easily separated from other influencing variables, such as emotional disorders, cognitive deficits, and environmental factors. However, the link between violence, drug abuse, and brain abnormality may be mediated by altered cognitive capacities, in particular those involving EFs such as attention, abstract reasoning, and planning goal-oriented behaviors (Fishbein, 2000).

5.11 Conclusion

According to a tentative model of the neurobiology of aggression and violence, aggression and violence, irrespective of the distal cause, reflect abnormalities in the neural circuitry of emotion regulation (Davidson, Putnam, & Larson, 2000). More specifically, aggression emerges when the "drives" of subcortical, limbic-mediated affective prefrontal responses to anger-producing stimuli are insufficiently constrained by inhibitory forces and are channeled into violent behaviors. Indeed, excessive reactivity in the amygdala (bottom-up), coupled with inadequate prefrontal regulation (top-down), serves to increase the likelihood of aggressive behavior (Siever, 2008).

Einstein once wrote that the best models should be "as simple as possible, but no simpler" (Goldsmith & Bartusiak, 2006, p. 292). The assumption that violent behavior emerges mainly from localized brain dysfunctions in individuals who are neurobiologically different is, arguably, too simplistic. In order to attribute violent behavior to activity or lack thereof in a specific brain region, the term "violent" must designate a homogenous behavior; however, violence designates a wide range of behaviors. Indeed, while violence is a universal phenomena, it takes its meaning from social norms, the law, and the particular contexts in which violent acts occur (Sapolsky et al., 2013). Therefore, despite the emphasis on biological causes of violence, ultimately it is not possible to understand the biology of violent behavior without understanding the context in which that biology arises. This is true of our understanding of violence; there are, as of yet, no highly accurate methods of determining the neuroscientific basis of violent behavior or identifying individuals likely to commit impulsive or premeditated violent acts (Sapolsky et al., 2013).

6

Violence and the Adolescent Brain

Age considers; youth ventures.

Rabindranath Tagore[1]

6.1 Introduction

One of the most important questions the juvenile justice system has been forced to answer is: Are juvenile offenders fundamentally different from adults? To answer this question, knowledge of the developmental timetable of certain phenomena, such as planning and self-control are of particular importance in determining the culpability of an adolescent offender (Steinberg, 2008). Neuroscience and, in particular, neuroimaging techniques have significantly improved our understanding of the relationship between adolescent brain function and violent behavior. The influence of advancements made in the neurosciences and the impact on the juvenile justice system is perhaps best illustrated in cases involving adolescents who have committed extreme violent crimes, like the following.

At the age of 17, Christopher Simmons committed murder, and nine months later, after he had turned 18, he was tried and sentenced to death. At trial the State introduced Simmons's confession, the videotaped reenactment of the crime, and testimony that Simmons had discussed the crime in advance and bragged about it later. The defense called no witnesses in the guilt phase, and after the jury had returned a guilty verdict the trial proceeded to the penalty phase.

The State sought the death penalty and, as aggravating factors, submitted that the murder was inhuman, horrible, and outrageously and wantonly vile. During closing arguments, both the prosecution and the defense addressed Simmons's age. More specifically, defense counsel argued that his age should make a difference in deciding what type of punishment was appropriate.

In contrast, the prosecutor argued that Simmons's youth should be considered aggravating rather than mitigating:

> Let's look at the mitigating circumstances. . . . Age, he says. Think about age. Seventeen years old. Isn't that scary? Doesn't that scare you? Mitigating? Quite the contrary I submit. Quite the contrary.[2]

The jury recommended the death penalty and, accepting the jury's recommendation, the trial judge sentenced Simmons to death. Simmons appealed his conviction, arguing that he had received ineffective assistance of counsel because information regarding his impulsivity and susceptibility to being easily influenced by others was not properly presented at the sentencing hearing. The trial court found no constitutional violation by reason of ineffective assistance of counsel and denied Simmons's motion for postconviction relief which the Missouri Supreme Court affirmed (*State v. Simmons*, 1997). In 2001, federal courts denied Simmons's petition for a writ of habeas corpus and, the following year, the US Supreme Court held in *Atkins v. Virginia* (2002) that "the 8th and 14th Amendments prohibit the execution of a person with mental retardation" (*Atkins*, 2002, p. 304). Simmons filed a new petition for state postconviction relief arguing that the Supreme Court's reasoning in *Atkins* (2002) should also be applied to juveniles. The Missouri Supreme Court agreed, set aside Simmons' death sentence, and resentenced him to life in prison without possibility for parole (*Simmons v. Roper*, 2003).

6.2 Adolescent Brain Development

In 2010, in *Graham v. Florida*, the US Supreme Court once again was asked to decide the fate of juvenile offenders. In 2003 Graham, age 16, along with two accomplices, attempted to rob a restaurant. Graham was arrested for the robbery attempt and was charged as an adult for armed burglary with assault and battery, as well as attempted armed robbery, with the first charge being a first-degree felony charge, punishable by life. Graham pled guilty and his plea was accepted. Six months later, Graham was arrested again for home invasion robbery. Although Graham denied any involvement, he acknowledged that he was in violation of his plea agreement. In 2006 Graham was sentenced to life in prison without the possibility for parole.

Graham challenged his sentence under the 8th Amendment's Cruel and Unusual Punishments Clause, but the State First District Court of Appeal affirmed. Subsequently, the US Supreme Court held that the 8th Amendment Clause does not permit a juvenile offender to be sentenced to life in prison without parole for a nonhomicide crime (*Graham v. Florida*, 2010).

Two years later, in *Miller v. Alabama* (2012) and *Jackson v. Hobbs* (2012), the US Supreme Court further held that mandatory life sentences without the possibility of parole are unconstitutional. These rulings extended beyond *Graham* (2010), in which the Court previously had ruled that for nonhomicide crimes a life without parole sentence imposed on a juvenile is unconstitutional under the 8th Amendment. As in *Graham* (2010), the Court reasoned that mandatory life without parole for those under the age of 18 at the time the crime was committed violates the 8th Amendment's prohibition on cruel and unusual punishments. More specifically, the Court contended that a mandatory life sentence without the possibility of parole precludes any consideration of the chronological age of juveniles and its characteristic features, such as immaturity and the failure to appreciate risks and consequences. As noted, "our decisions rested not only on common sense—on what 'any parent knows'—but on science and social science as well. Psychology and brain science continue to show fundamental differences between juvenile and adult minds," making their actions "less likely to be evidence of 'irretrievably depraved character' than are the actions of adults" (quoting *Roper v. Simmons*, 2005, p. 570).

As these cases illustrate, neuroscience related to adolescent brain development has invaded the legal system and has captured the attention of courts and legislatures. Indeed, in 2007 Senator Edward Kennedy convened a hearing on the juvenile justice implications of brain development, and in 2002 US Supreme Court Justice Stevens, *In re Stanford* (2002), signaled his interest in "[n]euroscientific evidence" that had revealed that adolescent brains are not fully developed (p. 971). Further, many scholars, commentators, and courts believe that neuroscience evidence played a dominant role in *Roper* (2005) and *Graham* (2010). More specifically, in reaching its decisions in the cited cases, the US Supreme Court relied in large part on neuroscientific studies presented by the American Psychological Association (APA) in their amicus briefs in support of defendants. In these briefs the APA argued that there is clear evidence that significant changes in brain structure and function occur during adolescence, with the most important changes occurring in the prefrontal cortex and in the connections between the prefrontal cortex and other brain structures (Casey, Giedd, & Thomas, 2000; Goldberg, 2001). Also, following the period immediately after puberty, important changes in the reward processing system of the brain occur, which have been linked to the tendency to engage in risky behaviors (Spear, 2010; Steinberg, 2010; see also Figure 6.1).

6.2.1 Cortical White and Gray Matter

Neuroimaging studies examining structural and microstructural indices of brain development have suggested that, throughout adolescence, cortical gray matter[3] volume decreases, while cerebral white matter[4] volume and organization, density, and integrity of white matter pathways increase (Barnea-Goraly et al., 2005; Fields, 2008; Sowell, Trauner, Gamst, & Jernigan, 2002; see Figure 6.2). Although these studies diverge in terms of the exact brain regions in which white matter density increases, the majority of studies have pointed to a steady, linear increase in white matter

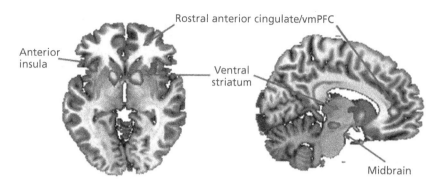

Figure 6.1 Main Components of the Human Reward Brain Circuit. See Color Plate 22 in insert.

Reprinted from Blakemore, S. J., & Robbins, T. W. (2012). Decision-making in the adolescent brain. *Nature Neuroscience, 15*, 1184–1191, with permission from Macmillan Publishers.

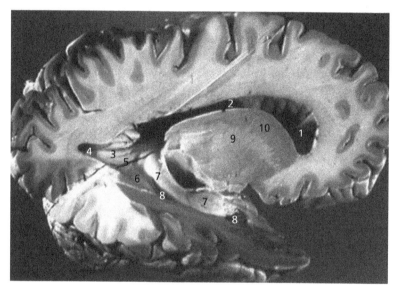

Figure 6.2 Grey and White Brain Matter

Image Courtesy of Wikimedia Commons, available at http://en.wikipedia.org/wiki/File:Human_brain_right_dissected_lateral_.

with age (Barnea-Goraly et al., 2005). While white matter development follows a gradual course, the changes in grey matter density seem to follow a region-specific, nonlinear pattern, progressive at certain times and regressive at other times, as evidenced by structural neuroimaging studies. For example, a magnetic resonance imaging (MRI) study of 35 normally developing children (7 to 11 years), adolescents (12 to 16 years), and young adults (23 to 30 years) found a significant decrease of grey matter in the parietal and dorsal prefrontal cortices between childhood and adolescence (Sowell, Thompson, Tessner, & Toga, 2001).).[5] Sowell and colleagues (2001) also found an inverse relationship between dorsal prefrontal cortex growth and grey matter density between childhood and adolescence. In fact, the regions exhibiting the most dramatic decrease in grey matter density also exhibited the most dramatic postpubescent increase in white matter density in the dorsal prefrontal cortex (Sowell et al., 2001). This gradual decrease in grey matter density has been attributed to postpubescent synaptic pruning (Sowell et al., 2001). Further, children with early-onset conduct disorder (CD) are presumed to be at a high risk for developing antisocial personality disorder due to primarily reduced gray matter in limbic brain structures, including the amygdala and the orbitofrontal cortex, thus supporting the notion that the latter plays an important role in regulating aggressive behavior (Huebner et al., 2008). Finally, a structural MRI study of regional gray matter volumes in incarcerated male adolescents found that psychopathic traits were correlated with decreased volumes in the orbitofrontal cortex, temporal poles and posterior cingulate (Ermer, Cope, Nyalakanti, Calhoun, & Kiehl, 2013).

Numerous research studies have also found developmental changes in white matter density in other brain regions. For example, Paus and colleagues (1999) analyzed the brain images of individuals between the ages of 4 and 17 and noted an increase in white matter density, specifically in the right internal capsule and left arcuate fasciculus, which was interpreted as reflecting increased connections between the speech regions. In addition, the corpus callosum, which connects the two hemispheres of the brain, has been found to undergo region-specific growth during adolescence and up until the mid-twenties (Barnea-Goraly et al., 2005). Furthermore, it has been suggested that, especially during childhood and early adolescence, the brain undergoes substantial synaptic pruning that ultimately leads to more efficient neural connections, significant improvement in executive functions, and substantial myelination (Casey, Giedd, & Thomas, 2000; Gogtay & Thompson, 2010; Spear, 2010). Neural connections that survive the pruning process become more adept at transmitting information through myelination.[6] This in turn allows nerve impulses to travel throughout the brain faster and more efficiently and increasingly facilitates the integration of various brain activities (Anderson, Anderson, Jacobs, & Spencer-Smith, 2008).

6.2.2 Connectivity

Continuing into late adolescence, connections among cortical areas and between cortical and subcortical regions that are important for emotion regulation also increase, and this increased connectivity is especially important for processing social and emotional information and for cognitive control (Steinberg, Cauffman, Woolard, Graham, & Banich, 2009). In fact, recent studies have emphasized the importance of examining the connectivity between key brain regions in antisocial behavior, and many of these studies have used diffusion tensor imaging to measure fractional anisotropy (FA)[7] in the uncinate fascicle (UF).[8] The uncinate fasciculus has the longest period of development in terms of FA; it continues to develop beyond the age of 30 (Lebel, Walker, Leemans, Phillips, & Beaulieu, 2008). It has also been suggested that the UF is developmentally vulnerable. For example, in 12-year-old males that were preterm, abnormalities measured by FA in the left anterior uncinate correlated with verbal and full-scale IQ and the Peabody Picture Vocabulary Test–Revised scores (Constable et al., 2008). Furthermore, a study of male adolescents with childhood-onset CD found increased FA in the UF (Passamonti et al., 2012). Sarkar and colleagues (2013) likewise found increased FA in a group of male subjects (ages 12 to 19) with CD[9] as well as an age by group interaction indicating that controls demonstrated age-related maturation in this tract, but those with CD did not (Sarkar et al., 2013). Finally, a diffusion tension imaging study of adolescents (mean age of 14 years) with CD or oppositional defiant disorder and psychopathic traits found no differences in FA in the UF but did find reduced functional connectivity between the amygdala and anterior cingulate cortex, insula, cingulate, and superior temporal gyrus during a learning task (Finger et al., 2012).

6.2.3 The Frontal Lobes

Changes in brain maturation occur at different times, with changes in the brain's reward and social processing systems occuring well before changes in areas that are associated with self-control and executive function (Steinberg et al., 2009). Indeed, studies have shown that the prefrontal cortex is among the last areas in the brain to fully mature (Gogtay & Thompson, 2010). These findings suggest that middle adolescence in particular may be a period of increased vulnerability to risky behavior due to the temporary disconnection between the rapid rise in dopaminergic activity around the time of puberty and the more gradual maturation of the prefrontal cortex and its connections to other brain regions (Steinberg et al., 2009). Further, MRI studies have established that the developmental process tends to occur in the brain in a back to front pattern, explaining why the prefrontal cortex develops last. These research findings have led to the idea of "frontalization," meaning that the prefrontal cortex gradually becomes able to regulate behavioral responses that are initiated by the more primitive limbic structures (Giedd, 2004; see Figure 6.3).

As previously discussed, the frontal lobes play a critical role in executive brain functions. These functions are considered to be the supervisory cognitive skills needed for goal-directed behavior, such as planning and response inhibition (Goldberg, 2001). Indeed, as Figure 6.4 illustrates, while both adolescents and adults activate a network of fronto-parietal regions implicated in cognitive control, during the Stroop test adults exhibit significantly greater

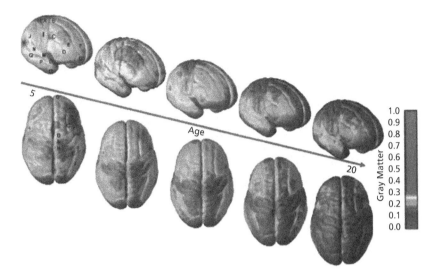

Figure 6.3 Time-Lapse Imaging Tracks Brain Maturation from Ages 5 to 20. Red indicates more gray matter, blue less gray matter. Areas that mediate "executive functioning" mature later than those responsible for basic functions. See Color Plate 23 in insert.

Reprinted from Giedd, J. N., & Rapoport, J. L. (2010). Structural MRI of pediatric brain development: what have we learned and where are we going? *Neuron, 67*(5), 728–734, with permission from Elsevier.

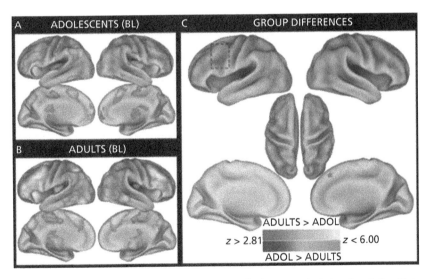

Figure 6.4 Between-Group Differences in Blocked Stroop Activity. See Color Plate 24 in insert.

Reproduced from: PLoSOne-Open Access Journal: A Andrews-Hanna, J. R., Mackiewicz Seghete, K. L., Claus, E. D., Burgess, G. C., Ruzic, L., & Banich, M. T. (2011). Cognitive control in adolescence: Neural underpinnings and relation to self-report behaviors. *PLoS One, 6*(6), e21598.

activity in lateral prefrontal regions, dorsal medial prefrontal cortex, and temporal-occipital regions (Andrews-Hanna et al., 2011). Although during adolescence, the size of the frontal lobes does not change significantly, their composition, consisting of white and gray brain matter, undergoes dynamic changes, resulting in improved cognitive functioning, which is presumed to be due to increased myelination (Gogtay et al., 2004). Any disruption of executive functions may lead to impairment in strategic thinking and risk management, which, in turn, has been associated with greater impulsivity. In fact, "one hallmark of frontal lobe dysfunction is difficulty in making decisions that are in the long-term best interests of the individual" (Damasio & Anderson, 2003, p. 434).

6.3 Adolescents and Criminal Behavior

As noted by Steinberg and Haskins (2008), during the mid-1980s the American public developed a fear of violent youth that almost bordered on paranoia. Since then the rate of crimes committed by adolescents has significantly decreased, with individuals under the age of 18 being responsible for only a small percentage of all crimes committed, as shown in Table 6.1.

As previously discussed, adolescents' tendency to engage in illegal behavior may stem, at least in part, from their inability to make mature decisions,

Table 6.1 Adolescent Arrests, 2010

Type of Crime Committed	Number of individuals arrested		
	Under the Age of 15 Years	Under the Age of 18 Years	18 Years of Age and Older
Murder and nonnegligent manslaughter	70	718	7,289
Forcible rape	683	2,072	12,398
Aggravated assault	9,894	31,976	269,438
Robbery	3,547	19,118	62,403
Burglary	13,386	48,557	167,783
Arson	2,070	3,506	5,036
Violent crime	14,194	53,884	351,528
Property crime	78,530	276,461	950,731
Other assaults	57,841	153,159	797,983
Vandalism	22,483	57,724	130,159

Adapted from the Uniform Crime Report—Crime in the U.S. 2010—Table 36.

and research has in fact shown that adolescents' decision-making differs from that of adults in several respects, including the ability to (a) weigh the risks and rewards of their conduct, (b) control impulses, and (c) resist negative external pressure.

6.3.1 Inability to Weigh Risks and Rewards

As the US Supreme Court in *Roper* recognized, adolescents have less capacity for mature judgment than adults and as a result are more likely to engage in risky behaviors:

> As any parent knows and as . . . scientific and sociological
> studies . . . tend to confirm, "a lack of maturity and an
> underdeveloped sense of responsibility are found in youth more
> often than in adults and are more understandable among the
> young. These qualities often result in impetuous and ill-considered
> actions and decisions." (*Roper v. Simmons*, 2005, p. 569)

Indeed, a recent study that employed a gambling task to measure reward-seeking and risk-avoiding behavior found that adolescents improved their performance over time by being drawn to the bets with the best rewards, while adults improved by avoiding bets with the worst losses (Steinberg, Cauffman, & Woolard, 2009). From these findings Steinberg and colleagues concluded that while the ability to make decisions improves throughout adolescence and into young adulthood, this improvement may not be due to cognitive maturation but rather to changes in affective processing. Further,

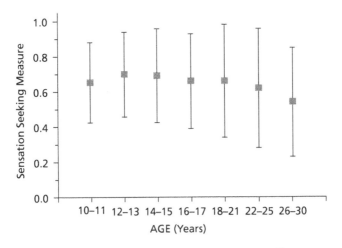

Figure 6.5 Sensation-Seeking as a Function of Age Based on Self-Report

Adapted from Steinberg, L., Albert, D., Cauffman, E., Banich, M., Graham, S., & Woolard, J. (2008). Age differences in sensation seeking and impulsivity as indexed by behavior and self-report: Evidence for a dual systems model. *Developmental Psychology, 44*(6), 1764–1778.

as shown in Figure 6.5, age differences in sensation-seeking as indexed by self-report followed a curvilinear trend, with sensation-seeking increasing between the ages of 10 and 15 and declining or remaining stable thereafter (Steinberg et al., 2008).

Many experts agree that the prefrontal cortex in particular is closely involved in the ability to assess the relative risks and rewards of a particular behavior (Spear, 2010; Stuss & Knight, 2013). For example, it has been shown that patients who suffer from frontal-lobe dysfunction tend to perform poorly on tasks that require the inhibition of a particular behavior (Stuss & Knight, 2013). Similarly, using functional MRI, Eshel, Nelson, Blair, Pine, and Ernst (2007) found that adolescents show decreased frontal cortical activity relative to adults while engaging in a monetary decision-making task. These results converge with behavioral research findings that have provided evidence that core brain regions, such as the prefrontal cortex, are recruited in children, but refinements in the working memory circuitry continue through adolescence into adulthood (Luna, Padmanabhan, & O'Hearn, 2010). These refinements include (a) changes in prefrontal cortex activation and (b) the integration with other regions, which are presumed to reflect ongoing neural maturation (Luna et al., 2010). Brain imaging studies have provided support for an increased strengthening in the connections of the dopamine-rich fronto-striatal circuitry across development. Using functional MRI and DTI, these studies (a) found greater strength in distal connections, within these circuits across development and (b) linked the connection strength between prefrontal and striatal regions with the capacity to successfully engage cognitive control (Asato, Terwilliger, Woo, & Luna, 2010; Casey et al., 2007).

6.3.2 Inability to Control Impulses

That youths are more likely than adults to act more impulsively and to "weigh the consequences of their options differently, by discounting risks and future consequences, and over-valuing peer approval, immediate consequences, and the excitement of risk taking" is well established (Scott & Steinberg, 2003, p. 830). The differences in thinking and behavior between adolescents and adults are presumed to reflect basic biological differences in neurophysiological maturation (Sowell et al., 2001). More specifically, adolescents' levels of cortical development may be directly related to the ability to perform well in situations requiring, in particular, executive cognitive skills, with younger, less cortically mature adolescents being at a greater risk for engaging in impulsive behavior (Gnaber & Yurgelun-Todd, 2006).

Impulsivity, defined as the tendency to react to the immediate environment with little deliberation before action, has been positively related to risk-taking behavior (Steinberg, 2003). Laboratory studies of age differences in impulse control have pointed to the gradual development of cognitive control mechanisms over the course of adolescence and into adulthood. More specifically, brain imaging studies examining performance on tasks requiring

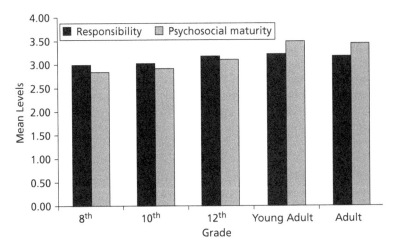

Figure 6.6 Age Differences in Responsibility and Psychosocial Maturity

Adapted from Cauffman, E., & Steinberg, L. (2000). (Im)maturity of judgment in adolescence: Why adolescents may be less culpable than adults. *Behavioral Sciences and the Law, 18,* 741–760.

cognitive control, such as the Stroop and Go/No-Go tests, have shown that between childhood and adulthood, improved performance on cognitive control tasks is gradual and is accompanied by an increase in focal activation of the dorsolateral prefrontal cortex (Adleman et al., 2002; Steinberg et al., 2008). Research examining the components of psychosocial maturity of judgment, such as responsibility, perspective, and temperance, have also shown that adolescents score significantly lower than adults on measures of responsibility and overall maturity (see Figure 6.6; Cauffman & Steinberg, 2000).

That adolescence is a time of sensation-seeking is by now also well established. In fact, sensation-seeking is most prominent during early to midadolescence but decreases thereafter, while impulse control appears to steadily improve throughout the teenage years, suggesting that they are subserved by different biological processes (Steinberg et al., 2008). Clearly, adolescents' tendencies to seek out novel experiences, even at the risk of physical harm, is not surprising, given their inability to assess risks or assess possible outcomes (Sturman & Moghaddam, 2011). However, it has also been suggested that during adolescence some individuals may be more prone to engage in risky behaviors due to a combination of developmental changes and variability in a given individual's predisposition to engage in risky behavior, rather than to changes in impulsivity alone (Casey & Jones, 2010).

6.3.3 Inability to Resist External Influences

Why do adolescents so easily give in to peer pressure? Two reasons have been cited for the increased significance of peers in adolescence. First, because there is an increased need to conform and fit in, peer pressure becomes increasingly important, and, second, group membership becomes more salient during adolescence (Steinberg & Monahan, 2007). It is, therefore, not surprising that, because of greater fear of being socially ostracized, adolescents experience greater anxiety and concern over the consequences of refusing to engage in risky conduct than adults do (Taylor-Thompson, 2003).

As the US Supreme Court recognized, "juveniles are more vulnerable . . . to negative influences and outside pressures, including peer pressure"(*Roper v. Simmons*, 2005, p. 569). In fact, antisocial acts committed by teenagers are much more likely to occur in groups, and peer pressure in particular has been hypothesized to be an important contributor to various deviant behavior in adolescence (see, e.g., Steinberg & Monahan, 2007; Warr, 2002). Also, consider the following:

One day in January 1992, Timothy Kane, a 14-year-old junior high school student who had never had any contact with the justice system, was playing video games with friends when a couple of older adolescents suggested that they break into a neighbor's house. Upon entering the house, they were surprised to find both the neighbor and her son at home. Subsequently, two of the older boys killed both of them, while Timothy watched from under the dining room table. In an interview years later, while he was serving a life sentence under Florida's felony murder law, Kane explained that he went along because he didn't want to stay behind alone and he didn't want his friends to call him a "scaredy-cat" (Liptak, 2005).

Not only do peer relationships become dominant during adolescence, but the inclination to seek out fun and exciting experiences also increases (Nelson, Leibenluft, McClure, & Pine, 2005). While a teenager may know right from wrong and may even have the capacity to control his or her impulses while alone, "resisting temptation while alone is a different task than resisting the pressure to commit an offense when adolescent peers are pushing for misbehavior and waiting to see whether or not the outcome they desire will occur" (Zimring, 2000, p. 280). Recent studies looking at the neural underpinnings of resistance to peer influence in adolescence have suggested that improvements in this capacity may be due to greater connectivity between cortical and subcortical regions, which may result in better coordination of cognition and affect (Grosbras et al. 2007, Paus et al. 2008). Ultimately, however, young adults become increasingly resistant to peer pressure, which suggests that this process of refraining from antisocial behavior may also be tied to the normative changes in peer relations that occur as individuals become more emotionally and socially mature (Monahan, Steinberg, & Cauffman, 2009).

6.4 Neuroscience and Juvenile Justice

Although the exact relationships between various aspects of brain maturation and behavior have not yet been clearly identified, research studies focusing on the neuroscience of adolescent development continue to expand on the behavioral findings both *Roper v. Simmons* (2005) and *Graham v. Florida* (2010) relied on. To that end, advocates of the use of neuroscience evidence have argued that (a) neuroscience validates the wealth of psychological studies on juveniles' immaturity, thus lending a "hard science" base to a "soft science" argument (Feld, 2007, p. 59), and (b) neuroimaging studies, in addition to psychological studies, are "the best, most sophisticated source of information about how children actually develop" (Buss, 2009, p. 507).

There is no doubt that the US Supreme Court relied heavily on neuroscientific research findings in reaching its decisions in *Roper* (2005) and *Graham* (2010). However, while many scholars approve of the use of such evidence in a court of law, others have cautioned against its use for various reasons. Justice Scalia's dissenting opinion in *Roper*, in which Chief Justice Roberts and Justice Thomas joined, addressed a number of these reasons, including the following:

- The Court never explained why these particular studies are methodologically sound, since not a single study was ever entered into evidence or tested in an adversarial proceeding. As explained by Chief Justice Roberts: "Methodological and other errors can affect the reliability and validity of estimates about the opinions and attitudes of a population derived from various sampling techniques. Everything from variations in the survey methodology, such as the choice of the target population, the sampling design used, the questions asked, and the statistical analyses used to interpret the data can skew the results" (*Roper*, 2005, p. 617).
- The APA, which in this case had claimed that scientific evidence has established that persons under the age of 18 lack the ability to take moral responsibility for their decisions, had previously taken the opposite position. In its brief in *Hodgson* v. *Minnesota* (1989), the APA, in fact, found a "rich body of research" showing that juveniles are mature enough to decide whether to obtain an abortion without parental involvement (APA, 1989, p. 18).
- Given the lack of a uniform scientific methodology and many conflicting views, courts, which can only consider the evidence before them, are arguably ill equipped to decide which view of is correct.
- Many of the studies relied on in *Roper* had small sample sizes and potential sample selection biases, and some of the studies were in fact flawed (Aronson, 2009).
- The studies cited by the *Roper* Court offer little support for a categorical exclusion of the death penalty for murderers under the age of 18. At most, these studies conclude that, on average or in most cases, persons under 18 are unable to take moral responsibility for their actions. Moreover, the cited studies describe only adolescents who engage in risky or antisocial behavior, as many young people do.

"Murder, however, is more than just risky or antisocial behavior" (*Roper*, 2005, p. 618).

These comments are instructive in that they clearly illustrate the problems courts face in determining the scientific validity of neuroscience evidence proffered in a court of law. They also make clear that any neuroscientific evidence to be admitted in a court of law must be scientifically valid. This is especially true in light of the fact that such evidence can drastically change the legal landscape, as evidenced in *Roper* and *Simmons*. Further, while data from research studies support conclusions at the aggregate level, they shed little light on the developmental status of a particular adolescent, except insofar as he or she is a member of the group (Maroney, 2011). More specifically, the problem with individualized assessments is that we currently lack the diagnostic tools to evaluate psychosocial maturity on an individual basis and thus are unable to separate adolescent career criminals from ordinary adolescents (Scott & Steinberg, 2008). In addition, despite the popular belief that neuroimaging techniques provide "objective truth" of brain functioning, these techniques involve an element of subjectivity, as previously noted. Establishing a causal relationship is much more complicated than it might seem, because there rarely is a one-to-one relationship between particular brain regions and their discrete functions.[10] Consequently, the relationships between an individual's brain structure, level of brain function, and behavior remains largely speculative (Maroney, 2011).

6.5 Conclusion

In 350 BC Aristotle observed that youth "are hot-tempered, and quick-tempered, and apt to give way to their anger" (Book II, Part 12, Paragraph 2). As noted throughout this chapter, there is a long history of empirical studies clearly indicating that adolescence is a time of increased risk-taking, impulsiveness, and recklessness. Consequently, numerous scholars have argued that since adolescents have neither the volitional capacity nor the cognitive capacity, equating their criminal responsibility with that of adults is unjustified (Feld, 2003).

Death is final and irreversible. It is, therefore, not surprising that it is in the context of the death penalty that many courts have most carefully examined the culpability of and deserved punishment for adolescents. In reaching their decisions, the *Roper* and *Graham* courts in particular relied heavily on findings from neuroscientific studies to make their final determinations. However, use of neuroscience evidence, and in particular the use of evidence based on neuroimaging scans, continues to pose evidentiary problems of accuracy, validity, and causation. While there is no doubt that neuroimaging techniques are essential for neuroscience research, there are innumerable questions about what can be stated with certainty about the images generated and the behavior in question. Furthermore, as has been noted: (a) images from all currently available functional neuroimaging techniques are not direct images of brain activity but theory-laden representations of the outcomes of statistical analyses performed in highly controlled settings when subjects respond to often very carefully constructed and artificial questions, and (b) responsibility is a normative concept that reflects social expectations and conventions about how people should or can act and is not simply an empirical finding about an individual's mental capacity (Glannon, 2005).

7

The Admissibility of Scientific Evidence

Act only according to that maxim whereby you can, at the
same time, will that it should become a universal law.

(Kant, 1929)

7.1 Introduction

Law and science both seek to ascertain the truth though they embrace dispa-
rate objectives. While law aims to resolve dispute between two parties, science seeks to understand and explain phenomena. Indeed, as once noted by
the Supreme Court "the balance struck by the Rule of Evidence is designed
not for the exhaustive search for cosmic understanding, but for the particu-
larized resolution of legal disputes" (*Daubert v. Merrell Dow*, 1993, p. 579).
Thus while science seeks a universal truth, law "seeks repose" (Dreyfuss,
1995, p. 1795).

Scientists have learned more about the brain in the last two decades than
in all previous centuries combined due to the increasing pace of research
dedicated to the behavioral and neurocognitive sciences and the development
of new research techniques, such as neuroimaging. It is, therefore, not surprising that the US Congress declared the 1990s the Decade of the Brain and
the European Brain Council made the decision to make 2014 the year of the
brain in Europe. That recent neuroscientific advances, such as neuroimaging techniques, have furthered our understanding of how the brain operates
by providing, for example, structural and functional images of both healthy
and diseased brains, is unquestionable. The proper legal application of these
advances, however, is still very much debated. For example, some judges
have argued that scientific evidence, which offers insight into an offender's
mental state, is crucial because it is the only way of determining whether an
offender's punishment is proportional to his crime. Other judges have argued

that "objective" evidence does not "wholly determine the controversy" and instead have focused on their duty as gatekeepers to independently evaluate scientific evidence (Baskin, Edersheim, & Price, 2007, p. 239). With respect to understanding the relationship between the brain and violent behavior, the state of scientific knowledge, while still relatively limited, is promising. However, while violence is most likely a multifactorial behavior that is not easily reducible to a specific neuropsychological test score, brain function, or brain region, the frontal cortex and executive dysfunction in particular have been linked to violent behavior.

The foundation for using neuropsychological test results and neuroimaging evidence in criminal trials lies in a massive body of scientific literature on the neuroanatomical, neurochemical, and neurocognitive bases of violence. For example, in 1998 and 1999, an interdisciplinary group of experts were convened to create a consensus statement on the relationship between the mind, the brain, and violence. To this end, the experts conducted an exhaustive literature survey of the role of the brain in violent behavior and in 2001 issued a statement noting that the frontal lobes and the limbic system "are thought to play preeminent roles in [violent] behavior" (Filley et al., 2001, p. 5). More specifically, aggressive behavior is presumed to result from the operations of the limbic system, with the amygdala being the structure most frequently implicated, while prefrontal functions provide an individual with the ability to exercise judgment in situations in which actions have significant consequences. Further, this capacity for judgment

> may serve the important function of inhibiting limbic
> impulses, which, if acted on, could be socially inappropriate or
> destructive. . . . Therefore, there exists a balance between the
> potential for impulsive aggression mediated by temporolimbic
> structures and the control of this drive by the influence of the
> orbitofrontal regions. (Filley et al., 2001, p. 5)

This view of aggression and violence has been supported by numerous neuroimaging studies. One such study, published by Raine, Lencz, Bihrle, LaCasse, and Colletti in 1994, used positron emission tomography (PET) to illustrate diminished glucose metabolism or reduced activity of the prefrontal cortex in criminal defendants accused of homicide. Other research studies have confirmed the association between prefrontal dysfunction and violence, and numerous articles and literature reviews written by prominent neuroscientists have reached similar conclusions (see, e.g., Barkataki et al., 2005; Bufkin & Lutrell, 2005). In addition, a significant area of research on the disposition to criminal violence concerns the neurobiological correlates of psychopathy and antisocial personality disorder. As noted in the amicus brief filed by the American Psychological Association in *Roper v. Simmons* (2005), "psychopathy is presumed to be deep seated, stable over time, and resistant, if not absolutely impervious, to change" (APA Amicus Curiae Brief, 1989, pp. 20–21). Antisocial personality disorder is a related diagnostic construct of the *Diagnostic and Statistical Manual of Mental Disorders* (fourth edition, text revision; American Psychiatric Association, 2000) that is based on behavioral characteristics such as "a pervasive pattern of disregard for, and violation of, the rights of others that begins in childhood or early adolescence and continues into adulthood" (p. 645). A survey of structural and functional neuroimaging studies relating to antisocial personality disorder and psychopathy concluded that the functional but not the structural neuroimaging studies strongly suggest dysfunction of the frontal and temporal lobes and possibly other structures, including the angular gyrus and corpus callosum, in psychopathy (Pridmore, Chambers, & McArthur, 2005). Many other neuroscientists likewise have undertaken inquiries using neuroimaging techniques to explore the potential connection between aggression and brain abnormalities and, by linking brain abnormalities such as executive dysfunction to specific behaviors and specifically to violent behavior, these studies have provided the foundation for the use of neuroimaging evidence in criminal trials.

7.2 Admissibility of Neuroscience Evidence

Science and law are said to exist on different dimensions: law operates through logic, deduction, and precedent; science, in contrast, is based on the scientific method, which values empirical and measurable phenomena as its core (Erickson, 2010). More specifically, "the evaluation of research on the neurobiology of violence demands conceptual clarity, along with careful analysis of methods and data to prevent misunderstanding and possible abuse of the results" (Brower & Price, 2000, pp. 145–146).

Challenges to the admissibility of scientific evidence are rare in criminal cases due to the longstanding practice of deferring to experts and the usually limited resources available to many criminal defendants (Mobbs, Lau, Jones, & Frith, 2007). However, while the reality of brain impairment and its effect on judgment is well accepted in the scientific community, how brain dysfunction may have contributed to the criminal offense may be open to challenges, particularly with respect to neuroimaging and neuropsychological test results. Clearly if judges and juries seek to rely on brain images and neuropsychological tests to assist them in making culpability determinations, conclusions based in part or in full on neuroscience evidence must meet pertinent legal standards for the admissibility of scientific evidence. To that end, there are number of legal rules and guidelines that assist courts in their admissibility determinations.[1]

7.2.1 Federal Rules of Evidence

Almost every state court has its own set of evidence rules, with a majority following the template of the Federal Rules of Evidence (FRE). In deciding whether or not to admit neuroscience evidence, most courts will consider the following: FRE 104(a), FRE 401, FRE 402, FRE 403, and FRE 702.

7.2.1.1 FRE 104(a)—Preliminary Questions

Before any evidence can be admitted, the court must decide preliminary questions of fact concerning the qualification of a person to be a witness, the existence of privilege, or the admissibility of evidence. In making its decision the court is not bound by the rules of evidence except those with respect to privileges; judges have full power to decide if a potential expert witness is qualified.

7.2.1.2 FRE 401—Test for Relevant Evidence

FRE 401 states that evidence is relevant if (a) it has any tendency to make a fact more or less probable than it would be without the evidence and (b) the fact is of consequence in determining the action. To be admissible, evidence need not be conclusive on a particular issue. For example, in a recent drug trial, testimony that a hotel clerk saw the defendant drop a little bag containing a white substance was relevant even without any evidence confirming the nature of this substance (*United States v. Burnett*, 2009). In affirming the admission of this testimony, the First Circuit Court explained the measure for relevant evidence, noting that "each specific item of evidence offered need not be sufficient to prove the case standing by itself before it is admissible. Rather, it is enough that the piece of evidence has some bearing on a matter of consequence to the case" (*United States v. Burnett*, 2009, pp. 132–133).

7.2.1.3 FRE 702—Testimony by Expert Witnesses

Judge Learned Hand, discontent with the increasing frequency of highly credentialed experts offering completely polarized opinions on the stand, questioned,—"How can the jury judge between two statements each founded upon an experience admittedly foreign in kind to their own?" (Learned Hand, 1902, p. 54).

FRE 702 rule permits a witness qualified as an expert by knowledge, skill, experience, training, or education to testify to scientific, technical, or other specialized knowledge if that knowledge can assist the trier of fact to understand the evidence or to determine a fact in issue. In 2000, an amendment to FRE 702 added the following language: if (a) the testimony is based on sufficient facts or data, (b) the testimony is the product of reliable principles and methods, and (c) the witness has applied the principles and methods reliably to the facts of the case. The 2000 amendment was enacted explicitly in response to *Daubert v. Merrell Dow Pharmaceuticals, Inc.*, the 1993 Supreme Court case that set the current standard for judicial application and interpretation of FRE 702 in many states. In 2011 Rule 702 was again amended, and the rule now reads: "a witness who is qualified as an expert by knowledge, skill, experience, training, or education may testify in the form of an opinion or otherwise if the (a) expert's scientific, technical, or other specialized knowledge will help the trier of fact to understand the evidence or to determine a fact in issue; (b) testimony is based on sufficient facts or data; (c) testimony is the product of reliable principles and methods; and (d) expert has reliably applied the principles and methods to the facts of the case."

7.2.1.4 FRE 403—Exclusion of Relevant Evidence

Expert testimony that survives scrutiny under FRE 702 may still be excluded under FRE 403. FRE 403 allows for the exclusion of evidence that "although relevant," has a probative value "substantially outweighed by the danger of unfair prejudice, confusion of the issues, or misleading the jury, or by considerations of undue delay, waste of time, or needless presentation of cumulative evidence." The rule sets out "a zone of discretion within which judges may exclude evidence" that is otherwise relevant and admissible (*United States v. Messino*, 1999). Although FRE 403 rarely operates to exclude expert testimony because FRE 702 itself excludes expert testimony that is unfairly prejudicial or has the potential to confuse the jury, the following case illustrates the operation of FRE 403.

Montgomery was convicted in federal district court for kidnapping and homicide and was subsequently sentenced to death (*United States v. Montgomery*, 2011). The defendant appealed the proceedings on a number of grounds, including that the trial judge had improperly excluded polygraph evidence proffered by the defense at both guilt and penalty phases. Montgomery had initially confessed that she acted alone in the killing of the victim and the kidnapping of an infant in December of 2004. In early 2007, however, she claimed that her brother was with her when the crimes were committed. She repeated the allegations during interviews with psychiatrists for the government and the defense, and her attorneys commissioned a polygraph examination to test the veracity of her allegations. The polygraph exam results, which indicated that Montgomery's answers were not indicative of deception, were then shared with the government, which moved to exclude all testimony related to the examination or its results, contending that the results were unreliable, that the questions were flawed, and that any evidence related to the polygraph examination should be excluded under FRE 403 and 702. The Circuit Court subsequently concluded that the trial judge did not abuse its discretion in excluding the polygraph evidence under FRE 403 and noted that since the evidence could be easily excluded without the use of FRE 702 and the principles of *Daubert*, there was no need to engage in an analysis of FRE 702. In doing so the Court reasoned in part that (a) Montgomery's polygraph evidence had minimal probative value and (b) the test was administered without the government's knowledge and without the possibility that the defendant might suffer negative consequences from a failed examination (*Montgomery*, 2011).

7.3 The *Frye* General Acceptance Test

Paralleling the manner in which science has been established throughout history, the legal community originally qualified and integrated science according to the general consensus and popularity of a given idea (Lopez, 2004). For example, in *The Church v. Galileo Galilei*, the court accepted the Aristotelian theory that the sun revolves around the earth without question (Faigman, 2000). Indeed, because the geocentric theory conformed to the Bible and the majority of the worldview, the court simply deferred to the theologically scientific community and maintained the generally accepted theory of geocentricism. As a result, the court found Galileo guilty of heresy as he wrote the *Dialogue on the Great World Systems,* which critiqued the geocentric theory and promoted a minority theory of Copernicus, which presumed that the earth revolves around the sun (Faigman, 2000). Based on the historical deference to the specified community and qualification of general acceptance for scientific theory, it is not surprising that the first primary legal standard would be a general acceptance test (Lopez, 2004).

Federal courts, since the early part of the last century, have attempted to limit the uncertainty surrounding novel scientific evidence by establishing an evidentiary standard of reliability for scientific proof. In *Frye v. United States* (1923), the Columbia District Court of Appeals established that standard for the admissibility of novel scientific evidence—the general acceptance standard.[2] Under this test, any novel form of scientific evidence admitted into evidence must be sufficiently established to have gained general acceptance in the particular field in which it belongs. More specifically, as the *Frye* Court noted: "while courts will go a long way in admitting expert testimony deduced from a well-recognized scientific principle or discovery, the thing from which the deduction is made must be sufficiently established to have gained general acceptance in the particular field in which it belongs" (*Frye*, p. 1014). However, "just when a scientific principle or discovery crosses the line between experimental and demonstrable stages is difficult to define. Somewhere in this twilight zone the evidential force of the principle must be recognized, and while courts will go a long way in admitting expert testimony deduced from a well-recognized scientific principle or discovery, the thing from which the deduction is made must be sufficiently established to have gained general acceptance in the particular field in which it belongs" (*Frye v. United States*, 1923, p. 1014). The following case illustrates the application of *Frye*.

In *Zink v. State* (2009), the defendant was charged with first-degree murder and asserted a voluntary manslaughter and diminished-capacity defense. Various defense experts had diagnosed Zink with paranoid personality disorder, narcissistic personality disorder; substance abuse disorder; personality disorder with narcissistic, paranoid, impulsive, and antisocial features; alcohol dependence; and obsessive-compulsive disorder. Consequently, Zink raised the issue of his personality disorders in the guilt phase to support a diminished-capacity defense. The jury, however, found him guilty of first-degree murder and sentenced him to death on the basis of the aggravating factors of his two prior convictions for rape, that the murder was committed heinously, and to avoid a lawful arrest. Following his conviction, Zink obtained a PET scan for the purpose of his postconviction proceeding, which indicated (a) an asymmetry between the right and left frontal and parietal lobes with the right frontal lobe generating excessive metabolic activity, (b) a reduction of metabolic activity in the cingulate gyrus, and (c) a deficit in the amygdala. In his motion for postconviction relief Zink claimed ineffective assistance of counsel; however, the motion court denied his motion and he appealed to the Supreme Court of Missouri. On appeal, he argued that the motion court erred in denying his multiple claims of ineffective assistance of counsel and in violating his constitutional rights. In particular, he claimed that his attorney failed to obtain and present a PET scan at the trial and sentencing phase, which would have revealed to the jury that he had "organic anatomical physiological brain damage" and bolstered his defense of diminished capacity (*Zink v. State*, 2009, p. 177).

The Missouri Supreme Court affirmed the motion court's judgment and in doing so noted that, because the PET scan results were at most consistent with defendant's diagnosed conditions and could not demonstrate any definite link to his behavior at the time of the murder, the evidence was irrelevant and inadmissible. More specifically, the Court argued that, in this case, the PET scan could not show that Zink suffered from a mental disease or defect. In fact, according to one defense expert, there is no generally accepted medical practice that would associate a brain scan with any diagnosis of a mental disease. Therefore, under *Frye*, the PET scan evidence would have been inadmissible in the guilt phase to show that the defendant suffered from a mental disease because there is no generally accepted medical practice making that link. Furthermore, this evidence was also irrelevant in the guilt phase because, as noted by another defense expert, none of the diagnostic criteria for personality disorders are related to the brain's physical dynamics. This evidence, therefore, could not have helped the jury to determine if Zink had a mental disease or defect because it does not address any of the diagnostic criteria.

7.4 The *Daubert* Trilogy

7.4.1 *Daubert v. Merrell Dow Pharmaceuticals, Inc.*

The plaintiffs in *Daubert v. Merrell Dow Pharmaceuticals, Inc.* (1993) were minors born with "serious birth defects" (p. 582), who claimed that Bendectin, a prescription drug sold by Merrell Dow and taken by the plaintiffs' mothers during their pregnancy to control nausea, caused their birth defects. Merrell Dow moved for summary judgment and offered an affidavit from a well-credentialed expert who contended that "maternal use of Bendectin during the first trimester of pregnancy has not been shown to be a risk factor for human birth defects" (*Daubert v. Merrell Dow Pharmaceuticals, Inc.*, 1993, p. 582). The plaintiffs offered opinions from eight experts of their own that Bendectin could cause human birth defects, and the federal district judge granted the defendants' motion for summary judgment (*Daubert v. Merrell Dow Pharmaceuticals, Inc.*, 1989).

The Ninth Circuit affirmed, citing *Frye* (1923), which upheld the exclusion of the result of a "systolic blood pressure deception test," commonly known as a lie detector test, offered by the defendant in a second-degree murder case. In this short opinion the D.C. Circuit stated that admissibility of "a scientific principle or discovery" depends on whether it is "sufficiently established to have gained general acceptance in the particular field in which it belongs" (*Frye v. United States*, 1923, p. 1013).[3] The US Supreme Court vacated the judgment of the Ninth Circuit that had upheld the district court's granting of defendant's summary judgment motion and remanded the case for further proceedings. All nine justices agreed that FRE 702 provides the standard for judging the admissibility of scientific evidence in federal courts and that 702 supersedes the *Frye* test. The Court looked at the "permissive backdrop" of the Federal Rules and concluded that the "austere standard" of the *Frye* test was incompatible with the Federal Rules and should not be the standard in federal courts (*Daubert v. Merrell Dow Pharmaceuticals, Inc.*, 1993, p. 589).

Justice Blackmun's opinion, joined by six other justices, attempted to provide some reassurance that the FRE 702 standard does not mean that trial judges are powerless to exclude any scientific evidence or that all scientific evidence is admissible; to be admissible under FRE 702 the scientific evidence must be "not only relevant, but reliable" (*Daubert v. Merrell Dow Pharmaceuticals, Inc.*, 1993, p. 589). Judges must determine that the proffered evidence is "scientifically valid" and that it "properly can be applied to the facts in issue" (*Daubert v. Merrell Dow Pharmaceuticals, Inc.*, 1993, p. 593). Justice Blackmun then identified the following five factors that judges might consider in ruling on offers of scientific evidence: (a) the "falsifiability, or refutability, or testability" of the expert's "reasoning or methodology," (b) "peer review and publication" of the expert's "theory or technique," (c) "the known or potential rate of error" of the particular scientific technique, (d) "the existence and maintenance of standards controlling the technique's operation," and (e) "general acceptance" in the "relevant scientific community" (*Daubert v. Merrell Dow Pharmaceuticals, Inc.*, 1993, pp. 592–594).

To those who might fear that abandoning the "general acceptance" test will result in pseudoscientific evidence confounding juries, Justice Blackmun pointed out the effectiveness of the "conventional devices" of "vigorous cross-examination, presentation of contrary evidence, and careful instruction on the burden of proof." To those who might fear that a gatekeeping role of judges "will sanction a stifling and repressive scientific orthodoxy and will be inimical to the search for truth," he noted the important differences between the quest for truth in the courtroom and the quest for truth in the laboratory. The fact that judges have to decide legal issues "finally and quickly" requires exclusion of "conjectures that are probably wrong" (*Daubert v. Merrell Dow Pharmaceuticals, Inc.*, 1993, pp. 595–597).[4] The following case illustrates the application of *Daubert*:

In *Gier v. Educational Service Unit No. 16* (1995), an action was brought against a school on behalf of mentally retarded students for emotional, physical, and sexual abuse. The District Court's *Daubert* assessment was based on its review of the psychological evaluations of the appellants conducted by Drs. Sullivan, Scanlan, and Jones, whose evaluations formed the foundation for their proffered testimony. The evaluation of the appellants consisted of (a) reviewing the Child Behavior Checklists completed by the appellants' parents, (b) conducting clinical interviews with appellants that involved role playing with anatomically correct dolls, and (c) interviewing appellants' parents and assessing their credibility. The clinical interviews purportedly were conducted in accordance with a protocol developed by Dr. Sullivan. The District Court first expressed general reservations regarding the use of psychological evaluations as evidence in cases of alleged child abuse, regardless of whether the abuse at issue is physical, emotional, or sexual. The court cited cases from a number of jurisdictions dealing with the use of psychological evaluations and observed that such evaluations tend to be founded on "vague psychological profiles and symptoms" (*Gier v. Educational Service Unit No. 16*, 1995, p. 1348). The court further observed that psychological evaluations based on a number of symptoms or indicators are "essentially irrefutable" because:

> An expert using this methodology may candidly acknowledge any inconsistencies or potential shortcomings in the individual pieces of evidence she presents, but can easily dismiss the critique by saying that her evaluation relies on no one symptom or indicator and that her conclusions still hold true in light of all the other available factors and her expertise in the field. In such a case, the expert's conclusions are as impenetrable as they are unverifiable. (*Gier v. Educational Service Unit No. 16*, 1995, p. 1348)

The plaintiffs intended to rely on evidence presented by three psychiatric experts whose testimony was based on evaluations of the children. At the *Daubert* hearing for the case, the court drastically limited the scope of the experts' testimony due to its determination that this testimony was unreliable because of problems of "testability" and high error rate (*Gier v. Educational Service Unit No. 16*, 1994, pp. 1351–1352). In its conclusion, the court cited

State v. Foret (1993), which held that such psychological syndrome theories are essentially unable to be tested. More specifically, the court noted that "this type of evidence is of highly questionable scientific validity, and fails to unequivocally pass the *Daubert* threshold test of scientific reliability" (p. 1127).

7.4.2 *General Electric Co. v. Joiner*

Following the *Daubert* ruling, some legal scholars began to argue that *Daubert* required courts to limit themselves to determining whether a scientific expert witness was relying on studies that used a methodology appropriate for inquiry into the general subject at issue, while others insisted that courts should also review the expert's reasoning in deducing from these studies issues, such as causation (Bernstein, 2001). This debate was resolved when the Supreme Court returned to the topic of admissibility of expert testimony four years later in *General Electric Co. v. Joiner* (1997), the second case in the trilogy. In *Joiner* the US Supreme Court granted certiorari in order to determine the appropriate standard an appellate court should apply in reviewing a trial court's *Daubert* decision to admit or exclude scientific expert testimony. Joiner and his wife sued three manufacturers of PCBs—the General Electric Company, Westinghouse Electric Corporation, and the Monsanto Company—in state court on theories of strict liability, negligence, and fraud (*General Electric Co. v. Joiner*, 1997). Joiner, a former cigarette smoker, alleged that tobacco smoke acted as an initiator of his cancer and that the PCBs acted as a promoter, transforming the initiated cells into malignant growths. The trial court applied the *Daubert* criteria, excluded the opinions of the plaintiff's experts, and granted the defendants' motion for summary judgment. The court of appeals reversed the decision, stating that "because the Federal Rules of Evidence governing expert testimony display a preference for admissibility, we apply a particularly stringent standard of review to the trial judge's exclusion of expert testimony" (*Joiner v. General Electric Company*, 1996, p. 529). The Supreme Court granted certiorari in response to a petition from the defendants complaining of the "particularly stringent" standard of review that the Court of Appeals claimed to apply to the district court's ruling that plaintiffs' experts' conclusions were inadmissible under *Daubert*. The Court subsequently held that abuse of discretion is the correct standard for an appellate court to apply in reviewing a district court's evidentiary ruling, regardless of whether the ruling allowed or excluded expert testimony. More specifically, the Court unequivocally rejected the suggestion that a more stringent standard is permissible when the ruling, as in *Joiner*, is "outcome determinative" (*General Electric Co. v. Joiner*, 1997, pp.142–143). Further, the Court concluded that it was within the district court's discretion to find that the statements of the plaintiff's experts with regard to causation were nothing more than speculation, since the plaintiff never explained "how and why the experts could have extrapolated their opinions" from animal studies far removed from the circumstances of the plaintiff's exposure (*General Electric Co. v. Joiner*, 1997, p. 144). In addition, the Court observed that the district court could find that the four epidemiological studies the plaintiff relied on were insufficient as a basis for his experts' opinions:

> Trained experts commonly extrapolate from existing data. But nothing in either *Daubert* or the Federal Rules of Evidence requires a district court to admit opinion evidence, which is connected to existing data only by the ipse dixit of the expert. A court may conclude that there is simply too great an analytical gap between the data and the opinion proffered. (*General Electric Co. v. Joiner*, 1997, p. 146)

7.4.3 *Kumho Tire Company, Ltd. v. Carmichael*

Carmichael was driving a minivan when the rear tire blew out, causing an accident that resulted in the death of one of the passengers and severe injuries to others. The plaintiffs' expert in tire failure analysis proposed to testify that a defect in the tire's manufacture or design caused the blowout. The trial court applied the *Daubert* analysis to the proffered testimony, even though the testimony could be considered "technical" rather than "scientific." The trial court concluded that the proffered testimony failed to satisfy the reliability factors of *Daubert* and granted Kumho Tire's motion to exclude the expert's testimony (*Carmichael v. Samyang Tire, Inc.*, 1996). The Eleventh Circuit reversed and in doing so held that the trial court erred by applying the *Daubert* analysis to nonscientific evidence. The proffered testimony was based not on the application of scientific principles but "on skill- or experience-based observations" (*Carmichael v. Samyang Tire, Inc.*, 1997, pp. 1435–1436). The tire manufacturer and distributor appealed to the Supreme Court. Numerous amicus briefs were filed, arguing that the *Daubert* test would limit expert testimony that relies on specialized knowledge derived from experience when such knowledge cannot be corroborated by "objective" tests or that such testimony should be subjected to the *Daubert* test to preserve the integrity of the system (see, e.g., Vidmar et al., 2000).[5] The Supreme Court reversed the Eleventh Circuit's decision to overrule the district court and in doing so held that *Daubert* applied to all expert testimony (*Kumho Tire Co. v. Carmichael*, 1999). The Court also noted that the four factors suggested in *Daubert* were factors that "may" be used by the trial judge in carrying out its gatekeeping requirement (*Kumho Tire Co. v. Carmichael*, 1999, p. 1175). The Court emphasized that the trial judge was not required to use each factor in making its decision:

> Rather, we conclude that the trial judge must have considerable leeway in deciding in a particular case how to go about determining whether particular expert testimony is reliable. That

is to say, a trial court should consider the specific factors identified in *Daubert* where they are reasonable measures of the reliability of expert testimony. (*Kumho Tire Co. v. Carmichael*, 1999, p. 1176)

7.5 Searching for the Truth

The intentions of science and law appear to be closely aligned. Like science, law seeks to ascertain the truth. Indeed, evidence is that which demonstrates, makes clear, or ascertains the truth of the very fact or point in issue, either on the one side or the other (*Ballantine's Law Dictionary*, 2010). The definition of relevant evidence in FRE 401 likewise suggests a similar purpose. There is no doubt that the adoption of the reliability standards for expert evidence in many state and federal courts has created a daunting task for trial judges who are now forced to decide complex questions concerning forensic expert evidence that is often a part of criminal trials. The following case illustrates the problems judges may face in determining the truth of scientific evidence proffered in a court of law.

On Halloween 2007, former fashion writer Peter Braunstein, dressed as a firefighter, set off a smoke bomb in the lobby of former coworker's New York apartment building and then knocked on her door, claiming that he had come to assess the damage to her apartment. When she let him in, Braunstein sedated her with chloroform, tied her to her bed, forced a pair of fashionable high-heeled shoes onto her feet, and sexually assaulted her for 13 hours. At trial, Dr. Monte S. Buchsbaum, testified for the defense that Braunstein's FDG-PET scan, which was acquired six months after the crimes were committed, showed abnormalities consistent with schizophrenia. He also suggested that this noticeable deficiency would have affected Braunstein's frontal lobes, which control, among other things, the capacity for making executive decisions (Applebaum, 2009).

Under cross-examination, Dr. Buchsbaum defended the reliability of the PET scan, which the assistant district attorney attacked for its lack of conclusive findings. Eventually, Dr. Buchsbaum conceded that the PET scan alone was not enough to make a formal diagnosis of schizophrenia; the mere showing of decreased glucose metabolism in the frontal lobes does not, automatically, imply a diagnosis of schizophrenia. Thus while he could show the differences between Braunstein's brain and a normal brain, he was unable to prove anything about the defendant's mental state at the time of the offense (Applebaum, 2009).

The fact that in both *Daubert* (1993) and *Kumho* (1999) the Court emphasized the flexibility of the factors a court should consider in determining whether expert testimony is reliable no doubt complicates the search for truth. The search for truth is further complicated by the fact that research studies have shown that judges apply different *Daubert* criteria according to the kind of evidence under review and that the decision about which criteria to use is closely related to the perceptions that some types of evidence are more scientific than others (Dahir et al., 2005). More specifically, in 2008 Merlino, Murray, and Richardson performed a content analysis of district court cases to investigate judges' evaluations of expert characteristics and evidence characteristics for toxicology, psychological/psychiatric, and damage testimony and found the following significant differences in the application of *Daubert* criteria:

- Of the factors associated with the *Daubert* guidelines, the most frequently mentioned was general acceptance, followed by falsifiability, peer review, and publication.
- The *Daubert* factors were mentioned most frequently in the toxicology cases.
- Falsifiability, peer review, and publication were evaluated twice as often in toxicology cases as psychological/psychiatric or damages cases.
- Error rate and general acceptance were the most frequently mentioned *Daubert* criteria in damages cases.
- *Daubert* factors were mentioned relatively infrequently in psychological/psychiatric cases, where general acceptance was the most frequently mentioned characteristic. (Merlino et al., 2008)

7.6 Conclusion

Unlike the law, which does not require a stringent standard for the admissibility of scientific evidence, science does require a rigorous standard for determining scientific validity. This is of particular importance in light of the fact that an aura of infallibility surrounds neuroscience, especially neuroimaging techniques. Clearly, connecting brain imaging to particular behaviors in the real world is, at best, problematic, since current methodologies employed for assessing the relationship between brain function and behavior vary too much from one study to the next to provide definite answers about this relationship. Furthermore, while structural or functional brain abnormalities may predispose an individual to violent behavior, there is no evidence that most people who commit violent crimes have any brain damage. Thus, as noted by Pustilnik (2009), the present challenge of neuroscience is not to create attractive simplifications but to illuminate complex and multifaceted realities. Indeed, even if a neuroimaging scan clearly shows a defendant's brain abnormality, the evidence still would not be useful in explaining why the particular defendant lacked the requisite mens rea. There is at present no test, measure, or technique that can reliably determine what was happening in a defendant's brain at the time the crime was committed, and, given the current state of the technology, establishing a direct and clear chain of causation between brain impairment and violent behavior will rarely if ever be possible.

The law demands finality and certainty and tends to force its participants to render decisions in binary pairs (e.g., responsible/not responsible), even where evidence is complex, uncertain, and ambiguous. Science, in contrast, tends to embrace probability and uncertainty and does not require the occasionally premature dichotomization of outcomes that are frequently required by the law (Vickers, 2005). There is no doubt that research findings can provide invaluable contributions to neuroscience as a broad field of inquiry; however, they can provide only correlations and generalized averages, which may not accurately reflect the causal mechanisms underlying a particular defendant's behavior. In other words, just because a particular pattern of neural activity has been associated on average with, for example, cognitive impairment, it cannot be concluded that a defendant whose brain scan has produced the same neural pattern has such a cognitive deficit. Thus the striking images produced by neuroimaging techniques convey a sense of objectivity that is unjustified. However, with 10^{10} neurons and 10^{14} connections in the cortex, the human brain clearly defies any simple explanation (Logothetis, 2008).

8

The Issue of Evidentiary Reliability

At the heart of science is an essential balance between two
seemingly contradictory attitudes—an openness to new
ideas, no matter how bizarre or counterintuitive they may
be, and the most ruthless skeptical scrutiny of all ideas, old
and new. This is how deep truths are winnowed from deep
nonsense.

(Carl Sagan, 1997)[1]

8.1 Introduction

Law does not occur in a vacuum; legal decisions involving science implicate
the legitimacy of both law and science (Moreno, 2009). There is no doubt
that the purposes of science and evidence are one and the same; like science, evidence is intended to assist in the search for truth. Indeed, "evidence
signifies that which demonstrates, makes clear, or ascertains the truth of the
very fact or point in issue either on the one side or on the other; and no evidence ought to be admitted to any other point" (Blackstone, 1979, p. 336).
However, while advancements in neuroscience are proceeding at an impressive pace, whether the reliability of various technologies such as neuroimaging techniques in detecting cognitive impairment have reached a point
where their use should be permitted in criminal trials has been a divisive
topic. While some scholars have suggested that neuroimaging modalities
"offer an objective, non-invasive, quantifiable image, which can provide useful information particularly when the clinical examination may otherwise be
normal" (Baskin, Edersheim, & Price, 2007, p. 247), others have argued that
neuroimaging is "fraught with uncertainties" (Roberts, 2007, p. 266), "indis-
tinct" (Vloet et al., 2008, p. 99), and, arguably, quite subjective. These views
are reflected in the results of a recent survey that sought to assess the public

and experts' understanding of the capabilities of neuroimaging. Of the 660 public respondents, 84% thought that neuroimaging could diagnose brain diseases such as tumors very well, but only 17% had the same confidence in the use of neuroimaging to diagnose mental illness (Wardlaw et al., 2011). Furthermore, while 59% of expert respondents thought that neuroimaging could improve understanding of cognitive functioning or improve treatment of psychiatric illnesses (23%), only 40% thought that neuroimaging might improve understanding of criminal behavior sometime in the distant future (Wardlaw et al., 2011).

A large number of potential jurors have also been found to mistrust expert testimony that is proffered for the purpose of providing an exculpatory mental status-related explanation for what would otherwise be criminal behavior (Skeem, Louden, & Evans, 2004). This mistrust is based on the concern that self-reported symptoms, such as "I hear voices" are inherently falsifiable and that testimony that depends on such self-reports is essentially untrustworthy. As noted in *Atkins v. Virginia* (2002):

> [Determination of a person's incapacity] is a matter of great difficulty, partly from the easiness of counterfeiting this disability . . . and partly from the variety of the degrees of this infirmity, whereof some are sufficient, and some are insufficient to excuse persons in capital offenses. (p. 351)

The questions of whether a given methodology is sufficiently reliable and accurate for use and whether that reliability and accuracy has been established by sufficiently valid methods are questions that demand skillful scientific analysis and irreducibly evaluative and normative answers (Schauer, 2010). Ultimately, however, due to the normative and nonscientific nature of the questions neither scientist nor science can provide definitive answers or be justifiably regarded as the law's exclusive or final decision-makers (Schauer, 2010). Indeed, in *Daubert v. Merrell Dow Pharmaceuticals, Inc.* (1993), the Court recognized that science remains theoretical and in doing so noted

> Of course, it would be unreasonable to conclude that the subject of scientific testimony must be "known" to a certainty; arguably, there are no certainties in science . . . Indeed, scientists do not assert that they know what is immutably "true"—they are committed to searching for new, temporary, theories to explain, as best they can, phenomena. (*Daubert v. Merrell Dow Pharmaceuticals, Inc.*, 1993, p. 590)

Based on the foregoing, it is crucial that all evidence proffered in a court of law meets the evidentiary reliability requirements set forth in *Daubert*. Indeed, the Court is interested in the nexus of the expert's conclusions and the methodology used to reach those conclusions (Hom, 2008).

In science, reliability refers to the repeatability and the reproducibility of measurement, while validity is defined as the extent to which a test measures what it claims to measure. In contrast, in law evidence is considered to be reliable if it proves what it purports to prove. Under *Daubert*, evidentiary reliability is construed as the "trustworthiness" of the data and "for scientific evidence *evidentiary reliability will be based on scientific validity*" (*Daubert v. Merrell Dow Pharmaceuticals, Inc.*, 1993, p. 2795; italics in original). In the years since *Daubert*, the standards for admissibility at trial of expert testimony in general and scientific evidence in particular have become more demanding. In fact, reviews of recent cases and empirical studies of federal judges' and attorneys' practices indicate that judges are more likely to consider the admissibility of expert evidence prior to trial, to inquire more deeply into the reasoning and methodology that supports the expert opinions, and to limit or exclude such evidence from presentation at trial (Cecil, 2005). Furthermore, courts' increasing skepticism concerning expert testimony and scientific evidence is apparent in the following case.

In *United States v. Flaherty* (2008), the defendant, after having been convicted by a jury of conspiracy to commit securities fraud, mail fraud, wire fraud, and money laundering, filed a motion for a new trial arguing that recently discovered evidence showed the defendant to be mentally incompetent. More specifically, after her conviction, the defendant retained new counsel, who immediately had the defendant evaluated by a psychiatrist and neuropsychologist, who performed neuropsychological testing. The results from these tests purportedly showed that the defendant suffered from a low IQ and significant cognitive impairments that negatively affected her ability to exercise judgment, participate in her defense, conform her conduct to the law, and form the requisite intent to defraud. The expert neuropsychologist also characterized defendant's neuropsychological profile as grossly abnormal and concluded that she was a naive individual with borderline intelligence with superimposed cognitive impairments that extended beyond her limited IQ.

The Court concluded that this newly discovered evidence of mental incompetence, clearly produced for the purpose of avoiding judgment, was biased and unreliable and therefore did not provide valid grounds for a new trial.[2] The Court reasoned that, aside from the neuropsychologist's inherent bias, his reports had the following methodological weaknesses, and thus results should be viewed with caution:

- The tests employed failed to adequately take into account the fact that the defendant is a Taiwanese immigrant whose native tongue is Mandarin, not English. Her poor performance on intelligence tests asking questions about American history and European literature and culture can thus be easily explained by her foreign upbringing.
- The defendant's low IQ of 73 is not valid because the score is made up of both culturally weighted English-language subtests as well as nonverbal subtests.

- The expert's conclusions did not fit with the other evidence regarding defendant's behavior in this case. For example, the defendant took an active role in managing the business entities, directed the corporation's promotional activities, and personally made several misrepresentations to investors in both the English and Mandarin languages and was actively involved in her legal defense.

Consequently, the Court denied the defendant's motion for a new trial.

8.2 The Issue of Validity and Reliability

8.2.1 Basic Principles

The principles of validity and reliability are fundamental cornerstones of the scientific methodology. Indeed, issues of research validity and significance are quite meaningless if the results of our experiments are not trustworthy. It is well recognized that reliability can vary greatly depending on the test, measures, and techniques being used. In general, science assumes no measurement is perfect, either in terms of reliability or accuracy. For these reasons, it is imperative that any scientific endeavor be aware of the limits surrounding the reliability of its measurements (Bennett & Miller, 2010).

In research, there are many definitions of validity, but in general there are two essential parts: internal and external validity. Internal validity refers to whether the results of a study, such as a mean difference between control and treatment groups, are legitimate because of the way the groups were selected, data were recorded, and analysis performed. For example, a study may have poor internal validity if the cognitive testing was not performed the same way in the control and treatment groups, or if confounding variables, such as level of education, were not accounted for in the study design or analysis. External validity, also referred to as "generalizability," refers to whether the results given by the study are transferable to other groups/populations of interest (Last, 2001). In other words, results from a study performed exclusively in a particular group, such as all male schizophrenics, should also be applicable to all female schizophrenics. Further, it is important to remember that without internal validity one cannot have external validity.

Another important point to be considered is the issue of ecological validity. Ecological validity is often confused with external validity. The question of ecological validity asks whether a simulation is conducted under conditions that are similar to the real-world situation such that the results from the simulation are generalizable to the world as it is. The question of external validity asks whether an experiment's results are robust enough to generalize across various experimental settings. More specifically, while external validity refers to the question of whether an effect that has been shown in one research setting would be obtained in other settings with different research procedures and participants, ecological validity asks whether the effect is representative of what happens in everyday life (Breau & Brook, 2007). Most of our knowledge about cognitive functioning and violent behavior is based on findings from research studies conducted in a laboratory setting. However, the lack of ecological validity in many laboratory-based studies with a focus on artificially controlled and constricted environments may be problematic when extrapolated to a particular legal case. Milgram's famous obedience experiment carried out in 1963 illustrates this point. In Milgram's study, participants were asked to inflict an electric shock on confederates to determine if people would listen to an authoritative figure even if what they were telling them to do was unethical. While results from this study may be reliable, the fact that his experiment took place in a laboratory setting suggests that it lacks ecological validity that could have affected results, as participants may have acted differently to how they would in a real-life situation due to the artificial environment.

A common threat to internal validity is reliability. Reliability refers to the degree to which a test score is free from measurement errors and is considered an indication of a test's consistency between two or more administrations or ratings of that test. In other words, the term "reliability" is generally used to indicate the precision of measurement across different times, places, subjects, and experimental conditions (Bryman, 2012). For example, if a test of cognitive functioning is applied in standard ways across a range of people and situations, it is desirable that the test be reliable across a range of people and situations being measured. However, reliability is often compromised when assessments are taken over time or performed by different people, or if the assessments are highly subjective. Therefore, test–retest reliability, which is the extent to which the same measurement procedure is used to examine the same subject for the same purpose yields the same result on repetition, must be considered. In addition, for those tests that require scoring on subjectively rated criteria, interrater reliability, which refers to the extent to which different examiners would draw the same conclusions about a given subject at a given time, must also be carefully considered (Trowbridge & Schutte, 2007). Another important aspect of reliability is internal consistency. A cognitive test may be judged to indicate dysfunction because of a particular score on the test. If the examinee shows similar result to other relevant questions about the same event or piece of information, the test is internally consistent. Neuroimaging scans, which provide a "real-life" representation of brain activity, impairment, or dysfunction, used in conjunction with neuropsychological tests, may either mitigate or exacerbate any potential reliability issues.

As discussed in chapter 7, the second *Daubert* factor involves the evaluation of the scientific validity and reliability of scientific testimony, which requires understanding the known or potential characteristics of error associated with using a particular scientific technique. *Daubert* referred to statistical standards of error rates to reject a hypothesis at a given confidence level[3] but gave discretion for the choice of the confidence level to the expert

(*Daubert v. Merrell Dow Pharmaceuticals, Inc.*, 1993). This flexible standard was based on the idea of "evidentiary reliability" or "trustworthiness" of the data. Rather than blanket exclusions, *Daubert* reasoned that "vigorous cross-examination, presentation of contrary evidence, and careful instruction on the burden of proof," coupled with the court's power to direct verdicts and grant summary judgment, were the "appropriate means of attacking shaky but admissible" evidence (*Daubert v. Merrell Dow Pharmaceuticals, Inc.*, 1993, p. 595).

Daubert offers no guidance as to what point imperfect precision and bias exceed what are acceptable for a reliability determination. Likewise, the scientific community has yet to establish an acceptable level of precision and bias for various neuroscientific tests and measures. Although a determination of, for example, cognitive impairment or malingering is generally not based solely on neuropsychological test results or on a single test score, the scientific validity and evidentiary reliability of each test must nevertheless be critically evaluated. Indeed, even if a test, measure, or technique is not being presented to the trier of fact for the purpose of alone influencing a judgment of, for example, cognitive dysfunction it nevertheless must meet the standard of the scientific validity (Vallabhajosula & van Gorp, 2001). Clearly, a test that fails to prove what it purports to prove when used in isolation cannot be deemed scientifically valid when used within a battery of tests or as part of a multimodal approach (Vallabhajosula & van Gorp, 2001). Judging the reliability and validity, however, is not easy. As noted by Saxe and Ben-Shakhar (1994):

> Reliability and validity are complex, multidimensional concepts and encompass the methodological requirements for research that can assess scientifically based techniques . . . The underlying question is as follows: What constitutes a proper evaluation of a technique and the theory from which it is derived? It is not sufficient to demonstrate that a technique has been tested; the key question is whether the test is adequate and what generalizations are appropriate. (p. 207)

8.2.2 Indices of Predictive Accuracy

In general, most classification research has focused on four indices of predictive accuracy or scientific validity: sensitivity, specificity, positive predictive power (PPP), and negative predictive power (NPP). Sensitivity is the probability of a person with a certain condition or trait being picked up by a test, while specificity is the probability that a person without a certain condition or trait is being identified by the test as not having that condition or trait. In other words, sensitivity is the proportion of true positives that are correctly identified by the test, while specificity is the proportion of true negatives that

Table 8.1 Calculation of Accuracy Indices

		Actual	
		Malingering	Honest
Predicted	Malingering	A	B
	Honest	C	D
	Sensitivity = A/(A + C)		
	Specificity = D/(B + D)		
	PPP = A/(A + B)		
	NPP = D/(C + D)		

Note. PPP = positive predictive power; NPP = negative predictive power.

are correctly identified by the test. PPP is the likelihood of a person identified by a test as having the condition or trait actually possessing that characteristic, and NPP indicates the probability of a person identified by a test as not having a certain condition or trait actually not having that characteristic (Butcher, 2002; see Table 8.1, which provides the formulas for how to calculate these indices).

Although the importance of these indices may vary depending on the type of prediction offered, it may be argued that in the case of cognitive dysfunction, PPP is the most clinically relevant index to consider. Indeed, erroneously classifying a genuinely impaired individual as not impaired may result in the individual being subject to prosecution despite neurocognitive impairment. The failure to identify cognitive impairment when it is present is also problematic since it may lead to a failure to prosecute a competent defendant. Similarly, in the case of risk assessment, the danger and damages from failing to detect potentially violent individuals represents a far greater harm than that inflicted by the unnecessary treatment and hospitalization of a nonviolent individual (Rosenfeld, Sands, & van Gorp, 2000). More specifically, while the involuntary hospitalization of nonviolent individuals may be considered harmful, it is less likely to result in permanent consequences. There may exist other scenarios in which different indices may be the most appropriate to optimize; however, many researchers attempt to optimize all of these indices, essentially presuming that each is equally important (Rogers, 1997; Rosenfeld et al., 2000; Vallabhajosula & van Gorp, 2001).

8.3 Neuropsychological Tests and Measures

8.3.1 The Issue of Base Rates

Base rate refers to the relative frequency with which a certain condition or state occurs in a population. A base rate is defined for and restricted to a specified population. In other words, a base rate is the a priori chance that a member of a specified population will have a certain characteristic, assuming that we know nothing else about this person other than that he or she is a member of the population we are examining (Kamphuis & Finn, 2002). Consider the following, well-known example of base rates and the base rate fallacy.

A witness testifies that she saw a blue cab. The witness gets the color of the cab right 80% of the time she testifies. In her area, 85% of the taxis are green cabs and 15% of the taxis are blue. What is the most probable color of the cab seen by the witness? The correct answer is green. The base rate of green cabs is much higher than that of blue cabs. The proportion of cabs that are green (85%) is much greater than the proportion of cabs that are blue (15%). Therefore, despite the witness's 80% reliability, the most likely explanation (59%) is that the witness is mistaken and she actually saw a green cab.

The issue of base rates in discussing the efficacy of neuropsychological tests is a crucial one. Indeed, over a half-century ago, Meehl and Rosen (1955) described how base rates can potentially impact the accuracy of clinical judgments in psychology, stating that the diagnostic utility of a test is based not only on the test's sensitivity and specificity but also on the base rate of the diagnosis in the population of interest. More specifically, it is well known that the predictive accuracy varies as the base rate varies, but, to date, few studies have considered the influence of base rates on these various accuracy indices. However, doing so is important, especially in light of the existing literature, which suggests that, regardless of the setting, the base rate of, for example, malingering is unlikely to exceed 30% (Rosenfeld, Sands, & van Gorp, 2000; Vallabhajosula & van Gorp, 2001). Consider the following.

With an original base rate of malingering of 48%, the nonverbal subtest of the Validity Indicator Profile was found to have 83% PPP, while the verbal subtest demonstrated 79% PPP. However, with a base rate of 30%, the PPP of the Nonverbal and Verbal subtests decreased to 69% and 63%, respectively. Further, if a conclusion of malingering is based on both subtests producing scores in the valid range, the Validity Indicator Profile quite accurately detects malingerers with a 53% base rate (90% PPP). With base rates of 30% and 15%, however, the PPP decreases to 78% and 60%, respectively (Vallabhajosula & van Gorp, 2001).[4] Since the diagnostic utility of a test is relative to the base rate of the diagnosis in the population of interest, the extensive use of tests in neuropsychological assessment makes knowledge of the base rates of various disorders and dysfunctions highly relevant. Unfortunately, to date, the base rates of various illnesses, disorders, and dysfunctions in the population has yet to be established.

8.3.2 The Issue of Cutoff Scores

Classification accuracy numbers are specific to the cutoff scores used in each study. However, widely applicable cutoff scores have been difficult to establish because (a) optimal cutoff scores vary across studies and (b) optimal cutoff scores are defined as those that best balance specificity and sensitivity. Further, as the consequences of Type I and Type II classification errors are likely to vary across settings, optimal cutoff scores also will vary, depending on which type of error is more important to minimize in each setting. Therefore clinicians who choose to use a different cutoff score in order to minimize a specific type of error may obtain different classification accuracy rates (Baer & Miller, 2002).

A 2008 study that examined the utility of the Halstead-Reitan Neuropsychological Test Battery to predict neuropsychological impairment in adults illustrates this point clearly. Using a cutoff score of 9, as recommended by Reitan and colleagues, the screening battery had excellent specificity but only fair sensitivity for identifying subjects with neuropsychological impairment. With a cutoff score of 8, the sensitivity and specificity of the screening battery was comparable to the findings of Reitan and Wolfson. From these results the authors concluded that optimal cutoff scores for the screening battery may vary with different populations (Horwitz, Lynch, McCaffrey, & Fisher, 2008). Similarly, in assessing the ability of the Digit Span score of the Wechsler Adult Intelligence Scale (third edition) in detecting malingering, the Digit Span recommended cutoff of 7 resulted in a sensitivity of 62% and a high false positive rate (23%). Dropping the cutoff to 6 raised the specificity to 93% but decreased the sensitivity to 45% (Babikian, Boone, Lu, & Arnold, 2006).

As the foregoing suggests, sensitivity, specificity, PPP, and NPP values can be manipulated. Indeed, depending on the cutoff score used, tests that lack sufficient predictive accuracy with one cutoff score may be found to be highly accurate if the cutoff score is changed. However, changing the cutoff score to maximize the predictive accuracy may arguably invalidate the test results. Also, depending on the sophistication of the cross-examination of an expert witness, opinions based on test results that have employed cutoff scores other than those recommended by the test developers may be open to a *Daubert* challenge. Further, reliability, validity, sensitivity, specificity, and other accuracy indices have emerged from a well-selected sample of individuals providing data in response to a uniform procedure in a uniform condition. When the instructions, test items, administration, or scoring are changed, attempts to draw on the actuarial base become questionable (Pope & Vasquez, 2005). Finally, unless a uniform methodology is used for the assessment of cognitive impairment, the exact relationship between brain function and aggressive behavior will remain uncertain.

8.3.3 Norms and Standardization

Almost all tests used in clinical psychological practice are norm referenced. This allows for a comparison of each patient's test score with typical test scores from a representative group of individuals (norms[5]; Meyer et al., 2001). Some clinicians may be using informal evaluation procedures to generate their own internal standards; however, these standards are less systematic and are more likely to be skewed by the type of patients seen in a particular setting, such as the forensic setting. As a consequence, idiosyncratic standards tend to suffer from a lack of reproducibility. Normed information accurately conveys how atypical a patient is on a given characteristic measurement, which in turn helps clinicians to more adequately consider base rates (Finn & Kamphuis, 1995). However, the results of a subject's performance on a norm-referenced test is of little value by itself; interpretations of test scores are meaningful only when the scores are compared with those of a group of similar individuals matched with regard to similar age, sex, and other important variables. To be more precise, when evaluating below-norm test scores, it is difficult to conclude that these poor performances are the result of brain dysfunction if the test norms included only normal individuals. Is a score that is one standard deviation below the norm for normal subjects really an indication of cognitive impairment when applied to an individual with severe mental retardation? Clearly test users must carefully evaluate the adequacy of a test's reference group data.

According to the American Psychological Association, the use of uniform, standardized evaluation procedures is one of the fundamental principles on which psychological assessment and testing is founded. Psychological tests have standardized administration and scoring procedures for a reason. Presenting each subject with a uniform stimulus that serves as a common gage to measure his or her characteristics allows the clinician to detect subtle behavioral cues that may indicate psychological or neuropsychological impairments (e.g., Lezak, 1995). While neuropsychological tests and measures can provide comprehensive information regarding, for example, cognitive dysfunction or impairment, there are several inherent drawbacks to this type of evaluation, such as the time involved in the administration. Consequently, the use of abbreviated test batteries or subtests to assess cognitive impairment has become more frequent. Unfortunately, to date, validation studies on the use of subtests and comparisons between abbreviated test batteries and the full version of test batteries are still limited. Administering neuropsychological tests in a nonstandardized manner, whose diagnostic utility and validity have not been established, may open the doors for a *Daubert* challenge with respect to the methodology employed and the results obtained.

8.3.4 The Use of Fixed Versus Flexible Test Batteries

In *Chapple v. Ganger* (1994), the *Daubert* standard was applied for the very first time to the use of fixed (standardized) versus flexible (nonstandardized) neuropsychological test batteries in the federal court. In this personal injury case, the *Chapple* court gave far greater weight to the results obtained from a fixed battery than to the results obtained from two flexible neuropsychological test batteries. More specifically, the district court noted the lack of medical and scientific evidence to support the conclusions made by the plaintiffs' two expert witnesses, a psychologist and a neuropsychologist, who had administered a comprehensive and flexible neuropsychological test battery and had based their conclusions on the test results. However, the judge accepted as scientific evidence the objective test results obtained from the fixed Halstead-Reitan Neuropsychological Test Battery administered by the defendants' expert witness and also accepted his scientific expert medical testimony, which was closely derived from these data. Applying the *Daubert* standard to the neuropsychological test results and opinions of the expert witnesses, the district court held that the entire reasoning process and not simply part of the reasoning process on which the expert witness derives a conclusion must reflect scientific methodology.

According to a survey conducted by Sweet, Nelson, and Moberg (2006), 76% of practicing neuropsychologists use a flexible battery while only 7 percent use a standardized battery, such as the Halstead-Reitan Neuropsychological Test Battery. As discussed previously, when it comes to neuropsychological testing, reliability equals validity. More specifically, courts will rarely accept the flexible battery as scientifically valid. Using tests that are not standardized for a specific population is also problematic since a test that measures one thing in a normal population may measure something different in a forensic population. Further, it may be argued that in the forensic setting, only psychologists who use standardized test batteries can provide dependable expert testimony regarding psychometric test results (Russell, Russell, & Hill, 2005).

8.3.5 The Use of Multiple Tests

The true positive diagnostic accuracy rates (sensitivity) of psychological tests are generally positively related to the rates of false negative diagnoses (specificity), the prevalence of exaggeration for the claimed disorder, and the complaints of the individual. Since the error rates of most currently available tests, measures, or techniques are unknown, many tests, measures, or techniques thus may lack sufficient diagnostic accuracy to be relied on when used in isolation. Consequently, it has been suggested that informed clinical practice requires that multiple sources of information are considered in the assessment of malingering, cognitive, and/or psychological deficits and/or mental disorders (Samuel & Mittenberg, 2005). Indeed, the use of multiple measures is often necessary and appealing, given the high rates of NPP associated with many tests (Samuel & Mittenberg, 2005). Furthermore, despite the frequent occurrence of inconsistent findings from different measures, research studies have demonstrated the importance of administering multiple measures of, for example, malingering (Larrabee, 2008; Rosenfeld, Green, Pivovarova, Dole & Zapf, 2010). Thus while clinicians may be tempted to reduce ambiguity by relying on a single measure, the diagnostic accuracy may be greatly improved by administering additional measures (Rosenfeld et al., 2010). This is of particular importance in light of the fact that many psychologists base their diagnostic reasoning on personal, implicit causal theories about disorders (Kim & Ahn, 2002). In other words, based on a few observations, psychologists appear to form a theory about a patient's problem and then use this theory to direct the gathering of additional information (Brammer, 1997). Since these implicit theories preclude the necessity to explicitly reason causally, psychologists thus may use pattern recognition to determine whether the pattern of complaints and/or problem behavior of a specific individual fits their personal, implicit, causal theory (Groenier, Pieters, Hulshof, Wilhelm, & Wittem, 2008). If this is the case, then explicitly testing and/or generating possible explanations would not only be redundant but also unnecessary (Groenier et al., 2008). Rosenhan's 1973 study "On Being Sane in Insane Places" exemplifies this point:

As previously noted, in this study, mentally healthy experts, including Rosenhan himself, presented themselves to different mental hospitals exhibiting anxiety and requesting admission based on a complaint of having auditory hallucinations. Consequently, all of them were admitted to the hospitals and received a diagnosis of schizophrenia or manic-depressive disorder. Shortly after having been admitted, all pseudo-patients stopped faking their symptoms to determine whether the staff would discover their sanity and discharge them from the hospitals. The pseudo-patients were discharged after an average stay of 19 days, each receiving the same diagnostic revision: the original condition was now classified as in remission. Rosenhan (1973), subsequently, reached a number of logical but questionable conclusions on the issue of diagnostic reliability. For example, Rosenhan claimed that "psychiatric diagnoses . . . carry with them personal, legal, and social stigmas" (p. 252). Consequently, once having been labeled schizophrenic, there is nothing a pseudo-patient can do to overcome this diagnosis. Rosenhan also claimed that, "in a more benign environment, one that was less attached to global diagnosis, [the staff's] behaviors and judgments might have been more benign and effective" (p. 257).

In response to Rosenhan's (1973) contentions, a number of researchers argued that he had used seriously flawed methodology, ignored relevant data, and reached unsound conclusions (Spitzer, 1976). More specifically, Rosenhan (a) failed to make appropriate comparative judgments, drawing instead on anecdotes selected from observational data; (b) frequently relied on speculative theory; (c) failed to provide scientific data in support of his conclusions; (d) made questionable inferences regarding others' perceptions with no independent corroboration; and (e) relied on consensus of opinion or other somewhat weak sources of evidence to support his claims (Dawes, 2001). This study also alludes to a fundamental difference between the practice of medicine and the practice of law. The practice of medicine requires patients to assume a patient's role, which includes being truthful. In law, this assumption is not given or is given with skepticism.

8.4 Neuroimaging Techniques

The ultimate goal of cognitive neuroscience is to understand the relationship between psychological processes and brain function. This, however, is particularly difficult because psychological processes are not directly observable, and human brain function can only be measured through the "highly blurred and distorted lens of neuroimaging techniques" (Poldrack, 2011, p. 692). Inherent in the biological model of mental disorder is the view that, if an individual truly has a diseased mind, he or she will also have some type of visible abnormality in brain structure and/or functioning (Pratt, 2005). It is therefore not surprising that advances in neuroimaging technologies over the last two decades have prompted their relatively widespread use in the study of structural and functional brain abnormalities and their use in legal trials. However, the visual "allure" of neuroimages can "dazzle" and "seduce" jurors (Khoshbin & Khoshbin, 2007, pp. 183, 185) in ways that may be "inappropriately persuasive" (Feigenson, 2006, p. 243). This view has been supported by a study in which participants were presented with descriptions of violent crimes and asked to decide whether the offenders should be found not guilty by reason of insanity. Some participants simply received a description of the crime along with expert testimony that the perpetrator was psychopathic, while other participants received the description of the crime plus one of the following: (a) evidence that the perpetrator has a history of brain trauma or (b) brain images suggesting damage to the frontal lobes. Perhaps not surprisingly, the percentage of participants who judged that the perpetrator was not guilty by reason of insanity was higher when accompanied by a brain image (37%), by testimony concerning brain injury (43%), or by both (50%) than they were when participants received neither (22%; Gurley & Marcus, 2008).

In light of the foregoing, it is of particular importance to evaluate the strength and weaknesses of neuroimaging techniques, the methodology used to generate a particular neuroimaging brain scan, and the soundness of conclusions reached regarding structural and functional brain abnormalities. Understanding the potential usefulness of brain images in a court of law requires some fundamental knowledge about the relationship between behavior and biology.[6] To that end, there are number of basic issues that bear consideration:

- All behavior is the result of chemical and physical activities of the brain; therefore, all behavior is biological. This however does not mean that behavior can be predicted in a reliably way.
- The brain is an organ that processes information based on various environmental inputs, which are unique to every individual and thus lead to differences in individual behaviors.
- Every person's brain is functionally specialized and is slightly different in size, shape, connectivity between neurons, and other anatomical features.

- Violent behavior arises from multiple areas of the brain, and, conversely, one area of the brain can affect the activity of other brain regions.
- Cognitive phenomena rarely originate from a single brain region, and different individuals may use different parts of the brain in different ways to perform the same cognitive task (Jones, Buckholtz, Schall, & Marois, 2009).

8.4.1 The Issue of Convergent Validity

It has been suggested, and I agree, that behavior is a complex phenomenon, neither attributable to single causes nor easily parsed among multiple causes (Jones et. al., 2009). Therefore, the assessment of brain function in the context of violent behavior necessitates a multimodal and cross-disciplinary approach. Since clinical psychology, psychiatry, or neuroscience cannot in isolation fully explain the relationship between brain dysfunction and violent behavior, neuropsychological tests and measures and neuroimaging scans must be regarded as convergent validity operations, with none of them being superior to the other (Rogers, Salekin, & Sewell, 1999). In other words, findings from neuroimaging scans must be related to functional status as measured in some other manner, such as neuropsychological testing, to establish that an identified neuroimaging abnormality is not simply an incidental finding. The significance of an unusual pattern of, for example, hypometabolism on a fluorodeoxyglucose positron emission tomography (FDG-PET) scan is unclear if the patient is asymptomatic and presents normal on neuropsychological tests or other measures. Likewise, the importance of findings of abnormal performances on neuropsychological tests and measures is unclear unless they are supported by other, arguably more objective measures, such as neuroimaging scans. For example, research studies have shown that in the majority of mild traumatic brain injury cases, conventional clinical neuroimaging findings are normal. More specifically, Borg and colleagues (2004) reported that only 5% of individuals who have a Glasgow Coma Scale score of 15, 20% with a score of 14, and 30% with a score of 13 have abnormal findings on computerized tomography (CT). Similarly, while magnetic resonance imaging (MRI) findings have been correlated with neuropsychological performance in mild traumatic brain injury, many symptomatic patients have normal MRI scans (Hofman et al, 2001; Hughes et al, 2004). The need for the assessment of both structure and function is also clearly indicated in Figure 8.1, which illustrates the dissociation between structure and function.

8.4.2 The Issue of Reliability and Validity

As is the case with all scientific evidence proffered in a court of law, the issue of the known or potential rate of error of currently available neuroimaging techniques is an important one. With respect to these techniques, sensitivity

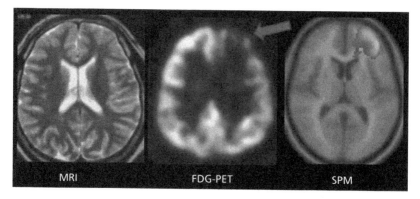

Figure 8.1 Comparison of FDG-PET with MRI in Epilepsy. In a patient with left frontal lobe epilepsy, brain MRI findings were normal (left), ^{18}F-FDG-PET indicated decreased metabolism in left frontal lobe (middle), and SPM (p <.05, corrected) gave the same finding (right). See Color Plate 25 in insert.

Reprinted from Kim, Y. K., Lee, D. S., Lee, S. K., Chung, C. K., Chung, J., & Lee, M. C. (2008). 18F-FDG PET in localization of frontal lobe epilepsy: Comparison of visual and SPM analysis. *Journal of Nuclear Medicine*, 43(9), 1167–1174, Figure 2, by permission of SNMMI.

refers to the ability of a diagnostic process such as CT, MRI, or PET scanning to detect the presence of abnormalities, such as brain lesions or functional deficits. Specificity refers to the capacity of the diagnostic process to determine the particular types of abnormalities detected and to differentiate between various types of abnormalities. For example, many violent subjects have decreased glucose metabolism in the areas of the prefrontal and temporal cortex. These hypoperfusions, however, may be completely independent of, for example, substance abuse or certain psychiatric disorders. In addition, the variability in brain physiology between experimental subjects and the inherent problems associated with defining normalcy make it extremely difficult to draw meaningful comparisons (Snead, 2007). Further, while some structural abnormalities, such as tumors, are easily identified, other structural abnormalities, such as abnormalities related to traumatic brain injury, may be much more difficult to recognize. In such cases determining whether or not a given scan is normal requires a comparison between the normative sample brain scan and the scan in question. However, deciding which measure[7] should be used for comparison is difficult, since there is no single measure that serves as a gold standard (Canli & Amin, 2002). Further, the decision whether a given sample is "normal" or "abnormal" is not absolute. Ultimately, the decision whether an individual's brain structure or function falls within the normal range may likely depend on the measures used (a structure or function may qualify as normal by one measure but not another; Canli & Amin, 2002). Finally, the conditions under which the scan was obtained may be idiosyncratic and impossible to compare in a meaningful way with data obtained at other imaging centers (Reeves, Mills, Billick, & Brodie, 2003).

8.4.3 Baseline and Activation

Another major problem arises when one attempts to define brain functions in terms of activation patterns. Indeed, the image of an activation pattern from a poorly designed study can be visually indistinguishable from one based on a sound methodology (Canli & Amin, 2002). As previously noted, when researchers identify a region as being active they mean to say that the activation in that region during one condition (e.g., performing the Wisconsin Card Sorting Test) is significantly different than during a control condition (e.g., at rest). What constitutes a significantly different activation is determined through statistical analysis. More specifically, activation under one condition will be called significantly greater than under another condition when a certain threshold of statistical certainty has been crossed (Canli & Amin, 2002). Raising the threshold will reduce the number of significant regions while lowering the threshold will create more regions that are statistically significant. Since the choice of the threshold is usually determined by convention among researchers, rather than an absolute standard, a given brain activation pattern is therefore primarily a statistical interpretation of a very complex dataset, which may be interpreted differently by different researchers (Canli & Amin, 2002).

Another factor that significantly influences the appearance of a brain activation pattern is the choice of tests and control conditions employed. To be more precise, the activation pattern is based on a comparison between a test and a control condition; however, there may be more than one control condition, and different control conditions may produce different patterns of activation. For example, in Stark and Squire's 2001 study, activity in the medial temporal lobe, as well as in other brain regions, was substantially higher during rest than during several alternative baseline conditions. This elevated activity during rest may, in effect, have reduced, eliminated, or even reversed the sign of the activity during task conditions relevant to cognitive functioning (Stark & Squire, 2001). In addition, many neuroimaging studies fail to use specific tasks that activate the brain area of interest or employ tests that are not designed to activate the area of interest. Performing activation studies in a scientifically sound manner is important since activation studies provide stronger and more reliable findings. Finally, the extent to which deficits are relative is often not assessed. Doing so, however, is crucial since data obtained from studies that demonstrate relative deficits constitute more powerful evidence of specific brain dysfunction.

8.4.4 The Issue of Data Analysis

After the data has been obtained from the scanner, image processing is required to extract the quantitative information from the images as requested by the clinician. This information may include brain volume, blood flow, size and shape of brain structures, thickness of cortex, or functional activation data. However, many layers of signal processing, statistical analysis, and interpretation separate imaged brain activity from the psychological traits and states inferred from it. In fact, the array of expertise required to produce a single neuroimage, such as physics, neuroscience, computer science, statistical analysis, and nuclear medicine, presents many opportunities for technical bias, variance, and error (Snead, 2007). More specifically, before the clinician can interpret the signals produced by a particular imaging modality, the data must be reconstructed by using a set of mathematical equations based on a variety of assumptions. This reconstruction involves (a) statistical analysis and comparisons from which clinical inferences or experimental conclusions may be drawn and (b) many assumptions, corrections, and compromises (Reeves et al., 2003). Since these steps are not standardized, the image to be interpreted varies, depending on the color, signal threshold, contrast, or coordinates that have been chosen. For example, changes in regional cerebral glucose metabolism rates can be expressed in absolute glucose metabolic rates. Functional MRI blood oxygenation-level dependent responses, however, measure only the relative change from the baseline or control condition. For these measurements, "zero" is not absolute but is entirely dependent on what each particular experimenter chooses to use as his or her experimental baseline (Binder et al., 1999; Stark & Squire 2001). In addition, because color-coding can be arbitrary, the image display may suggest that there is a big differences in brain activity when in fact there is not (Reeves et al., 2003). As noted by Brodie (1996), the problem is that, as more detail is visualized, the data can become more confounded.

An additional concern is that the use of cognitive neuroimaging data to diagnose psychiatric disorder relies on the soundness of the diagnostic criteria that, given the absence of specific biological markers for any psychiatric disorder, may be open to a *Daubert* challenge (Snead, 2007). Further, since certain concepts that are integral to the interpretation of cognitive neuroimaging, such as self, vary widely from culture to culture, the analysis of data acquired in neuroimaging studies is further complicated (Snead, 2007). Finally, the reality is that neuroimaging is fraught with uncertainties (Roberts, 2007), and the steps used in the production and presentation of neuroimaging evidence are "not only . . . not standardized, they are easily manipulated by a person with knowledge of the technology" (Reeves et al., 2003, p. 90).

8.4.5 Effects of Psychotropic Medications and Substance Abuse

Although neuroimaging is an important tool for better understanding the neurobiological basis of various psychiatric disorders and diseases, many potential study participants are often receiving psychotropic medications that can confound the imaging data. In fact, Reeves and colleagues (2003) stress that "psychotropic drugs affect functional imaging of the brain" and the effects of such drugs "are not always short-lived" (p. 90). For example, decreased glucose metabolism has been shown for at least one month after ingestion of cocaine (Volkow et al., 1991). Similarly, while treatment with monoamine oxidase inhibitors may have been discontinued prior to neuro-imaging, it can take months to return to pretreatment levels (Fowler et al., 1994). It has also been shown that moderate to high alcohol doses acutely interfere with brain activity (Anderson et al., 2011). Indeed, Volkow and colleagues (2008) observed that alcohol shifts activity from cortical to limbic regions, while other studies have reported decreased prefrontal and parietal activity at higher levels of alcohol (Soderlund, Grady, Easdon, & Tulving, 2007; Van Horn, Yanos, Schmitt, & Grafton, 2006).

8.4.6 The Issue of Reversed and Forward Inference

One common goal of functional neuroimaging studies is to use imaging data to identify the mental/cognitive processes that are engaged when subjects perform specific mental tasks. However, interpretation of functional neuroimaging scan can potentially lead to inferential failure. More specifically, two types of inferences can be applied to functional neuroimaging data: (a) reversed inference and (b) forward inference.

8.4.6.1 Reversed Inference

As previously noted, functional neuroimaging techniques are frequently used to better understand brain functioning, including the nature of cognition. One particular practice that has become common is "reverse inference," which means that the engagement of a particular cognitive process is inferred from the activation of a particular brain region (Poldrack, 2006). It is difficult, however, to infer the involvement of a specific cognitive process from the activation, since various cognitive processes can activate the brain region. Thus, as noted by Poldrack (2011), brain activation patterns are considered as a weak indicator of the presence of a cognitive process, and reverse inference is assumed to be intrinsically weak (Fox & Friston, 2012).

Furthermore, Poldrack (2006) has argued that cognitive neuroscientists should be circumspect in the use of reverse inference, especially when selectivity of the region in question is known to be weak or cannot be established. However, most recently Hutzler (2014) concluded that reverse inference should not be disregarded as a fallacy per se: "Rather, the predictive power of reverse inference can even be 'decisive'—dependent on the cognitive process of interest, the specific brain region activated, and the task-setting used" (p. 1061).

8.4.6.2 Forward Inference

While the reverse inference is a (probabilistic) assignment of a cognitive process to activation of a specific brain region, forward inference is a data-driven method that uses qualitatively different patterns of brain activation to distinguish between competing cognitive theories (Henson, 2006). An important feature of forward inference is that it does not require strong selectivity of brain regions. More specifically, as long as there is a qualitative difference in the overall pattern of brain activity, it may not matter which brain regions differ in the two conditions or even if numerous regions differ (Henson, 2006). However, because this is a correlational approach, one cannot infer that the activated regions are necessary or sufficient for the engagement of the mental process (Poldrack, 2008). For example, the hippocampus has been shown to be activated during classical conditioning; however, lesion studies have demonstrated that classical conditioning can occur without hippocampus involvement (Knight, Smith, Cheng, Stein, & Helmstetter, 2004).

8.5 Correlation Versus Causation

As noted by Justice Breyer (2011), "there is an increasingly important need for law to reflect sound science" (p. 5). To that end, perhaps the most important point to remember is that correlation does not equal causation. Indeed, identifying an association between two variables does not imply a causal link between them since it is entirely possible that both measures are caused by another factor that has yet to be identified. In other words, neuroscience is unable to provide complete, or even sufficient, explanations of criminal violence by reference primarily to purported neurobiological dysfunctions within isolated parts of an offender's brain (Pustilnik, 2009). The following case clearly illustrates this point.

A Texas jury convicted James Irvin Quick of the murder of Michelle Denise Melton (*Quick v. State*, 2011). Quick admitted to the murder in a videotaped custodial statement with detectives, and a jury subsequently found him guilty of murder. Quick then appealed his conviction, contending that the trial court abused its discretion by allowing the State to mention his failure to testify at trial during the prosecution's closing argument and by barring his three experts from testifying regarding his ability to form the requisite intent to commit murder. The Texas Court of Appeals affirmed Quick's conviction and the trial court's denial of his neuroscience experts.

Before deciding whether to admit the testimony of the three experts proffered by Quick, the trial court conducted an evidentiary hearing on the admissibility of the experts' testimony. After reviewing the experts' reports, the trial court concluded that the experts failed to prove that Quick could not form the requisite intent for murder. More specifically, the court held that the experts failed to adequately connect Quick's alleged diminished executive functioning to an inability to form the necessary mental state to commit murder, as required by the Texas evidentiary standard.

Since it may be argued that the admissibility and immediacy of neuro-imaging data create a misleading aura of scientific infallibility when, in fact, "there is not, and will never be, a brain correlate for responsibility" (Aharoni, Funk, Sinnott-Armstrong, & Gazzaniga., 2008, p. 145), it is of particular importance that the interpretation of neuroimaging scans is sound. Further, while neuroscience continues to discover a great deal about the correlates and etiology of violent behavior, causation is not in and of itself an excusing condition. Indeed, given the substantial obstacles associated with the study of cognitive neuroscience, it is difficult to show a direct relationship between a particular brain region's function or a neuropsychological test score and any associated cognitive processes or behaviors (Snead, 2007). In addition, numerous concerns have been raised about the notion of functional specialization of brain regions, a premise that is central to neuroimaging studies. If, in fact, certain brain regions serve multiple cognitive functions or, alternatively, multiple cognitive functions activate the same region of the brain, the risk of error in drawing inferences from neuroimaging data about the brain and behavior is further increased (Snead, 2007).

8.6 Conclusion

Although the search for scientific truth is not a search for scientific accuracy, there are many issues related to the reliability and validity of neuroscience evidence that bear consideration. The well-known case of *United States v. Gigante* (1997) highlights many of these issues. Gigante, a reputed Mafia leader, was charged with numerous counts of murder, conspiracy to commit murder, and RICO violations.

In 1997, after having been found guilty by a jury of various charges and having his motion to set aside the verdict denied, Gigante moved for an order declaring him to be incompetent to be sentenced. Based on the results of neurological and neuropsychological assessments, and CT, SPECT, and functional PET scans, which showed bilateral parietal metabolic decrease, eight experts for the defense diagnosed Gigante with (a) vascular dementia, in the absence of any neurological deficits and structural impairment, as assessed by CT; (b) dementia of the Alzheimer's type, based on a functional PET scans; and (c) cognitive dysfunction and found him incompetent to be sentenced (*United States v. Gigante*, 1997).

With regard to the alleged abnormalities found on the PET, SPECT, and CT scans by the defense witnesses, Dr. Brodie, an expert for the government, explained that

- Although all scans were read as "abnormal," the abnormalities described were neither consistent with each other, with the present clinical impression of vascular dementia, or with Gigante's clinical history.
- The available information suggested that Gigante's prescribed psychotropic medication, if he took them at the time of the PET scan, would have had a profound effect on the PET metabolic images.[8]
- The typical clinical reference state for most dementia studies has been the resting state as opposed to the task state. Therefore, it is unclear if the apparent temporoparietal hypometabolism found on Gigante's PET scan was absolute or a consequence of the task state.
- Hypometabolism, which is essentially restricted to the temporoparietal area and roughly bilaterally symmetrical, is not consistent with a vascular process. Similarly, the CT scan provided no evidence of a vascular lesion, much less multiple lesions sufficient to compromise global brain function, consistent with the descriptions of the severity of Gigante's cognitive and behavioral deficits. According to the diagnostic criteria of the National Institute of Neurological Disorders and Stroke, a diagnosis of vascular dementia cannot be made without evidence for dementia, as well as radiological evidence of vascular lesions, by either CT or MRI scans. (*United States v. Gigante*, 1997, Gov. Exh. W-1, at 2)

In conclusion Dr. Brodie noted that (a) the description of a nearly catatonic defendant in the courtroom makes sense only if the diagnosis is malingering, since it is not the presentation of dementia and is inconsistent with Gigante's behavior and appearance at his psychiatric examinations and (b) to suggest that this is part of the normal fluctuation of classical dementia is incredulous. "I am struck by the details of the inconsistencies, for it is always in the details that the imperfections of an actor playing a role become manifest" (*United States v. Gigante*, 1997, Gov. Exh. W-1, at 4).

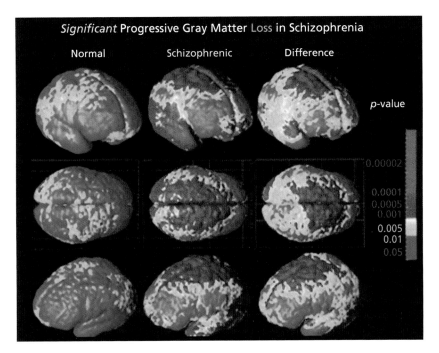

Color Plate 1 Significance of Dynamic Gray Matter Loss in Normal Adolescents and Schizophrenia. Highly significant progressive loss occurs in schizophrenia in the parietal, motor, supplementary motor, and superior frontal cortices. Broad regions of the temporal cortex, including the superior temporal gyrus, experience severe gray matter attrition. By comparison of the average rates of loss in disease (middle column) with the loss pattern in normal adolescents (first column), the normal variability in these changes can also be taken into account, and the significance of disease-specific change can be established (last column).

Reproduced with permission from Thompson et al., 2001. Mapping adolescent brain change reveals dynamic wave of accelerated gray matter loss in very early-onset schizophrenia. *Proceedings of the National Academy of Science*, 98(20), 11650–11655. Copyright (2001) National Academy of Sciences, U.S.A.

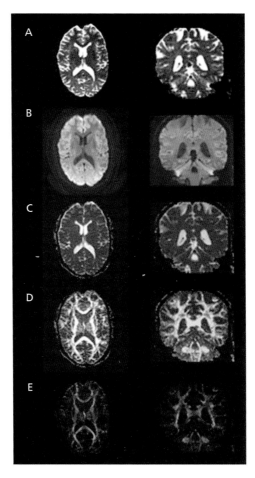

ColorPlate 2 Diffusion Tensor Based Images. T2-weighted MRI (A), diffusion-weighted images (B), apparent diffusion coefficient maps (C), fractional anisotropy maps (D), and direction-coded fractional anisotropy maps (E) in axial (left column) and coronal (right column) views. In the direction-coded fractional anisotropy maps, red represents fibers crossing from left to right, green crossing in the posterior anterior direction, and blue crossing in the inferior–superior direction in a normal head coordinate system.

Images courtesy of H. U. Voss and N. D. Schiff, Weill Medical College of Cornell University.

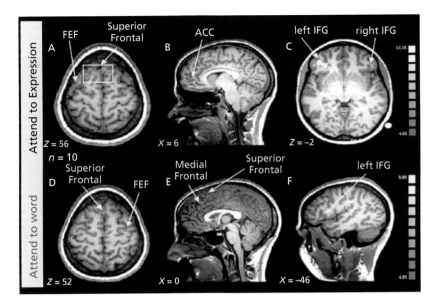

Color Plate 3 fMRI BOLD Activation in an Emotional Stroop Task. Activation from incongruent blocks compared with congruent blocks in the expression (A-C) and word instruction conditions (D-F).

Courtesy of Wikimedia Commons, available at http://en.wikipedia.org/wiki/File:FMRI_BOLD_activation_in_an_emotional_Stroop_task.jpg

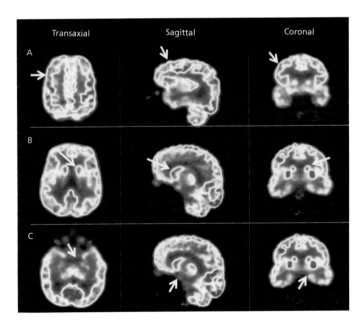

Color Plate 4 FDG-PET scan of Normal Human Brain. Scan shows the brain at the level of mid frontal gyrus (A), caudate head (B), and amygdala (C).

Adapted from images available from the Whole Brain Atlas at http://www.med.harvard.edu/AANLiB/cases/.caseNA/pb9.htm.

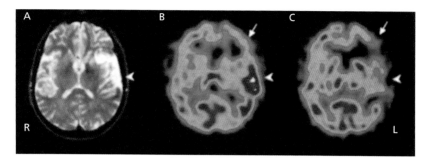

Color Plate 5 Comparison of Brain SPECT with MRI Scan. Left temporal lobe infarction (arrowhead) in MRI-T2 scan (A). 99mTc-HMPA SPECT obtained 1 week after stroke shows luxury perfusion (B) but hypoperfusion 1 month after stroke (C). Perfusion changes (arrow) also seen in frontal right lobe (B and C).

Reprinted by permission of SNMMI from Catafau, A. M. (2001). Brain SPECT in clinical practice. Part I: Perfusion. *Journal of Nuclear Medicine*, *42*(2), 259–271, Figure 5.

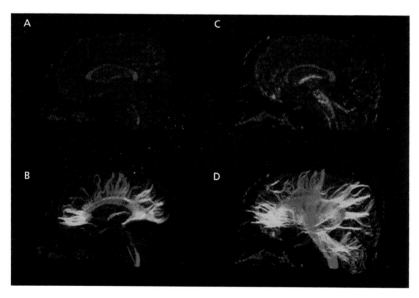

Color Plate 6 DTI Brain Tractography. DTI direction-coded fractional anisotropy map and tractography of a female patient with history of idiopathic basilar artery occlusion producing multifocal brain lesions (A and B) and a healthy volunteer (C and D). Fiber tracts are originating from the shown direction-coded fractional anisotropy slice centered on the midline of the brain only and do not reflect all fiber tracts of the brain.

Images courtesy of H. U. Voss and N. D. Schiff, Weill Medical College of Cornell University.

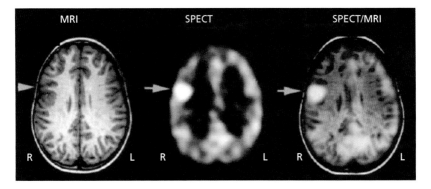

Color Plate 7 MRI vs. ^{99m}Tc-HMPAO Brain Perfusion SPECT. MRI scan (left) is normal, while SPECT shows hyperemia (increased rCBF) at the time of the epileptogenic seizure. A SPECT/MRI fusion image (right) identifies the location of the focus.

Reprinted with permission of Anderson Publishing from Mountz, J. M. (2007). PET/CT neuroimaging applications for epilepsy and cerebral neoplasm. *Applied Radiology, 36*(11), 44–52. © Anderson Publishing Ltd.

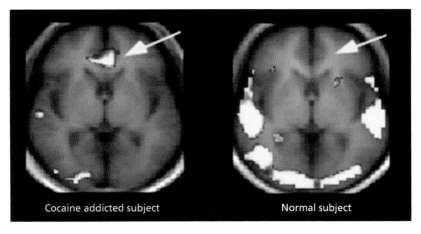

Color Plate 8 The Brain's Response to Cocaine Cues Imaged by fMRI. Arrows point to the activation of the anterior cingulate cortex, a region associated with emotional processing, while cocaine-addicted subjects watched videotapes containing cocaine-associated cues, even if they did not experience craving.

Reproduced from National Institute of Health: Fowler, J. S., Volkow, N. D., Kassed, C. A., & Chang, L. (2007). Imaging the addicted human brain. *Science and Practice Perspectives, 3*(2), 4–16.

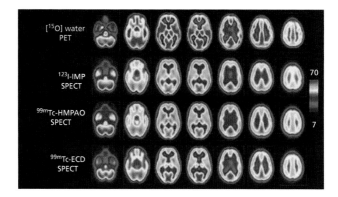

Color Plate 9 Estimation of rCBF Based on [^{15}O]water-PET. Comparison of rCBF measured with three different SPECT tracers. Anatomically standardized averaged CBF images are transaxial sections. Scale maximum and minimum values for all images are 70 and 7 ml/100 ml/min, respectively.

Reproduced from Fro, H., Inoue, K., Goto, R., Kinomura, S., Taki, Y., Okada, K., . . . Fukuda, H. (2006). Database of normal human cerebral blood flow measured by SPECT: I. Comparison between I-123-IMP, Tc-99m-HMPAO, and Tc-99m-ECD as referred with O-15 labeled water PET and voxel-based morphometry. *Annals of Nuclear Medicine, 20*(2), 131–138, Figure 2, with permission from Springer Science and Business Media.

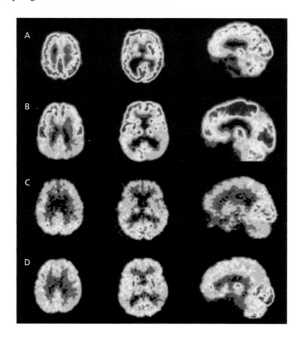

Color Plate 10 FDG-PET of Normal Subject and Subjects with DAT and FTLD. Normal subject (A), patient with DAT (B and D), and patient with frontotemporal lobar degeneration (FTLD) (C).

Reproduced with permission from Jagust, W., Reed, B., Mungas, D., Ellis, W., & Decarli, C. (2007). What does fluorodeoxyglucose PET imaging add to a clinical diagnosis of dementia? *Neurology, 69*(9), 871–877. Copyright © 2007, Wolters Kluwer Health

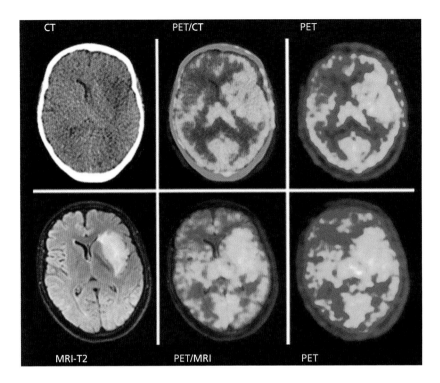

Color Plate 11 Hybrid PET/MRI of Intracranial Masses. PET/MR and PET/CT images of patient with low-grade glioma extending on left side from insular cortex to temporal lobe and frontal operculum. Top row: PET/CT data: low-dose noncontrast-enhanced CT image (left), fusion image (center), and PET images (right). Bottom row: PET/MRI data: T2-weighted FLAIR image (left), fusion image (center), and 11C-methionine PET image (right).

Reprinted by permission of SNMMI from Boss, A., Bisdas, S., Kolb, A., Hofmann, M., . . . Stegger, L. (2010). Hybrid PET/MRI of intracranial masses: Initial experiences and comparison to PET/CT. *Journal of NuclearMedicine*, *51*(8), 1198–1205, Figure 4.

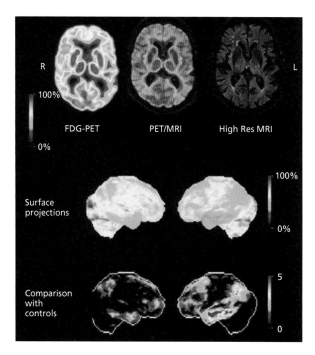

Color Plate 12 Simultaneous PET/MRI Study in Patient with Alzheimer's Disease. Areas with reduced metabolism representing impaired neuronal function are visible in the left temporoparietal cortex (green). Surface projections of cerebral metabolism and of z score images (comparison with controls) are shown in middle and bottom rows.

Reprinted by permission of SNMMI from: Catana, C., Drzezga, A., Heiss, W. -D., & Rosen, B. (2012). R.PET/MRI for neurologic applications. *Journal of Nuclear Medicine 53*(12), 1916–1925. Figure 5.

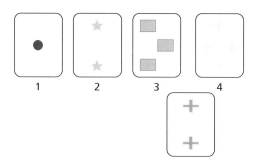

Color Plate 13 Illustration of Wisconsin Card Sort Test. This test uses stimulus and response cards that show various forms in various colors and numbers. Individually administered, it requires the subject to sort the cards according to different principles (i.e., by color or number). As the test progresses, there are unannounced shifts in the sorting principle that require the subject to change his or her approach.

BLUE RED GREEN
PURPLE BLUE PURPLE
RED PURPLE RED

Color Plate 14 Illustration of the Stroop Color and Word Test. The subject is presented with names of colors written in the same color or in a different color. When the name of a color (e.g., "blue" or "red") is printed in a color not denoted by the name (e.g., the word "red" printed in blue ink instead of red ink), naming the color of the word takes longer and is more prone to errors than when the color of the ink matches the name of the color.

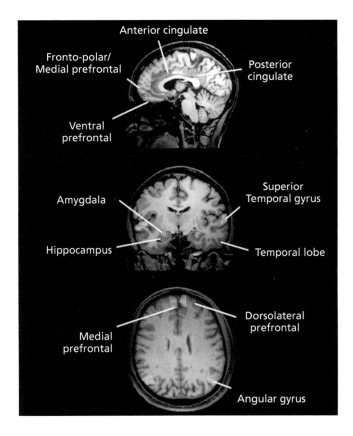

Color Plate 15 Brain regions that are presumed to be impaired in antisocial groups only (red), activated only in moral decision-making (green), and regions common to both antisocial behavior and moral decision-making (yellow).

Reproduced from Raine, A., & Yang, Y. (2006). Neural foundations to moral reasoning and antisocial behavior. *Social Cognitive & Affective Neuroscience*, *1*(3), 203–213, with permission from Oxford University Press.

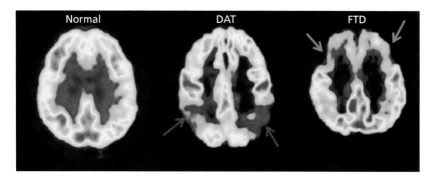

Color Plate 16 FDG-PET Scans in Normal and Dementia Subjects. In subject with DAT, significant hypometabolism is seen in the temporo-parietal areas (red arrows). In contrast, in the subject with FTD, hypometabolism is found in the frontal areas (blue arrows).

Adapted from Jacobs, A. H., Winkler, A., Castro, M. G., & Lowenstein, P. (2005). Human gene therapy and imaging in neurological diseases. *European Journal of Nuclear Medicine and Molecular Imaging, 32*, S358–S383, with permission from Springer Science and Business Media.

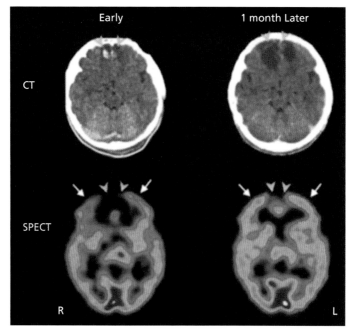

Color Plate 17 CT and SPECT Scans of Patient with TBI. At time of admission, a CT scan showed focal defects due to frontal lobe hemorrhage (orange arrows), while ^{99m}Tc-HMPAO SPECT showed markedly decreased regional cerebral blood flow in frontal lobes (orange and white arrows). One month later, CT showed resolution of the hematomas while SPECT still showed focal abnormalities (orange arrows).

Reprinted from Catafau, A. M. (2001). Brain SPECT in clinical practice. Part I: Perfusion. *Journal of Nuclear Medicine, 42*(2), 259–271, Figure 4, with permission from SNMMI.

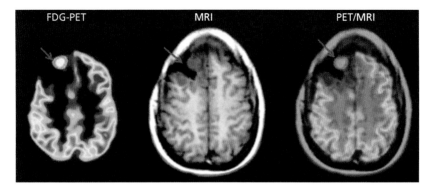

Color Plate 18 Brain Tumor Imaging. FDG-PET scan (left) shows focal metabolic abnormality involving the right frontal lobe. Contrast MRI scan (middle) shows enhancement in the right frontal lobe. PET/MRI fused image (right).

Reprinted from Herholz, K., Langen K. J., Schiepers C., & Mountz J. M. (2012). Brain tumors. *Seminars in Nuclear Medicine*, *42*, 356–370, with permission from Elsevier.

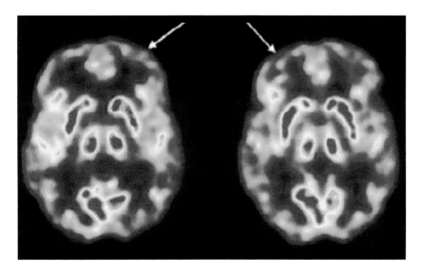

Color Plate 19 FDG-PET Scan of Patient with Schizophrenia. The scan shows mild global decrease, particularly in the frontal regions (arrows), consistent with some of the reported findings in the literature.

Image Courtesy of Open Access Publications: Hayempour, B. J., Cohen, S., Newberg, A., & Alavi, A. (2013). Neuromolecular imaging instrumentation demonstrating dysfunctional brain function in schizophrenic patients. *Journal of Alzheimer's Disease and Parkinsonism*, *3*, 114.

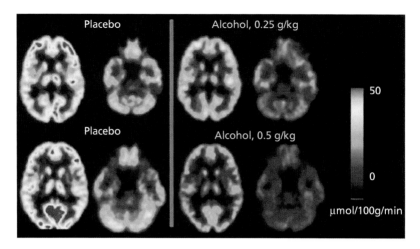

Color Plate 20 FDG-PET images of brain glucose metabolism for a subject tested at baseline (placebo) and after 0.25 g/kg alcohol consumption and for a subject tested at baseline and after 0.5 g/kg alcohol consumption.

Reprinted from Volkow, N. D., Wang, G.-J., Franceschi, D., Fowler, J. S., Thanos, P. K., Maynard, L., . . ., Li, T. K. (2006). Low doses of alcohol substantially decrease glucose metabolism in the human brain. *NeuroImage*, *29*, 295–301, with permission from Elsevier.

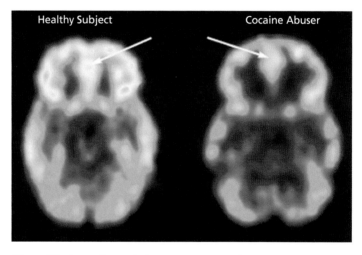

Color Plate 21 Cortical Metabolism in Cocaine Abusers. FDG-PET scan shows reduced brain glucose metabolism, especially in the OFC, compared to healthy control subject. Red and yellow represent the highest level of metabolic activity, while blue and purple are the lowest level.

Reproduced from National Institutes of Health: Fowler, J. S., Volkow, N. D., Kassed, C. A., & Chang, L. (2007). Imaging the addicted human brain. *Science & Practice Perspectives*, *3*(2), 4–16.

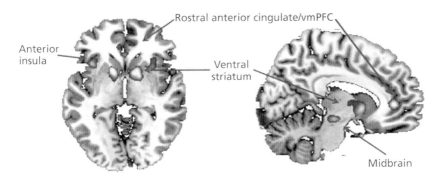

Color Plate 22 Main Components of the Human Reward Brain Circuit

Reprinted from Blakemore, S. J., & Robbins, T. W. (2012). Decision-making in the adolescent brain. *Nature Neuroscience*, *15*, 1184–1191, with permission from Macmillan Publishers.

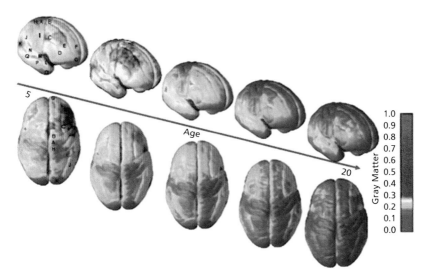

Color Plate 23 Time-Lapse Imaging Tracks Brain Maturation from Ages 5 to 20. Red indicates more gray matter, blue less gray matter. Areas that mediate "executive functioning" mature later than those responsible for basic functions.

Reprinted from Giedd, J. N., & Rapoport, J. L. (2010). Structural MRI of pediatric brain development: what have we learned and where are we going? *Neuron*, *67*(5), 728–734, with permission from Elsevier.

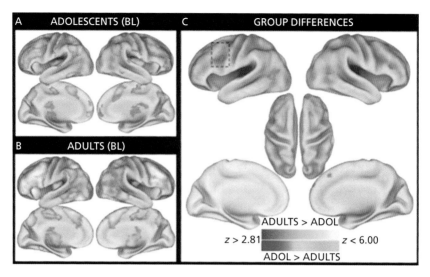

Color Plate 24 Between-Group Differences in Blocked Stroop Activity

Reproduced from: PLoSOne-Open Access Journal: A Andrews-Hanna, J. R., Mackiewicz Seghete, K. L., Claus, E. D., Burgess, G. C., Ruzic, L., & Banich, M. T. (2011). Cognitive control in adolescence: Neural underpinnings and relation to self-report behaviors. *PLoS One*, 6(6), e21598.

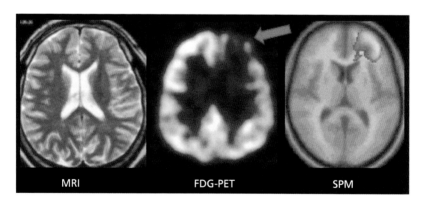

Color Plate 25 Comparison of FDG-PET with MRI in Epilepsy. In a patient with left frontal lobe epilepsy, brain MRI findings were normal (left), ^{18}F-FDG-PET indicated decreased metabolism in left frontal lobe (middle), and SPM ($p < .05$, corrected) gave the same finding (right).

Reprinted from Kim, Y. K., Lee, D. S., Lee, S. K., Chung, C. K., Chung, J., & Lee, M. C. (2008). ^{18}F-FDG PET in localization of frontal lobe epilepsy: Comparison of visual and SPM analysis. *Journal of Nuclear Medicine*, 43(9), 1167–1174, Figure 2, by permission of SNMMI.

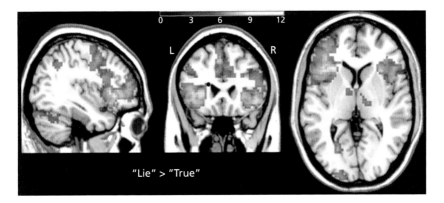

Color Plate 26 Brain Regions Showing Increased Activity During Lying. Brain regions found to be involved in lying, as assessed with blood-oxygen-level dependent fMRI: the insula bilaterally, the middle temporal gyrus bilaterally, the left supplementary motor areas, the left occipital gyrus, the left supramarginal gyrus, the right inferior frontal gyrus, the right middle frontal gyrus, and the right cerebellum.

Open Access Publications: Marchewka, A., Jednorog, K., Falkiewicz, M., Szeszkowski, W., Grabowska, A., & Szatkowska, I. (2012). Sex, lies and fMRI—Gender differences in neural basis of deception. *PLoSOne*, *7*(8), e43076.

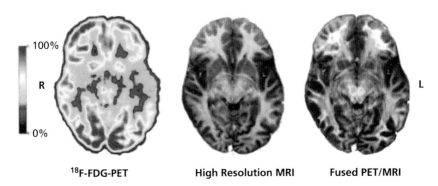

¹⁸F-FDG-PET   **High Resolution MRI**   **Fused PET/MRI**

Color Plate 27 Simultaneous PET/MRI Scan of Epilepsy Patient. Shown from left to right are axial FDG-PET, high-resolution MRI scan, and fusion image. Distinct hypometabolism is visible in polar region of left temporal lobe, corresponding to epileptogenic focus.

Reprinted from Catana, C., Drzezga, A., Heiss, W.-D., & Rosen, B. R. (2012). PET/MRI for neurologic applications. *Journal of Nuclear Medicine*, *53*(12), 1916–1925, Figure 7, by permission of SNMMI.

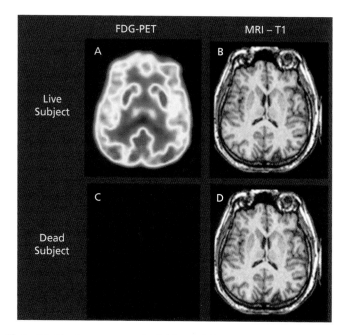

Color Plate 28 The Importance of a Multimodal Assessment. As the figure clearly illustrates, functional neuroimaging modalities, such as FDG-PET, can only provide an in vivo image of metabolic activities, while structural imaging with CT or MRI cannot differentiate viable tissue from dead tissue.

9

Malingering and its Assessment

It is the essence of truth that it is never excessive. Why
should it exaggerate? There is that which should be
destroyed and that which should be simply illuminated and
studied. How great is the force of benevolent and searching
examination! We must not resort to the flame where only
light is required.

(Victor Hugo, 1862)

9.1 Introduction

Mary Doherty was 13 years old when she was charged with the murder of her
father by repeatedly hitting his head with an axe. Her father's body was discovered four days later buried under the floorboards of the house, and it was
obvious that efforts had been taken to clean up the crime scene. She was held
in jail for about four months prior to the trial, during which time she did not
speak a word. The trial procedures of the time required a jury to first rule on
the issue of her being mute. If the jury found her mute by visitation of God,
then a special trial would be held and an automatic plea of not guilty entered.
If, in contrast, she was found mute of malice then she would stand trial and
the malice would be considered an attempt to evade justice. Doherty was
found mute by visitation of God, and the jury consequently found her not
guilty. The jury's decision was based in large part on the fact that she was too
young to have the ability to commit the crime. However, a note affixed to the
case stated that the day after the trial she was found outside the courthouse
animated and smiling at the judges in a way that suggested her pleasure with
the deception (*State v. Mary Doherty*, 1806).

The *Diagnostic and Statistical Manual of Mental Disorders* (fourth
edition, text revision [*DSM–IV–TR*]; American Psychiatric Association,

2000) does not list malingering as a mental disorder but rather as "additional conditions that may be a focus of clinical attention" (p. 739). Malingering is defined as "the intentional production of false or grossly exaggerated physical or psychological symptoms, motivated by external incentives such as avoiding military duty, avoiding work, obtaining financial compensation, evading criminal prosecution, or obtaining drugs" (American Psychiatric Association, 2000, p. 739).[1] The *DSM–IV–TR* also provides the following additional factors that should lead professionals to strongly suspect malingering: (a) an individual is presenting with symptoms within a medico-legal context, (b) there are marked discrepancies between objective findings and the person's subjective account of stress/disability, (c) the individual is noncompliant with the prescribed treatment regimen or uncooperative during evaluation, and (d) there is a presence of antisocial personality disorder (APD).

That mental illnesses and cognitive deficits can be feigned has been known since ancient times. Indeed, according to Homer, Ulysses feigned madness to avoid participating in the Trojan War, while in the Hebrew Bible David feigns insanity to escape from a king who views him as an enemy. Two Shakespearean plays also contain accounts of feigned madness: Edgar in King Lear, who feigned madness in order to escape the persecutions of his brother, and Hamlet, when he was attempting to escape the machinations of his uncle (Chesterman, Terbeck, & Vaughan, 2008). While malingering of deficits has a long history, determining exactly how to detect an individual who feigns cognitive or other impairments has proven to be difficult. Rosenhan's 1973 study clearly demonstrated the inability of mental health professionals to distinguish mental illness from normal behavior. In this classic study eight volunteer pseudo-patients—a psychology student, a pediatrician, three psychologists, a psychiatrist, a housewife, and a painter—all were admitted to psychiatric hospitals after claiming to hear voices. Although all claims of hearing voices stopped immediately following admission, all were diagnosed as suffering from schizophrenia and remained in the hospital from 9 to 52 days. From these findings Rosenhan concluded: "It is clear we cannot distinguish the sane from the insane in psychiatric hospitals" (p. 250).

Forensic mental health experts are frequently asked to determine the nature and severity of cognitive, neurological, and/or psychological deficits of individuals. Consequently, forensic clinicians bear considerable responsibility to society in differentiating true disease from malingered madness (Resnick, 1999). This is particularly true in light of the fact that the base rate of malingering in criminal settings may be as high as 50% (Larrabee, Greiffenstein, Greve, & Bianchini, 2007). It is thus not surprising that professional interest in methods of detecting suboptimal effort or malingering has flourished, and, as the literature has matured, the following three primary methods of detecting suboptimal effort or malingering have emerged:

- Unusual poor performance on tests designed specifically to detect poor effort or malingering, such as the Test of Memory Malingering (TOMM) and the Portland Digit Recognition Test (PDRT);
- Unusual patterns of errors on tests originally designed to assess some aspect of neurocognitive ability, such as the California Verbal Learning Test (CVLT) or the Wechsler Adult Intelligence Scale–Revised; and
- Unusual patterns of variability within the same tests across time (Williamson, Green, Allen, & Rohling, 2003).

Given the abundance of available tests and techniques currently available, deciding exactly which test or technique to employ to obtain the most reliable information is difficult. To make this decision, a careful examination of each test's predictive accuracy is therefore necessary. A number of issues bear consideration in this regard. Many of the currently available tests were developed using normal samples simulating impairment rather than clinical samples. While this is a helpful starting point, normal samples simulating impairment and clinical samples may not behave in identical ways (Rogers & Cruise, 1998). Thus a clinician's confidence in the generalizability of these test or techniques is limited. Many of the clinical samples used to validate tests have limitations as well. For example, some are limited to patients without severe neurocognitive impairment; consequently, the extent to which one may encounter "false positives" in the face of severe impairment is unknown (Curtiss & Vanderploeg, 2000). In addition, the contexts in which many clinical validation studies are performed bear little similarity to the context often encountered by the practicing clinician: that is, when the results of the evaluation are explicitly linked to the possibility of a subject receiving secondary gains (Binder & Rohling, 1996).

There is no doubt that the assessment of malingering of cognitive deficits, psychiatric disorders, and/or psychopathology must be an integral part of forensic evaluations since failure to detect malingering of disorders and dysfunctions can have serious adverse consequences. Indeed, defendants who successfully feign cognitive and/or other impairments may avoid criminal prosecution if acquitted by reason of insanity. In addition, successful malingering of disorders or deficits may result in the imposition of shorter sentences due to the mistaken finding that the feigned symptoms mitigated the offenses. Falsely concluding that a defendant is malingering, when he or she does present with a genuine impairment is also problematic since it may result in denial or delay in the provision of much needed health care (Kucharski, Duncan, Egan, & Falkenbach, 2006). Therefore it is crucial that forensic mental health evaluators employ valid methods for the identification of malingering.

Since malingering is not a syndrome, it has no specifiable inclusion and exclusion criteria and is therefore fundamentally different from other clinical assessments (Drob, Meehan, & Waxman, 2009). It has been suggested that although assessment measures such as the Structured Interview of Reported Symptoms (SIRS) are used to detect feigning, such measures do not identify an individual's motivation for feigning and therefore can never be used in isolation to detect malingering (DeClue, 2002). When making judgments about malingering of cognitive deficits or psychiatric or personality disorders, psychologists and psychiatrists are making a judgment about an individual's intentions, motives, and behavior. Consequently, mental health experts must utilize the same principles that are utilized in a court of law; the individual's conduct must be placed within the broadest psychological and motivational context possible, being mindful that a broader context may ultimately expose an initial judgment to have been in error (Drob et al., 2009). Clearly, clinicians who fail to consider a variety of data, such as behavioral observations and review of historical records, run a high risk of false-positive attributions (DeClue, 2002). Further, given that many currently available tests of malingering lack adequate predictive accuracy when used in isolation, employing a multimodal approach to the assessment of malingering is not only justified but also necessary.

The need to assess malingering using a multimodal approach that employs valid and reliable tests, measures, and techniques and the inherent difficulties associated with making a determination of malingering is perhaps no better illustrated that in the case of *United States v. Gigante* (1996). During Gigante's trial, four psychiatrists testified that Gigante was incompetent, although reservations were expressed that he might be malingering. The trial judge, Judge Nickerson, had also received testimony from former members of the Mafia and, subsequently, made the factual findings that "Gigante was a forceful and active leader of the Genovese family from at least 1970 on" and that Gigante had put on a "crazy act" for many years in order "to avoid apprehension by law enforcement" (*United States v. Gigante*, 1996, p. 976). After being presented with these findings, two of the examining psychiatrists changed their opinion, indicating that they now thought Gigante was malingering; one said Gigante was competent to stand trial, and the other said it was quite possible that Gigante was competent. The remaining experts held to their earlier findings of incompetence.[2] The trial judge subsequently found the weight of medical opinion to show that Gigante was mentally competent to stand trial (*Unites States v. Gigante*, 1996).

In 1997 Gigante moved for a new trial based on new evidence as to his competency to stand trial, arguing that the district court erred in finding that he was competent to stand trial. More specifically, Gigante presented new evidence of incompetence in the form of a positron emission tomography (PET) scan of his brain and the results of a battery of tests designed to identify malingering. The defense experts testified that Gigante was incompetent to be tried.[3] In contrast, the government's expert testified that it was possible that the results of these tests were due to the drugs Gigante was receiving.[4] The new trial judge consequently found Gigante competent and ordered that the trial proceed. The court subsequently concluded that the defense experts' findings were (a) not consistent with other evidence in this case, (b) unreliable, and (c) based on speculative scientific theories lacking full development, research, and support. More specifically the court noted that

- One of the defense expert's findings were based upon speculative assumptions; the expert argued that since defendant seemed to be trying on the cognitive tests and scored slightly above the score of "chance" guessing, the conclusion was valid that malingering was not probable.
- Defendant's experts failed to take into account the extensive testimony received by Judge Nickerson, proving that defendant's mental difficulties had been feigned for many years (*United States v. Gigante*, 1997, pp. 147–148).

Many years later, Vincente Gigante signed a statement in which he admitted that he had been faking mental illness in order to avoid conviction.

9.2 The Assessment of Malingering

Since the *DSM–IV–TR* does not view malingering as a specific disorder, guidelines rather than diagnostic criteria are provided for the assessment of malingering.[5] These guidelines include (a) medicolegal context of presentation, (b) marked discrepancy between objective findings and claimed disability, (c) lack of cooperation in assessment and treatment, and (c) the presence of APD. Malingering is not an all-or-nothing phenomenon, however; it exists on several levels. Indeed, an individual who is exaggerating genuine symptoms in an attempt to create the appearance of a more severe form of psychopathology or cognitive impairment represents one level, while a person who uses deceit to extend legitimate symptoms back to the time of the criminal activity in order to reduce culpability involves a different level of malingering. Further, there are those individuals who completely fabricate symptoms for the sole purpose of receiving external incentives. These incentives include but are not limited to (a) a finding of not guilty by reason of insanity, diminished capacity, incompetency to stand trial, or incompetency to be executed and (b) mitigating factors. Finally, criminal charges may be dismissed entirely (Frederick, Crosby, & Wynkoop, 2000).

The difference between simple unreliable reporting and malingering of cognitive dysfunction or mental illness is a matter of the individual's intent. More specifically, feigning, by definition, is deliberate. In contrast, where intentionality is in doubt, the individual may be classified as simply being unreliable. In other words, the information provided may be inaccurate in that it does not present a valid portrait of the individual's impairment or illness but this is not due to purposeful distortion (Rogers, 1997). Further mental illness[6] or cognitive impairment and malingering are not mutually exclusive phenomena. In fact, research has shown that some of the more effective malingerers are those individuals who have experienced or are experiencing actual symptoms of mental illness and/or cognitive impairment. Thus malingering and neurological, psychiatric, and psychological disorders may coexist with some malingerers simply exaggerating the symptoms of genuine disorders (Rogers & Bender, 2003).

The concept of malingering also should not be confused with somatoform and factitious disorders. The major difference between malingering and somatoform disorder is motivation. When the feigning of a mental illness or a cognitive deficit is due to a conscious effort, it can be referred to as malingering, whereas unconscious or involuntary processes motivate somatoform disorder. Factitious disorders can be distinguished from malingering in that there are no external incentives present (Rogers, 1997). In response to the *DSM–IV–TR*'s broad categorization, a number of criteria have been proposed to more precisely define malingering, but the most thoroughly outlined proposal has been provided by Slick, Sherman, and Iverson (1999). Slick and colleagues define malingering as "the volitional exaggeration or fabrication of cognitive dysfunction for the purpose of obtaining substantial material gain, or avoiding or escaping formal duty or responsibility" (p. 552). The authors describe three categories of malingering: (a) possible, (b) probable, and (c) definite. For a patient to classify into one of these categories, a combination of four criteria must be met:

- *Criterion A: Presence of a substantial external incentive*—at least one clearly identifiable and substantial external incentive is present at the time of testing.
- *Criterion B: Evidence from neuropsychological testing*—evidence of exaggeration or fabrication on neuropsychological tests as evidenced from at least one of the following: (1) definite response bias—below chance performance ($p < .05$) on one or more forced-choice measures; (2) probable response bias—performance on a well-validated test is consistent with fabrication or exaggeration; (3) discrepancy between test data and known patterns of brain functioning; (4) discrepancy between test data and observed behavior; (5) discrepancy between test data and reliable collateral reports; and (6) discrepancy between test data and documented background history.
- *Criterion C: Evidence from self-report*—significant inconsistencies or discrepancies in a patient's self-reported symptoms that suggest exaggeration or fabrications as evidenced by one of the following: (1) self-reported history is discrepant with documented history; (2) self-reported symptoms are discrepant with known patterns of brain functioning; (3) self-reported symptoms are discrepant with behavioral observations; (4) self-reported symptoms are discrepant with information obtained from collateral informants;

and (5) evidence of exaggerated or fabricated psychological dysfunction—performance on well-validated validity scales or indices on self-report measures of psychological adjustment are strongly suggestive of exaggeration or fabrication.
* *Criterion D: Behaviors meeting necessary criteria from groups B or C are not fully accounted for by psychiatric, neurological, or developmental factors*—behaviors are the product of an informed, rational, and volitional effort aimed at least in part toward achieving or acquiring external incentives.

To qualify as definite malingerer, a subject must meet criteria A, B1, and D (there must be substantial external incentive, the presence of a definite negative response bias on neuropsychological test[s], and no psychiatric, neurological, or developmental factor that would significantly diminish one's capacity to appreciate laws or mores against malingering; Slick et al., 1999). To qualify as a probable malingerer, a subject must meet criterion A, two or more from B1 through B6, and D, or criterion A, one from B1 through B6, one from C1 through C5, and D; someone can be classified as probable malingerer in two ways: (a) by having the presence of external incentive, two pieces of evidence from neuropsychological testing, and no psychiatric, neurological, or developmental disorder or (b) by having external incentive, one piece of evidence from neuropsychological testing, one piece of evidence from self-report, and no psychiatric, neurological, or developmental disorder). There are also two ways in which an individual can qualify as a possible malingerer: (a) the person must either meet criterion A, one from C1 through C5, and D (external incentive, evidence from self report, and no psychiatric, neurological, or developmental disorder) or (b) the person must meet criteria that would classify him or her as a definite or probable malingerer with the exception of criterion D (Slick et al., 1999). Although suggestions for improving this system have been made, these proposed definitions and criteria have gained support in the research community, and several studies have classified subjects according to these criteria (e.g., Aguerrevere, Greve, Bianchini, & Ord, 2011; Greve & Bianchini, 2006; O'Bryant et al., 2008).

It has been suggested that approximately 75% of attorneys prepare their clients for forensic neuropsychological evaluations by discussing the purpose and content of various tests and measures (Essig, Mittenberg, Peterson, Stauman, & Cooper, 2001). There is also evidence that attorneys brief their clients on the inclusion of measures designed to detect malingering with the most frequently reviewed tests being the Minnesota Multiphasic Personality Inventory-2 (MMPI-2; 29%), the PDRT (6%), and the Rey 15-Item Memory Test (Rey-15). In addition to direct warnings of neuropsychological and effort measures, approximately 10% of attorneys also inform their clients of what types of information to disclose concerning their injury, and 12% tell their clients what information not to disclose (Essig et al., 2001). Coaching has also been a controversial topic among psychologists. While some professionals contend that clients are not able to give proper informed consent to proceed with psychological testing until all information is disclosed to them, the American Psychological Association specifically forbids the practice of coaching by its members (Suhr & Gunstad, 2007). In addition, individual neuropsychologists differ even in their willingness to specify which particular tests will comprise the battery they will be administering to a particular subject in an effort to foil the malingering efforts of coached malingerers (Larrabee et al., 2007).

Few studies have examined the susceptibility of effort measures to attorney coaching. For example, Suhr and Gunstad (2000) reported that providing simulated malingerers with brain-injury information had no effect on their performance on the Auditory Verbal Learning Test. Similarly, a computerized version of the PDRT was found to be resilient to coaching (Rose, Hall, Szalda-Petreem, & Bach, 1998). In contrast, Lamb, Berry, Wetter, and Baer (1994) demonstrated the susceptibility of the MMPI-2 to both coaching and brain-injury information. In fact, simulated malingerers who were provided with information regarding brain-injury and/or information regarding the ability of the MMPI-2 to detect a "fake bad" profile produced valid profiles with significantly elevated clinical scales similar to those obtained by individuals with true head injuries. More believable profiles were also observed on the Nonverbal Forced Choice Test, 21-Item Test, PDRT, and Recognition Memory Test after participants were provided with information on how to beat these measures (Cato, Brewster, Ryan, & Guiliano, 2002; Dunn, Shear, Howe, & Ris, 2003).

Another issue to be considered is the fact that the vast majority of malingering research has relied on simulation designs that utilize nonclinical subjects, typically university undergraduates, asked to feign or malinger dysfunctions. Although it has been suggested that simulated malingerers are comparable to actual malingerers, studies utilizing the simulation design have historically been criticized for their lack of generalizability to actual malingerers (Brennan & Gouvier, 2006). A particular concern of this design is that the subjects usually employed in these studies have little or no experience with head injury. This is considerably different from individuals involved in actual criminal cases; a large number of criminal defendants who are malingering have had experience with and recovered from, for example, traumatic brain injury (TBI).[7]

According to Rogers and Correa (2008), tests designed to assess malingering are different for individuals malingering cognitive impairment and those malingering mental disorder or illness. More specifically, in the former case malingerers must put forth a convincing effort and make believable errors on cognitive measures, while in the latter malingerers must create a convincing story about the onset and course of their disorder, deciding on the order, frequency, and effects of symptoms. Consequently, different detection strategies are needed for distinct domains of malingering (Rogers & Bender, 2003). Any assessment of cognitive impairment in the context of violent and aggressive behavior therefore must include tests of cognitive malingering as well as tests designed to assess malingering of mental illness or psychological disorders. The importance of doing so is underscored by the fact that a well-designed study that seeks to assess cognitive impairment requires the use of a valid and reliable psychological test known to activate the brain area of interest. For example, in assessing frontal lobe dysfunction, a finding of below chance performance on tests of frontal lobe dysfunction and/or on tests designed to assess cognitive impairment can result in a diagnosis of frontal lobe dysfunction in the absence of any structural or functional abnormality. In addition, a finding of functional abnormality without collateral information is not sufficient to diagnose an individual with frontal lobe dysfunction since a link between any cognitive impairment and functional abnormality can only be inferred.

9.3 Standard Detection Strategies

Assessment of malingering is not an easy task. There are, however, a number of strategies available to assist the clinician in making an informed decision. One technique frequently used in the assessment of malingering is the performance curve analysis. The performance curve compares the probability of correctly answering easy items versus more difficult items (Rogers, 1997). In individuals who are not malingering impairment or dysfunction, the clinician should expect to see a decrease in correct responding as task difficulty increases. Evidence has shown that simulated malingerers do not generate the typical performance curve. In other words, malingerers fail a more-than-expected proportion of easy items compared to their performance on more difficult items (Frederick & Foster, 1991). One malingering measure that relies on the performance curve is the Dot Counting Test. This measure presents stimuli of varying (and randomly ordered) levels of difficulty to determine the consistency of an individual's response time and error rate (Lezak, 1995). In nonmalingering subjects, typically no errors are committed and a positive correlation is observed between difficulty level and time to respond. If there is more than one pronounced discrepancy between the expected and observed patterns of response time and/or if more than two errors are made, malingering should be suspected. Overall, empirical evidence supports error rate (performance curve) as a strong indicator of malingering (Binks, Gouvier, & Waters, 1996; Frederick, 2002).

Another strategy frequently employed is the floor effect. More specifically, there are many tasks that are easily accomplished by most individuals, including those with brain damage, and malingering detection utilizes this knowledge by examining floor effects. Floor effects are extremely low performances observed when malingerers misjudge the difficulty of easy tasks and perform more poorly than brain-damaged patients (Millis & Kler, 1995). One of the most frequently used floor-effect measures is the Rey-15. A major drawback of this test is that it is, in fact, sensitive to true memory impairment and correlates considerably with measures of cognitive competence (Lezak, 1995; Vallabhajosula & van Gorp, 2001).

A third strategy, atypical test performance, suggests that test performance that is markedly different from accepted models of normal and abnormal brain functioning should alert the clinician to the possibility of malingering.[8] The theory behind this method is that the automatic and intentional uses of memory can be separated and that "conscious control can be measured as the difference between performance when a person is trying *to* as compared with trying *not to* use information from some particular source" (Jacoby, 1991, p. 527). Therefore, any impairment on measures of implicit learning may be indicative of malingering.

Researchers have also looked at the predictive accuracy of validity indices designed to assess malingering. More specifically, many self-report measures of psychological functioning contain validity scales designed to detect if a subject is answering in a manner that invalidates the overall results. For example, the MMPI-2 has at least two indices that can be used to assist in the detection of malingering. The Infrequency (F) scale measures the extent to which a person answers in an atypical and deviant manner. A score of 70 or above is suggestive of possible malingering. The Dissimulation or F-K index determines the likelihood and direction of exaggeration. A score of 12 or greater indicates a fake bad profile, while a score of –12 or less indicates a fake good profile (Groth-Marnat, 1997). Similarly, the Personality Assessment Inventory (PAI) contains scales appropriate for use in the detection of malingering, such as the Negative Impression Management scale (NIM), which measures the degree to which a subject has presented an exaggerated, unfavorable impression of distress (Morey, 2003).

Finally, most of the literature aimed at defining assessment techniques that reliably assess malingering has been devoted to the development and validation of symptom validity tests (SVTs),[9] which were created on the tenet that, with adequate effort, all patients with the exception of the most severely neurologically impaired will score within the normal range (Weinborn, Orr, Woods, Conover, & Feix, 2003). To be more precise, symptom validity testing is a simple strategy based in binomial distribution theory; an individual with a legitimate impairment who cannot discriminate between the two stimuli presented should perform at chance levels over many trials. In contrast, malingerers are likely to select the wrong response deliberately and thus perform significantly below chance (Rogers, Harrell, & Liff, 1993). Perhaps most commonly known for their use in forensic settings, SVTs can be crucial when making diagnostic decisions in situations involving criminal defendants. In addition, SVTs are more commonly being added to research protocols to screen out possibly invalid data. Without the support of passing SVT scores, lowered scores on other cognitive measures remain suspect because the possibility of malingering makes valid conclusions difficult, if not impossible, to ascertain (Gierok, Dickson, & Cole, 2005).

Literature has suggested that symptom validity testing is the best-validated strategy to assess for malingered cognitive impairments (e.g., Bush et al., 2005).[10] In fact, it has been argued that the clinician should be prepared to justify a decision not to assess symptom validity as part of a neuropsychological assessment (Bush et al., 2005). However, according to a survey of members of the National Academy of Neuropsychology, the International Neuropsychological Society, and the American Psychological Association Division 40, SVTs are not among the top 40 most frequently administered assessment instruments. This may be due to the lack of knowledge that some psychologists have about the existence of SVTs, differential emphasis in training programs, philosophical opposition to utilization of these instruments, as well as limitations in survey methodology utilized (Rabin, Barr, & Burton, 2005).

A major criticism of symptom validity testing is that of its low sensitivity. This method is extremely conservative, and only the most blatant malingerers are caught. In response to this low sensitivity came the derivation of cutoff scores (Haines & Norris, 1995). A cutoff score typically represents the lowest score achieved by subjects with documented brain damage. Therefore if a patient with minor or no documented brain injury performs significantly worse than the cutoff, malingering is to be suspected (Haines & Norris, 1995). Utilizing cutoff scores improves the sensitivity of the forced-choice method but at the cost of reduced confidence in the interpretation (specificity is lowered because of the increase in false positives; Rogers, 1997). A major advantage of symptom validity measures is that demographic variables do not affect test scores. For example, research findings have shown that age and intelligence do not impact performance on the Word Memory Test (WMT; Brockhaus & Merten, 2004). Further, Delain, Stafford, and Ben-Porath (2003) found no significant demographic differences between individuals passing or failing the TOMM with respect to age, gender, ethnicity, or years of education in a sample of criminal defendants, while Tombaugh (1997) found the TOMM to be insensitive to age and years of education in a sample of community dwelling adults.

There is, at present, no single test that acts as the gold standard in the detection of malingering or symptom exaggeration, and this lack of a gold standard is clearly illustrated by the following: A 2007 study investigating neuropsychologists' beliefs and practices with respect to assessing malingering found that the five most frequently used measures were the TOMM, MMPI-2 F-K ratio and Fake Bad scale, the Rey-15, and the CVLT. However, the TOMM, Validity Indicator Profile (VIP), WMT, and Victoria Symptom Validity Test (VSVT) were rated as most accurate for detecting suboptimal effort.[11] In addition, only approximately 79% of the respondents reported using at least one specialized technique for detecting malingering (Sharland & Gfeller, 2007).

It must be noted that numerous studies have shown that some of the currently available malingering tests lack sufficient specificity, sensitivity, positive predictive power (PPP), and negative predictive power (NPP) to be relied on as a sole measure of malingering. Therefore since a single test of malingering may yield incorrect results (misclassifies an honest respondent as malingerer or the reverse), the use of multiple measures to provide converging evidence of malingering has been highly recommended (Farkas, Rosenfeld, Robbins, & van Gorp, 2006; Vallabhajosula & van Gorp, 2001). In fact, it may be argued that testifying to a jury that a defendant is malingering based solely on a single test result is unduly prejudicial. Indeed, Federal Rules of Evidence requires the potential prejudicial effect of scientific testimony to be carefully balanced against its probative value. Thus the use of multiple malingering measures might provide this balance in a manner that is more consistent with the legal standards set for the admissibility of scientific evidence (Saxe & Ben-Shakhar, 1999). Further, by employing multiple tests the likelihood for a subject who has been coached to convincingly feign impairment across multiple measures is decreased. Also, by using more than one test it is more likely that a particular malingering test will

> be relevant to a specific patient's functional or genuine complaints, or both. Thus the best use of a single test will be in combination with other tests—always within the context of a patient's history and clinical presentation—which together will reduce the likelihood of prediction error. (Lezak, 1995, p. 792)

Clearly, expert testimony that is based on the fact that a defendant passed multiple malingering measures would help a court to decide with a high degree of certainty that a claimed cognitive dysfunction and/or mental illness is valid and would more likely withstand a *Daubert* challenge.

9.4 Symptom Validity Tests Designed to Assess Malingering of Cognitive Impairment

9.4.1 Portland Digit Recognition Test

The PDRT is a 72-item (two sets of 36 items) test employing visual recognition of auditorily presented five-digit number strings. The first 36 trials are referred to as the "easy" items and the second 36 are the "hard" items based on their apparent difficulty. The published cutoff scores for the easy, hard, and total items sets have been associated with a 0% false positive error rate (100% specificity) in noncompensation-seeking moderate to severe TBI patients (Bianchini, Mathias, & Greve, 2001). In terms of the test's sensitivity, Bianchini and colleagues found the PDRT to be positive in about 30% of compensation-seeking head trauma patients. Further, a study using data from 262 TBI patients who were classified as not malingering, possibly malingering, and malingering based on the Slick et al. (1999) criteria found that the original PDRT cutoff scores detected between 20% and 50% of malingering TBI patients with a false positive error rate of 5% or less. When the false positive error rate was held at 5%, across all item sets, sensitivity was found to be as high as 70% (Greve & Bianchini, 2006). However, while it is highly likely that someone whose profile indicates malingering is actually feigning, the PDRT has also shown to yield a large number of false negatives (Rogers & Bender, 2003). Furthermore, Greve, Ord, Curtis, Bianchini, & Brennan (2008) in examining the individual and joint malingering detection accuracy of the PDRT, the TOMM, and the WMT in subjects with TBI and chronic pain found that (a) at published cutoff scores, the PDRT and TOMM were very specific but failed to detect approximately 50% of malingerers; (b) the WMT was sensitive but prone to false positive errors; and (c) the joint classification accuracy was superior to that of the individual tests.

9.4.2 Test of Memory Malingering

The TOMM was developed to help detect feigned cognitive impairment. The TOMM requires examinees to memorize 50 simple pictures and then identify correct pictures from 50 two-picture items after two learning trials and a retention trial (15-minute delay). Examinees are given feedback on the correctness of their answers to facilitate learning. The probability of feigned memory impairment is said to increase if a subject scores significantly lower than 45 on Trial 2 or the retention trial on the TOMM, particularly if they score below chance levels (Tombaugh, 1996). Individuals showing sustained effort on the TOMM generally do not score below 45 on Trial 2 or the retention trial, including those with genuine neurological impairment, such as dementia, TBI, and mild retardation (e.g., Merten, Bossink, & Schmand, 2007; Simon, 2007; Tombaugh, 1997).

Studies evaluating the reliability of the TOMM indicate that this test is highly sensitive to malingering but insensitive to true neurological and cognitive impairments. Indeed, sensitivity estimates range from 60% to 84%, and specificity estimates range from 90% to 100% (e.g., Bounds, 2005; Weinborn, Orr, Woods, Conover, & Feix, 2003).[12] Furthermore, Powell, Gfeller, Hendricks, and Sharland (2004) explored the effects of coaching on TOMM scores. Using the recommended cutoff score of 45 out of 50 correct to classify suboptimal performance, the TOMM accurately classified 92.6% of the symptom-coached simulators and 96% of the test-coached simulators. In addition, a review of four studies found the TOMM to have 100% PPP, irrespective of the base rates of malingering in these studies (Vallabhajosula & van Gorp, 2001). More recently it has been suggested that Trial 1 may only be used in predicting overall performance on the TOMM (O'Bryant et al., 2008). Recent studies have also suggested that cutoff scores higher than those originally recommended for the TOMM can produce excellent classification and diagnostic accuracy (Jones, 2013a; Stenclik, Miele, Silk-Eglit, Lynch & McCaffrey, 2013). However, it may be argued that the use of any nonstandard administration is inappropriate and may not satisfy *Daubert* criteria.

9.4.3 Validity Indicator Profile

Results of the VIP test indicate whether the individual's performance on other tests of cognitive capacity should be considered a valid representation of his or her abilities. The VIP consists of two subtests, each of which can be administered and scored separately: (a) the Nonverbal subtest presents 100 picture-matrix problems that require simple matching, complex matching, analogous decision making, progression, addition, subtraction, and abstraction, and (b) the Verbal subtest consists of 78 word-definition problems. Test-takers are presented with a stimulus word and are asked to choose which of two possible answers is most similar in meaning to the stimulus. For both subtests, the items have a hierarchy of difficulty but are presented randomly with respect to item difficulty. Once administered, the items are reordered in terms of difficulty level and then scored (Frederick, Crosby, & Wynkoop, 2000).

The overall effectiveness of the VIP in correctly classifying the initial validation sample resulted in 73.5% sensitivity and 85.7% specificity rates. The sensitivity of the nonverbal subtest was 66% with a specificity of 90% while the sensitivity and specificity for the verbal subtest were 59% and 94% (Frederick, 1997). In general, this test has received favorable reviews and comments although some concerns, criticisms, and cautions have been voiced (Gebart-Eaglemont, 2001; Vallabhajosula & van Gorp, 2001). More specifically, depending on the base rate of malingering, the VIP may or may not have sufficient sensitivity, specificity, PPP, and NPP (Vallabhajosula & van Gorp, 2001). More recently it has also been suggested that the use of the VIP with psychotic-disordered individuals will generate increased invalid performance profiles compared to the TOMM, which is more resilient in this subject population (Hunt, Root, & Bascetta, 2013).

9.4.4 Victoria Symptom Validity Test

The VSVT is a computer-administered two-alternative forced-choice SVT designed to assess cognitive functioning. This test consists of a total of 48 items, which are presented in three blocks of 16 items. For each item administered, a five-digit study number is first presented on a computer screen during the study trial and then is immediately followed by the retention interval during which a blank computer screen is shown. At the recognition trial, two five-digit numbers are presented on the computer screen, one of which was shown initially in the study trial. The subject is then required to identify which of the two five-digit numbers was shown during the study trial. Subjects are also instructed to make their selection as quickly as they can without making mistakes (Slick, Hopp, Strauss, & Thompson, 1997).

To date few researchers have investigated the scientific validity of this test; however, the VSVT is presumed to have almost 100% specificity, which is paramount in any test assessing symptom validity. Additionally, because the VSVT cutoff scores are based on binomial probability theory and are not norm-referenced, it is very unlikely that a patient who scores in the invalid range on the VSVT will do so for any reason other than response bias or malingering (Slick et al., 1997). A 2013 study of 404 patients with medically intractable epilepsy has also suggested that the VSVT hard item scores may be impacted by working memory difficulties and/or low intellectual functioning (Keary et al., 2013). Further, examining the ability of the VSVT to discriminate between a control group and a group of simulated malingerers, researchers found that the VSVT exhibited excellent sensitivity and specificity as it correctly classified 88% of the controls and 89% of the simulated malingerers (Strauss et al. 2000). It has also been suggested that much higher cutoffs scores than those originally recommended for the VSVT by the developers based on binomial probability theory can produce excellent classification and diagnostic accuracies when a psychometrically defined nonmalingering group is compared with two psychometrically defined malingering groups (Probable and Probable to Definite; Jones, 2013b). The results from this study also indicated that while reaction times have some utility, they are constrained by a lack of sensitivity (Jones, 2013b).

9.4.5 Word Memory Test

The WMT is a computer-based test that is designed to measure both verbal memory and biased responding (malingering). It measures memory on a number of dimensions and contains hidden scales that serve to check the validity of the person's test scores. More specifically, this test was designed to assess a person's ability to learn a list of 20 word pairs and to evaluate a person's effort to perform well during testing.

The claims for validity advanced by the authors of this test are scientifically provocative. It has been suggested that effort, as measured by the WMT, (a) explains a substantial portion of variance in cognitive outcome after TBI and (b) interacts with injury severity to produce patterns of scores after TBI that cannot be explained by injury severity alone (Green, Lees-Haley, & Allen, 2002). Research findings on the diagnostic efficacy of the WMT, however, have been mixed. For example, a functional magnetic resonance imaging (fMRI) study employing the WMT has suggested that this test activates numerous cortical regions that are critical for cognitive effort. More specifically, given the extensive neural network necessary to perform the WMT, this study raised questions about what a WMT failure truly means in patients with TBI, who have an increased likelihood of disruption within this neural network of vision, language, attention, effort, and working memory (Allen, Bigler, Larsen, Goodrich-Hunsaker, & Hopkins, 2007). In contrast, a study assessing the individual and joint malingering detection accuracy of the PDRT, TOMM, and WMT has shown that at published cutoff scores, the PDRT and TOMM are very specific. In addition, joint classification accuracy was superior to that of the individual tests (Greve et al., 2008). Also, according to Green (2003), the WMT is failed more often by people with mild than severe brain injury. Finally, it has been suggested that this test is fairly resistant to attempts at coaching (Dunn et al., 2003).

9.4.6 Rey 15-Item Memory Test

The Rey-15 consists of five rows of three characters each on a card (e.g., A B C, 1 2 3) (see Figure 9.1). Subjects are shown the card for 10 seconds and told to study it carefully in order to later recall as many of the items as possible. The Rey-15 is presented to subjects as a very difficult memory test but is, in fact, very simple because of the redundancy among items. Therefore, even individuals with significant impairments can perform the test without difficulty. However, it is assumed that malingerers will not know this. Instead, they will reason that, in order to register a result of being memory impaired, they should recall only a few items (Reznek, 2005).

Research findings have established some variability in performance among individuals with genuine memory impairment. Consequently, different cutoff scores have been proposed. For example, Lezak (1995) argued that only in cases of severe brain damage should an individual be unable to recall fewer than nine items, while Lee and colleagues (1992) concluded that a cutoff score of 7 should arouse suspicion of malingering of mental deficits. Research studies have also indicated that adjusting the cutoff higher increases the Rey-15's sensitivity but decreases its specificity; therefore, a cutoff score of 7 has been recommend to increase diagnostic efficiency (Lee, Lohring, & Martin, 1992).

A meta-analysis of available studies using the Rey-15 has shown that this test has high specificity but low sensitivity (with a cutoff score of 7 the specificity is 95% and the sensitivity is 10%; with a cutoff score of 8 the specificity decreases to 92% and the sensitivity decreases to 9%; when employing the usual cutoff score of 9 the specificity drops to 85% and the sensitivity increases to 36%; Rezneck, 2005). Indeed, Rüsseler, Brett, Klaue, Sailer, and Münte (2008) contend that the sensitivity of the Rey-15 is too low for clinical use in the assessment of malingering, while Vallabhajosula

Figure 9.1 Illustration of the Rey-15

and van Gorp (2001) have argued that if used as a single procedure, this test appears to be insufficiently sensitive to detect malingering of cognitive impairment, irrespective of the cutoff score applied. Ideally, a test designed to detect malingering of cognitive deficits should be sensitive to malingering but insensitive to genuine cognitive dysfunction. The Rey-15 falls short of this ideal precisely because of its sensitivity to genuine impairment (Vallabhajosula & van Gorp, 2001).

9.4.7 California Verbal Learning Test

The CVLT is a list-learning task that requires the subject to learn a list of 16 words throughout five trials and evaluates recall and recognition after a delay. Unlike some neuropsychological tests, the CVLT quantifies numerous cognitive components of verbal learning memory within a single test. More specifically, it examines retroactive and proactive interference in a number of ways, as well as the strategy that the individual employs to remember information presented to him or her verbally (Lezak, Howieson, & Loring, 2004). Although the CVLT is among the most frequently used methods for evaluating learning, its utility in the detection of cognitive malingering has also been investigated. In fact, this test is presumed to be effective in detecting malingering because malingerers often overestimate the amount of memory impairment that is associated with head injuries and disorders characterized by brain pathology (Coleman, Rapport, Millis, Ricker & Farchione, 1998).

In 1994, Trueblood examined the classification accuracy of Total Correct from Trials 1 through 5 (Total 1–5) and Recognition Hits using a known-groups design of mild TBI patients and found the CVLT's sensitivity to be approximately 70%, with a false positive error rate of 5% to 10%. Millis and Kler (1995), also using a known-groups design, studied the same two variables along with Long Delay Cued Recall and Recognition Discriminability and correctly identified about 85% of TBI patients, with a false positive error rate of only about 8%. In contrast, the CVLT has demonstrated an average sensitivity of 51% in clinical TBI patients and 64% in simulators, with an average false positive error rate in moderate-severe TBI of about 15% (Sweet et al., 2000). In another study the CVLT was shown to have 80% sensitivity and 97% specificity in correctly identifying patients attempting to feign memory deficits (Delis, Kramer, Kaplan, & Ober, 2000). More recently, however, this test was found to have sensitivity of only 50% but excellent specificity (> 95%; Curtis, Greve, Bianchini, & Brennan, 2006). The Forced Choice Recognition and the Critical Item Analysis indices of the second edition of the CVLT have also been identified as being potentially useful brief screening indicators of effort or malingering in neuropsychological assessment. Indeed, while a negative finding should not be relied on as evidence of adequate effort, a positive finding, in the absence of frank dementia, is strongly suggestive of inadequate effort and indicates the need for further testing (Root, Robbins, Chang, & van Gorp, 2006).

9.4.8 Wechsler Adult Intelligence Scale, Third Edition

Numerous investigators have sought to determine if the Digit Span (DS) subtest of the Wechsler Adult Intelligence Scale (third edition; WAIS-III) can accurately detect feigned cognitive impairment. For example, Mathias, Greve, Bianchini, Houston, and Crouch (2002), using the DS subtest as an indictor of effort in patients with TBI, obtained a 67% sensitivity rate and a 93% specificity rate. In contrast, using a cutoff score of ≤7 on this subtest yielded an overall correct classification rate of 62.5% with a false positive rate of 0% (Schwarz, Gfeller, & Olivieri, 2006), while Strauss and colleagues (2002) obtained a 47% true positive rate and a false positive rate of 5%. Iverson and Tulsky (2003) examined the WAIS-III Vocabulary and DS indicators of six clinical groups with chronic alcohol abuse, Korsakoff's syndrome, left temporal lobectomy, right temporal lobectomy, TBI, and dementia of the Alzheimer's type. Their findings provide further support that it is clinically rare for individuals with neurological impairment to score below the established DS cutoff scores that are indicative of low effort.

Researchers have also utilized discrepancy scores between the DS and Vocabulary subtests on the Wechsler Adult Intelligence Scale–Revised and the WAIS-III to detect malingering. For example, using the WAIS-III Vocabulary–DS subtests discrepancy cutoff of ≥2 (established by Mittenberg, Fichera, Zielinski, & Heilbronner, 1995) has shown to yield an overall correct classification rate of 78.1%. However, while the classification rate was relatively high, the Vocabulary–DS discrepancy score also produced a false positive rate of 36.6%. Thus an unacceptably high number of individuals who were not malingering impairment were labeled as malingerers.

9.5 Tests Designed to Assess General Response Style

9.5.1 Miller Forensic Assessment of Symptoms Test

This brief, structured interview contains 25 items and is designed to detect malingering by assessing an individual's general response style. The Miller Forensic Assessment of Symptoms Test (M-FAST) contains seven subscale scores and an overall total score. The seven subscales are based on strategies used to detect malingerers: reported versus observed symptoms, extreme symptoms, rare combinations, unusual hallucinations, unusual symptom course, negative image, and suggestibility. A cutoff total score of 6 has been used to suggest dishonest responding, and research using the M-FAST has found this cut score to be most effective (Miller, Guy, & Davila, 2000; Miller, 2001). Examining the ability of the

M-FAST to differentiate a group of undergraduate students simulating schizophrenia, bipolar, major depressive, and posttraumatic stress disorder from a clinical sample comprising individuals with the same diagnosis, Guy, Kwartner, and Miller (2006) found that (a) across all diagnostic conditions, the simulators obtained higher M-FAST total scores than the clinical comparison group and (b) the M-FAST was most efficient at distinguishing feigned from genuine schizophrenia. In addition, while the internal consistency of the total score was high ($\alpha = 0.88$), the inter-item correlations were lower than the values reported in previous research; however, the M-FAST was able to identify malingerers even at relatively low base rates (Guy et al., 2006).

9.5.2 Diagnosis of Antisocial Personality Disorder and Psychopathy

As previously noted, the *DSM–IV–TR* (American Psychiatric Association, 2000) advises that malingering should be considered whenever there is a lack of cooperation, the distress reported exceeds observed disability, or APD is present. Indeed, studies have shown that criminal defendants diagnosed with APD score significantly higher than defendants diagnosed with a personality disorder other than APD or no personality disorder on validated measures of malingering (Kucharski, Falkenbach, & Duncan, 2004). However, Kucharski and colleagues also found that a high percentage (>40%) of those diagnosed with APD did not score above accepted cutoffs for suspecting malingering and that a diagnosis of APD was, in fact, a poor discriminator of malingerers from those believed to be responding honestly.

Although there is little research that supports this association, it has been suggested that a diagnosis of psychopathy may be a good indicator of malingering. For example, Poythress, Edens, and Watkins (2001) found that psychopathic prison inmates were no better at avoiding detection of malingering than nonpsychopathic subjects. Subjects with severe psychopathy were also found to score higher than those with low psychopathy on measures of malingering. However, these findings are significantly diminished by the observation that while psychopaths score higher on validated measures of malingering, a high proportion of those with severe psychopathy did not show evidence of exaggeration (Kucharski et al., 2006). Based on these findings, Kucharski and colleagues concluded that while psychopathy appears to discriminate malingerers from nonmalingerers, the relatively poor sensitivity and specificity of psychopathy calls into question its clinical and forensic utility in the detection of malingering. More specifically, "there is a strong likelihood that the reliance on psychopathy as a basis for opining that a defendant is malingering would not clear any evidentiary standard for admissibility if a test of its scientific merit were conducted (Kucharski et al., 2006, p. 642).

9.6 Tests Designed to Assess Malingering of Psychiatric Disorders/Symptoms

9.6.1 Structured Inventory of Malingered Symptomatology

The Structured Inventory of Malingered Symptomatology (SIMS) is a self-report measure designed to screen for malingering of psychiatric symptoms, such as psychosis or depression, and/or cognitive impairments, such as memory complaints and low intelligence. The SIMS consists of 75 dichotomous (i.e., true/false) items that can be grouped into five subscales, each subscale containing 15 items. Subscales tap malingered symptoms in the following areas: low intelligence, affective disorders, neurological impairment, psychosis, and amnestic disorders (Merckelbach & Smith, 2003; Smith & Burger, 1997). As noted in the Test Manual, internal consistency alpha coefficients for all SIMS scales range from .82 (Psychosis scale) to .88 (Total score), while test–retest reliability was adequate ($r = .72$) for the Total score over a 3-week interval. The SIMS has also demonstrated moderate to high correlations with other indexes of malingering, including the MMPI-2 validity scales ($r = -.47-.50$), the SIRS scales ($r = .43-.80$), and the M-Fast ($r = .58-.67$). Furthermore, in the SIMS cross-validation sample, efficiency was found to be .95, while sensitivity and specificity were .96 and .88, respectively (Smith & Burger, 1997).

Previously recommended SIMS total cutoff scores (>14 or >16) have shown to have excellent sensitivity but low specificity (Clegg, Fremouw, & Mogge, 2009). Further, in a 2008 study, both the M-FAST and SIMS were found to have high sensitivity and NPP when discriminating probable psychiatric feigning versus honest groups, suggesting effectiveness in screening for this condition. However, neither tests were effective when applied to probable neurocognitive feigners versus honest groups, suggesting caution when using these tests for this purpose (Alwes, Clark, Berry, & Granacher, 2008). In addition, a study in which undergraduate students were administered the TOMM and the SIMS and asked to respond honestly or instructed to feign cognitive dysfunction due to head injury showed that both tests were relatively resistant to coaching (Jelicic, Ceunen, Peters, & Merckelbach, 2011). Finally, research findings have suggested that a higher cutoff score on the SIMS for identification of malingering may be appropriate for use with a forensic population (Wisdom, Callahan, & Shaw, 2010).

9.6.2 Structured Interview of Reported Symptoms

The SIRS was developed to assist in the evaluation of feigning of psychosis. It is administered orally, in less than an hour, and includes interpretation instructions. This 172-item generalized measure of feigning mental illness includes eight primary scales and five supplementary scales. Scores from the primary scales are classified into one of four categories: honest responding, indeterminate, probable feigning, and definite feigning (Rogers, Bagby, & Dickens, 1992). Rogers and colleagues' validation study yielded a PPP of 99% and a NPP of 64.9% with a base rate of 51%. With a base rate of 20% to 25%, PPP remained in the range of 96% to 97%, while the NPP increased to between 86% and 89%. Further, the SIRS manual, summarizing the studies available at the time of its publication, states that the SIRS sensitivity is 48.5% and its specificity is 99.5%. Therefore, if the recommended cutoff scores are used, the scale tends to underidentify malingering but is unlikely to falsely identify an individual as malingering (Rogers, Bagby, & Dickens, 1992). The relatively low sensitivity supports the developers' recommendation that the SIRS be used in conjunction with other indicators of malingering. Meta-analyses revealed that research published since the initial validation studies demonstrate higher sensitivity but lower specificity rates than those reported in the SIRS manual (Green & Rosenfeld, 2011). Studies in which feigners were composed of simulators yielded higher classification rates than studies sampling actual suspected malingerers. Furthermore, genuine patient samples were significantly more likely than nonclinical samples to be misclassified as feigning. Abbreviated versions of the SIRS also demonstrated equivalent accuracy with the standard measure (Green & Rosenfeld, 2011).

Most recently, Green, Rosenfeld, and Belfi (2013) evaluated the accuracy of the second edition of the SIR (SIRS-2) in a criterion-group study using a sample of forensic psychiatric patients and a community simulation sample, comparing it to the original SIRS and to results published in the SIRS-2 manual. The SIRS-2 yielded an impressive specificity rate (94.3%) that exceeded that obtained using the original SIRS scoring method (92.0%) and approached that observed in the SIRS-2 normative data (97.5%). However, changes in scoring resulted in markedly lower sensitivity rates of the SIRS-2 (36.8% among forensic patients and 66.7% among simulators) compared with the SIRS (47.4% and 75.0%, respectively; Green et al., 2013). Further, a study focusing on the applicability of the original and revised versions of the SIRS in a sample of participants with genuine intellectual disabilities, all of whom were asked to respond honestly, found that a considerable proportion of these respondents were misclassified as feigning psychiatric symptoms. These misclassifications were most frequent when the respondents had comorbid psychiatric diagnoses. The updated scoring algorithm of the SIRS-2 generated a rate of misclassifications that was substantially lower but that still exceeded published normative data (Weiss, Rosenfeld, & Farkas, 2011).

9.7 Tests Designed to Assess Malingering of Personality Disorders

9.7.1 Minnesota Multiphasic Personality Inventory-2

The MMPI-2 is one of the most widely used personality tests designed to assist mental health professionals in identifying psychopathology and personality structure. Further, validity indicators, in particular the F scales (F, Fb, Fp) and the F-K ratio, can be used to generate hypotheses regarding the potential for malingering. Although the MMPI-2 and its predecessor the MMPI were not constructed to identify the presence of malingering specifically, a substantial body of research has focused on the utility of these indicators to detect malingering. For example, a meta-analysis has found the F scale to be an effective scale but questioned the routine use of Fb (Rogers, Sewell, Martin, & Vitacco 2003). Similarly, the F scale has proven to be the best at distinguishing psychiatric patients from research participants instructed to malinger (Bagby, Nicholson, Bacchiochi, Ryder, & Bury, 2002). Further, a study by Kucharski and colleagues (2004) revealed that neither the Fp scale nor the revised Fp scale added to the F scale in predicting group membership. More specifically, the F scale alone correctly classified 80.8% of cases with no incremental accuracy added by either Fp or the revised Fp.

Investigations of detection of malingering in neuropsychological settings have also demonstrated superior sensitivity of the Fake Bad scale in comparison to F and related scales (e.g., Larrabee, 2003; Nelson, Sweet, & Demakis, 2006). However, other authors have expressed concern over the scale's specificity. More specifically, Butcher, Arbisi, Atlis, and McNulty (2003) concluded that the scale "is likely to classify an unacceptably large number of individuals who are experiencing genuine psychological distress as malingerers" (p. 473).[13] Furthermore, the F scale is not intended to assess cognitive effort and is generally thought to be insensitive to feigning of neurocognitive impairment (Greene, 2000; Larrabee, 2003). In addition, it has been suggested that the MMPI-2 validity scales are measuring a different construct than tests of malingered memory deficits and therefore should be interpreted with caution (McCaffrey, O'Bryant, Ashendorf, & Fisher, 2003). Although numerous studies have found that the F and F-K ratio indices demonstrate large effect sizes for discriminating between honest respondents and those who are feigning, cutoff scores for detecting malingering have greatly varied across these studies (Greene, 2000; Rogers et al., 2003). Regardless of the cutoff scores being used, however, the F-K ratio was found to lack sufficient scientific validity to be relied on as a measure of malingering (e.g., Boccaccini, Murrie, & Duncan, 2006).

A new version of the MMPI-2, the MMPI-2-Restructured Form (RF), also includes validity scales (L-r and K-r) designed to assess underreporting of symptoms (Ben-Porath, 2012).[14] Research data has indicated that the L-r and K-r are able to differentiate between individuals instructed to underreport from those who responded honestly. More specifically, the effect sizes derived from this study were mean $ds = 1.19$ and 1.13 for L and K, respectively (Sellbom & Bagby, 2008). In addition, results from a sample of 125 criminal defendants who were administered the MMPI-2-RF and the SIRS during their evaluations showed that the two MMPI-2-RF validity scales specifically designed to detect overreported psychopathology, F-r and F(P)-r, best differentiated between the malingering and nonmalingering groups (Sellbom,

Toomey, Wygant, Kurcharski, & Duncan, 2010). Also, examining the effectiveness of the MMPI-2-RF for differentiating feigned mental disorder and feigned cognitive impairment in patients with genuine disorders, Rogers and colleagues (2011) found that most MMPI-2-RF validity scales had limited effectiveness with the feigned cognitive impairment group (Rogers, Gillard, Berry, & Granacher, 2011).

9.7.2 Millon Clinical Multiaxial Inventory, Third Edition

This inventory includes 175 true/false items scored on 24 content scales intended to correspond to major *Diagnostic and Statistical Manual of Mental Disorders* (fourth edition) Axis I disorders, such as autism, Axis II personality disorders, and mental retardation. The two scales most often used to detect malingering are the Disclosure Index, which assesses willingness to admit to difficulties, and the Debasement Index, which identifies a tendency to overstate emotional and personal problems. Although the test's manual proposes that raw scores above 178 on the Disclosure Index denote excessive symptom exaggeration, no cutoff scores are recommended for use with the Debasement Index beyond the suggestion that base rate scores above 85 tend to be associated with malingering (Millon, Davis, & Millon, 1997). Few studies have examined the ability of the MCMI-III to detect malingering, and those that have reported poor classification accuracy for this measure (e.g., Daubert & Metzler, 2000; Schoenberg, Dorr, & Morgan, 2003).

9.7.3 Personality Assessment Inventory

This 344-item self-administered inventory is organized into 11 clinical scales (Somatic Complaints, Anxiety-Related Disorders, Depression, Mania, Paranoia, Schizophrenia, Borderline Features, Antisocial Features, Alcohol Problems, Drug Problems), five treatment scales (Aggression, Suicidal Ideation, Stress, Nonsupport, Treatment Rejection), and two interpersonal style scales (Dominance and Warmth). It also contains four validity scales (Inconsistency, Infrequency, Negative Impression (NIM), and Positive Impression (PIM), and four additional validity indexes (Malingering Index [MAL], Rogers Discriminant Function [RDF], Defensiveness Index, Cashel Discriminant Function) that have been developed since the original introduction of the PAI (Morey, 1996). In addition, the PAI has norms based on correctional populations, which is something the MMPI-2 lacks (Morey, 1996). It has been suggested that the PAI is useful as a measure of psychopathology in forensic settings for the following three reasons: (a) completion of the PAI requires only a fourth-grade reading level, (b) it is not limited to those fluent in English, and (c) it provides broad assessment of response styles, including carelessness, random responding and minimization, or exaggeration of symptoms (Edens, Hart, Johnson, Johnson, & Oliver, 2000).

Bagby, Nicholson, Bacchiochi, Ryder, and Bury (2002), found the RDF to be clearly superior to other PAI validity indicators for use with a nonforensic population. In fact, neither the NIM scale nor the MAL effectively detected malingered profiles. In contrast, a regression analysis using malingering versus nonmalingering as criterion found that the NIM scale but not the RDF or the MAL significantly differentiated the malingering from the nonmalingering group (Kucharski, Toomey, Fila, & Duncan, 2007). Further, it has been suggested that the NIM scale has the greatest utility as a faking detection scale as the level of pathology increases, while the RDF scale is better suited to identify subtler and/or more sophisticated attempts at feigning that go overlooked by the NIM scale (Morey & Lanier, 1998; Rogers, Sewell, Morey, & Ustad, 1996). Indeed, the NIM and RDF scales were found to be most sensitive to unsophisticated attempts to dissimulate by inpatient psychiatric patients (Baity, Siefert, Chambers, & Blais, 2007).

To date, few studies have examined the ability of the PAI to detect malingering in a forensic sample. However, one study, using the SIRS to classify forensic patients as honest or malingering, found that with the recommended cutoff score of ≥77 the NIM correctly classified 84% of malingerers and 74% of honest respondents. MAL was clearly less effective as a screening measure, with a cutoff score of ≥3 correctly identifying only 47% of malingerers and 86% of honest respondents. The performance of RDF was also poor, with the recommended cutoff score correctly identifying only 51% of malingers and 72% of honest respondents (Rogers, Ustad, & Salekin, 1998). In addition, with the recommend cutoff score of ≥77, the NIM was found to have 91% sensitivity, 65% specificity, PPP of 53%, and NPP of 95%, while the MAL, with the recommended cutoff score of ≥5, demonstrated 13% sensitivity, 97% specificity, PPP of 67%, and NPP of 72% (Boccaccini et al., 2006). Finally, Dell'Anno & Shiva (2006) found a positive correlation between the NIM scale score and the category of crime and a positive correlation between the MAL index and crime severity and concluded that as the severity of the crime increases, so does the likelihood of malingering of symptoms for secondary gain.

9.8 Other Techniques Used to Detect Malingering

As previously noted, measures designed to assess malingering have become an integral part of many neuropsychological assessments, especially in forensic settings. However, because many malingering measures have been found to be vulnerable to coaching and manipulation, research studies have attempted to identify physiological indices of cognitive functioning that are less susceptible to overt manipulation.

9.8.1 Polygraph Test

Current technologies for detecting malingering/deception are epitomized by the polygraph test, a test that measures the activity of a subject's autonomic nervous system (galvanic skin response, respiration rate, heart rate, etc.) in response to questions. More specifically, the polygraph rests on the assumption that psychophysiological changes consisting of increases in heart rate, respiratory rate, and electrical conductivity of the skin in response to certain questions are the result of deception/lying, rather than other mental states, such as fear of being suspected or fear of being tested. However, the polygraph test does not directly measure brain activity associated with deception and is subject to countermeasures by knowledgeable and/or trained subjects. In addition, the scientific basis and validity of the polygraph test is often challenged, and results of polygraph tests are not admissible as evidence in criminal court proceedings. Furthermore, critics of polygraph testing worry that some criminals may be able to stay calm during the examination, while innocent people who are vulnerable to anxiety and/or intimidation may appear to be deceptive because their stress level rises while undergoing the polygraph examination. Finally, the polygraph test is considered by the US National Academy of Sciences to be unreliable (Adelson, 2004).

9.8.2 Electroencephalograph

Another strategy used to detect malingering has been to identify psychophysiological markers associated with deception using electroencephalogram (EEG) recording to measure event-related potentials (ERPs). An ERP is an averaged EEG signal recorded from the scalp that appears in response to a discrete event, such as presentation of or psychological reaction to a stimulus. Research studies have attempted to demonstrate that the ERPs can be used to detect deception in human subjects. More specifically, these efforts have focused on developing ERPs, specifically the P300, a positive ERP component with a latency of at least 300 ms, as a tool to reveal when a subject has certain information in his or her memory. To date, a number of studies have investigated the application of P300 and the pattern of visual evoked potentials to detect malingering of memory impairment (Rosenfeld, Sweet, Chuang, Ellwanger, & Song, 1996; Tardiff, Barry, & Johnstone, 2002). Results from research studies have been mixed and limited in part by the relatively rare inclusion of a neurologic patient group answering honestly. For example, Vagnini, Berry, Clark, and Jiang (2008) found that the ERP mean amplitude was largest for honestly responding healthy adults and that the effect of malingering in non-brain-injured subjects reduced ERP mean amplitude, such that these subjects looked similar to subjects with TBI. Other studies, however, found that malingerers had a larger P300 than subjects who responded honestly (Ellwanger, Tenhula, Rosenfeld, & Sweet, 1999).

Although this technique has not yet been found to be scientifically valid under *Daubert* or *Frye*, it was successfully used in 2000 to free Terry Harrington after he had served 22 years of a life sentence for a murder he did not commit (*Harrington v. State, 2001*). EEG is presumed to be a particularly good indicator of neural abnormality due to its objective nature and inability to fake (Gaetz & Bernstein, 2001). Indeed, ERP components (< 300 ms) are an excellent measure of neural abnormalities because they reflect early and automated attentional processes that are affected by brain pathology (Reinvang, Nordby, & Nielsen, 2000; Rowe, 2005). More specifically, these early automated processes precede the subject's conscious awareness of the need to respond (Libet, 2002; Pollen, 2004) and therefore cannot be faked. However, the low spatial resolution inherent in ERP methodology limits the ability to localize the underlying brain regions involved in deception (Gonzalez-Andino, Blank, Lantz, Thut, & Grave de Peralta Menendez, 2001).

9.8.3 Magnetic Resonance Imaging

Structural MRI studies have demonstrated increases in frontal white matter, particularly in the orbitofrontal lobes, in populations with marked deceitful traits as measured by the Psychopathy Checklist–Revised. For example, Yang and colleagues (2007) examined white matter volumes in four prefrontal sub-regions using MRI in 10 pathological liars, 14 antisocial controls, and 20 normal controls and found that pathological liars showed a relatively widespread increase in white matter (23%–36%) in orbitofrontal, middle, and inferior but not superior frontal gyri compared with normal and antisocial controls. In another study, liars showed a 22% to 26% increase in prefrontal white matter and a 36% to 42% reduction in prefrontal grey/white ratios compared with both antisocial controls and normal controls (Yang et al., 2005, 2007). In contrast, a 2006 study comparing individuals with conduct disorder with normal youths did not find prefrontal differences in lying youths but did find suggestion of corpus callosum difference (Kruesi & Casanova, 2006).

9.8.4 Functional Magnetic Resonance Imaging

An association between ERP and lying on a standard test, such as the Guilty Knowledge Test, suggests that deception may be associated with changes in other measures of brain activity such as regional blood flow (Langleben et al., 2002; Mochizuki, Oishi, & Takasu, 2001). As discussed in chapter 3, fMRI enables researchers to create maps of the brain in action as it processes thoughts, sensations, motor commands, and memories. More recently, researchers have claimed that fMRI can provide insight into the cognitive operations behind behaviors, such as malingering. For example, fMRI studies have examined neural activity under task situations that are presumed to approximate the malingering of cognitive deficits, specifically, purposefully poor performance on visual memory tasks (i.e., malingered omissive memory errors) and confabulatory-like false endorsement of task foil stimuli (i.e., malingered inclusive memory errors; Abe et al., 2006; Lee et al., 2002). These studies have shown that the prefrontal cortex in particular plays a predominant role in deception (see, e.g., Spence et al., 2001). More specifically, converging evidence from various sources has suggested that the prefrontal cortex organizes the processes of inhibiting true responses and making deceptive responses, which is consistent with the hypothesis that lying involves executive control processes, in particular working memory (Christ, Van Essen, Watson, Brubaker, & McDermott, 2009). More recently, research findings have indicated that the bilateral dorsolateral prefrontal cortex extending to the middle frontal gyrus, the left inferior parietal lobe, and the bilateral anterior cingulate gyrus/medial superior frontal gyrus are associated with deception among offenders with APD (Jiang et al., 2013; see also Figure 9.2).

The hypothesis underlying fMRI as a lie detector is that telling the truth is a normal response of the brain and one would not expect to see increased activity over and above the normal background level of brain activity. However, when a subject begins to prevaricate, more brain activity is needed and more oxygenated blood is directed to those areas of the brain that are processing the deception (Woodruff, 2010). In other words, the absence of this blood-oxygen-level dependent response in those areas of the brain associated with deception is presumed to be an indication of the truthfulness of a subject's responses (Bles & Haynes, 2008). However, despite these research findings, using fMRI to detect deception is problematic for a number of reasons. Research has shown the following:

- Studies have a limited number of participants and lack diversity, thus little is known about whether or how exactly the results obtained may differ across a large and diverse population.

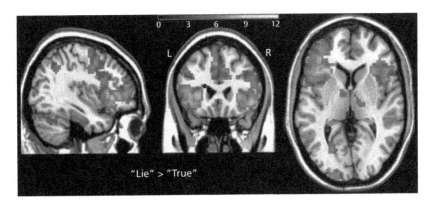

Figure 9.2 Brain Regions Showing Increased Activity During Lying. Brain regions found to be involved in lying, as assessed with blood-oxygen-level dependent fMRI: the insula bilaterally, the middle temporal gyrus bilaterally, the left supplementary motor areas, the left occipital gyrus, the left supramarginal gyrus, the right inferior frontal gyrus, the right middle frontal gyrus, and the right cerebellum. See Color Plate 26 in insert.

Open Access Publications: Marchewka, A., Jednorog, K., Falkiewicz, M., Szeszkowski, W., Grabowska, A., & Szatkowska, I. (2012). Sex, lies and fMRI—Gender differences in neural basis of deception. *PLoSOne*, 7(8), e43076.

- Group-averaged studies have shown that on average certain areas of the brain are more active during lying than during truth-telling; however, group-averaged studies do not directly address whether a particular subject is lying at a particular time.
- Studies that have attempted to apply models built from group-averaged studies to individual responses have met with some success, reporting accuracies from 76% to 90%, specificities of 42% to 85%, and sensitivities of 69% to 85%.
- The replication of studies has been difficult due to variance in the methodologies employed.
- All current studies lack ecological validity and have failed to address the issue of countermeasures (Adelsheim, 2011).

Furthermore, just because the prefrontal cortex is activated during deception does not mean that every time the prefrontal cortex activates the individual is lying (Fox, 2009). Also, assuming that increased blood flow in specific brain regions denotes deception, scientists have yet to agree with some degree of precision as to what these specific regions are (Gerard, 2008). In addition, it has been argued that the current status of fMRI studies on lie detection meets neither basic scientific nor legal standards (Rusconi & Mitchener-Nissen, 2013). Indeed, a recent fMRI study showed that activity patterns in specific prefrontal regions can distinguish lies from truth-telling with great accuracy in individual subjects; however, that same study showed that when experimenters instructed the subjects to use countermeasures designed to defeat the test, there was a dramatic reduction in the ability of fMRI responses to distinguish lies from truth (Ganis, Rosenfeld, Meixner, Kievit, & Schendan, 2011). Since countermeasures are a significant concern in real-world settings, the authors of this study, consequently, advised caution in applying fMRI-based lie detection outside the laboratory (Ganis et al., 2011). Finally, fMRI lie detection is still in its infancy, and only limited conclusions can be drawn from the various studies undertaken to date (Pardo, 2006).

9.8.5 Positron Emission Tomography

Findings of the involvement of the prefrontal cortex have also been supported by studies that have used PET to detect deception. For example, Abe, Suzuki, Mori, Itoh, and Fujii (2007) found that the left dorsolateral and right anterior prefrontal cortices were associated with the process of falsifying the truthful responses, while the left ventromedial prefrontal cortex and amygdala were associated with the process of deceiving the interrogator. Further, a study comparing the pattern of brain activities of two men with hysterical motor symptoms affecting their left arm and two healthy individuals who were instructed to feign difficulty moving their upper left limbs, as well as six healthy individuals who did movement tasks normally, found that malingerers had hypoactivity of the right anterior prefrontal cortex (Spence, Crimlisk,

Cope, Ron, & Grasby, 2000). To date, however, the evidence of the relationship between malingering and pattern of brain activities as documented with PET is weak at best.

As previously noted, the use of neuroscience in the search for truth presents evidentiary problems of, for example, causation, validity, and inferential conclusions unsupported by data. These problems are equally important to consider when using EEG and neuroimaging techniques to assess deception/malingering. This is particularly true in light of the fact that (a) research findings have suggested that fMRI lie-detection evidence may lead to more guilty verdicts than lie-detection evidence based on, for example, polygraph evidence or a control condition that did not include lie-detection evidence, and (b) when the validity of the fMRI lie detection evidence was called into question on cross-examination, guilty verdicts were reduced to the level of the control condition (McCabe, Castel, & Rhodes, 2011).

9.9 Malingering and the Law

There is no doubt that the assessment of malingering in the forensic context must be comprehensive and should not rely on a single test, measure, or technique because of the consequences associated with a misclassification. Therefore, in addition to the standard clinical interview, acquiring collateral information to verify the veracity of a claim of cognitive impairment or mental illness is crucial. Although the evaluation of malingering occurs in many criminal cases, to date it has not been specifically addressed in statute. However, in terms of case law, *United States v. Greer* (1998), a federal case decided by the Fifth Circuit Court of Appeals, clearly emphasizes the importance of malingering assessment. Consider the following.

In 1994 Greer was arraigned on federal charges of kidnapping and firearms violations. State charges had initially been dismissed after Greer was determined to be incompetent as the result of a mental disorder. The federal prosecutor pursued the case, and Greer was hospitalized at a federal medical center for mental health evaluation. The evaluating psychologist testified that Greer was competent and malingering psychopathology and cognitive impairment, and the judge consequently ruled that Greer was competent. However, Greer was so disruptive in jail while awaiting trial that he was reevaluated on an outpatient basis, ruled to be incompetent after another hearing, and committed to a different federal medical center for restoration of competence. After a period of hospitalization Greer was evaluated again by a psychologist, who concluded that Greer was malingering and competent. A third competency hearing was held, and the court agreed that Greer was malingering and competent. Geer was eventually convicted on all counts.

At sentencing, the government asked the court to increase the offense level for purposes of sentencing pursuant to the US Sentencing Guidelines based on the premise that Greer had obstructed justice by pretending to be incompetent. The court granted an enhancement and increased the sentence from 185 to 210 months. Greer appealed to the US Fifth Circuit Court of Appeals, claiming that the sentence enhancement undercut his right to be tried only if competent. The appellate court affirmed the finding of obstruction of justice by malingering, reasoning that malingering constitutes obstruction of justice because it involves egregiously wrong behavior that requires a significant amount of planning and inherent high risk that justice will indeed be obstructed. The court ruled that feigning incompetency is similar to altering evidence and creating a false record: "A defendant who playacts . . . essentially tries to create a record that includes inaccurate testimony and factual conclusions" (*United States v. Greer*, 1998, p. 235).

The publication of a National Academy of Neuropsychology position paper on symptom validity assessment also recognizes the importance of considering the appraisal of effort in neuropsychological practice, stating: "clinicians should be prepared to justify a decision not to assess symptom validity as part of a neuropsychological evaluation" (Bush et al., 2005, p. 421). Furthermore, as Iverson (2003) stated in the context of forensic practice, "any neuropsychological evaluation that does not include careful consideration of the patient's motivation to give their best effort should be considered incomplete" (p. 138). Yet according to a survey, malingering tests failed to appear among the top 40 most frequently administered assessment instruments by practicing neuropsychologists (Rabin et al., 2005). Results from a 2006 meta-analysis also called into question the ability of psychologists to detect intentional lying by finding that psychologists are only slightly more accurate in detection deception than are student research participants (62% accuracy compared with 54%, respectively; Aamodt & Custer, 2006).

9.10 Conclusion

Jason Miears, after having pled pleaded guilty to charges of murder and aggravated robbery, was sentenced to 50 years in prison and subsequently filed an appeal challenging the trial court's admission of the state's expert witness testimony. More specifically, Miears contended that Dr. Skop had insufficient facts or data with which to form his opinion that Miears was malingering and that the opinion was, therefore, unreliable (*Miears v. State*, 2013). The Appellate Court affirmed the trial court's judgment and in doing so reasoned as follows.

Dr. Skop attempted five interviews with Miears, three of which were unsuccessful because Miears refused to cooperate. During the first interview, Miears appeared to be psychotic, had hallucinations or delusions, and became so agitated and threatening that Dr. Skop had to end the interview after 45 minutes. During the second interview, which lasted 75 minutes, Dr. Skop administered a malingering test, which indicated that Miears was, in fact, malingering. In reaching his opinion Dr. Skop also relied on the fact that during both interviews Miears was very uncooperative and exhibited aberrant and aggressive behavior. In addition, Miears's own expert described the malingering test given by the state's expert as the gold standard. Therefore, because Dr. Skop adequately demonstrated the basis for his testimony and refrained from offering an opinion he could not professionally justify, the trial court did not abuse its discretion in admitting his testimony (*Miears v. State*, 2013).

As both this case and the *Gigante* case highlight, judges and juries face a complex task when asked to assign weight to frequently conflicting scientific expert testimony. The assessment of the validity of neuropsychological testing, which is of particular importance in the forensic setting, is often accomplished by using tests specifically designed to assess the malingering or exaggeration of disorders and diseases or the presence of a valid effort. Indeed, because performance on neuropsychological measures of, for example, memory, attention, and cognitive functioning depend greatly on the amount of effort put forth, in the absence of demonstrated good effort the results may be meaningless or highly misleading (Green et al., 2002). In other words, unless clinicians administer tests of exaggeration or malingering of disorders and/or deficits as part of their neuropsychological evaluation, the results of neuropsychological tests must be interpreted with caution. Furthermore, since most tests of malingering are moderately sensitive (they will detect most though not all malingerers) but highly specific (few if any legitimate patients will fail them), using at least two and preferably three tests of effort has been recommended (Meyers & Volbracht, 2003). As has been noted by many scholars and systematized by the Slick et al. (1999) criteria, a formal diagnosis of malingering should be based on the integration of diverse clinical information. Indeed, while the research literature on malingering is ever expanding, our knowledge is still somewhat limited and, therefore, conclusions should be drawn conservatively, bearing in mind that evidence of malingering does not necessarily rule out neurological or psychological pathology (Conroy & Kwartner, 2006).

10

Neuroscience and the Law

> All scientific inquiry is subject to error, and it is far better to
> be aware of this, to study the sources in an attempt to reduce
> it, and to estimate the magnitude of such errors in findings,
> than to be ignorant of the errors concealed in the data.
>   (Hyman, Cobb, Feldman, Hart, & Stember, 1954, p. 4)

10.1 Introduction

The first publicized functional magnetic resonance imaging (fMRI) evidence admitted into a US court was used to prove that a murderer was a psychopath. In 2009 Brian Dugan, already serving a life sentence for two murders, was indicated in the 1983 rape and murder of Jeanine Nicarico. Dugan pleaded guilty to killing the young girl, and during the sentencing hearing Dugan's lawyer introduced fMRI scans as evidence that his client suffered from a clear case of psychopathy. In addition, according to the defense expert Dugan scored 37 out of 40 on the Hare Psychopathy Checklist, placing him in the 99.5 percentile. Dugan's lawyers hoped to use the fMRI brain scan images in an attempt to reduce sentencing from the death penalty to life in prison, arguing that Dugan was born with a mental illness, psychopathy, which should be considered a mitigating factor because it impaired his ability to control his behavior (Hughes, 2010).

The prosecution, with the help of its own expert Dr. Brodie, argued that a mental illness such as psychopathy does not mitigate the results of Dugan's actions and that a scan in 2009 could not accurately reflect the state of mind of someone in 1983. In fact, according to Dr. Brodie, relying on fMRI to draw conclusions about psychopathic behavior is a risky oversimplification of the workings of the brain. The brain is "a complex orchestra," Dr. Brodie testified, "and if all we're measuring is one instrument, we're missing the sound of the entire piece" (Gregory, 2009). The jury sentenced Dugan to death; however, in 2011 the Illinois governor abolished capital punishment, and Dugan's sentence was commuted to life in prison.

Functional brain imaging is frequently used in the neurosciences since it provides the means for identifying brain damage or disease in the absence of physical damage. However, as critics of functional brain imaging have pointed out, the results of these scans are not entirely dispositive, since a causal relationship between specific brain function and criminal behavior has not yet been definitively determined (Brown & Murphy, 2010). In fact, some scholars, troubled by defense attorneys using brain dysfunctions to demonstrate their clients lacked the requisite mens rea, have argued that the mind can still be guilty, since most people with brain defects or damage have some ability to restrain their actions (Lamparello, 2011). Other scholars have argued that "researchers, clinicians, and lawyers are seduced into becoming true believers in the merits of brain imaging for understanding the relationship between brain and behavior" (Tancredi & Brodie, 2007, p. 289), while critics have questioned the reliability and validity of the underlying science of functional neuroimaging (e.g., Aronson, 2010). Regardless of one's position, it is clear that neuroscientific techniques have and will continue to change the legal landscape, and, despite limits to the technology, defendants will continue to attempt to introduce neuroscience evidence at all points throughout the legal process (Snead, 2007).

Whether or not there is a direct link between a specific behavior and a brain structure or functional response has yet to be determined. Further, determining what is or is not a normal response when assessing brain function is complicated, and once something is determined to be atypical, understanding the implications of that atypicality frequently remains uncertain (Schweitzer & Saks, 2011). In addition, because brain function can change over time, a neuropsychological test or neuroimaging scan performed today does not necessarily tell us anything about the brain functioning at the time the criminal offense was committed. It has also been contended that no explanation of any kind, brain based or otherwise, has direct implications for mitigation, justification, or exculpation in law; legal responsibility for behavior is not a scientific finding—it is a legal conclusion (Schweitzer & Saks, 2011).

Most states have their own set of rules of evidence, with the majority relying on the Federal Rules of Evidence (FRE) in deciding whether or not to admit neuroscience-based evidence of cognitive impairment. To that end, the majority of courts consider three rules: (a) FRE 702, which governs the admission of expert testimony; (b) FRE 401, which requires the evidence to be relevant; and (c) FRE 403, which balances probative value against unfair prejudice. FRE 702 is of particular importance since it requires that expert testimony be sufficiently reliable. However, reliability is not merely a generalized concept about a particular technique's or test's functional accuracy; it is the specific concern about whether or not the proffered evidence is reliable as applied to a particular issue in question (Moriarty, 2008). Indeed, "reliability cannot be judged 'as drafted,' but must be judged only specifically 'as applied'" (Risinger, Saks, Thompson, & Rosenthal, 2002, p. 4).

While at present the admissibility of neuroscience-based evidence remains fluid, the courts' concerns regarding the scientific validity and evidentiary reliability of neuroimaging evidence in particular is clearly reflected in cases that have sought to admit evidence of cognitive, neurological, and psychological impairments. Indeed, numerous legal cases illustrate the trend toward utilizing neuroimaging evidence as objective evidence of brain injury and the difficulty surrounding admissibility of such evidence. Not surprisingly, a review of the current literature regarding such evidence proffered in a court of law reveals a broad array of positions taken by the courts and opinions expressed by expert witnesses. What follows is a discussion of various issues related to the admissibility of neuroscience evidence as illustrated by case law.

10.2 Admissibility of Neuroscience-Based Evidence

> Circuit Judge David Eddy ordered that a PET scan be
> performed on Michael Bargo and granted defense attorneys'
> motion to continue Bargo's trial. (Persaud, 2013)

Fueled by technological advances, neuroscience-based evidence has found its way into criminal trials and is now quite frequently offered to help resolve a number of issues, including competence and insanity (Applebaum, 2009; Erickson, 2010; Vincent, 2011). Indeed, neuroscientists are frequently called as expert witnesses in criminal cases to provide testimony concerning the cause and extent, if any, of cognitive impairment and/or psychological and psychiatric disorders and diseases. However, the admissibility of such testimony is often challenged as being scientifically unreliable under evidentiary standards established by the US Supreme Court. Although courts have yet to directly address the admissibility of many specific tests and measures, there are a number of legal cases that illustrate the inherent problems associated with expert opinions that are based on findings from neuropsychological test results and/or neuroimaging scans.

10.2.1 Ineffective Assistance of Counsel

The Sixth Amendment to the US Constitution gives a person who is being prosecuted for a crime the right to effective assistance of counsel. Claims of ineffective assistance of counsel are reviewed under a two-part test: (a) a demonstration that counsel's performance fell below an objective standard of reasonableness, based on prevailing professional norms and (b) a showing that the deficient performance resulted in prejudice (*Strickland v. Washington*,

1984). To date, only a few cases have addressed the issue of ineffective assistance of counsel as it relates to neuroscience evidence. Consider the following.

In 2003, a jury found Earl Forrest guilty of three counts of first-degree murder and recommended three death sentences that the Supreme Court of Missouri affirmed (*State v. Forrest*, 2006). Forrest subsequently filed an appeal seeking postconviction relief, arguing that the motion court clearly erred in denying the ineffective assistance of counsel claim for failing to obtain a positron emission tomography (PET) scan. More specifically, Forrest alleged that the PET scan would have show brain damage, thereby creating a reasonably probability that the jury would have imposed a life rather than a death sentence.

In the penalty phase, a psychiatric pharmacist and a clinical neuropsychologist presented evidence of brain damage and substance dependence. In the guilt phase, a clinical psychologist testified that Forrest was diagnosed with dysthymic disorder (long-term depression), cognitive disorder (brain injury or brain damage), and addiction to methamphetamine and alcohol. The defense attorney had decided weeks before the trial commenced not to pursue a PET scan, despite considering it earlier, since she could not obtain the PET scan ex parte and because of concerns that the PET scan might undermine other mitigating evidence, if it is negative (*Forrest*, 2006). After Forrester's conviction a PET scan was obtained that showed chemical injury and brain damage. Nevertheless, the Court, after hearing the evidence, found that trial counsel was not ineffective for not seeking a PET scan. The Court reasoned that (a) the PET scan and expert testimony regarding the findings was inadmissible because the PET scan, in and of itself, can not demonstrate any connection to Forrest's behavior at the time the crime was committed, and (b) no scientific evidence was presented to show that the PET scan would definitively confirm that Forrest was suffering from a mental defect or disease (*Forrest v. State*, 2009).

Similarly, in *Zink v. State* (2009), the appellate court rejected an ineffective assistance of counsel claim for failure to obtain and present a PET scan. More specifically, on appeal Zink's principal claims of ineffective assistance of counsel was the failure of his trial attorney to obtain and utilize at trial and sentencing a PET scan that indicated a brain abnormality that might have bolstered his defense of diminished capacity and mitigated the death sentence he received. The State Supreme Court concluded that PET-scan expert testimony in support of a claim of diminished capacity did not meet the *Frye* standard of admissibility and thus defense counsel was not ineffective.

However, in *Awkal v. Mitchell* (2009), a capital murder case, the Sixth Circuit US Court of Appeals held that defense counsel's decision to call a mental health expert witness who testified that the defendant was sane at the time the crime was committed constituted ineffective assistance of counsel. The Appellate Court also found that the Ohio Supreme Court mischaracterized the expert's testimony as helpful and erred in failing to recognize how harmful the decision to call the expert had been to the defense.

10.2.2 General Acceptance

Courts who regard neuroscience evidence, in particular neuroimaging evidence, as too novel may deny its admission into evidence under the *Frye* standard on the grounds that this evidence has not yet achieved "general acceptability." This was the case in *People v. Protsman* (2001), in which the defendant sought to admit PET-scan evidence and psychiatric testimony to argue that he was suffering from decreased frontal lobe activity and therefore could not formulate the necessary intent. However, since the evidence had not yet achieved general acceptance, it was not admitted. Similarly, in *People v. Yum* (2003), the defendant, after having been convicted of second-degree murder, argued on appeal that the trial court erroneously refused to admit his single photon emission tomography (SPECT) brain scan, which showed diminished activity in his left temporal lobe and damage caused by brain trauma, causing him to kill his mother and sister. Because of the novelty of the diagnostic approach, using a SPECT scan to diagnose posttraumatic stress disorder and brain trauma, the defendant failed to satisfy the court that the scientific evidence was "generally accepted." Further, in *Jackson v. Calderon* (2000), the district court excluded the defendant's PET scan, since the use of PET scans to diagnose chronic PCP abuse is not generally accepted by the scientific community and because the defendant's PET scan "is susceptible to conflicting interpretations" (p. 1165).

The exclusion of neuropsychological evidence, based on the failure to administer a reliable test battery, has also been addressed in case law. For example, in *Baxter v. Temple* (2008) the plaintiff alleged that she sustained permanent cognitive impairment as a result of exposure to lead paint and consequently retained an expert who found that the plaintiff demonstrated a 20-point decline in her full-scale IQ between the first test, administered in 2002, and the second test, given in 2004. Before trial, the plaintiff's expert testified that she employed a neuropsychological testing technique called the Boston Process Approach (BPA).[1] The defendant challenged the reliability of the BPA methodology and the specific battery of tests chosen by Dr. Bruno-Golden as being scientifically unreliable because the battery had not been subjected to peer review and publication, had no known rate of error, and was not generally accepted in the scientific literature. Subsequently, Dr. Bruno-Golden conceded that (a) this particular battery had never been tested and (b) the results of the BPA could not be independently verified because the methodology varied between neuropsychologists. The court subsequently precluded Dr. Bruno-Golden from testifying, noting that the proffered testimony did not meet the requirements for the admission of expert testimony set forth in *Daubert*. However, the New Hampshire Supreme Court later concluded that the exclusion of the neuropsychological testimony was in error (*Baxter v. Temple*, 2008).

In contrast, in *State v. Griffin* (2005) a clinical psychologist was precluded from testifying as to defendant's competency based on a test battery that had not been peer reviewed or generally accepted as scientifically valid. Further, in *United States v. Eff* (2006), the court held that although the expert's opinion of insanity was not a reliable conclusion, the battery of tests administered to measure the defendant's cognitive abilities, including the Wechsler Adult Intelligence Scale (third edition) and the Wisconsin Card Sorting Test, was reliable because the individual tests had been widely administered, had reasonable confidence levels, and could be repeated.

10.2.3 The Right to Present Evidence

Neuroscience evidence can be introduced only through expert witnesses who can explain what exactly a neuropsychological test result or a neuroimaging scan means. The right to an expert was first addressed by the US Supreme Court almost three decades ago, in *Ake v. Oklahoma* (1985), with the Court ruling that an indigent criminal defendant who makes a threshold showing that insanity is likely to be a significant factor at trial is constitutionally entitled to a psychiatrist's assistance (470 U.S. 68, p. 74). More specifically, the Court noted that it had "long recognized that when a State brings its judicial power to bear on an indigent defendant in a criminal proceeding, it must take steps to insure that the defendant has a fair opportunity to present his defense" (*Ake v. Oklahoma*, 1985, p. 76).

Courts have been divided about whether or not a defendant has a right to an expert to perform psychological testing and have been hesitant to extend *Ake* to requests for funding for neuroimaging tests (Perlin, 2010). For example, in *People v. Jones* (1994), the appeals court reversed a murder conviction because the defendant was denied neurological testing that would have supported his claim that he was suffering from brain damage, which impaired his ability to think quickly and flexibly and to perceive risks. Similarly, in *United States v. Sandoval-Mendoza* (2006), the Ninth Circuit ruled that the district court abused its discretion when it excluded the defendant's functional neuroimaging evidence. The court reasoned that, without this evidence, the jury would not be able to reach a reasonable conclusion about whether the defendant possessed the requisite mental state or had a valid defense, and because the district court excluded the evidence, the defendant was "deprived . . . of a fair opportunity to defend himself" (*United States v. Sandoval-Mendoza*, 2006, p. 656). In contrast, in *Allen v. Hickman* (2005), a convicted murderer on death row claimed that the State's refusal to administer a SPECT or MRI scan was a violation of due process; however, the US District Court denied the defendant's claim (see also *Rogers v. State*, 2001).[2]

10.2.4 Determination of Guilt

10.2.4.1 The Doctrine of Mens Rea

With few exceptions, criminal culpability cannot be established solely by demonstrating that a particular crime was committed. More specifically, the doctrine of mens rea allows for the notion that, under certain circumstances such as mental illness or disease, a defendant's moral responsibility is reduced. A substantive obstacle in the path of any defendant seeking to introduce neuroscience-based evidence is demonstrating impaired capacity at the time of the offense. As the definition of "impaired capacity" stands, the defendant must prove that he was unable to conform his actions to the requirements of the law when he committed the offense. Therefore, the effects of the brain dysfunction or impairment must be present at the time the crime was committed for the mitigating factor to be satisfied. The importance of this obstacle diminishes when an anatomical brain defect is detected before the commission of the crime and after the brain is generally considered fully mature (Barth, 2007). If such a defect is detected during that time frame, then the defendant has a strong argument establishing that his brain dysfunction existed when he committed the crime (*United States v. Llera Plaza*, 2001).

There are a few cases in which neuroscience-based evidence has been introduced at the guilt phase to support claims of lack of requisite culpable mental state. For example, in *People v. Weinstein* (1992), the defendant, accused of strangling his wife, successfully introduced PET scan images, which he asserted showed reduced brain function in and around an arachnoid cyst in his frontal lobe. The evidence was presented in support of the defense's theory that Weinstein was not responsible for his actions as a result of mental disease/defect. Shortly after the judge ruled the PET scan to be admissible, the prosecution agreed to negotiate a plea bargain for a reduced charge of manslaughter. Some defendants, however, have not been as successful in demonstrating a lack of mens rea by relying on neuroimaging evidence. For example, in *State v. Anderson* (2002), the defendant presented expert testimony, supported by neuroscience evidence, that brain damage induced depression and paranoia precluded him from being able to premeditate and deliberate in a manner sufficient to justify the charge of first-degree murder. However, the jury was not persuaded, and Anderson was found guilty on all counts and sentenced to death. Also, consider the following.

In 2005, Stephen Stanko was charged with the murder of his girlfriend and raping and attempting to murder her daughter and in August 2006 was convicted and sentenced to death. Stanko was subsequently indicted for another murder and armed robbery and during the trial argued that he suffered from central nervous system dysfunction at the time of the murder and therefore did not understand right from wrong. The defendant's psychiatric expert testified that Stanko demonstrated (a) mild signs consistent with brain dysfunction, including central nervous system dysfunction, and (b) the typical signs of antisocial personality disorder or psychopathy and therefore could not understand moral or legal right from wrong (*State v. Stanko*, 2008). In addition, a medical doctor with expertise in PET scans and neuropsychiatric disorders testified that the defendant's brain dysfunction played a crucial role in impulse control and judgment. In 2009, Stanko was found guilty of murder and armed robbery and sentenced to death by lethal injection.

More recently, in *Quick v. State* (2011), Quick, after having been found guilty of murder and sentenced to 15 years in prison, argued on appeal that the trial court abused its discretion by barring his three psychological and psychiatric experts from testifying regarding his ability to form the requisite intent to commit murder.[3] The Texas Court of Appeals, however, affirmed his conviction and the trial court's denial of his neuroscience experts.

10.2.4.2 The Doctrine of Excuses

The law excuses criminal behavior if there are circumstances that negate the moral blameworthiness of the actor. More specifically, "our collective conscience does not allow punishment where it cannot impose blame" (*Holloway v. United States*, 1945, p. 65). There are a number of different excuses that can serve as an affirmative defense, including insanity, guilty but mentally ill (GBMI), and diminished capacity.

10.2.4.2.1 Insanity

The insanity defense is based on the idea that some defendants may have a lack of criminal intent, or mens rea, making them not legally accountable for the crime committed. Relying on the right to present psychiatric evidence, defendants have offered neuroscience evidence, including neuroimaging scans of brain dysfunction, as part of an insanity defense, and the plea has succeeded in a number of high-profile cases, including the following.

In *United States v. Hinckley* (1981), Hinckley, after attempting to assassinate President Reagan, sought to rely on neuroscience evidence to support a not guilty by reason of insanity defense, and at trial a defense expert introduced a CT scan that showed a "widening" of sulci in Hinckley's brain, in support of a diagnosis of schizophrenia. Other defense experts testified that (a) the degree of atrophy was abnormal and possibly indicated the presence of an organic brain disease and (b) the evidence of atrophy increased the statistical likelihood that the defendant was suffering from schizophrenia. The court admitted this evidence in order to give the jury all possibly relevant evidence bearing on cognition, volition, and capacity in considering the claim of insanity, and the defendant was, subsequently, found not guilty by reason of insanity.[4]

Studies have shown that the insanity defense is used in less than one percent of cases, and only about a quarter of those cases are successful, as the following demonstrate. In 1999, Andrew Goldstein, a schizophrenic, shoved Kendra Webdale from the platform of a New York subway station onto the train tracks in front of an oncoming train. The defendant's first trial ended in a mistrial, and at retrial the jury rejected his insanity plea, found him guilty, and sentenced him to 25 years to life in prison. On appeal Goldstein argued that the court improperly excluded evidence in the form of a PET scan that would have supported a defense expert's opinion that Goldstein's brain physically manifested schizophrenia in the form of a massive reduction in metabolism in the frontal lobes and basal ganglia. The appellate court affirmed the conviction, noting that the scan test results could not conclusively prove schizophrenia but could only show an abnormality in the brain, which would not be probative of the key issue of whether the defendant comprehended either the nature and consequences of his actions or that his actions were wrong, since a diagnosis of schizophrenia does not preclude that a defendant is capable of such comprehension (*People v. Goldstein*, 2004). In 2005, Goldstein's conviction was overturned on appeal, and, in 2006, prior to the start of his third trial, Goldstein pled guilty to manslaughter and admitted for the first time that he knew what he was doing when he pushed the victim to her death.

Similarly, after having been indicted for killing his mother in 2005, Michael Carreiro pled not guilty by reason of insanity. At trial, two defense experts testified that Carreiro did not know the moral wrongfulness of his acts because the voice of God commanded him to kill his mother, and, while Carreiro knew that his actions violated the law, his lack of any attempt in hiding the murder weapon and his bloody clothes or locking the apartment door showed that he did not appreciate the moral "wrongfulness" of his acts. In contrast, a forensic psychologist testified that while he believed that the defendant suffered from a severe mental illness, the defendant did understand the wrongfulness of his actions. The jury ultimately rejected the insanity defense, found the defendant guilty of aggravated murder, and sentenced him to life in prison with parole eligibility after 20 years. In 2013, Carreiro's conviction was affirmed by the Ohio Court of Appeals (*State v. Carreiro*, 2013).

10.2.4.2.2 Guilty but Mentally Ill

States may also provide juries with the option of returning a verdict of GBMI when the jury finds that the defendant suffers from a mental illness but does not find that he or she was insane. In fact, there are a number of reported cases in which it appears that the jury's GBMI verdict was based, in large part, on evidence of the defendant's brain impairment. For example, in *Ward v. Sternes* (2003), the defendant, after having been arrested and charged with his wife's murder, presented neurological expert testimony that, because of a traumatic brain injury he had sustained nine months before the murder, he was GBMI. More specifically, two neurologists testified that Ward's temporal-lobe injury resulted in his aphasia and that the frontal-lobe injury severely impeded his ability to control his impulses. The defense also called two psychiatrists who testified that Ward was legally insane when he killed his wife. In response the state argued that Ward's inability to restrain his impulses on the day of the murder was caused by his voluntary intoxication rather than any mental defect. On cross-examination, one of the defense's psychiatrists agreed with the prosecution's suggestion that alcohol was a "necessary component" of Ward's inability to control his actions, while the other psychiatrist suggested that Ward's dementia would have made it highly unlikely that he would have been able to control his violent impulses toward his wife if he had been sober. Ward was subsequently found GBMI and received a 40-year sentence.

Also, in *State v. Downs* (2004), the defendant pled guilty to the crimes of kidnapping, criminal sexual conduct with a minor, and murder. At the hearing to determine whether or not he was GBMI, a court-appointed expert in forensic psychiatry testified that she had evaluated the appellant for a GBMI determination on six prior occasions from May 2001 to June 2002 and her diagnoses included antisocial personality disorder, pedophilia, paraphilia, substance abuse, and mild depression. She further stated that none of these diagnoses impacted Downs's ability to understand the proceedings or communicate with his attorney. After considering the evidence, the court ruled that the defendant had failed to prove he was GBMI. Downs was sentenced to death, and the sentence was subsequently affirmed by the Supreme Court of South Carolina.

10.2.4.2.3 Diminished Capacity

The diminished capacity defense is based on the belief that certain individuals, because of mental disease or impairment, are incapable of possessing the mental state required to commit a certain crime. In the example of murder and manslaughter, diminished capacity states that a certain defendant is incapable of intending to cause a death and therefore must have at most caused such a death recklessly. Thus a successful plea of diminished capacity in a murder trial may likely result in the charge being reduced to manslaughter. This was the case in one of the most well-known diminished capacity cases, the "Twinkie defense" case—*People v. White* (1981). In *White,* the defendant, a former city supervisor, shot and killed San Francisco Supervisor Harvey Milk and San Francisco Mayer George Moscone. At the trial, a psychiatrist testified that White had been depressed at the time of the crime and pointed to several behavioral changes indicating White's depression: he shunned his wife and quit his job, and, although usually clean-cut, his appearance had become slovenly. In addition, White, previously a health-food advocate and fitness fanatic, had begun consuming junk food and sugar-laden soft drinks (Pogash, 2003). The jury subsequently found the defendant guilty of two counts of voluntary manslaughter, a lesser included offense than the crime of murder.[5]

Likewise, in *Samayoa v. Ayers* (2011), the defendant, after having brutally murdered a mother and her two-year-old daughter during a burglary, presented evidence of diminished capacity at the trial and sentencing phases. More specifically, four psychologists, after having performed neuropsychological evaluations and testing, which included the administration of the Luria-Nebraska test battery, the Canter Background Interference Procedure, the Bender-Gestalt visual motor test, and the Wechsler Adult Intelligence Scale, testified that the defendant was suffering from brain damage of the left hemisphere of the brain, including damage to the frontal, temporal, and parietal lobes. The experts also offered various descriptions of how this type of damage may lead to aggressive behavior, poor impulse control, and lack of awareness. However, the diminished capacity defense failed, and the jury found the defendant guilty of the homicides (See also *United States v. Pineyro*, 2005).[6]

10.2.5 Imposition of Punishment

Courts have been somewhat hesitant to admit neuroscience-based evidence as part of a defense to a crime; however, this type of evidence is now quite frequently admitted at the penalty phases of capital cases. In fact, while there are only a few reported cases in which defendants have secured acquittals on the strength of neuroscience-based evidence, defendants have enjoyed some measure of success in the context of sentencing. For example, in early 2004, MRI and PET scan evidence helped to defeat two separate death sentences for Simon Pirela. In April of 1983, and in a separate murder trial in May of 1983, the defendant received two death sentences, and the conviction and sentences were confirmed on direct appeal (*Commonwealth v. Pirela*, 1986). When the second death sentence was vacated due to reversible error for prosecutorial misconduct and resentencing ordered, defense attorneys introduced MRI and PET scans as evidence in support of mitigating factors of diminished capacity, brain damage, and mental impairment. In 2004, the jury unanimously recommended that Pirela be resentenced to life in prison rather than executed, and the judge noted that the expert testimony on the brain scans, combined with the testimony of neuropsychologists, was rather convincing (*Commonwealth v. Morales*, 2004).[7] Similarly, in *McNamara v. Borg* (1991), PET scan evidence was introduced in support of the defendant's mitigation claim that he was suffering from schizophrenia. The defendant received a sentence of life in prison rather than death, and, according to postsentencing interviews, jurors acknowledged that they were significantly influenced by the neuroimaging evidence in their decision to spare the defendant's life.

10.2.6 Competence-Related Issues

It has been suggested that legal competence is specific to the task at hand and requires the ability to deliberate and/or reason, appreciate one's circumstances, hold appropriate goals and values, understand information one is given, and be able to communicate a choice (Buchanan, 2004). Since the law acknowledges that mental ability is a continuous quality that may be present to a greater or lesser extent at different times, the issue of incompetency can be raised throughout the trial and penalty phases and may include questions regarding competency to (a) stand trial, (b) be executed, and (c) waive constitutional rights.

10.2.6.1 Competence to Stand Trial

The Due Process Clause of the 14th Amendment prohibits the prosecution of an incompetent person. Although a defendant's mental competency is difficult to assess and quantify, the US Supreme Court in *Dusky v. United States* (1960) enunciated a legal standard governing the minimum competency required of a defendant before he or she may be put to trial. The Dusky Court held that the test must be whether a defendant has sufficient present ability to consult with his or her lawyer with a reasonable degree of rational understanding and whether he or she has a rational as well as factual understanding of the proceedings against him or her. For example, when a defendant's frontal lobe dysfunction is severe or present alongside other mental impairments, it may form the basis for a finding of adjudicative incompetence (see also *State v. Hall*, 2001). Also, consider the following.

In September 2004, while screaming "die," James Phillips attacked his wife in the lobby of her apartment building, stabbed her 17 times, and then fled the scene. Minutes after the attack he was caught by the police and, after having been indicted on several charges, including attempted second-degree murder, he was ordered to undergo a competency examination. At the initial examination, Phillips was found unfit for trial. Several months later at a competency hearing, the defendant and the people proffered expert medical testimony regarding defendant's fitness for trial. Both parties agreed that Phillips suffered from a permanent brain injury that affected his speech and language, as evidenced by MRI scans indicating a permanent lesion in the left hemisphere of his brain. However, the experts were in disagreement about the defendant's ability to comprehend the trial proceedings. After the hearing, Phillips was found competent to stand trial. Phillips was convicted of all charges and moved to set aside the verdict and for a new trial. The Appellate Court affirmed the verdict and in doing so noted that while the defendant suffered from transcortical motor aphasia, he did not exhibit any severe mental imbalance or impairment in his current mental state (*People v. Phillips*, 2011).

10.2.6.2 Competency to be Executed

In *Ford v. Wainwright* (1986), the US Supreme Court upheld the common law rule that the insane cannot be executed. Many years later in *Panetti v. Quarterman* (2007), the. Supreme Court reiterated the holding in *Ford* and explained that the prohibition applies despite a prisoner's earlier competency to be (a) held responsible and (b) be tried for the crime committed. In other words, according to *Ford*, "prior findings of competency do not foreclose a defendant from proving he is incompetent to be executed because of his present mental condition" (*Panetti*, 2007, pp. 934–935). Further, as noted by Supreme Court Justice Frankfurter in *Ford* (1986), a determination of sanity as a lawful foundation to executions calls for "no less stringent standards than those demanded in any other aspect of a capital proceeding" (p. 412). This standard is particularly demanding in light of the fact that "the present state of the mental sciences is at best a hazardous guess however conscientious" (*Solesbee v. Balkcom*, 1950, p. 23). *Panetti* (2007) clearly illustrates this point.

Scott Panetti was convicted of murdering his parents-in-law and was sentenced to death. Before his scheduled execution, he petitioned the state court for a determination of his competency to be executed, and the state habeas court appointed a psychiatrist and a clinical psychologist to assess Panetti's competency. The experts then filed a joint report in which they concluded that Panetti knew that he would be executed and that he had the ability to understand the reason why he would be executed. Based on this report the state court found Panetti competent to be executed. Following his direct appeals and initial petition of writ of habeas corpus, all of which were rejected, Panetti filed a subsequent habeas writ petition in which he alleged that he did not understand the reasons for his pending execution, which also was rejected and affirmed by the Fifth Circuit Court (*Panetti v. Dretke*, 2006; *Panetti v. Dretke*, 2004). The US Supreme Court reversed in a 5–4 decision and noted that "the beginning of doubt about competence in a case like petitioner's is not a misanthropic personality or an amoral character, it is a psychotic disorder. It was the prisoner's severe, documented mental illness that is the source of gross delusions preventing him from comprehending the meaning and purpose of the punishment to which he has been sentenced" (*Panetti*, 2007, p. 2862). The following case is also instructive.

John Ferguson, after having been convicted of eight murders, filed numerous appeals and a federal habeas petition asserting an insanity defense, claiming incompetency to stand trial and to assist counsel, and seeking relief from his convictions and death sentences, all of which were denied. The denials were affirmed on appeal (e.g., *Ferguson v. State*, 2001; *Ferguson v. State*, 1992). On October 19, 2012, Ferguson filed a federal habeas petition along with an emergency motion for a stay of execution claiming that he was mentally incompetent to be executed under the Eighth Amendment, as interpreted in *Ford* and *Panetti*. The US Court of Appeals issued a stay of execution and held a two-day evidentiary hearing, during which Ferguson presented evidence from a psychiatric expert and an expert in forensic psychology and malingering.

At the hearing, the psychiatrist described Ferguson as a late-life schizophrenic who, despite his psychosis, did not require medication and would not necessarily exhibit any outward manifestations of his illness because the positive symptoms of paranoid schizophrenia diminish with age. The forensic psychologist, having evaluated Ferguson in September of 2012 for the sole purpose of determining whether he was currently malingering or feigning psychotic symptoms, acknowledged that, at that time, two of the test scores were elevated, suggesting that Ferguson was malingering. However, at the hearing he testified that based on the totality of the results of the administered tests, he was of the opinion that Ferguson was not currently malingering but incompetent to be executed. A board-certified psychiatrist testifying for the state opined that Ferguson displayed lucid thinking, had average intelligence, and was functioning well in his day-to-day life. The expert also contended that even if Ferguson's delusions were genuine, he would still not meet the diagnostic criteria for schizophrenia, since the delusions were not disrupting his daily life. Two other state experts, a professor of forensic psychiatry and a neuropsychologist, similarly concluded that Ferguson did not meet the diagnostic criteria for schizophrenia and was most likely malingering.

On rebuttal, Ferguson's psychiatric expert stuck to his diagnosis and opinion that Ferguson was incompetent. The state trial court subsequently issued an order finding that Ferguson had failed to meet his burden of proving that he was mentally incompetent to be executed (*State v. Ferguson*, 2012). Ferguson appealed that decision to the Florida Supreme Court, which affirmed the trial court's decision. On October 20, 2012, the district court granted a temporary stay of execution to permit a "fair hearing" on Ferguson's latest habeas claim; however, two days later the State's emergency motion to vacate that stay of execution, was granted. Then, shortly before Ferguson's scheduled execution on October 23, 2012, the district court issued a summary order denying the habeas petition but granted Ferguson a certificate of appealability on the following two issues: (a) whether the decision of the Florida Supreme Court involved an unreasonable application of the US Supreme Court's decision in *Ford* and *Panetti* and (b) whether the Florida Supreme Court's affirmance of the state trial court was based on an unreasonable determination of the facts in light of the evidence presented. The US Court of Appeals for the Eleventh Circuit granted a temporary stay of execution, and the State moved to vacate the stay and to dismiss Ferguson's appeal. However, the State's motion to vacate the stay of execution was denied (*Ferguson v. Florida Department of Corrections*, 2013).

10.2.6.3 Competency to Waive Constitutional Rights

The US Constitution guarantees significant rights to a defendant during a criminal trial, including the prohibition of compulsory self-incrimination, and the right to (a) a jury trial, (b) confront one's accusers, and (c) assistance of counsel. Although these rights are guaranteed, a defendant may waive them, and evidence of brain dysfunction or impairment is frequently used to challenge, for example, a defendant's competence to waive constitutional rights, as the following cases illustrate.

10.2.6.3.1 Competency to Waive Presentation of Mitigation

In *State v. Delahanty* (2011), the defendant, after having been convicted of first-degree murder, attempted arson, conspiracy to commit first-degree murder, and solicitation to commit first-degree murder, was sentenced to death for murder and to prison terms for the other offenses. After conviction, both the defendant and the State waived a jury trial, and, shortly after the penalty phase began, Delahanty sought to waive presentation of mitigation. The trial judge then appointed a psychologist to determine whether the defendant was competent to do so and, after having reviewed the expert's report, concluded that the defendant had knowingly, intelligently, and voluntarily waived his right to present mitigation. The jury determined that Delahanty should be sentenced to death; however, the defendant subsequently claimed that the Court erred in not ordering a competency prescreening. Since the record was replete with evidence that the defendant understood the proceedings and was able to assist in his own defense, the Court disagreed. In fact, even before ordering a psychological evaluation, the Court made it clear that it had no doubts about defendant's ability to understand the proceedings. The Court also noted that, even though the sentencing expert suggested that Delahanty suffered from brain damage and that this type of brain damage reduces an individual's ability to control impulsive violent urges, volatility and mental incompetence to stand trial are not equivalent.

10.2.6.3.2 Competency to Enter a Plea

Henry Marshall, after having been charged with the shooting death of a pub owner, pled guilty against the advice of his attorney. He then sought to withdraw his guilty plea, arguing that he was incompetent to enter a plea because of frontal lobe dysfunction and other serious mental disorders. Subsequently, a competency hearing was held to determine whether the plea was entered voluntarily, given the evidence of Marshall's significant mental impairment, which included an MRI scan that showed that the decision-making area of his brain had shrunken significantly and was considerably smaller than that of a normal brain. In addition, an EEG showed that Marshall's brain electrical activity was at a much slower frequency than that of a normal person, and a SPECT scan indicated abnormal blood flow to the brain. On appeal the Washington Supreme Court vacated the guilty plea because of the lower court's failure to allow Marshall to withdraw his plea or order a formal competency hearing (*Washington v. Marshall*, 2001).

10.2.6.3.3 Competency to Waive Miranda Right

Evidence of frontal lobe dysfunction has also been used to argue that a defendant's confession should be suppressed because the Miranda rights waiver was not given knowingly, voluntarily, or intelligently (*People v. Wilson,* 2000); however, these claims are seldom successful. Indeed, in *State v. Mears* (2000), the court held that despite frontal lobe dysfunction and other mental impairments, the defendant's understanding was sufficient to establish a knowing, voluntary, and intelligent waiver of his Miranda rights. However, in *Garner v. Mitchell* (2007), the US Court of Appeals for the Sixth Circuit reversed an inmate's convictions and death sentence after concluding that the inmate did not knowingly and intelligently waive his Miranda rights. More specifically, in 1992 Garner was convicted and sentenced to death on five counts of aggravated murder. On direct appeal, the Ohio Court of Appeals affirmed his convictions and sentence, which were affirmed by the Ohio Supreme Court. Subsequently, the US Supreme Court denied certiorari after which Garner filed two petitions for postconviction relief, both of which were denied, with the denials affirmed by the Appellate Court. In 1998, Garner filed a petition for a writ of habeas corpus in the federal district court raising numerous claims; however, the district court denied all the claims and dismissed Garner's petition. In 2007, he filed an appeal, and one of the issues raised on appeal was whether or not he knowingly and intelligently waived his Miranda rights. In reversing Garner's conviction and death sentence, the Court of Appeals for the Sixth Circuit relied on a report from a mental health expert for the defense who, after having interviewed and tested Garner and reviewed reports of prior mental health experts, concluded that Garner did not have full comprehension of the Miranda warning or his right to remain silent.

10.2.6.3.4 Competency to Proceed pro se

In 1999 Ahmad Edwards was charged with several crimes, including attempted murder and, after his arrest, received a diagnosis of schizophrenia, was found incompetent to stand trial, and was hospitalized at a forensic state hospital for restoration of competency. Following two hospitalizations for competency restoration, Edwards's trial began, at which time he asked to represent himself. However, his request was denied, and he was subsequently convicted of criminal recklessness and theft. Because the jury was unable to reach a verdict on the charges of attempted murder and battery with a deadly weapon, the state sought to retry Edwards on these remaining charges, and he again asked to represent himself. His request again was denied, with the trial judge ruling that Edwards remained competent to stand trial but was not competent to defend himself. Edwards was convicted of the remaining charges and was sentenced to 30 years imprisonment. After another unsuccessful appeal, the US Supreme Court granted certiorari to determine whether the trial court was constitutionally required to allow Edwards to represent himself and in 2008 vacated the Indiana Supreme Court's decision and remanded the case for further proceedings (*Indiana v. Edwards*, 2008).

10.2.6.3.5 Competency to Waive Statutory Right to Appeal

The standard for determining whether an individual is mentally competent to waive the right to appeal is a two-pronged test, set forth in *Singleton v. State* (1993): the first test is whether a convicted defendant can understand the nature of the proceedings, what he or she was tried for, the reason for the punishment, or the nature of the punishment, and the second test is whether the convicted defendant possesses sufficient capacity or ability to rationally communicate with his or her counsel. The following case illustrates *Singleton*.

In 1995 Hughes was convicted of murder, armed robbery, criminal conspiracy, possession of a firearm during the commission of a violent crime, and possession of a stolen vehicle and was sentenced to death. Hughes's conviction and death sentence were subsequently affirmed (*Hughes v. South Carolina*, 2000; *State v. Hughes*, 1999). At a competency hearing in 2004, three psychiatrists diagnosed Hughes as suffering from undifferentiated schizophrenia and concluded that he did not (a) understand the nature of a postconviction relief proceeding or the nature of the punishment, and (b) possess sufficient capacity or ability to rationally communicate with his attorney. Nevertheless, the circuit court ruled that Hughes was mentally competent to waive his right to pursue postconviction relief with counsel's assistance and that his decision to do so was knowing and voluntary. In 2006 the Supreme Court of South Carolina concluded that Hughes was not mentally competent, pursuant to the *Singleton* standard, to waive the right to pursue postconviction relief and remanded this case to the circuit court for further proceedings (*Hughes v. State*, 2006).

10.2.6.3.6 Competency to Plead Guilty

Kevin Wayne Dunlap pled guilty to three counts of capital murder, capital kidnapping, and tampering with physical evidence and one count each of attempted murder, first-degree kidnapping, first-degree rape, first-degree arson, and first-degree burglary. He was sentenced to death for each of the six capital crimes, life imprisonment for kidnapping, rape, and arson, 20 years' imprisonment for attempted murder and burglary, and 5 years imprisonment for each of the tampering convictions. Dunlap subsequently appealed, contending, among other things, that the trial court violated his 14th Amendment right by accepting his guilty plea since an abnormality in his brain severely affected his judgment and the capacity to waive his rights. One month prior to trial, a CT scan revealed two nonspecific hyperattenuated punctuate foci on the right frontal lobe of Dunlap's brain. Counsel for the defense then requested a PET and MRI scan, which revealed that Dunlap had an arterial venous malformation[8] on his right frontal lobe. The Appellate

Court affirmed the trial court's decision and in doing so noted that, according to the psychiatrist who had supervised Dunlap's month-long competency evaluation in 2010, the neurological examination was normal and none of his psychological tests indicated any problems with impulse control or anything else that might suggest problems in the right frontal lobe. The Court further noted that although Dr. Trivette's testimony was rendered shortly before the arterial venous malformation was officially discovered, it is undisputed that Dunlap had it at the time Trivette evaluated him (*Dunlap v. Commonwealth of Kentucky*, 2013).

10.2.7 Mitigation

For a jury to accept a mitigating factor, only one juror needs to find that the defendant established the factor by a preponderance of the evidence (*Simmons v. South Carolina*, 1994). This standard differs dramatically from the standard required for aggravating factors, which is a unanimous jury finding beyond a reasonable doubt. The standard of proof for mitigating evidence is significant because of the high degree of deference that jurors generally give to expert witnesses. With only one juror misunderstanding the neuroscience-based testimony of an expert, a mitigating factor will be established and thus be weighed against aggravating factors in the sentencing phase. Clearly, such a low standard places an increased burden on expert witnesses to be cautious when presenting neuroscience-based testimony (Barth, 2007).

Under the Supreme Court's decision in *Lockett v. Ohio*, (1978), all mitigating evidence must be heard in a capital case. Statutory mitigating evidence has been defined by the Federal Death Penalty Act to include impaired capacity defined as: "The defendant's capacity to appreciate the wrongfulness of the defendant's conduct or to conform conduct to the requirements of law was significantly impaired, regardless of whether the capacity was so impaired as to constitute a defense to the charge" (18 U.S.C. § 3592(a)(1) (2006).

The choice of language, "significantly impaired," leaves plenty of room for interpretation, and thus courts have the option of admitting much more evidence than they can in the guilty phases of trials (Moriarty, 2008). Indeed, having recognized that "death is different" (*Ford v. Wainright*, 1986, p. 411), judges are more likely to err on the side of allowing neuroscience-based testimony in death penalty hearings; however, juries frequently are not swayed by this type of evidence, as the following cases suggest.

Philian Eugene Lee was convicted of first-degree murder and, during the penalty phase of the trial, introduced as mitigation evidence expert testimony of a clinical psychologist. The defense expert, after having administered a number of neuropsychological tests, concluded that the defendant suffered from brain damage in three separate areas, that such damage could cause problems with learning and controlling anger, and that alcohol consumption exacerbates the effects of the damage. After the penalty trial, the jury returned a verdict of death and, on automatic appeal, the California Supreme Court affirmed the judgment (*People v. Lee*, 2011).

Similarly, more than two and a half years after having been charged with and convicted of four counts of murder and numerous other felonies, Ronald Davis entered into a plea agreement with the State and, following a lengthy sentencing hearing in 2010, the trial court sentenced him to 245 years in prison. Davis then filed a motion to correct error; however, in 2011 the trial court issued a detailed order denying the motion and clarifying its original sentencing order. Davis appealed, arguing that the trial court failed to consider his significant brain damage as a mitigating factor. The Appellate Court affirmed the sentence, noting that the trial court fully considered the medical evidence relating to Davis's brain damage, signs of paranoid schizophrenia, and symptoms of posttraumatic stress disorder (*Davis v. State*, 2012).

Some courts have taken an entirely different view regarding neuroscience-based evidence offered as mitigation evidence, as illustrated in *Sears v. Upton* (2010). In 1993, a jury convicted Sears of armed robbery and kidnaping with bodily injury, which also resulted in death. During the penalty phase, Sears's attorney portrayed the defendant's life as that of a well-adjusted member of society, a strategy that was meant to show how harmful a death sentence would be to Sears's family. This strategy, however, backfired, and Sears was sentenced to death.

Evidence offered during the state postconviction relief process revealed that Sears suffered significant frontal lobe abnormalities and had substantial deficits in mental reasoning and cognition, including problems with planning and impulse control. One expert also noted that from an etiological standpoint Sears's history was replete with multiple head traumas, substance abuse, and traumatic experiences of the type expected to lead to significant cognitive impairments (*Sears v. State*, 1997). In 2010 the US Supreme Court found that the initial mitigation hearing was constitutionally inadequate because it did not consider this evidence, vacated the judgment, and remanded the case for further proceedings. The Court concluded that a proper analysis of prejudice would have taken into account the evidence of significant mental and psychological impairments, along with the mitigation evidence introduced during Sears's penalty phase trial (*Sears v. Upton*, 2010).

10.3 Conclusion

As these cases suggest, while the reality of brain dysfunction and its effect on behavior and judgment is well accepted in the scientific community, the reliability of a diagnosis of brain dysfunction and evidence about how it may have contributed to a criminal offense may be open to *Daubert*[9] or *Frye*[10] challenges, particularly with respect to neuroimaging-based testimony. Indeed, neuroimages are not direct visualizations of the brain. Rather, they "simplify complicated data about the brain, but . . . are mutable, constructed representations, far more similar to charts and line graphs than to photographs" (Reeves, Mills, Billick, & Brodie, 2003, p. 96). There are also, at present, no uniform or well-defined criteria for differentiating normal from abnormal imaging scans or for quantifying the extent of cognitive impairment in the context of violent behavior. In addition, neuroimages' ability to produce false positives is particularly problematic for both evidence and science, since, as *Daubert* recognized, the potential error rate of a scientific methodology is a crucial aspect of its evidentiary reliability (Moriarty, 2008). Furthermore, as discussed in chapter 4, many neuropsychological tests lack the scientific validity to be relied on as a sole measure of cognitive impairment. This is particularly problematic in light of the fact that mock jurors are more likely to find a defendant not guilty by reason of insanity when provided with neuroimaging scans showing brain dysfunction than when presented with clinical testimony alone (Gurley & Marcus, 2005).

This singular persuasiveness of neuroimaging evidence is clearly illustrated in the dissenting opinion of a Florida Supreme Court Justice, who complained that the experts' conclusions, based largely on the defendant's history and neurological examinations, were not based on objective testing, such as brain scans, as differentiated from an experts' subjective conclusions (*Crook v. State*, 2002). The belief that neuroimaging scans convey the absolute truth hampers the objective evaluation of the limitations of tests and techniques currently used to assess cognitive functioning in the context of violent behavior. In fact, "the forensic application of non-replicated, unpublished or anecdotal SPECT or positron emission tomography (PET) observations is inappropriate and has ominous implications; it can lead to unsupportable conclusions if introduced as 'objective evidence'" (Society of Nuclear Medicine Brain Imaging Council, 1996, p. 1257). Finally, as noted in FRE 102, the federal rules must be construed "to the end of ascertaining the truth and securing a just determination." The failure to base expert testimony on reliable methodologies, tests, measures, and techniques clearly furthers none of these objectives.

11

Linking Brain Function and Behavior

A science of the mind must reduce . . . complexities (of
behavior) to their elements. A science of the brain must point
out the functions of its elements. A science of the relations of
mind and brain must show how the elementary ingredients
of the former correspond to the elementary functions of the
latter. (James, 1890, p. 103)

11.1 Introduction

The premises on which medicine and law rest are incommensurate: a mentally
impaired patient presents along a continuum, while a criminal defendant is
either innocent or guilty according to a code of justice (Schwarz, 2009). It
is, therefore, not surprising that some scholars have expressed concern that
many of the assertions made in support of some uses of neuroscience testimony in courts are, in fact, unsupportable (Moriarty, 2009).

When a computerized tomography (CT) or magnetic resonance imaging
(MRI) scan shows a gross structural abnormality, such as a brain tumor, the
distinction between normal and abnormal is clear, since the presence of a
brain tumor, at least statistically, points to an abnormal state. Similarly, when
a subject scores significantly below the norm on neuropsychological tests,
impairment can easily be inferred. The problem arises when one attempts to
determine the relationship between an abnormal neuroimage and/or below
normal test performance and past behavior (Brown & Eyler, 2006). There is
no doubt that neuroimaging techniques can provide powerful visual evidence of cognitive impairment; however, because results may differ due to
the conditions under which the scan was obtained or the imaging technique
employed, differentiating normal from abnormal results can be difficult

(Stuss & Knight, 2002). Indeed, the use of neuroscience in the search for the truth poses consistent evidentiary problems of definition, validity, accuracy, causation, and inferential conclusions unsupported by data and real-world complications (Moriarty, 2009). Further, as previously noted, an image of, for example, diminished cerebral blood flow in the frontal lobes, indicating hypometabolism, is simply a computer-generated reflection of physiological signals gathered by a camera geared to that specific signal. This neuroimage does not and cannot fully tell us what is happening in that particular brain region, nor does it reveal the impact of the diminished blood flow on other neuronal tissues or circuitry. Furthermore, just as an abnormal neuroimaging scan does not necessarily imply cognitive dysfunction, a normal scan does not necessarily mean that there are no cognitive deficits.

Neuroimaging techniques alone cannot establish a definitive relationship between violent behavior and brain functioning or forensically relevant abilities, such as competency to stand trial. Therefore, while neuroimaging techniques can be helpful in the identification of brain injuries or dysfunctions, the behavioral consequences of an injury or dysfunction can only be fully appreciated in the context of other information, such as neuropsychological testing (Reeves, Mills, Billick, & Brodie, 2003). Furthermore, neuroimaging scans, in particular those used in the forensic context, compare an individual's brain against the average of a group of controls, which is meant to represent the normal population. However, "normal" is merely a statistical creation, which is problematic since we do not know the population base rate of most disorders and diseases. This problem of normal range becomes amplified when working with any particular neuroimaging technique. Clearly, without knowing the actual base rate for a specific functional brain abnormality in the population, little can be said about the positive predictive value of a particular neuroimaging scan that seeks to establish an abnormality (Brown & Murphy, 2010).

11.2 The Algorithm

Despite the fact that the potential of neuroimaging techniques to be utilized in criminal trials is now no longer just a theoretical topic for scholars to contemplate, caution must nevertheless be applied when intruding neuroscience-based evidence, in particular neuroimaging scans, for evidentiary purposes. In fact, because every currently available test, measure, or technique designed to assess cognitive impairment, malingering, and neurological, psychiatric, and psychological disorders has limitations, a multimodal approach for the assessment of cognitive functioning is not only warranted but also necessary. The following algorithms attempt to illustrate how best to assess (a) competency-related issues; (b) cognitive abilities to support pleas of not guilty by reason of insanity, diminished capacity, and guilty but mentally ill; and (c) cognitive impairment for purpose of providing mitigating evidence employing the most valid and reliable tests, measures, and techniques currently available.

11.2.1 Assessing Competency

Clearly the methodology used to assess cognitive dysfunction, no matter how sound, and the subsequent results obtained cannot be dispositive of most questions posed by the law. However, functional and structural neuroimaging scans can be a useful addition to the assessment of cognitive functioning in the context of competency-related issues. For example, in *Dusky v. United States* (1960) the Court noted that the test to determine whether or not a defendant is competent to stand trial must be "whether he has sufficient present ability to consult with his lawyer with a reasonable degree of rational understanding— and whether he has a rational as well as factual understanding of the proceedings against him" (p.780).[1] More specifically, it has been contended that competency is ultimately a capacity that is based, at least in part, on cognitive processes (Nestor, Daggett, Haycock, & Price, 1999). It has also been suggested that competency to stand trial, in fact, consists of the following two-pronged test: (a) the interpersonal/behavioral prong, which consists of several clinical factors, including mood disorders, that while not directly impairing a defendant's understanding of the legal process may instead impinge on his or her ability to act in the socially appropriate manner necessary to effectively assist in one's defense, and (b) the cognitive prong, which consists of mental faculties, including memory and understanding (Martell, 1992). Similarly, to find that an individual has properly waived his or her Miranda rights, it must be determined that the individual has done so knowingly, intelligently, and voluntarily. Competence to waive Miranda rights, thus, encompasses both a volitional and a cognitive prong (Burton & Chamberlain, 2010).

Although specific assessment instruments are available to evaluate competency to stand trial and have been found to be highly reliable and valid in research settings, their practical applicability in improving clinical practice has been questioned (Pinals, Tillbrook, & Mumley, 2006). For example, the MacArthur Competence Assessment Tool–Criminal Adjudication (MacCAT-CA) scores were found to sometimes underestimate defendants' actual abilities, in part as a function of the items' complexity (many of the items require substantial attentional and abstract reasoning abilities). Consequently, defendants with even mild impairments in frontal lobe functions, such as attention, mental control, and abstract reasoning, may perform poorly on the MacCAT-CA, which may not equate to absolute deficits in competence-related abilities (Pinals, Tillbrook, & Mumley, 2006).[2] In addition, while competency assessment instruments focus on functional aspects of, for example, competency to stand trial, they do not measure capacity or whether there is an underlying condition that contributes to a defendant's poor functioning. Neuropsychological tests and neuroimaging scans are, therefore, particularly useful in assessing whether or not any deficits shown are (a) genuine or malingered, (b) associated with cognitive deficits due to structural or functional abnormalities, (c) the result of mental retardation, or (d) caused by psychotic or mood disorders (Stafford & Sellbom, 2012). In other words, whereas competency assessment instruments identify possible impairments in competency-related functions, traditional neuropsychological tests and neuroimaging scans may clarify the cause of these impairments and/ or dysfunctions (Stafford & Sellbom, 2012). Indeed, as noted by Nicholson and Kugler (1991), "both legal abilities and psychological or psychiatric functioning are important correlates of competency decisions" (p. 366). Further, usually individuals diagnosed with mental retardation are not automatically considered to be incompetent; the cognitive impairment must be linked to deficits in the defendant's functional abilities necessary to stand trial, including the ability to rationally or factually understand the nature of the charges or to make rational decisions regarding some aspects of his or her defense (Zapf, 2011). Finally, it has been noted that since there is no single determinant of an individual's capacity, the ethical evaluation of competency requires a multipronged approach to the assessment (Moberg & Kniele, 2006).

Although competency is a legal concept, the following algorithm is intended to provide a methodology for assessing competency to stand trial that not only would likely withstand a *Daubert* challenge but that would also provide much needed clarification on the link between cognitive functioning and behavior (see Figure 11.1).

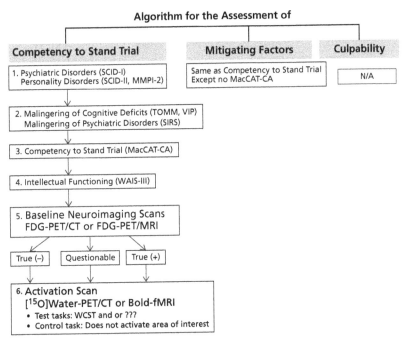

Figure 11.1 The Algorithms

While there is, at present, little empirical evidence as to what underlying capacities are necessary for competency status, it is generally accepted that the ability to reason or make proper decisions is essential. In addition, it is believed that decision-making capacity is a multidimensional construct that requires a combination of intact cognitive abilities, including attention, memory, general intellectual functioning, abstract reasoning, problem solving, and the ability to regulate emotions (Moberg & Kniele, 2006). Further, some neuropsychologists agree that measures of executive functioning provide the most reliable findings in capacity evaluations (Moberg & Kniele, 2006). Since at present there is a lack of established methodological and procedural guidelines for competency evaluations, the assessment of competency to stand trial should include the following tests, measures, and techniques, based on the following rationales (see, Figure 11.1):

- As discussed in detail in chapter 4, the SCID-I and SCID-II were designed to assess the major Axis I and Axis II disorders. The rational for using the SCID-I and SCID-II is based on the fact that many individuals within the forensic setting are diagnosed with psychiatric and personality disorders and the fact that these tools produce relatively good to excellent interrater agreement on Axis I and Axis II disorders. In addition, case law and research findings have indicated that major personality disorders, in particular those with psychotic features, and psychotic disorders, such as schizophrenia, can result in adjudicative incompetency (Moberg & Kniele, 2006). Therefore, to assess the presence of *Diagnostic and Statistical Manual of Mental Disorders* (fourth edition, text revision, 2000) Axis I and Axis II disorders the evaluation should include the SCID-I and SCID-II. Further, because no single measure can reliable establish the presence of these disorders, it is highly recommended that additional measures be employed to determine the presence of psychiatric and personality disorders, such as the Minnesota Multiphasic Personality Inventory-2, the Millon Clinical Multiaxial Inventory-III, and/or the Personality Assessment Inventory.
- Since as previously noted the rate of malingering within the forensic setting is presumed to be as high as 30%, any neuropsychological evaluation must also determine whether or not subjects are malingering. Failure to assess for malingering can call into the questions the findings of other neuropsychological tests employed. The decision to use the Test of Memory Malingering, Validity Indicator Profile, and Structured Interview of Reported Symptoms is based on the fact that these tests have relatively high positive predictive power and that, unlike the Minnesota Multiphasic Personality Inventory-2, these tests were specifically designed to assess malingering of cognitive deficits (executive function deficits) and malingering of psychiatric disorders.

- The use of measures specifically designed to assess competency to stand trial, such as the MacCAT-CA, is also highly recommended, since these types of measures may be helpful in revealing specific competence-related capacities. Further, because standard neuropsychological tests have generally been validated in the diagnostic but not the forensic realm, the question remains whether they have sufficient ecological validity to be used in competency assessments (Moberg & Kniele, 2006).
- Neuropsychological testing can play an important role in evaluating cognitive impairment, especially when findings from interviews or other measures are ambiguous or when there is a question of neuropsychological impairment or mental retardation. In addition, a number of neurological, psychiatric, and psychological disorders and diseases have cognitive impairment as part of their symptomatology. Therefore, intellectual ability must also be assessed using measures of intelligence, such as the Wechsler Adult Intelligence Scale, Third Edition.
- Regardless of the results on the aforementioned neuropsychological tests and measures, the presence or absence of any gross brain abnormality, such as a brain tumor, should also be ascertained with neuroimaging tests, such as fluorodeoxyglucose positron emission tomography/computed tomography (FDG-PET/CT).[3] Indeed, even if a single one of these tests, or all of them, suggest the possibility of cognitive impairment or suggest no cognitive impairment, the assessment process must continue, since these measures alone cannot always establish the presence or absence of any dysfunction or impairment with a high degree of certainty. However, some images alone may show the pathology of a severe dysfunction (e.g., a scan can show the characteristics of a severe neurodegenerative disease or multifocal brain injury). In addition, since the error rate of some of these tests and measures has yet to be systematically established, and because neuroimaging techniques are arguably more objective and reliable, assessments including neuroimaging scans may more likely withstand a *Daubert* challenge than assessments based solely on neuropsychological tests and measures. Further, FDG-PET/CT is arguably the most appropriate modality to employ, since it allows for the simultaneous assessment of structure and function, thereby eliminating the possibility of errors in image interpretation.
- Irrespective of whether the FDG-PET/CT scan is abnormal, questionable, or normal, the decision to continue the assessment is based on the fact that even if an individual has a gross structural abnormality, cognitive impairment can only be inferred. A brain activation scan based on [15O]water-PET/CT or blood-oxygen-level-dependent functional MRI should, therefore, be obtained using an appropriate distractor task (control task) and the Wisconsin Card

Sort Test (WCST) to activate the frontal lobes. The decisions to use the WCST is based on the facts that the WCST (a) is known to activate the dorsolateral prefrontal cortex, which is of particular importance for performing executive function tasks, and (b) is known to also activate the orbitofrontal cortex, which has been primarily linked to aggression. The decision to rely on fMRI or [^{15}O]water-PET/CT to assess functional impairment is based on the following:

- PET/CT is currently the only available neuroimaging technique that is truly quantitative. However, fMRI with the addition of arterial spin labeling can be quantitative and may eventually become a global standard for routine clinical use for measuring brain perfusion.
- The activation value is obtained by scanning the subject multiple times while the subject is alternately performing the distractor task and the WCST and then averaging the values.[4] [^{15}O]water is currently the most established technique for brain perfusion imaging, and since ^{15}O has a short half-life, multiple scans can be obtained relatively quickly. However, because the temporal resolution of fMRI is higher than that of PET/CT, it may eventually become the technology of choice for this purpose.
- Because of the neuronal activity during activation, blood flow increases. More specifically, blood flow is one of the first physiological responses to changes in neuronal activity and occurs almost instantaneously. Therefore, because activation tasks last only a few seconds to minutes, blood flow, rather than metabolism, is the most appropriate to assess. Further, the FDG-PET metabolism tracer does not allow for multiple activations in a single setting; the activation period must be significantly longer because of the slow FDG uptake. In addition, while single photon emission tomography (SPECT) also measures regional cerebral blood flow, this technique is not optimal since the SPECT blood flow tracer has a long half-life, allowing only one measure per day in ordinary medical settings.[5] Finally, SPECT has relatively poor spatial and temporal resolution compared to fMRI and [^{15}O]water-PET and is not a true quantitative measure.

11.2.2 Assessing Cognitive Functioning

In law, a mitigating factor is any evidence or information presented to the court regarding a defendant or the circumstances of the crime that may result in reduced charges or a reduced sentence. Courts have stressed that, because of the constitutional requirement of the fundamental respect for human dignity set out by the 8th Amendment, information must be provided on previous history and the character of the defendant, as well as the circumstances surrounding the particular criminal offense (Melton, 1997). In the United States, the issue of mitigating factors is of particular importance in death-penalty cases, and most mitigating evidence is based on clinical evaluations of a particular defendant involving neuroscientific analysis. However, while abnormal brain functioning may be a mitigation factor for judges and jurors to consider, neither mental illness nor severe cognitive impairment automatically leads to a reduction in sentence. In fact, trial courts vary greatly in their approach to neuroscience evidence offered for purpose of mitigation. Consider the following:

- In *Rogers v. State* (2001), the Florida Supreme Court held that, because an MRI scan had already been conducted that showed no impairments, the defendant was not entitled to a PET scan.
- In *Smith v. Anderson* (2005), the defendant's sought to have his death sentence vacated by introducing CT and MRI scans; the federal appellate court, however, found that the evidence was not compelling enough to prove organic brain injury, because it was not conclusive.
- In *State v. Reid* (2006) the Supreme Court of Tennessee affirmed the jury's decision to impose the death penalty even though defense experts testified that (a) the defendant had difficulty in language skills, lacked reasoning in complicated situations, and lost motor skills due to brain injury, and (b) due to atrophy of the left temporal lobe, as shown on PET and MRI scans, psychotic and cognitive disorders impacted the criminal acts.

Another case further illustrates the problems inherent in introducing neuroscience evidence for purpose of mitigation. In 2009 a neuroscientist testifying for the defense in the sentencing hearing of Brian Dugan, who had pled guilty to the rape and murder of a young girl, stated that on a diagnostic checklist and an fMRI scan the defendant showed responses and abnormal brain functioning similar to other psychopaths, and, therefore, Dugan's psychopathic disorder should be a mitigating factor. The prosecution's expert witness, however, criticized the defense's use of brain imaging, contending that it was not possible to draw conclusions about psychopathic behavior based on fMRI data, much less about behavior that took place 26 years ago. After deliberating for 10 hours, the jury sentenced Dugan to death.

Despite the fact that many legal scholars and scientists disagree about what conclusions can be drawn from neuroimaging scans, the use of this type of evidence will continue to increase, because the threshold for admitting neuroscientific evidence is lower at the penalty phase than it is at the trial phase. This, however, does not mean that a less vigorous standard should be applied in assessing cognitive functioning for purpose of mitigation than that used to assess, for example, competency to stand trial. Indeed, as noted throughout this book, relying on a single measure, test, or technique to make competency and/or culpability determinations or establish mitigating factors is problematic since, at present, the error rate of most tests, measures, and techniques is not well established. Therefore, to determine the presence/absence of cognitive dysfunction for the purpose of mitigation, all tests, measures, and techniques used to determine competency to stand trial, with the exception of tests specifically designed to determine competency to stand trials, such as the MacCAT-CA, should be used (see Figure 11.1).

11.2.3 Not Guilty by Reason of Insanity, Diminished Capacity, and Guilty But Mentally Ill

As previously noted, neuroimaging results demonstrate the condition of a defendant's brain at the time the scan was obtained. Likewise, neuropsychological test results and results from personality inventories and other measures indicate the defendant's cognitive functioning and/or the presence or absence of neuropsychiatric or personality disorders at the time of the evaluation. In contrast, the defenses of not guilty by reason of insanity, diminished capacity, and guilty but mentally ill focus on the defendant's state of mind at the time the crime was committed. Although definitions of legal insanity differ from state to state, generally an individual is considered insane and therefore not responsible for the criminal conduct if, at the time of the offense, as a result of a severe mental disease or defect, he or she was unable to appreciate the nature and quality or the wrongfulness of the acts.[6] Several states have eliminated the insanity defense, and a number of other states have adopted a verdict that allows for a defendant to be mentally ill but also guilty of his or her criminal acts. However, unlike not guilty by reason of insanity, guilty but mentally ill is not a criminal defense but rather an alternative verdict in cases in which the insanity defense is employed. Diminished capacity is a partial defense that requires that the defendant acted with a particular state of mind. To be more precise, at the time the crime was committed, the defendant must have acted with premeditation, deliberation, and the specific intent to harm. If there is sufficient evidence to create a reasonable doubt as to whether the defendant did not have the capacity to premeditate, deliberate, or form the specific intent to kill, the state cannot convict the defendant of first-degree murder.[7]

Brain areas that are likely to be of interest in mens rea related defenses are the prefrontal cortex, parietal association cortex, and other areas, including the hippocampus and amygdala, which are among the most studied yet most complex areas of the human brain (Brown & Murphy, 2010). However, because these areas are responsive to a great variety of stimuli and are engaged in nearly all of human behavior, even the most reliable and valid methodology cannot, as of yet, provide a causal link between violent behavior and cognitive functioning. Further, as alluring as neuroimaging scans can be, these scans vary too much from one individual to the next to serve as a basis for assessing culpability because "'normal' brain features have yet to be determined (Gurley & Marcus, 2008).

In August of 1966, Charles Whitman, a student at the University of Texas at Austin, climbed to the top of an observation tower and killed 14 people before being killed by the police. Shortly before the incident, Whitman wrote: "lately (I can't recall when it started), I have been a victim of many unusual and irrational thoughts. These thoughts constantly recur and it requires a tremendous mental effort to concentrate on useful and progressive tasks" (Whitman, 1966). During Whitman's autopsy doctors found that he had a malignant brain tumor compressing his amygdala, an area of the brain that is presumed to be involved in the regulation of fear and emotional responses (Lavergne, 1997). While a structural neuroimaging scan that clearly shows a lesion may provide useful evidence, for the purpose of, for example, mitigation, functional neuroimaging scans such as a PET scan, introduced to suggest that his or her brain made him/her do it, cannot explain much (Valeo, 2012). Further, even if a gross structural brain abnormality such as a lesion is identified shortly after the crime is committed, cognitive impairment can only be inferred. In addition, while the diagnosis of a mental disorder can only rarely be made solely on the basis of neuroimages,[8] whether or not a particular defendant has a mental illness is often irrelevant to his or her capacity to distinguish right from wrong. Clearly, not everyone with a mental disorder or disease is, by definition, legally insane. Further, while currently available imaging modalities may identify cognitive dysfunction, the technology is not sophisticated enough to demonstrate the existence of cognitive impairments, as set out in the *M'Naghten* rule.[9] It has also been argued, and I agree, that the complex situations that give rise to criminal and violent behavior cannot be replicated or even approximated in a laboratory setting (Brown & Murphy, 2010). Clearly, "perfect unison between the experimental task and the criminal setting is impossible to reach" since there is no way to recreate the emotions and cognitive processes at the time the crime was committed to determine contemporaneous mens rea as is required by law (Brown & Murphy, 2010, p. 1196). Therefore, relying on findings from research studies that have demonstrated a link between violent behavior and cognitive impairment for the purpose of establishing a lack of culpability or mens rea is inappropriate.

Recall that *Daubert* (1993) and its progeny provide guidelines for determining the admissibility of expert testimony under Rule 702 and in doing so emphasize that, when evaluating the validity of proffered expert opinion, federal courts must assess four factors: (a) error rate, (b) falsifiability, (c) peer review and publication, and (d) general acceptance within the relevant scientific community. Reliability and relevance, however, are not the only criteria for determining the admissibility of scientific evidence; FRE 403 also requires judges to balance the probative value of the proffered evidence against the risk that the evidence may confuse the issues or mislead the jury. Indeed, as the court noted in *United States v. Pohlot* (1987), "presenting defense theories or psychiatric testimony . . . that do not truly negate mens rea may cause confusion about what the law requires" (p. 890). Based on the foregoing, the algorithm for determining culpability proceeds as set forth in Figure 11.1.

11.3 Conclusion

It may be argued that, while the algorithms used to assess competency to stand trial and cognitive functioning for the purpose of mitigation are theoretically sound, their practical applications may be limited, since PET/CT and fMRI are not yet widely available and/or relatively expensive to use. It may also be argued that the data derived from a single subject may lack statistical reliability. However, neuroimaging techniques such as MRI and PET/CT used to determine structural and functional abnormalities have been shown to have high sensitivity and specificity in routine clinical practice. In addition, since most currently available measures when used in isolation are unreliable, the algorithms were specifically designed to counter this argument by employing a multimodal/multidisciplinary approach to the assessment of cognitive functioning. This is of particular importance, since to date not a single study has been able to reliably demonstrate a characteristic pattern of cognitive dysfunction based on neuropsychiatric, neuropsychological, and neuroimaging techniques and measures that is predictive of a loss of control or the emergence of violent behavior that is applicable to an individual case (Sinnott-Armstrong, Roskies, Brown, & Murphy, 2008).

Accepting poor reliability and validity of neuroscientific expert testimony proffered in a court of law can be costly, in that it may undermine the goals of equitable justice. A number of courts have responded to the problem of scientifically unreliable expert testimony by (a) allowing the defense and prosecution to introduce an expert witness solely for the purpose of refuting the science underlying an earlier stated opinion and (b) using cautionary jury instructions to educate jurors about the problems and risks associated with expert testimony presented during trial (Compton, 2010). However, as first articulated in *Frye* (1923), judges should bow to scientific experts. Therefore, it is crucial that prosecution and defense counsel not abandon their duty of assisting courts at arriving at the truth by proffering expert testimony based on unreliable science.

12

A Cautionary Tale

Brain Scans Might Predict Future Criminal Behavior

A new study conducted by the Mind Research Network in Albuquerque, N.M., shows that neuroimaging data can predict the likelihood of whether a criminal will reoffend following release from prison. (Duke University, March 29, 2013)

12.1 Introduction

Developments in neuroscience and neuroimaging in particular have produced an extraordinary amount of literature and commentaries, and one is likely to see a news report headlining neuroimaging, like the one at the start of this chapter, quite frequently. There is no doubt that colorful neuroimages have led some scientists to make claims that far outpace reliable scientific data; nevertheless, many legal scholars and the general public are often tempted to believe these statements. Although neuroimaging scans have provided evidence of changes in brain structures and functions associated with many disorders and diseases, as of yet neuroimaging cannot be used to reliable diagnose most disorders and diseases, nor can this technology be used to determine exactly where in the brain many disorders and diseases originate.

Questions about the nature and origin of human behavior have been the focus of philosophical debates dating back to antiquity; however, it is only in the past few centuries that scientists have attempted to understand the intricacies of the structures and functions of our nervous system and, more recently, the nature of mind and brain (Zimmer, 2004). Some scholars worry that neuroscientific findings about how brain dysfunction results in violent behavior will change our views of conscious intent and, ultimately, moral and legal responsibility. Others have argued that although neuroscience offers a look into how humans think and behave, "nothing in neuroscience will make the idea of criminal responsibility disappear" (Hotz, 2009). As has been noted:

> In truth, neuroscience can offer very little to the understanding of responsibility. Responsibility is a human construct that exists only in the social world, where there is more than one person. It is a socially constructed rule that exists only in the context of human interaction. No pixel in the brain will ever be able to show culpability or nonculpability. (Gazzaniga, 2006, p. 100)

Morse (2004), similarly, has argued that while neuroscientific evidence may provide assistance in performing the culpability evaluation, neuroscience can "never tell us how much control ability is required for responsibility. That question is normative, moral and, ultimately, legal" (p. 179).

Regardless of one's point of view, the fact remains that our current lack of practical and theoretical knowledge will continue to impose substantial limits on the application of neuroscientific evidence, in particular neuroimaging evidence, to law (Silva, 2013). Furthermore, while neuroscientific advances may provide new types of evidence for parties within the legal system, any novel and complex technology has the potential to be misunderstood and misused (Compton, 2010). In fact, "scientific evidence is likely to be shrouded with an aura of near infallibility, akin to the ancient oracle of Delphi" (*United States v. Alexander*, 1975, p. 168).

12.2 The Pitfalls of Neuroscience

In 2006 Williams was indicted for felony murder based on his role in the alleged beating and killing of his five-year-old daughter. In July 2008, the government filed a motion to (a) exclude defendant's mental health expert witnesses at the guilt-phase of trial and (b) for an evidentiary *Daubert* hearing. At the *Daubert* hearing, defense experts Dr. Stewart, a clinical psychiatrist, and Dr. Young, a neuropsychologist, opined that the defendant suffered from borderline intellectual functioning and "brain damage," which impaired his ability to understand and adapt to highly stressful situations and, consequently, did not have the capacity to form the requisite intent (*United States v. Williams*, 2009).

On rebuttal, the government's experts, Dr. Resnick, a forensic psychiatrist, and Dr. Hall, a psychologist and forensic neuropsychologist, offered their opinions regarding Drs. Young and Stewart's diagnoses and methodology, concluding they were unreliable and unfounded.[1] The Court found Dr. Young's methodology reliable; however, it contended that Dr. Young failed to conduct crucial tests that would have significantly impacted the reliability of her overall methodology. More specifically, the government argued that Dr. Young failed to conduct a functional magnetic resonance imaging (fMRI) scan and a quantitative EEG (QEEG) that could have the potential to definitively prove or disprove the defendant's claim of brain damage (*United States v. Williams*, 2009). At the conclusion of the *Daubert* hearing, the government requested that the defendant undergo the fMRI and QEEG testing, but the Court made it clear that it would order the testing only if both parties agreed to it. The defendant objected to the government's request, and the Court refused to order the defendant to undergo the tests. The government subsequently asserted that Dr. Young's methodology remained inadequate and unreliable as a result of her failure to support her opinions with results from an fMRI and QEEG and sought to exclude her testimony (*United States v. Williams*, 2009). The Court concluded that while it may be true that additional testing may have uncovered the extent of defendant's brain damage, there was nothing inherently unreliable about the testing Dr. Young conducted. Consequently, the government could use Dr. Young's failure to administer the fMRI and QEEG to go to the weight of her testimony but it did not preclude the admissibility of her testimony (*United States v. Williams*, 2009).

This case clearly underscores (a) the importance of employing a multimodal approach for the assessment of brain functioning in the context of violent behavior, (b) the need for experts to understand and acknowledge the inherent limitations of neuropsychological tests and neuroimaging techniques, and (c) the difficulty of making a valid and reliable admissibility determination of scientific evidence proffered in a court of law. This case also illustrates a number of common methodological shortcomings. For example, defense experts did not administer malingering tests to ensure that the results of the neuropsychological tests were not compromised. Further, the defense experts' sole reliance on neuropsychological tests that formed the basis of their opinion is problematic, since these tests in isolation cannot establish "brain damage" with a high degree of certainty. Since brain damage can only be reliably ascertained with neuroimaging techniques, the government's assertion that the defense expert's methodology was inadequate and unreliable as a result of her failure to support her opinions with results from an fMRI and QEEG was, therefore, especially appropriate. However, with regard to QEEG, the current position of both the American Academy of Neurology and the American Clinical Neurophysiology Society is that, due to its methodological and technical limitations, QEEG is not recommended for use in criminal proceedings (Martell, 2009).

12.2.1 The Pitfalls

The brain, your honor, will take the witness stand: Researchers probe how the mind determines crime and punishment, but the science isn't beyond a reasonable doubt. (Hotz, 2009)

The ability to view the human brain in action has triggered strong reactions, ranging from the extremes of euphoria at the notion that we will no longer have to guess what an individual is thinking (Bandes, 2008) to panic that the law's fundamental assumptions of responsibility and autonomy may eventually be upended (Pardo & Patterson, 2010). Indeed, it has been argued that research into the neural workings of the human brain, aided by sophisticated brain imaging techniques such as positron emission tomography (PET), will "probably completely change . . . nearly every area of law" (Chorvat & McCabe, 2006, p. 128) and, in due time, neuroscience will "dominate the entire legal system" (Gazzaniga, 2006, p. 88). However, as Morse (2006) cautioned, those who look to neuroscience to help resolve questions of criminal law need to guard against what he has termed "brain overclaim syndrome." Consider the following.

James Fallon, professor emeritus of anatomy and neurobiology and professor of psychiatry and human behavior at the University of California, Irvine, School of Medicine, has spent decades studying the brain activity, psychology and genetics of psychiatric patients, and the brain scans of psychopathic serial killers. A few years ago, while studying brain scans of several family members, he made a startling discovery: one of the scans perfectly matched the pattern he had observed in the brains of serial killers. Perhaps most disturbing, however, was the fact that the scan in question was his own (Fallon, 2013).

It has been argued that, "the evaluation of research on the neurobiology of violence demands conceptual clarity, along with careful analysis of methods and data to prevent misunderstanding, and possible abuse of the results" (Brower & Price, 2000, p. 146). Clearly, there are limits to the objectivity of neuroimaging scans and neuropsychological tests and measures that must be acknowledged, addressed, and overcome. The following list of issues is presented for the purpose of demonstrating the problems associated with and the limitations inherent in proffering cognitive neuroscience evidence in a court of law:

12.2.1.1 Correlating Violent Behavior with Brain Dysfunction

- A brain abnormality does not necessarily imply dysfunction since the brain has more than one way to execute a function. Neuroscientific data allows only correlation, not causality, to be inferred.
- Even if a structural neuroimaging scan is abnormal, this does not necessarily imply functional abnormality and vice versa.
- There is no reliable baseline for determining whether an individual's brain functioning qualifies as normal (Snead, 2007).
- An inherent problem with all neuroimaging testimony offered in a court of law is that no neuroimaging scan can capture the individual's brain under the same condition that existed at the time the crime was committed.

12.2.1.2 The Issue of Individuality

- Research findings can provide only generalized averages and correlations that may not reliably reflect the causal mechanisms at work in a particular defendant.
- Brain structures vary significantly within the normal population, as does the degree to which an individual's brain may compensate for pathology.
- To the extent that data links reduced activity in a particular brain area to cognitive dysfunction, the findings are almost always based on correlations between aggregate data and outcome measures, which can obscure the full extent of individual differences (Morse, 2006).
- Advances in research have revealed the troubling variability of tests normed on mainstream cultures but routinely used with diverse populations (see Hicks, 2004). Therefore, care must be taken to choose assessment measures normed on populations that accurately reflect the subject.

12.2.1.3 Issues Associated with Data Acquisition

- The utility of functional imaging depends on the questions the subject is being asked. Scientists and clinicians must choose tasks that provide theoretical insight into the psychological and neural processes of interest and must avoid the influence of neural processes unrelated to the question of interest (Wager, Hernandez, & Lindquist, 2009).
- Psychometric tests should only be used if they are (a) relevant to the legal issue or psychological construct underlying the legal issue and (b) used for the purpose for which they were designed and validated (Heilbrun, 1992).
- Inappropriate use of neuropsychological test norms undermines the validity of the test results and the expert opinion based on those results.
- Multimodal assessment allows the potential limitations of any one test, measure, or technique to be overcome.
- Neuroimages are thought to be "real-time" images; however, the temporal resolution of the hemodynamic response is several seconds while events relevant to information processing are at least three orders of magnitude faster. Similarly, the spatial resolution of PET, single photon emission tomography (SPECT), and fMRI is measured in millimeters while nerve cells and axons are three orders of magnitude smaller (Blakemore, 2005).

12.2.1.4 Issues Associated with Data Analysis and Data Interpretation

- Neuroimaging data are reconstructed by using a set of mathematical assumptions that are framed by an experimental paradigm. Image reconstructions involve statistical analyses of comparisons; however, these steps are not standardized from one technology to the next or from one laboratory or equipment to another (Baskin, Edersheim, & Price, 2007).
- Brain mapping experiments generally rely on a method known as cognitive subtraction. However, recent research has indicated that a basic assumption underlying this approach—that brain activation is due to the additional processes triggered by the experimental task—is wrong (Case Western Reserve University, 2013).
- Neuroimaging scans tend to represent statistical maps of the probability of a change in local blood flow or glucose metabolism correlated with some task being carried out by the subject, as is the case with fMRI (Baskin et al., 2007).
- Since no study can achieve perfectly consistent results between experimental trials or among subjects, due to the complex ways in which areas of the brain interact with each other and with the subject's external environment, it is impossible to attribute a particular action to a single, specific, and consistent neurological cause (Nugent, 2009).
- Psychiatric neuroimaging studies have established a high degree of variability within groups of healthy and ill subjects, often with considerable overlap between the distributions of the two groups. In the language of diagnostic tests, imaging studies are usually not highly sensitive to the difference between illness and health (Farah & Gillihan, 2012).
- All currently available neuroimaging techniques have their respective strengths and weaknesses; even the most modern machines "are not diagnostic in that they do not perfectly predict who is violent and who is not" (Raine, 2002, p. 73).
- A neuroimaging scan is the product of a complex set of techniques, subjective decisions (e.g., what type of image should be acquired), technical choices (e.g., how thin or thick the slices should be), and informed interpretations (Baskin et al., 2007).

12.2.1.5 The Problem with Demonstrating Causality

- By design, human functional neuroimaging studies are necessarily correlational and as such cannot address which brain regions are necessary for a given function but highlight only those regions or networks that are sufficient (Chatterjee, 2005; Friston & Price, 2003).

- Current models suggest that higher level brain functions typically are dependent on interactions among a distributed web of neural centers; however, the ability of other brain regions to take over from injured areas suggests limits to the conclusions that can be drawn from localized deficits (Appelbaum, 2009).
- There is no one-to-one correspondence between a neuropsychological test and a brain area or cognitive function; tests can be failed for a number of reasons (Snowden, 2010).

12.2.1.6 Evidentiary Reliability and Neuroscientific Evidence

- Although neuroscience can shed some light on the legal questions of capacity and responsibility, it cannot provide legally dispositive answers or render the questions superfluous (Bandes, 2010).
- Courts may find neuroimaging scans to be quite suggestive in certain mental status determinations; however, neuroimaging results viewed in isolation cannot and should not be considered dispositive (Nugent, 2009).
- While it is possible that certain brain lesions can disable various capacities, few criminal cases will involve a precise, identifiable neurological mechanism that will demonstrate that criminal responsibility was not present (Morse, 2006).

12.2.1.7 Neuroscientific Expert Testimony

- Uttal (2012) warns cognitive neuroscientists about making claims that brain images generated by new brain imaging technologies reflect, correlate, or represent cognitive processes. Despite its utility in anatomic and physiological applications, neuroimaging research has yet to consistently provide evidence for correlation with cognition.
- Both attorneys and federal judges have cited experts' abandoning of objectivity and becoming advocates for the side that hired them as the most frequent problem with expert testimony (Treadway Johnson, Krafka, & Cecil, 2000).
- Awareness of psychometric properties, groups norms and culturally influenced variability is important, especially if the expert testimony may be open to cross-examination by opposing attorneys (Kalmbach & Lyons, 2006).
- Many problems have been identified regarding the performance of psychologists as expert witnesses. These include the (a) absence of collateral sources of information; (b) use of psychological tests that are outdated, irrelevant, and/or psychometrically unsound; and (c) failure to link data, reasoning, and conclusions (Heilbrun, Marczyk, DeMatteo, & Goldstein, 2008).

12.2.1.8 General Issues

- While flexible study designs and data analysis can dramatically increase the likelihood of obtaining nominally significant results, conclusions drawn from these results can be false (Simmons, Nelson, & Simonsohn, 2011).
- Many experiments that investigate the relationship between violent behavior and brain dysfunction are conducted in a laboratory setting. Thus findings from these studies cannot be easily generalized to real-world situations.
- None of the currently available imaging modalities or any of the currently available neuropsychological tests have any independent predictive value.
- To draw valid conclusions about the results from brain imaging scans or neuropsychological tests, one must determine whether the test, measure, and/or technique is sensitive, accurate, valid, and reliable and whether or not the results are reproducible.

The above is by no means a complete list of the problems associated with the acquisition, analysis, and interpretation of neuroimaging scans in the clinical and forensic setting. In fact, there are ongoing debates regarding other critical issues, such as whether or not observations made under resting conditions have privileged status as a fundamental measure of brain functioning (Morcom & Fletcher, 2007; Stark & Squire, 2001) or whether or not multivariate pattern analysis is more effective than classical general linear model analysis for detecting response patterns (Todd, Nystrom, & Cohen, 2013).

Researchers have also begun to question the reliability and validity of many neuroimaging studies undertaken to date. For example, a 2010 study focusing on the reproducibility of fMRI brain scan studies concluded that, on average, there is only a 50% correlation between the brain regions that light up in the first and second tests in the same individual, suggesting that results from a single fMRI study may not be very reliable (Bennett & Miller, 2010). Similarly, a team at the Massachusetts Institute of Technology in Cambridge argued that high correlations between brain activity and inherently ambiguous concepts, such as personality, are simply not possible (Vul, Harris, Winkielman, & Pashler, 2009). More specifically, Vul and colleagues noted that correlations reported in many fMRI studies are frequently overstated because researchers tend to report only the highest correlations or only those correlations that exceed some threshold. In addition, it has been suggested that null-hypothesis testing is insufficient for most goals of neuroscience because it can only indicate that a specific brain region is involved to some nonzero degree in a particular task contrast (Kriegeskorte, Lindquist, Nichols, Poldrack, & Vul, 2010). Further, to reliably determine exactly how the brain produces behavior and cognition, neuroscientists must answer a number of questions, including (a) which brain area is most responsible for this cognitive function or (b) what particular cognitive function is this brain area most involved in. These questions necessitate an evaluation of effect sizes and a comparison of effect sizes across tasks and regions (Kriegeskorte et. al., 2010). Finally, it must be pointed out that because researchers typically report only those results that attain statistical significance, the effect sizes reported in the literature tend to be substantially inflated (Ioannidis, 2008; Yarkoni, 2007). Indeed, a 2013 meta-analysis concluded that the median statistical power in neuroscience is 21%, while fMRI studies of brain volume abnormalities were found to have a median statistical power of 8% (Button et al., 2013).

Despite these significant scientific limitations and unresolved methodological issues, neuroscientific data is increasingly being used as legal evidence in criminal cases for various purposes, including establishing a lack of mens rea. Clearly this is problematic for a number of reasons. First, it may be argued that while *Daubert* (1993) does not specify what error rate of a test, measure, or technique is acceptable, and the scientific community likewise has yet to establish an acceptable error rate, even a statistical power of 80% is unacceptable. Second, the seductive allure of neuroscience explanations may lead to jurors' inability to differentiate good from poor explanations of psychological phenomena, even when an irrelevant statement about brain function is added (Weisberg, Keil, Goodstein, Rawson, & Gray, 2008). Third, in science, validity equals reproducibility and, in law, scientific validity equals evidentiary reliability.

One of the major tenets of the scientific method is reproducibility, the ability to replicate or reproduce experimental research findings. Unfortunately, most results have not been subjected to the test of precise replication. This, however, is problematic, since findings from a single study may merely reflect idiosyncrasies in subject population or research methods or may simply be due to random chance. Further, reliance on small and/or nonreproducible studies limits our ability to draw valid conclusions about the relationship between brain function and violent behavior and arguably cannot satisfy the admissibility criteria set forth in *Daubert* (1993). Finally, and perhaps most important, it must always be remembered that no currently available test, measure, or technique is capable of determining what was going on in the brain of a particular defendant at the time he or she committed the crime. While it is possible that an underlying brain disorder or abnormality, such as a gross structural abnormality that affected brain function, may have influenced a particular violent act, even this correlation is, at best, tenuous.

12.3 The Future of Cognitive Neuroscience

The ultimate goal of neuroscience is to observe the human brain at all levels of structure and function, from large networks of brain cells to neurotransmitter and receptor molecules, with time scales ranging from milliseconds to minutes. To achieve this goal would provide neuroscientists with biological building blocks not unlike those that the human genome project has provided geneticists (Ganis & Kosslyn, 2002). However, accomplishing the tasks of identifying all the building blocks associated with brain functions and behavior is arguably even more complicated than that of identifying our genetic makeup. In fact, whereas the human genome contains an estimated 3×10^9 base pairs within approximately 10^5 genes, the human brain contains approximately 10^{14} synapses on about 10^{10} neurons (Ganis & Kosslyn, 2002).

12.3.1 Neuroreceptor and Neurotransmitter Imaging

It has been suggested, and I agree, that the true correlates between the brain and behavior are located at a much more microscopic level of analysis—the networks of neurons that make up the brain (Uttal, 2012). Indeed, the area from which every kind of emotion and behavior, including violent behavior, originate is the brain, which in turn is governed by chemical messengers called neurotransmitters. Abnormal levels of extracellular neurotransmitter concentrations and/or abnormalities in the regulation of neurotransmitter release, in fact, continue to remain fundamental components of hypotheses on the neuronal foundations of cognitive, behavioral, neuropsychiatric, and neurodegenerative disorders (Sarter, Bruno, & Parikh, 2007). Imaging of neuroreceptors in vivo can be accomplished using SPECT or PET, both of which require a solution containing a radioligand that binds to the target neuroreceptor, to be injected intravenously, after which the emitted radioactivity is detected using rings of detectors around the head. In contrast to conventional diagnostic imaging procedures, which provide only anatomical or structural information, to date SPECT and PET are the only tools available to visualize the distribution, density, and activity of neurotransmitters, receptors, or transporters in the brain (Shen, Liao, & Tseng, 2012). In addition, PET and SPECT can be used to measure dynamic changes in neurotransmission that occur in response to regional fluctuations in the endogenous neurotransmitter, induced by experimental challenges, either in terms of a physiologic stimulus or as a consequence of pharmacological intervention (Paterson, Tyacke, Nutt, & Knudsen, 2010). More specifically, utilization of radiotracers that label specific receptor sites allows for the examination of neurotransmitter markers in vivo, both under baseline conditions and in response to a variety of experimental manipulations, such as performing a cognitive task.

12.3.2 Hybrid Neuroimaging

It has been contended that to achieve the ultimate goal of neuroimaging requires a combination of imaging techniques with complementary strengths that can provide better temporal and/or spatial resolution than any one technique by itself, but doing so is challenging because different techniques often measure different aspects or consequences of neural activity (Ganis & Kosslyn, 2002). With the introduction of SPECT/CT,

PET/CT, and most recently PET/MRI, hybrid neuroimaging devices have become the modality of choice within the research and medical communities because of the unmatched levels of diagnostic information provided by these hybrids (Zaidi & Mawlawi, 2007). Hybrid neuroimaging modalities are highly synergistic: the sum of, for example, PET and CT is more than its parts. However, while PET/CT has the ability to provide clinically critical anatomic correlation, resulting in increased sensitivity and specificity and attenuation[2] correction, a major limitation of the current PET/CT technology is that data are acquired sequentially rather than simultaneously (Alavi, Mavi, Basu, & Fischman, 2007; von Schulthess, Kuhn, Kaufmann, & Veit-Haibach, 2013). Consequently, PET/MRI may become the method of choice for neuroimaging due to its ability to combine metabolic information, such as glucose metabolism for various functional investigations provided by PET imaging with the various morphological and functional parameters measured by MRI (Garibotto et al., 2013; see also Figure 12.1). Indeed, the simultaneous acquisition of different functional parameters using, for example, PET/MR provides new opportunities to study biochemical processes and pathology in vivo that two stand-alone systems and PET/CT cannot provide (Judenhofer et al., 2008). However, the PET/MRI technique, at present, still has many limitations and weaknesses, and research studies have yet to establish this techniques' effectiveness and ability to image physiologic and pathophysiologic processes simultaneously. Nevertheless, hybrid neuroimaging techniques have the potential to increase specificity and decrease the error rate, which is of great importance in the clinical and forensic setting.

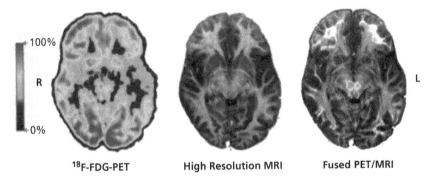

¹⁸F-FDG-PET   High Resolution MRI   Fused PET/MRI

Figure 12.1 Simultaneous PET/MRI Scan of Epilepsy Patient. Shown from left to right are axial FDG-PET, high-resolution MRI scan, and fusion image. Distinct hypometabolism is visible in polar region of left temporal lobe, corresponding to epileptogenic focus. See Color Plate 27 in insert.

Reprinted from Catana, C., Drzezga, A., Heiss, W.-D., & Rosen, B. R. (2012). PET/MRI for neurologic applications. *Journal of Nuclear Medicine*, 53(12), 1916–1925, Figure 7, by permission of SNMMI.

12.4 The Future of Neuroscience and the Law

As noted throughout this book, there is not now, nor will there ever be, a neuroimaging scan or neuropsychological test that can reliably assess what was going on in a defendant's brain at the time he or she committed a crime. Even if a defendant's brain scan obtained after the crime was committed detects a structural and/or functionality abnormality, it is difficult to reliably infer that this abnormality was present at the time of the offense or, even if it was present at that time, that it would have affected the individual's behavior in a significant way. Indeed, because (a) brains scans are obtained long after the violent behaviors that gave rise to these scans have occurred and (b) some individuals will likely develop structural or functional impairment with the passing of time, drawing causal conclusion is not only problematic but also inappropriate. Further, our ability to accurately identify individuals who may commit a violent crime sometime in the future has been and remains very limited due to the technological and methodological problems, and limitations noted here.

Whether a structural and/or a functional brain abnormality renders a particular defendant not responsible for the crime committed is a legal question that can only be answered by the trier of fact. However, there is place for neuroscience evidence in law. With the caveat that the methodology and tests employed to reach an opinion or conclusion are valid and reliable, cognitive neuroscience, and specifically neuroimaging, can be a valuable tool for (a) determining competency related issues, such as competency to stand trial or competency to waive an appeal, (b) assessing structure and function of a defendant's brain for the purpose of mitigation, and (c) determining cognitive functioning within the general and forensic population for the purpose of advancing our understanding of the relationship between brain function and violent behavior.

12.5 Conclusion

In 2011, France took the controversial step of banning the commercial use of brain imaging but permitting its use in court. More specifically, a new law provides that "brain-imaging methods can be used only for medical or scientific research purposes or in the context of court expertise" (Oullier, 2012, p. 7). Of particular interest is the fact that none of the neuroscientists consulted during the drafting process of this law encouraged the courtroom use of neuroimages (Oullier, 2012). Science is dynamic, and the scientific enterprise is cumulative; advances in science build directly on previous research studies and findings. Science is also a collective enterprise; the overall functioning of a system as complex as the human brain cannot be easily inferred from isolated investigations of a few variables (Yarkoni, Poldrack, Van Essen, & Wager, 2010). Indeed, no single experiment can control for most or all extraneous variables and, even if it were possible to isolate and

Figure 12.2 Skull Diagram of Phineas P. Gage

Image Courtesy of Wikimedia Commons: http://en.wikipedia.org/wiki/Phineas_Gage.

control, for example, a single psychological factor or brain region, neuroscientific research findings would allow for only very limited inferences about human behavior to be made (Yarkoni, Poldrack, Van Essen, & Wager, 2010).

To be sure, neuropsychological or neuroimaging evidence cannot establish a lack of criminal responsibility, which is a legal determination, not a medical one. Taken together, however, this evidence can provide a more complete picture of a defendant's brain functioning and its potential causal role in the criminal behavior in question. Further, while brain injury or dysfunction may impair decision-making or influence violent tendencies, there is no single violent brain region. As the case of Phineas Gage illustrates, it is possible to suffer a traumatic brain injury, even one that results in extreme personality changes, and still refrain from engaging in anything remotely violent (see Figure 12.2). While neuroscience has contributed greatly to our understanding of brain structures and functions, there is still no consensus as to whether impairment of a particular brain region provides a direct link to behavior. Currently, the best neuroscience can offer is to provide yet another piece of the puzzle (Batts, 2009).

Regardless of what one thinks about the ultimate value of neuroscience as evidence in a court of law, neuroscience research has increased our understanding of the neural basis of psychiatric disorders, addiction, and cognitive, and emotional processing (Brown and Murphy, 2010). However, courts must be aware that the connection between what scientists know about general brain physiology and functioning and what clinicians can determine by studying an individual brain is tenuous and unsupported by significant scientific data (Compton, 2010). Similarly, neuroscientists asked to provide expert testimony must acknowledge the inherent limitations of all currently available measures to assess cognitive functioning in the context of violent behavior. Clearly, only a true appreciation of the limits of neuroscientific techniques will allow for an objective evaluation of their usefulness in a court of law.

Further, while studies reviewed in this book and the resulting algorithms may appear to be simplistic in their approach to delineating the potential causes of violent behavior, they should, in fact, be interpreted within the framework of Barak's (1998) interdisciplinary criminology, where different points of view relevant to a specific behavior are treated as being complimentary. Indeed, understanding that each perspective in fact provides another piece of the puzzle from a different yet interrelated point of view will result in a more complete explanation and capture all of the dimensions of the phenomena of violence (Walsh & Hemmens, 2010). Thus, the purpose of this book is to further elucidate the phenomena of violence, without reducing

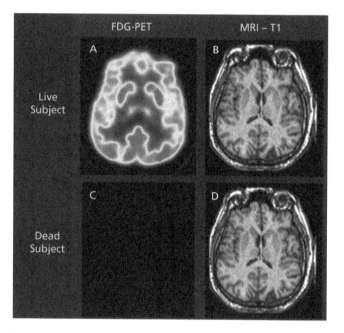

Figure 12.3 The Importance of a Multimodal Assessment. As the figure clearly illustrates, functional neuroimaging modalities, such as FDG-PET, can only provide an in vivo image of metabolic activities, while structural imaging with CT or MRI cannot differentiate viable tissue from dead tissue. See Color Plate 28 in insert.

violent behavior to cognitive impairments. More specifically, the intent is to inform the legal and scientific communities of limitations inherent in all currently available neuropsychological tests, measures, and neuroimaging techniques, and their importance to future research studies.

Finally, I would like to leave readers with an image that further illustrates some of the issues discussed in the preceding chapters (see Figure 12.3). To advance our understanding of the relationship between brain function and violent behavior requires the collaboration of various disciplines; a multimodal approach to the assessment of cognitive dysfunction in the context of violent behavior; valid and reliable tests, measures, and techniques; acknowledgment of a technique's limitation; and the transparent disclosure of research methods and findings.

Notes

Chapter 1

1 The Ramayana, an ancient Sanskrit epic, tells the story of Rama, whose wife Sita is abducted by the king of Sri Lanka. Thematically, the Ramayana explores human values and the concept of dharma (that which upholds, supports, or maintains the regulatory order of the universe).
2 The Mahabharata tells the story of a dynastic battle for the throne of Hastinapura, the kingdom ruled by the Kuru clan. The battle produces complex conflicts of kinship, friendship, and family loyalty and duty taking precedence over what is right and what is wrong.
3 As of 2006, 17 states and the Federal government have adopted a version of the M'Naghten test; 10 states have adopted a streamlined version, which asks whether the defendant could appreciate the wrongfulness of his actions; and 15 jurisdictions, inspired by the Model Penal Code, have in place a combination of the volitional incapacity test and some variant of the moral incapacity test, satisfaction of either being enough to excuse. Three states apply the full M'Naghten test, while New Hampshire applies a test that simply asks whether the defendant's conduct was a "product" of the defendant's mental illness (*Clark v. Arizona*, 2006).
4 This comment does not imply that quantum physics was conceived or developed on notions of individual behaviors and actions. This is merely an analogy made by the author.
5 Even though the Model Penal Code is a statutory work, no jurisdiction is required to adhere to its guidelines.

Chapter 2

1 The sulci (or fissures) are the grooves and the gyri are the bumps that can be seen on the surface of the brain.
2 Each lobe can also be divided into areas that serve very specific functions (e.g., right vs. left frontal lobe).
3 Tables 2.1 and 2.2 do not imply that any specific function is localized or that any specific behavior has been reliably linked to a specific brain region or neurotransmitter/neuroreceptor abnormality.
4 This term refers to the ability or tendency of an organism or cell to maintain internal equilibrium by adjusting its physiological processes.
5 Gap junctions permit changes in the electrical properties of one neuron to effect the other, and vice versa, so the two neurons, in effect, behave as one.
6 The blood–brain barrier is a dynamic interface that separates the brain from the circulatory system and protects the CNS from potentially harmful chemicals while maintaining a stable environment and regulating the transport of essential molecules.
7 Even seemingly mild head injuries can result in impairment, though there can be significant improvement depending on several factors related to the insult, the patient, and other factors.

Chapter 3

1 Glucose is the only sugar used by the brain as a fuel to produce energy.
2 CBF refers to the blood supply to the cerebral cortex in a given time (Tolias & Sgouros, 2006).
3 Because of the tight coupling between blood flow and neural activity, scientists are able to use the blood flow changes as a measure for brain activity.
4 The specificity and sensitivity for different parameters defines the limitations and the unique properties of each imaging technique.
5 Temporal resolution refers to how fast images can be produced, while spatial resolution refers to the size of an object that can be imaged clearly.
6 Tomography refers to imaging by sections/sectioning through the use of any type of penetrating wave. The device used in tomography is called a tomograph, and the image produced is called a tomogram.
7 CT scanning is primarily limited to the transverse plane because of the mechanics of the scanning system. All other image planes are synthesized from the volume image constructed from these transverse slices.
8 Spiral CT is a CT technology involving movement in a helical pattern for the purpose of increasing image resolution.
9 In 1944 he received the Nobel Prize in physics for his resonance method for recording the magnetic properties of atomic nuclei.
10 The Larmor or precessional frequency in MRI refers to the rate of precession of the magnetic moment of the proton around the external magnetic field.
11 The term "contrast resolution" refers to the ability to distinguish the differences between two arbitrarily similar but not identical tissues.

12 This image weighting is particularly useful for assessing the cerebral cortex, characterizing focal liver lesions, and identifying fatty tissue and for post-contrast imaging.

13 T2 weighted imaging is useful for detecting edema, revealing white matter lesions, and assessing zonal anatomy in the prostate and uterus.

14 This term refers to the formation of new blood vessels from preexisting vessels.

15 Brownian motion is the presumably random moving of particles suspended in a fluid (a liquid or a gas) resulting from their bombardment by the fast-moving atoms or molecules in the gas or liquid.

16 A voxel represents a single point or sample on a regularly spaced three-dimensional grid.

17 This is a condition in which there is insufficient blood flow to the brain to meet metabolic demands.

18 Brain tissue is made up of cell bodies (gray matter) and the filaments that extend from the cell bodies (white matter). The density of cells (volume of gray matter) in a particular region of the brain appears to correlate positively with various abilities and skills. The density of cells is determined by both genes and environmental factors, such as experience, while the speed with which we can process information is governed by the white matter (Bergman & Afifi, 2005).

19 This type of radiation is composed of particles that individually carry enough kinetic energy to free an electron from a molecule or atom, ionizing it.

20 Hemodynamics, meaning literally "blood movement," is the study of blood flow or blood circulation.

21 Hemoglobin is the protein molecule in red blood cells that carries oxygen from the lungs to the body's tissues and returns carbon dioxide from the tissues to the lungs.

22 Other kinds of fMRI exist; however, these forms of fMRI imaging have not gained as much widespread usage and acceptance as BOLD.

23 Nuclear medicine or radionuclide imaging procedures are noninvasive tests that help physicians diagnose medical conditions. These imaging scans use radioactive agents called radiopharmaceuticals or radiotracers.

24 More specifically, a substance is labeled by including radionuclides in its chemical composition. When the radionuclides decay, their presence can be determined by detecting the radiation emitted by them.

25 Baseline is defined as a rest state, during which the subject lays quietly with eyes closed and ears plugged, during image acquisition.

26 Control state is defined as a state when the transient changes in neuronal activity are due to a control task (subject is performing a task during image acquisition).

27 Activation is defined as a transient increase in neuronal activity due to motor, sensory, or cognitive stimulation task (subject is performing a task that is known to activate the brain region of interest).

28 A radioligand is a radioactive biochemical substance that is used to study the receptor systems of the body.

Chapter 4

1 A true structured interview asks questions in a specific way and leaves little room for interviewers to use their own clinical judgment. Semistructured interviews also have specified questions, but they allow interviewers to use their own skills in eliciting more information and include more open-ended questions.

2 Axis I disorders relevant to this discussion include delirium, dementia, bipolar and major depressive disorder, and schizophrenia. Axis II disorders relevant to this discussion include antisocial, borderline, and obsessive-compulsive personality disorders.

3 Egodystonic refers to feelings, behaviors, and values that are in conflict with one's own self-image.

4 Egosyntonic refers to feelings, behaviors, and values that are in harmony with, or acceptable to, the needs and goals of the ego, or consistent with one's own self-image.

5 Kappa ranges between zero and 1, with zero indicating agreement no better than chance and 1 indicating perfect agreement. It has been suggested that coefficients above 0.75 indicate excellent agreement, those between 0.60 and 0.74 indicate good agreement, those between 0.40 and 0.59 indicate fair agreement, and those below 0.40 indicate poor agreement (Messina et al., 2001).

6 Cluster B disorders include antisocial, borderline, histrionic, and narcissistic personality disorder. Cluster C disorders include avoidant, dependent, and obsessive-compulsive personality disorder.

7 Internal consistency refers to how well the item in a scale measures an identified construct.

8 Test–retest reliability refers to the consistency with which one would obtain the same test results over time.

9 MMPI-2 norms are based on community samples.

10 The MCMI-III was updated in 2008, with a new norming sample of 752 individuals with a wide variety of clinical disorders.

11 Forty-two percent of respondents thought that the BR cutoff score was 70 or lower (Bow et al., 2010).

12 Wise and colleagues (2010) noted that it is not desirable for the two excluded scales to have high alpha coefficients, because these scales are measuring carelessness and not theoretical constructs.

13 In statistics, effect size is a measure of the strength of the relationship between two variables.

14 The Stroop is presumed to be a general measure of executive functioning and dorsolateral prefrontal functioning in particular.

15 In 2006 the Florida Supreme Court affirmed the circuit court's denial of Burns's postconviction motion and the order on mental retardation.

16 The Flynn effect has been demonstrated across a large number of tests, studies, and cultures (Weiss, 2010).

17 Intellectual deficiency is defined as a FSIQ of two or more standard deviations below the mean (FSIQ < 70; Taub & Benson, 2013).

18 Keen was sentenced to death in 1991 after pleading guilty to murder and rape. In 2012 he filed a motion to reopen his postconviction proceeding and provided an affidavit from an expert who took issue with the validity of the scores he had received on earlier IQ tests in support of his motion. The affidavit stated that Keen's WISC score of 111 was inflated due to the practice effect and that his WISC score of 83 should be adjusted to 76 due to the Flynn effect. The expert further opined that Keen's WAIS-III score of 76 should be adjusted to 71 due to the Flynn effect and that his WAIS-IV score should be adjusted from 67 to 66 due to the Flynn effect.

19 For example, only eight patients who had undergone temporal lobectomy were included in the sample (Lohring & Bauer, 2010).

Chapter 5

1 Neil deGrasse Tyson is an American astrophysicist. He is currently the Frederick P. Rose Director of the Hayden Planetarium at the Rose Center for Earth and Space and a research associate in the Department of Astrophysics at the American Museum of Natural History.

2 Structural imaging techniques consist of computerized tomography (CT) and magnetic resonance imaging (MRI). These techniques look at brain architecture and are specifically designed to assess the presence or absence of gross abnormalities such as brain tumors. Functional imaging techniques include functional magnetic resonance imaging (fMRI), single photon emission tomography (SPECT), and positron emission tomography (PET). These techniques add the dimension of live neural activity and are used primarily to assess regional blood flow and/or glucose metabolism, or to study neurotransmitter and neuroreceptor biochemical systems. Functional imaging studies can be done under activation or while the subject/patient is resting. However, only fMRI and PET can generate absolute quantitative data, while SPECT generates semiquantitative data.

3 This region is most often the subject of study and frequently implicated in aggressive and violent behavior.

4 This is not an exhaustive list; other psychiatric disorders have been linked to dysfunction in these areas.

5 A neuromodulator modifies or makes more or less efficient the synaptic action of a neurotransmitter.

6 The *Diagnostic and Statistical Manual of Mental Disorders* (fifth edition; American Psychiatric Association, 2013) has kept the diagnosis of antisocial personality disorder, but it is now on the same axis as the other mental disorders.

7 This is the primary white matter connection between the anterior temporal lobe and the vmPFC.

8 The onset of Korsakoff's syndrome (also called Korsakoff's dementia, Korsakoff's psychosis, or amnesic-confabulatory syndrome) has been linked to chronic alcohol abuse and/or severe malnutrition.

Chapter 6

1 Rabindranath Tagore (1861–1941) was an Indian composer, poet, philosopher, artist, playwright, and novelist and India's first Nobel laureate (in 1913 he won the Nobel Prize for literature).
2 Transcript of Record on Appeal (filed December 19, 1994) at 1156-57, *State v. Simmons*, 944 S.W.2d 165 (Mo. 1997) (en banc) (No. 77269).
3 Grey matter, which is composed of neurons, is associated with processing and cognition.
4 White matter consists mostly of glial cells and myelinated axons that transmit signals from one region of the cerebrum to another and between the cerebrum and lower brain centers. White matter controls the distribution of action potentials, acting as relay and coordinating communication between various brain regions (Fields, 2008).
5 Between adolescence and adulthood, the decrease in grey matter density in the frontal lobes was even more pronounced (Sowell et al., 2001).
6 Myelination, which is the process through which neural pathways are insulated with a white fatty tissue called myelin, leads to a significant increase in cerebral white matter volume (Goldberg, 2001).
7 FA is a measure frequently used in diffusion imaging where it is thought to reflect axonal diameter, fiber density, and myelination in white matter.
8 The UF is a white matter tract in the brain that connects parts of the limbic system (e.g., the amygdala and hippocampus) with, for example, the orbitofrontal cortex. Although its precise function is unknown, it is affected in several psychiatric conditions.
9 Participants in the CD group had a history of serious aggressive and violent behavior, including burglary, robbery, and sexual assault.
10 As previously noted, a given brain region can be involved in many different cognitive processes, and many types of cognitive processes may be subserved by a particular brain structure (Snead, 2008).

Chapter 7

1 Because the admissibility of scientific evidence is a very broad topic, a general discussion is beyond the scope of this book; this discussion is limited to the Federal Rules of Evidence and other legal guidelines that bear on the admissibility of neuroscience evidence.
2 In *Frye*, the defendant appealed his second-degree murder conviction after the trial court refused to allow expert testimony concerning a systolic blood pressure deception test taken by the defendant.
3 This brief statement provided the dominant test for admissibility of scientific evidence for 70 years, including the years after the adoption of the Federal Rules of Evidence in 1975.
4 Two additional states, Arizona and Wisconsin, adopted the *Daubert* standard for the admission of expert testimony in 2012, bringing the number of state court systems that follow the federal rule to 32. Although the *Daubert* standard is now the law in federal court in over half of the states, the *Frye* standard still remains the law in a few jurisdictions, including New York.

5 Briefs of amici curiae were also filed for the Defense Research Institute and the National Academy of Engineering. In addition, briefs of amici curiae urging reversal or affirmance were filed for the American Automobile Manufacturers Association, the American Tort Reform Association, the Washington Legal Foundation, the Association of Trial Lawyers of America, Trial Lawyers for Public Justice, and the Attorneys Information Exchange Group, Inc.

Chapter 8

1 Carl Sagan was an American author, astronomer, astrophysicist, and cosmologist best known for his contributions to the research of extraterrestrial life.
2 Bypassing a number of psychologists and psychiatrists nearby, the defendant employed two doctors from the East Coast who are particularly known to the criminal defense bar for producing favorable diagnoses and opinions. Given the defendant's obvious motivations in retaining these professionals and the doctors' history of testifying favorably for similarly situated criminal defendants, the opinions of these doctors should not be relied on as newly discovered evidence mandating a new trial.
3 Statistical significance is a statistical assessment of whether observations reflect a pattern rather than just chance. The significance level is usually denoted by the Greek symbol α (lowercase alpha). The alpha level is the probability value that researchers decide to accept before they are confident enough to release a finding.
4 These accuracy values were calculated using data from the Validity Indicator Profile validation study.
5 Normative data are supplied by the test manufacturer and are available in the test manual.
6 Detailed discussions of the anatomy and physiology of the human brain and the neurobiology of violence are provided in chapters 2 and 5, respectively.
7 Should it be brain size, overall volume, or the ratio of white matter to grey matter instead?
8 By definition, drugs that are psychotropic affect the brain and, therefore, brain chemistry.

Chapter 9

1 For purpose of this discussion the terms "malingering" and "feigning" are used synonymously.
2 Dr. Rappeport testified that these findings made him think that it is quite possible that Gigante is competent to stand trial and that much or all of his mental illness may have been malingered. Dr. Schwartz stated that the findings convinced him that Gigante is fit to proceed. Likewise, after reading the findings, Dr. Portnow concluded that in 1991 Gigante was, in fact, competent to stand trial. However, he believes to a reasonable

degree of medical certainty that Gigante has been incompetent to stand trial since 1995. Before reading the findings, Dr. Portnow had attributed Gigante's incompetency to the combined effects of schizo-affective disorder and organic brain disease, but he now believes that Gigante suffers only from organic brain disease. In contrast, Dr. Halpern testified that these findings had not changed his opinion that Gigante was incompetent to stand trial. He also stated that he could not accept the finding that Gigante was competent and malingering in 1991. He felt that accepting this finding would require him to accept that Gigante is presently competent and malingering, a point that he was unwilling to concede (*United States v. Gigante*, 1997).

3 One of the defense experts concluded that Gigante was suffering from organic brain dysfunction, possibly due to dementia of the Alzheimer's type or multi-infarct dementia. Although the expert was not able to pinpoint the exact cause of the abnormality, nor could he quantify its level, he nevertheless claimed that Gigante was incompetent to stand trial. A second defense expert, who had based his opinion on neuropsychological tests designed to assess malingering, concluded that Gigante was not feigning incompetency but, in fact, suffered from severe cognitive impairment.

4 At the time of the examination, Gigante was taking Thorazine, Restoril, Lanoxin, Teneormin, Pamelor, Dalmane, and other drugs and had been taking potent psychotropic medications for an extended period of time. Dr. Brodie, testified that (a) the defense produced no convincing testimony about the specific effects the various drugs taken by defendant may have had on the PET scans and neuropsychological tests, and (b) from the limited information presented, there was no way to tell if, or how much, the results of the tests were skewed by the medication (*United States v. Gigante*, 1997).

5 The *Diagnostic and Statistical Manual of Mental Disorders* (fifth edition), published in 2013, also does not view malingering as a specific disorder.

6 These terms refer to disorders and illnesses that have functional but no structural abnormalities, such as schizophrenia.

7 Previous literature has, in fact, suggested that the inclusion of individuals with a history of head injury would be more generalizable to real-world malingerers (Cato et al., 2002).

8 One measure that utilizes this concept is the Word Completion Memory Test (Hilsabeck, LeCompte, Marks, & Grafman, 2001).

9 In order to place maximum confidence in the ability to accurately interpret results from cognitive measures and/or tests of personality, a determination must be made that the examinee puts forth appropriate effort on tasks and responds honestly to questions. Symptom validity assessment is the process through which such determinations are made.

10 Binder (2002) also argued that the strongest psychometric evidence of faking impairment occurs when a forced-choice test result is significantly below chance performance.

11 According to a 2004 survey, the Rey-15 and TOMM were the most frequently reported measures (Slick, Tan, Strauss, & Hultsch, 2004).

12 Ideally, all tests should have high sensitivity, specificity, NPP, and PPP; however, to date, few such tests exist. Consequently, Vallabhajosula and

van Gorp (2001) have suggested that, to meet the *Daubert* standard of admissibility of scientific evidence, a test must have, at a minimum, a PPP of ≥80%. It has also been argued that, in clinical practice, malingering tests should have a specificity of at least 90% (Rüsseler et al., (2008).

13 Butcher and colleagues (2003) also concluded that FBS is more likely to measure general maladjustment and somatic complaints than malingering.

14 The MMPI-2-RF scales are based on the assumption that psychopathology is a homogeneous condition that is additive (Sellbom, Ben-Porath, & Stafford, 2007).

Chapter 10

1 The BPA is a flexible battery approach in which the clinician utilizes a collection of standardized neuropsychological tests to assess various brain functions.

2 In *Rogers v. State* (2001) the court refused to overturn a lower court's denial of a motion for a PET scan where the defendant had not shown a particular need for the test and the court had already found statutory mitigating circumstance pertaining to defendant's mental condition without reliance on a scan.

3 Quick argued that his impaired executive functioning prevented him from forming the requisite mental state at the time of the alleged murder.

4 It has been argued that the use of a CT scan in the psychiatric diagnosis of schizophrenia lacks any real scientific justification (Taylor, 1982). Further, even if CT scans were valid and reliable tools for psychiatric diagnosis, Hinckley's brain scan did not show the enlarged ventricles that research indicates are the more highly correlated morphological feature of schizophrenia (Stone, 1984).

5 The actual legal defense used was that White's mental capacity was diminished, and White's consumption of junk food was presented to the jury as one of many symptoms, not a cause, of his depression.

6 In *United States v. Pineyro* (2005) the district court found, based on the testimony of a psychologist, that defendant's frontal-lobe damage constituted "diminished capacity" (p. 139).

7 "Morales" was an alias used by Simon Pirela.

8 A tangle of arteries and veins existed where cortical matter would be on a normal brain.

9 In *Daubert v. Merrell Dow Pharmaceuticals* (1993) the US Supreme Court held that the Federal Rules of Evidence superseded *Frye* as the standard for admissibility of expert evidence in federal courts. However, some states still adhere to the *Frye* standard (e.g., California, Minnesota, New Jersey, New York, Pennsylvania, and Washington).

10 The *Frye* standard, or general acceptance test, provides that expert opinion based on a scientific technique is admissible only where the technique is generally accepted as reliable in the relevant scientific community (*Frye v. United States*, 1923).

Chapter 11

1 Although the exact wording differs, all states use a variation of the *Dusky* standard to define competency.
2 Since all instruments designed specifically for assessing competence to stand trial have variable validity, reliability, and usefulness, it has been suggested that these instruments be used in concert with, rather than as a substitute for, a more comprehensive clinical examination (Mossman et al., 2007).
3 A detailed discussion about the various currently available neuroimaging modalities can be found in chapter 3.
4 As previously discussed, obtaining a baseline scan is crucial, since the baseline value will be subtracted from the average activation value. However, with an "at rest" baseline scan there is a lack of control over what the person is thinking. Therefore, a distractor task is used in an attempt to ensure that the subject is not activating the brain area of interest, either willfully or inadvertently.
5 Activation studies with SPECT take significantly longer than PET activation studies.
6 Some states employ the irresistible impulse test, which encompasses not only whether the defendant knew right from wrong but also whether he or she could control the impulse to commit wrongdoing.
7 It may be argued that all adolescents would qualify for an insanity defense simply because of their biological immaturity. However, it has been contended that while this immaturity may mitigate culpability and justifies a more lenient punishment, it is not generally a basis for excuse, except in the case of very young, preadolescent offenders (Steinberg & Scott, 2003).
8 Some conditions, such as dementia of the Alzheimer's type, Parkinson's disease, seizures, multiple sclerosis, and multi-infarct dementia, can be diagnosed solely based on neuroimaging scans.
9 Under the *M'Naghten* rule, legal insanity is defined as the inability to distinguish right from wrong (at the time the crime was committed).

Chapter 12

1 Dr. Young administered a variety of tests to assess defendant's neural functioning. These procedures tested, among other things, the defendant's intellectual functioning, his attention, motor, and learning skills, and his executive functioning and included the Wechsler Adult Intelligence Scale–Third Edition and the Test of Non-Verbal Intelligence.
2 Attenuation occurs when photons emitted by the radiotracer inside the body are absorbed by intervening tissue between the detector and the emission of the photon.

References

Prologue

Coccaro, E. F., Sripada, C. S., Yanowitch, R. N., & Phan, K. L. (2011). Corticolimbic function in impulsive aggressive behavior. *Biological Psychiatry, 69*, 1153–1159.

Fazel, S. (2012). Severe mental illness in 33,588 prisoners worldwide: Systematic review and meta-regression analysis. *The British Journal of Psychiatry, 200*, 364–373.

Gordon, H. L., Baird, A. A., & End, A. E. (2004). Functional differences among those high and low on a trait measure of psychopathy. *Biological Psychiatry, 56*, 516–521.

Greene, J., & Cohen, J. (2004). For the law, neuroscience changes nothing and everything. *Philosophical Transactions Royal Society: Biological Sciences, 359*, 1775.

Macmillan, M. (2000). Restoring Phineas Gage: A 150th retrospective. *Journal of the History of the Neurosciences, 9*(1), 42–62.

Mobbs, D., Lau, H. C., Jones, O. D., & Frith, C. D. (2007). Law, responsibility, and the brain. *PLoS Biology, 5*(4): e103.

Morse, S. J. (2006). Brain overclaim syndrome and criminal responsibility: A diagnostic note. *Ohio State Journal of Criminal Law, 3*, 397.

Roper v. Simmons, 543 U.S. 551 (2005).

Siegel, A., & Victoroff, J. (2009). Understanding human aggression: New insights from neuroscience. *International Journal of Law and Psychiatry, 32*, 209–215.

Snead, O. C. (2008). Neuroimaging and capital punishment. *The New Atlantis, 19*, 35–63.

Yang, Y., & Raine, A. (2009). Prefrontal structural and functional brain imaging findings in antisocial, violent, and psychopathic individuals: A meta-analysis. *Psychiatry Research, 30,* 174(2).

Chapter 1. Violence, Free Will, and Legal Responsibility

Aggarwal, N. K. (2009). Neuroimaging, culture, and forensic psychiatry. *Journal of the American Academy of Psychiatry and the Law, 37*(2), 239–244.

Al-Issa, I. (2000). *Al-Junun: Mental illness in the Islamic world.* Madison, CT: International Universities Press.

Barak, G. (2003). *Violence and nonviolence. Pathways to understanding.* Thousand Oaks, CA: SAGE.

Barlow, D. H., & Durand, V. M. (2004). *Abnormal psychology: An integrative approach* (6th ed.). Stamford, CT: Wadsworth.

Benedict, R. (1934). *Patterns of culture.* Boston: Houghton Mifflin.

Bhugra, D. (1992). Psychiatry in ancient Indian texts: A review. *History of Psychiatry, 3*(10), 167–186.

Blackmore S. (2006). *Conversations on Consciousness.* Oxford: Oxford University Press.

Blackstone, W. (1893). *Commentaries on the laws of England in four books.* Retrieved from http://www.scribd.com/doc/130888012/Blackstone-Commentaries-on-the-Laws-of- England-in-Four-Books-Vol-2

Bohr, N. (1934). *Atomic theory and the description of nature.* Cambridge, UK: Cambridge University Press.

Bohr, N. (1963). *Essays 1958–1962 on atomic physics and human knowledge.* New York: Wiley.

Bohr, N. (1958). *Atomic physics and human knowledge.* New York: Wiley.

Boldt, R. C. (1992). The construction of responsibility in the criminal law. *University of Pennsylvania Law Review, 140,* 2245–2247.

Carson, D., Milne, R., Pakes, F., Shaley, K., & Shawyer, A. (2007). *Applying psychology to criminal justice.* Portsmouth, UK: University of Portsmouth.

Cashmore, A. R. (2010). The Lucretian swerve: The biological basis of human behavior and the criminal justice system. *Proceedings of the National Academy of Sciences, 107*(10), 4499–4504.

Clark v. Arizona, 548 U.S. 735 (2006).

Crabtree, V. (1999). The illusion of choice: Free will and determinism. Retrieved November, 20, 2012, from http://www.humantruth.info/free_will.html.

Crick, F., & Koch, C. (2003). A framework for consciousness. *Nature Neuroscience, 6,* 119–126.

Coonan, C. (2007, December 13). The scars of Nanking: Memories of a Japanese outrage. *The Independent* (London). Retrieved from http://www.independent.co.uk/news/world/asia/the-scars-of- nanking-memories-of-a-japanese-outrage-764827.html.

Cooper, J. R., Bloom, F. E., & Roth, R. H. (1996). *The biochemical basis of neuropharmacology* (7th ed.). Oxford: Oxford University Press.

Dressler, J. (2000). Does one mens rea fit all? Thoughts on Alexander's unified conception of criminal culpability. *California Law Review, 88,* 955.

Ewing, C. P., & McCann, J. (2006). *Minds on trial: Great cases in law and psychology.* New York: Oxford University Press.

Farah, M. J. (2005). Neuroethics: The practical and the philosophical. *Trends in Cognitive Sciences, 9*(1), 34–40.

Ferrer v. State, 2 Ohio St. 54, 54 (1853).

Galtung, J. (1993). Kulturelle Gewalt. *Der Bürger im Staat, 43*(2), 106.

Gazzaniga, M. S., & Steven, M. S. (2004). Free will in the twenty-first century: A discussion of neuroscience and the law. In Brent Garland (Ed.), *Neuroscience and the law* (pp. 51–71). New York: Dana Press.

Gillihan, S. J., & Farah, M. J. (2005). Is self special? A critical review of evidence from experimental psychology and cognitive neuroscience. *Psychology Bulletin, 131,* 76–97.

Glancy, G. D., Bradford, J. M., & Fedak, L. (2002). A comparison of *R. v. Stone* with *R. v. Parks*: Two cases of automatism. *Journal of the American Academy of Psychiatry and Law, 30,* 541–547.

Glannon, W. (2009). Neuroscience, free will and responsibility. *Journal of Ethics in Mental Health, 4*(2), 1–6.

Grzywal, A., Morylowska-Topolska, J., & Gronkowski, M. (2012). Culture and mental disorders. *Current Problems in Psychiatry, 13*(1), 44–48.

Henry, S. (2000). What is school violence? An integrated definition. *Annals of the American Academy of Political and Social Science, 567,* 16–30.

Hippocrates (1886). *The genuine works of Hippocrates.* Vol. 2 (pp. 344–345). (Francis Adams, Trans.). Baltimore: Williams & Wilkins (1939).

Howorth, H. H. (1965). *History of the Mongols from the 9th to the 19th century.* 4 vols. Burt Franklin Research and Source Work Series 85. London: n.p., 1876–1927.

Huxley, T. (1871, November 1). Administrative nihilism. *Fortnightly Review,* 525–543.

Levi, M., & Maguire, M. (2002). Violent crime. In M. Maguire, R. Morgan, & R. Reiner (Eds.), *The Oxford handbook of criminology* (pp. 795–843). Oxford: Oxford University Press.

Lucretius (1951). *On the nature of the universe.* (R. E. Lanthan, Trans.). Harmondsworth, UK: Penguin.

Matsumoto, A. (1995). A plea for consideration of culture in the American criminal justice system: Japanese law and the Kimura case. *Journal of International Law and Practice, 4,* 507.

McElroy, D. (2008, March 31). Saudi woman killed for chatting on Facebook. *The Daily Telegraph.* Available from http://www.telegraph.co.uk/news/worldnews/1583420/Saudi-woman-killed-for-chatting-on-Facebook.html.

McFarlane, T. J. (2000). *Quantum physics, depth psychology, and beyond* (rev. ed.). Retrieved November, 21, 2012, from: http://www.integralscience.org/psyche-physis.html

Miller v. Alabama, 567 U. S. ____ (2012), Nos. 10–9646 and 10–9647.

Morissette v. United States, 342 U.S. 246, 250, 252 (1952).

Morse, S., & Hoffman, M. B. (2007). The uneasy entente between insanity and mens rea: Beyond *Clark v. Arizona. Journal of Criminal Law and Criminology, 97*(4), 1071–1149.

Morse, S. J. (2003). Inevitable mens rea. *Harvard Journal of Law and Public Policy, 27*(1), 51–64.

Nordstrom, C. (2004). The tomorrow of violence. In L. N. Whitehead (Ed.), *Violence* (pp. 223–242). Santa Fe, NM: School of American Research Press.

People v. Kimura, (No. A-09133 (L.A. Super. Ct. 1985).

Reisig, J. A., & Miller, M. K. (2009). How the social construction of "child abuse" affect immigrant parents: Policy changes that protect children and families. *International Journal of Social Inquiry, 2*(1), 17–37.

Riches, D. (1986). *The anthropology of violence.* Oxford: Blackwell.

Roskies, A. (2006). Neuroscientific challenges to free will and responsibility. *Trends in Cognitive Sciences, 10*(9), pp. 419–423.

Rovelli, C. (2013). Free will, determinism, quantum theory and statistical fluctuations: A physicist's take. Retrieved from http://www.edge.org/conversation/free-will-determinism- quantum-theory-and-statistical-fluctuations

Schwartz, J. M., Stapp, H. P., & Beauregard, M. (2005). Quantum physics in neuroscience and psychology: A neurophysical model of mind–brain interaction. *Philosophical Transaction of the Royal Society B, 360*, 1309–1327

Sendor, B. B. (1986). Crime and communication: An interpretive theory of the insanity defense and the mental elements of crime. *Georgetown Law Journal, 74*, 1371–1434.

Siegela, A., & Douard, J. (2011). Who's flying the plane: Serotonin levels, aggression and free will. *International Journal of Law and Psychiatry, 34*(1), 20–29.

Simpson, D. (2005). Phrenology and the neurosciences: Contributions of F. J. Gall and J. G. Spurzheim. *Journal of Surgery, 75*(6), 475–482.

Stapp, H. P. (1999). Attention, intention, and will in quantum physics. *Journal of Consciousness Studies, 6*(8–9), 143–164.

Stern, C. A. (2012). *The heart of mens rea and the insanity of psychopaths.* Retrieved from http://ssrn.com/abstract=2118130 or http://dx.doi.org/10.2139/ssrn.2118130

Sullivan, W. (1972, March 29). The Einstein papers: A man of many parts was long involved in the cause of peace. *New York Times.*

United States. v. Mest, 789 F.2d 1069 (1986).

United States v. Torniero, 570 F. Supp. 721, 729 (D. Conn. 1983).

Waddington, P. A. J., Badger, D., & Bull, R. (2004). Appraising the inclusive definition of workplace "violence." *British Journal of Criminology, 45*, 141–164.

Wagner, R. F., & Reinecker, H. (2003). Problems and solutions: Two concepts of mankind in in cognitive-behavior therapy. *American Journal of Psychotherapy, 57*(3), 401–413.

Weiner, N. (1989). *Violent criminal careers and "violent career criminals". An overview of the research literature.* In N. A. Weiner & M. E. Wolfgang (Eds.), *Violent crime, violent criminals* (pp. 35–138). Newbury Park: CA. SAGE.

Wells, C. (2012, November 24). Pakistani man says he's proud of "honor killing." Retrieved from http://www.nydailynews.com

Werth, B. (2006). *31 days: Gerald Ford, the Nixon pardon and a government in crisis.* New York: Anchor.

Williams, P. (2005). Convictions overturned for mom who drowned 5 kids. Retrieved from http://www.msnbc.msn.com/id/6794098/ns/us_news-crime_and_courts/

Chapter 2. The Human Brain and Cognition

Alivisatos, A. P., Chun, M., Church, G. M., Greenspan, R. J., Roukes, M. L., & Yuste, R. (2012). The Brain Activity Map Project and the challenge of functional connectomics. *Neuron, 74*(6), 970–974.

Asimov, I. (1970, June). In the game of energy and thermodynamics you can't even break even. *Smithsonian*, p. 10.

Barnes, N. M., & Sharp, T. (1999). A review of central 5-HT receptors and their function. *Neuropharmacology, 38*, 1083–1152.

Bear, M. F., Connors, B. W., & Paradiso, M. A. (2001). *Neuroscience: Exploring the brain*. Baltimore: Lippincott.

Bear, M. F., Connors, B. W., & Paradiso, M. A. (2006). *Neuroscience: Exploring the brain* (3rd ed.). Philadelphia: Lippincott Williams & Wilkins.

Blair, R. J. R. (2008). The amygdala and ventromedial prefrontal cortex: Functional contributions and dysfunction in psychopathy. *Philosophical Transactions of the Royal Society, 363*(1503), 2557–2565.

Blumberg, H. P., Kaufman, J., Martin, A., Whiteman, R., Zhang, J. H., Gore, J. C., . . . Peterson, B. S. (2003). Amygdala and hippocampal volumes in adolescents and adults with bipolar disorder. *Archives of General Psychiatry, 60*(12), 1201–1208.

Book: Human Brain. http://en.wikipedia.org/wiki/Book:Human_brain.

Clark, L., Bechara, A., Damasio, H., Aitken, M. R. F., Sahakian, B. J., & Robbins, T. W. (2008). Differential effects of insular and ventromedial prefrontal cortex lesions on risky decision-making. *Brain, 131*, 1311–1322.

Davidson, R. J., Putnam, K. M., & Larson, C. L. (2000). Dysfunction in the neural circuitry of emotion regulation—a possible prelude to violence. *Science, 289*(5479), 591–594.

Donegan, N. H., Sanislow, C. A., Blumberg, H. P., Fulbright, R. K., Lacadie, C., Skudlarski, P., . . . Wexler, B. E. (2003). Amygdala hyperreactivity in borderline personality disorder: Implications for emotional dysregulation. *Biological Psychiatry, 54*(11), 1284–1293.

Draper, K., & Ponsford, J. (2008). Cognitive functioning ten years following traumatic brain injury and rehabilitation. *Neuropsychology, 22*, 618–625.

Ethofer, T., Kreifelts, B., Wiethoff, S., Wolf, J., Grodd, W., Vuilleumier, P., & Wildgruber, D. (2009). Differential influences of emotion, task, and novelty on brain regions underlying the processing of speech melody. *Journal of Cognitive Neuroscience, 21*(7), 1255–1268.

Federative Committee on Anatomical Terminology. *Terminologia anatomica: International anatomical terminology*. (1998). New York: Thieme Medical.

Gage, G. J., Parikh, H., & Marzullo, T. C. (2008). The cingulate cortex does everything. *Annals of Improbable Research, 14*(3), 12–15.

Goghari, V. M., Macdonald, A. W., & Sponheim, S. R. (2014). Relationship between prefrontal gray matter volumes and working memory performance in schizophrenia: A family study. *Schizophrenia Research, 153*(1–3), 113–1121.

Greenfield, S. (1998). *The human brain*. Phoenix: Orion.

Guo, X., Li, J., Wang, J., Fan, X., Hu, M., Shen, Y., . . . Zhao. J. (2014). Hippocampal and orbital inferior frontal gray matter volume abnormalities and cognitive deficit in treatment-naive, first-episode patients with schizophrenia. *Schizophrenia Research, 152*(2–3), 339–343.

Gur, R. C., Turetsky, B. I., Matsui, M., Yan, M., Bilker, W., Hughett, P., & Gur, R. E. (1999). Sex differences in brain gray and white matter in healthy young adults: Correlations with cognitive performance. *Journal of Neuroscience, 19*(10), 4065–4072.

Honea, R., Crow, T.J., Passingham, D., & Mackay, C. E. (2005). Regional deficits in brain volume in schizophrenia: A meta-analysis of voxel-based morphometry studies. *American Journal of Psychiatry, 162*(12), 2233–2245.

Horgan, J. (2004, October). The myth of mind control: Will anyone ever decode the human brain? *Discover Magazine.*

Jagust, W. (2006). Positron emission tomography and magnetic resonance imaging in the diagnosis and prediction of dementia. *Alzheimer's and Dementia, 2,* 36–42.

Kircher, T., & Thienel, R. (2006). Functional brain imaging of symptoms and cognition in schizophrenia. In S. Laureys (Ed.), *The boundaries of consciousness* (pp. 299–309). Amsterdam: Elsevier.

Kuhnen, C. M., & Knutzon, B. (2005). The neural basis of financial risk taking. *Neuron, 47,* 763–770.

Lamb, F., Anderson, J., Saling, M., & Dewey, H. (2013). Predictors of subjective cognitive complaint in post-acute older adult stroke patients. *Archives of Physical and Medical Rehabilitation, 94*(9), 1747–1752.

Looney, J. W. (2010). Neuroscience's new techniques for evaluating future dangerousness: Are we returning to Lombroso's biological criminality? *University of Arkansas Little Rock Law Review, 32,* 301.

Martin, A. (1999). Automatic activation of the medial temporal lobe during encoding: lateralized influences of meaning and novelty. *Hippocampus, 9,* 62–70.

Mendez, C. V., Hurley, R. A., Lassonde, M., Zhang, L., Taber, K. H. (2005). Mild traumatic brain injury: neuroimaging of sports-related concussion. *Journal of Neuropsychiatry Clinic Neuroscience, 17*(3), 297–303.

Newschaffer, C. J., Croen, L. A., Daniels, J., Giarelli, E., Grether, J. K., Levy, S. E.,...Windham, G. C. (2007). The epidemiology of autism spectrum disorders. *Annual Review of Public Health, 28,* 235–258.

Nolte, J. (2009). *The human brain. An introduction to its functional anatomy* (6th ed.). Philadelphia: Mosby Elsevier.

Paulus, M. P., & Stein, M. B. (2006). An insular view of anxiety. *Biological Psychiatry, 60*(4), 383–387.

Paulus, M. P., Rogalsky, C., Simmons, A., Feinstein, J. S., & Stein, M. B. (2003). Increased activation in the right insula during risk-taking decision making is related to harm avoidance and neuroticism. *NeuroImage, 19,* 1439–1448.

Petroff, O. A. (2002). GABA and glutamate in the human brain. *Neuroscientist, 8*(6), 562–573.

Preuschoff, K., Quartz, S. R., & Bossaerts, P. (2008). Human insula activation reflects risk prediction errors as well as risk. *Journal of Neuroscience, 28,* 2745–2752.

Purves, D., Augustine, G. J., Fitzpatrick, D., Katz, L. C., LaMantia, A. S., McNamara, J. O., & Williams, S. M. (2001). *Neuroscience* (2nd ed.). Sunderland, MA: Sinauer Associates.

Purves, D., & Lichtman, J. (1985). *Principles of neural development*. Sunderland, MA: Sinauer Associates.

Rauch, S. L., Whalen, P. J., Shin, L. M., McInerney, S. C., Macklin, M. L., Lasko, N. B., . . . Pitman, R. K. (2000). Exaggerated amygdala response to masked facial stimuli in posttraumatic stress disorder: A functional MRI study. *Biological Psychiatry, 47*(9), 769–776.

Ribas, G. C. (2010). The cerebral sulci and gyri. *Neurosurgery Focus, 56*(2), E2.

Seymour, B., Singer, T., & Dolan, R. (2007). The neurobiology of punishment. *Nature Reviews Neuroscience, 8,* 300–311.

Smith, B. W., Mitchell, D. G. V., Hardin, M. G., Jazbec, S., Fridberg, D., Blair, R. J. R., & Ernst, M. (2009). Neural substrates of reward magnitude, probability, and risk during a wheel of fortune decision-making task. *NeuroImage, 44,* 600–609.

Spitz, G., Maller, J. J., O'Sullivan, R., & Ponsford, J. L. (2013). White matter integrity following traumatic brain injury: The association with severity of injury and cognitive functioning. *Brain Topography, 26*(4), 648–660.

Stephens, S., Kenny, R. A., Rowan, E., Allan, L., Kalaria, R. N., Bradbury, M., & Ballard, C. G. (2004). Neuropsychological characteristics of mild vascular cognitive impairment and dementia after stroke. *International Journal of Geriatric Psychiatry, 19*(11), 1053–1057.

Squire, L., Berg, D., Bloom, F. E., du Lac, S., Ghosh, A., & Spitzer, N. C. (2012). *Fundamental neuroscience* (4th ed.). New York: Academic Press.

Tau, G. Z., & Peterson, B. S. (2010). Normal development of brain circuits. *Neuropsychopharmacology, 35*(1), 147–168.

Thayer, J. F., & Lane, R. D. (2000). A model of neurovisceral integration in emotion regulation and dysregulation. *Journal of Affective Disorders, 61*(3), 201–216.

The Royal Society. (2011). Brain Waves Module 4: Neuroscience and the law. Retrieved from http://www.scribd.com/doc/109642320/Neuroscience-and-the-Law

Thompson, P. M., Vidal, C., Giedd, J. N., Gochman, P., Blumenthal, J., Nicolson, R., . . . Rapoport, J. L. (2001). Mapping adolescent brain change reveals dynamic wave of accelerated gray matter loss in very early-onset schizophrenia. *Proceedings of the National Academy of Science, 98*(20), 11650–11655.

van Os, J., & Kapur, S. (2009). Schizophrenia. *Lancet, 374*(9690), 635–645.

Wenk, G. L. (2003). Neuropathologic changes in Alzheimer's disease. *Journal of Clinical Psychiatry, 64*(9), 7–10.

Whitnall, L., McMillan, T. M., Murray, G. D., & Teasdale, G. M. (2006). Disability in young people and adults after head injury: 5-7 year follow up of a prospective cohort study. *Journal of Neurology, Neurosurgery & Psychiatry, 77,* 640–645.

Chapter 3. The Basics of Neuroimaging

Alexander, A. L., Lee, J. E., Lazar, M., & Field, A. S. (2007). Diffusion tensor imaging of the brain. *Neurotherapeutics, 4*(3), 316–329.

Altshuler, L., Bookheimer, S., Townsend, J., Proenza, M., Sabb, F., Mintz, J., & Cohen, M. S. (2008). Regional brain changes in bipolar I depression: A functional magnetic resonance imaging study. *Bipolar Disorders, 10*(6), 708–717.

Amaro, E., & Barker, G. J. (2006). Study design in fMRI: Basic principles. *Brain and Cognition, 60*(3), 220–232.

Andreasen, N. C., O'Leary, D., Flaum, M., Nopoulos, P., Watkins, G. L., Boles-Ponto, L. L., & Hichiwa, R. D. (1997). Hypofrontality in schizophrenia: Distributed dysfunctional circuits in neuroleptic-naive patients. *Lancet, 349,* 1730–1734.

Ashburner, J., & Friston, K. J. (2000). Voxel-based morphometry—The methods. *NeuroImage, 11*(6), 805–821.

Barkataki, I., Kumari, V., Das, M., Taylor, P., & Sharma, T. (2006). Volumetric structural brain abnormalities in men with schizophrenia or antisocial personality disorder. *Behavioral Brain Research, 169*(2), 239–247.

Baskin, J. H., Edersheim, J. G., & Price, B. H. (2007). Is a picture worth a thousand words? Neuroimaging in the courtroom. *American Journal of Law & Medicine, 33,* 239–269.

Basser, P. J., & Jones, D. K. (2002). Diffusion-tensor MRI: Theory, experimental design and data analysis-a technical review. *NMR in Biomedicine, 15*(7–8), 456–467.

Beaulieu, C. (2002). The basis of anisotropic water diffusion in the nervous system—a technical review. *NMR in Biomedicine, 15*(7–8), 435–455.

Bergman, A. K., & Afifi, A. (2005). *Functional neuroanatomy: Text and atlas* (2nd ed.). New York: McGraw-Hill Medical.

Belmaker, R. H., & Agam, G. (2008). Major depressive disorder. *New England Journal of Medicine, 358,* 55–68.

Bernal, B., & Altman, N. R. (2003). Evidence-based medicine: Neuroimaging of seizures. *Neuroimaging Clinics of North America, 13,* 211–224.

Bonte, F. J., Harris, T. S., Hynan, L. S., Bigio, E. H., & White, C. L. (2006). Tc-99m HMPAO SPECT in the differential diagnosis of the dementias with histopathologic confirmation. *Clinical Nuclear Medicine, 31*(7), 376–378.

Branstetter, B. F., Blodgett, T. M., Zimmer, L. A., Snyderman, C. H., Johnson, J. T., Raman, S., & Meltzer, C. C. (2005). Head and neck malignancy: Is PET/CT more accurate than PET or CT alone? *Radiology, 235*(2), 580–586.

Brenner, D. J., & Hall, E. J. (2007). Computed tomography: An increasing source of radiation exposure. *New England Journal of Medicine, 357,* 2277–2284.

Brodie, J. D. (1996). Imaging for the clinical psychiatrist: Facts, fantasies and other musings. *American Journal of Psychiatry, 153,* 145–149.

Brown, G. G., & Eyler, L. T. (2006). Methodological and conceptual issues in functional magnetic resonance imaging: Applications to schizophrenia research. *Annual Review of Clinical Psychology, 1,* 51–81.

Bushberg, J. T., Seibert, J. A., Leidholdt, E. M., & Boone, J. M. (2002). Nuclear magnetic resonance. In J. T. Bushberg, J. A. Seibert, E. M. Leidholdt Jr., & J. M. Boone (Eds.), *The essential physics of medical imaging* (2nd ed., pp. 373–413). Philadelphia: Lippincott Williams & Wilkins.

Cacioppo, J. T., Berntson, G. G., Lorig, T. S., Norris, C. J., Rickett, E., & Nusbaum, H. (2003). Just because you're imaging the brain doesn't mean you can stop using your head: A primer and set of first principles, *Journal of Personality and Social Psychology, 85*, 650–661.

Calzada-Reyes, A., Alvarez-Amador, A., Galán-García, L., & Valdés-Sosa, M. (2013). EEG abnormalities in psychopath and non-psychopath violent offenders. *Journal of Forensic and Legal Medicine, 20*(1), 19–26.

Calzada-Reyes, A., Alvarez-Amador, A., Galán-García, L., & Valdés-Sosa, M. (2012). Electroencephalographic abnormalities in antisocial personality disorder. *Journal of Forensic and Legal Medicine, 19*(1), 29–34.

Camargo, E. E. (2001). Brain SPECT in neurology and psychiatry. *Journal of Nuclear Medicine, 42*(4), 611–623.

Catafau A. (2001). Brain SPECT in clinical practice. Part I: Perfusion. *Journal of Nuclear Medicine, 42*, 259–271.

Catana, C., Drzezga, A., Heiss, W. T., & Rosen, B. R. (2012). PET/MRI for neurologic applications. *Journal of Nuclear Medicine, 53*, 1916–1925.

Cha, S. (2006). Update on brain tumor imaging: From anatomy to physiology. *American Journal of Neuroradiology, 27*, 475–487.

Chen, J. J., Wieckowska, M., Meyer, E., & Pike, G. B. (2008). Cerebral blood flow measurement using fMRI and PET: A cross-validation study. *International Journal of Biomedical Imaging.* doi: 10.1155/2008/516359

Cherry, S. R., Louie, A. Y., & Jacobs, R. E. (2008). The integration of positron emission tomography with magnetic resonance imaging. *Proceedings of the IEEE, 96*(3), 416–438.

Cipolla, M. J. (2009). Control of cerebral blood flow. In *The cerebral circulation* (pp. 27–32). San Rafael, CA: Morgan & Claypool Life Sciences. Retrieved from http://www.ncbi.nlm.nih.gov/books/NBK53082/

Cohen, J. D., & Tong, F. (2001). The face of controversy. *Science, 293*, 2405–2407.

Crosson, B., Ford, A., McGregor, K. M., Meinzer, M., Cheshkov, S., Li, X., . . . Briggs, R. W. (2010). Functional imaging and related techniques: An introduction for rehabilitation researchers. *Journal of Rehabilitation Research and Development, 47*(2), 1–33.

Davidson, R. J., Putnam, K. M., & Larson, C. L. (2000). Dysfunction in the neural circuitry of emotion regulation: A possible prelude to violence. *Science, 289*, 591–594.

Daw, N. D., Kakade, S. & Dayan, P. (2002). Opponent interactions between serotonin and dopamine. *Neural Networks, 15*, 603–616.

de Oliveira-Souza, R., Hare, R. D., Bramati, I. E., Garrido, G. J., Azevedo Ignacio, F., Tovar-Moll, F., Moll. J. (2008). Psychopathy as a disorder of the moral brain: Fronto-temporolimbic grey matter reductions demonstrated by voxel-based morphometry. *Neuroimage, 40*(3), 1202–1213.

Detre, J. A. (2006). Clinical applicability of functional MRI. *Journal of Magnetic Resonance Imaging, 23*(6), 808–815.

Detre, J. A., Rao, H., Wang, D. J., Chen, Y. F., & Wang, Z. (2012). Applications of arterial spin labeled MRI in the brain. *Journal of Magnetic Resonance Imaging, 35*(5), 1026–1037.

Donahue, M. J., Lu, H., Jones, C. K., Pekar, J. J., & van Zijl, P. C. (2006). An account of the discrepancy between MRI and PET cerebral blood flow measures: A high-field MRI investigation. *NMR in Biomedicine, 19*, 1043–1054.

Dong, Q., Welsh, R. C., Chenevert, T. L., Carlos, R. C., Maly-Sundgren, P., Gomez-Hassan, D. M., & Mukherji, S. K. (2004). Clinical applications of diffusion tensor imaging. *Journal of Magnetic Resonance Imaging, 19*(1), 6–18.

Edwards, J. C. (2009). Principles of NMR. Danbury, CT: Process NMR Associates. Retrieved from http://process- nmr.com/pdfs/NMR%20Overview.pdf

Entertainment Software Association v. Blagojevich, 404 F. Supp. 2d 1051 (N.D. Ill. 2005).

Eriksson, S. H., Rugg-Gunn, F. J., Symms, M. R., Barker, G. J., & Duncan, J. S. (2001). Diffusion tensor imaging in patients with epilepsy and malformations of cortical development. *Brain, 124,* 617–626.

Fayed, N., Olmos, S., Morales, H., & Modrego, P.J. (2006). Physical basis of magnetic resonance spectroscopy and its application to central nervous system diseases. *American Journal of Applied Science, 3,* 1836–1845.

Foong, J., Maier, M., Clark, C. A., Barker, G. J., Miller, D. H., & Ron, M. A. (2000). Neuropathological abnormalities of the corpus callosum in schizophrenia: A diffusion tensor imaging study. *Journal of Neurology, Neurosurgery & Psychiatry, 68,* 242–244.

Forster, G. J., Laumann, C., Nickel, O., Kann, P., Rieker, O., & Bartenstein, P. (2003). SPET/CT image co-registration in the abdomen with a simple and cost-effective tool. *European Journal of Nuclear Medicine and Molecular Imaging, 30,* 32–39.

Fowler, J. S., Volkow, N. D., Kassed, C. A., & Chang, L. (2007). Imaging the addicted human brain. *Science Practice and Perspectives, 3*(2), 4–16.

Friston, K. J. (2011). Functional and effective connectivity: A review. *Brain Connectivity, 1*(1), 13–36.

Friston, K. J., Ashburner, J. T., Kiebel, S. J., Nichols, T. E., & Penny, W. D. (2007). *Statistical parametric mapping: The analysis of functional brain images.* New York: Elsevier/Academic Press.

Frith, C. D., Friston, K. J., Herold, S., Silbersweig, D., Fletcher, P., Cahill, C., ... Liddle, P. F. (1995). Regional brain activity in chronic schizophrenic patients during the performance of a verbal fluency task. *The British Journal of Psychiatry, 167,* 343–349.

Gazzaniga, M. S. (2005). *The ethical brain.* New York: Dana Press.

Glannon, W. (2005). Neurobiology, neuroimaging, and free will. *Midwest Studies in Philosophy, 29,* 68–82.

Goldberg, E. (2001). *The executive brain: Frontal lobes and the civilized mind.* New York: Oxford University Press.

Grossman, R. I., & Yousem, D. M. (2003). *Neuroradiology: The requisites* (2nd ed.). St. Louis, MO: Mosby.

Gusnard, D. A., & Raichle, M. E. (2001). Searching for a baseline: Functional imaging and the resting human brain. *Nature Reviews: Neuroscience, 2,* 685–694.

Heiss, W. D., & Herholz, K. (2006). Brain receptor imaging. *Journal of Nuclear Medicine, 47,* 302–312.

Herholz, K., & Heiss, W. D. (2004). Positron emission tomography in clinical neurology. *Molecular Imaging and Biology, 6,* 239–269.

Herholz, K., Herscovitch, P., & Heiss, W. D. (2004). *NeuroPET: Positron emission tomography in neuroscience and clinical neurology.* Berlin: Springer.

Hoeffner, E. G., Case, I., Jain, R., Gujar, S. K., Shah, G. V., Deveikis, J. P., . . . Mukherji, S. K. (2004). Cerebral perfusion CT: Technique and clinical application. *Radiology, 231,* 632–644.

Hoerst, M., Weber-Fahr, W., Tunc-Skarka, N., Ruf, M., Bohus, M., Schmahl, C., & Ende, G. (2010). Correlation of glutamate levels in the anterior cingulate cortex with self- reported impulsivity in patients with borderline personality disorder and healthy controls. *Archives of General Psychiatry, 67*(9), 946–954.

Holmes, A., Murphy, D. L., & Crawley, J. N. (2003). Abnormal behavioral phenotypes of serotonin transporter knockout mice: Parallels with human anxiety and depression. *Biological Psychiatry, 54,* 953–959.

Hugdahl, K., Rund, B. R., Lund, A., Asbjørnsen, A., Egeland, J., Ersland, L., . . . Thomsen, T. (2004). Brain activation measured with fMRI during a mental arithmetic task in schizophrenia and major depression. *American Journal of Psychiatry, 161,* 286–293.

Huisman, T. A. (2010). Diffusion-weighted and diffusion tensor imaging of the brain, made easy. *Cancer Imaging, 10,* S163–S171.

Illes, J., & Racine, E. (2005). Imaging or imagining? A neuroethics challenge informed by genetics. *American Journal of Bioethics, 5*(2), 5–18.

Ito, H., Inoue, K., Goto, R., Kinomura, S., Taki, Y., Okada, K., . . . Fukuda, H. (2006). Database of normal human cerebral blood flow measured by SPECT. I: Comparison between I-123-IMP, Tc-99m-HMPAO, and Tc-99m-ECD as referred with O-15 labeled water PET and voxel-based morphometry. *Annals of Nuclear Medicine, 20*(2), 131–138.

Jagust, W., Reed, B., Mungas, D., Ellis, W., & Decarli, C. (2007). What does fluorodeoxyglucose PET imaging add to a clinical diagnosis of dementia? *Neurology, 69*(9), 871–877.

Jones, D. K., Dardis, R., Ervine, M., Horsfield, M. A., Jeffree, M., Simmons, A., . . . Strong, A. J. (2000). Cluster analysis of diffusion tensor magnetic resonance images in human head injury. *Neurosurgery, 47,* 306–313.

Kandel, E. R., Schwartz, J. H., & Jessell, T. M. (Eds.). (2000). *Principles of neural science* (4th ed.). New York: McGraw-Hill.

Kidwell, C. S., & Wintermark, M. (2008). Imaging of intracranial hemorrhage. *Lancet Neurology, 7,* 256–267.

Kim, J. J., Kwon, J. S., Park, H. J., Youn, T., Kang, D. H., Kim, M. S., . . . Lee, M. C. (2003). Functional disconnection between the prefrontal and parietal cortices during working memory processing in schizophrenia: A [15O]H2O PET study. *American Journal of Psychiatry, 160,* 919–923.

Kirchmeier, J. L. (2004). A tear in the eye of the law: Mitigating factors and the progression toward a disease theory of criminal justice. *Oregon Law Review, 83,* 631–730.

Kirsch, P., Lis, S., Esslinger, C., Gruppe, H., Danos, P., Broll, J., . . . Gallhofer, B. (2006). Brain activation during mental maze solving. *Neuropsychobiology, 54,* 51–58.

Klunk, W. E., Engler, H., Nordberg, A., Bacskai, B. J., Wang, Y., Price, . . . Mathis, C. A. (2003). Imaging the pathology of Alzheimer's disease: Amyloid-imaging with positron emission tomography. *Neuroimaging Clinics of North America, 13,* 781–789.

Kronenberger, W. G., Mathews, V. P., Dunn, D. W., Wang, Y., Wood, E. A., Giauque, A. L., . . . Li, T. Q. (2005). Media violence exposure and executive functioning in aggressive and control adolescents. *Journal of Clinical Psychology, 61,* 725–737.

Kumari, V., Aasen, I., Taylor, P., Ftyche, D. H., Das., M., Barkataki, I., . . . Sharma, T. (2006). Neural dysfunction and violence in schizophrenia: An fMRI investigation. *Schizophrenia Research, 84*(1), 144–164.

Levin, C. S. (2005). Primer on molecular imaging technology. *European Journal of Nuclear Medicine and Molecular Imaging, 32*(2), 325–345.

Lotfipour, S., Mandelkern, M., & Brody, A. L. (2011). quantitative molecular imaging of neuronal nicotinic acetylcholine receptors in the human brain with A-85380 Radiotracers. *Current Medcal Imaging Reviews, 7*(2), 107–112.

Malhi, G. S., & Lagopoulos, J. (2008). Making sense of neuroimaging in psychiatry. *Acta Psychiatrica Scandinavica, 117*(2), 100–118.

Malonek, D., & Grinvald, A. (1996). Interactions between electrical activity and cortical microcirculation revealed by imaging spectroscopy: Implications for functional brain mapping. *Science, 272,* 551–554.

Matthews, P. M., Honey, G. D., & Bullmore, E. T. (2006). Applications of fMRI in translational medicine and clinical practice. *Nature Reviews/Neuroscience, 7,* 732–744.

Mayberg, H. S. (1996). Medial-legal inferences from functional neuroimaging evidence. *Seminars in Clinical Neuropsychiatry, 1*(3), 195–201.

Miles, K. A., & Griffiths, M. R. (2003). Perfusion CT: A worthwhile enhancement? *British Journal of Radiology, 76,* 220–231.

Miller, B. L., Cummings, J. L., Villanueva-Meyer, J., Boone, K., Mehringer, C. M., Lesser, I. M., & Mena, I. (1991). Frontal lobe degeneration: Clinical, neuropsychological, and SPECT characteristics. *Neurology, 41,* 1374–1382.

Miller, J. D., & Bell, B. A. (1987). Cerebral blood flow variations with perfusion pressure and metabolism. In J. H. Wood (Ed.), *Cerebral blood flow: Physiologic and clinical aspects* (pp. 19–130). New York: McGraw-Hill.

Mobbs, D., Lau, H. C., Jones, O. D., & Frith, C. D. (2007). Law, responsibility, and the brain. *Biology, 5*(4), 693–700.

Müller, J. L., Gänssbauer, S., Sommer, M., Döhnel, K., Weber, T., Schmidt-Wilcke, T., & Hajak, G. (2008). Gray matter changes in right superior temporal gyrus in criminal psychopaths: Evidence from voxel-based morphometry. *Psychiatry Research, 163*(3), 213–222.

Naqvi, N. H., & Bechara, A. (2005). The airway sensory impact of nicotine contributes to the conditioned reinforcing effects of individual puffs from cigarettes. *Pharmacological and Biochemical Behavior, 81*(4), 821–829.

Neve, K. A., Seamans, J. K., & Trantham-Davidson, H. (2004). Dopamine receptor signaling. *Journal of Receptor Signal Transduction Research, 24,* 165–205.

O'Connor, M. K., & Kemp, B. J. (2006). Single-photon emission computed tomography/computed tomography: Basic instrumentation and innovations. *Seminars in Nuclear Medicine, 36,* 258–266.

Ogawa, S., & Sung, W. (2007). Functional magnetic resonance imaging. *Scholarpedia, 2*(10), 3105.

Parsey, R. V. (2010). Serotonin receptor imaging: Clinically useful? *Journal of Nuclear Medicine, 51,* 1495–1498.

Phelps, M. E. (2000). PET: The merging of biology and imaging into molecular imaging. *Journal of Nuclear Medicine, 41,* 661–681.

Phelps, M. E., Hoffman, E. J., Mullani, N. A., & Ter-Pogossian, M. M. (1975). Application of annihilation coincedence detection to transaxial reconstruction tomography. *Journal of Nuclear Medicine, 16*(3), 210–224.

Pivonello, R., Ferone, D., Lombardi, G., Colao, A., Lamberts, S. W., & Hofland, L. J. (2007). Novel insights in dopamine receptor physiology. *European Journal of Endocrinology, 156*(1), S13–S21.

Pooley, R. A. (2005). Physics tutorial for residents: Fundamental physics of MR imaging. *Radiographics, 25*(4), 1087–1099.

Potkin, S. G., Alva, G., Fleming, K., Anand, R., Keator, D., Carreon, D., . . . Fallon, J. H. (2002). A PET study of the pathophysiology of negative symptoms in schizophrenia. *American Journal of Psychiatry, 159*, 227–237.

Prante, O., Maschauer, S., & Banerjee, A. (2013). Radioligands for the dopamine receptor subtypes. *Journal of Labelled Compounds and Radiopharmaceuticals, 56*(3–4), 130–148.

Provenzale, J. (2007). CT and MR imaging of acute cranial trauma. *Emergency Radiology, 14*, 1–12.

Ragland, J. D., Gur, R. C., Glahn, D. C., Censits, D. M., Smith, R. J., Lazarev, M. G., . . . Gur, R. E. (1998). Frontotemporal cerebral blood flow change during executive and declarative memory tasks in schizophrenia: A positron emission tomography study. *Neuropsychology, 12*, 399–413.

Raichle, M. E., & Snyder, A. Z. (2007). A default mode of brain function: A brief history of an evolving idea. *NeuroImage, 37*, 1083–1090.

Raine, A. (1993). *The psychopathology of crime: Criminal behavior as a clinical disorder.* San Diego: Academic Press.

Rapoport, S. I. (2005). In vivo approaches and rationale for quantifying kinetics and imaging brain lipid metabolic pathways. *Prostaglandins & Other Lipid Mediators, 77*, 185–96.

Reeves, D., Mills, M. J., Billick, S. B., & Brodie, J. D. (2003). Limitations of brain imaging in forensic psychiatry. *Journal of the American Academy of Psychiatry and Law, 31*, 89–96.

Riehemann, S., Volz, H. P., Stutzer, P., Smesny, S., Gaser, C., & Sauer, H. (2001). Hypofrontality in neuroleptic-naive schizophrenic patients during the Wisconsin Card Sorting Test—A fMRI study. *European Archives of Psychiatry and Clinical Neuroscience, 251*, 66–71.

Roelstraete, B., & Rosseel, Y. (2011). FIAR: An R package for analyzing functional integration in the brain. *Journal of Statistical Software, 44*(13), 1–32.

Roper v. Simmons, 543 U.S. 551 (2005).

Rosenbloom, M., Sullivan, E. V., & Pfefferbaum, A. (2003). Using magnetic resonance imaging and diffusion tensor imaging to assess brain damage in alcoholics. *Alcohol Research & Health, 27*(2), 146–152.

Ross, A. J., & Sachdev, P. S. (2004). Magnetic resonance spectroscopy in cognitive research. *Brain Research Reviews, 44*(2–3), 83–102.

Sarter, M., Berntson, G. G., & Cacioppo, J. T. (1996). Brain imaging and cognitive neuroscience: Toward strong inference in attributing function to structure. *American Psychologist, 51*, 13–21.

Schiffer, B., Müller, B. W., Scherbaum, N., Hodgins, S., Forsting, M., Wiltfang, J., . . . Leygraf, N. (2011). Disentangling structural brain alterations associated with violent behavior from those associated with substance use disorders. *Archives of General Psychiatry, 68*(10), 1039–1049.

Shafi, N. (2009). Neuroscience and law: The evidentiary value of brain imaging. *Graduate Student Journal of Psychology, 11*, 27–39.

Siever, L. J. (2008). Neurobiology of aggression and violence. *American Journal of Psychiatry, 165*, 429–442.

Silverman, D. H. (2004). Brain 18F-FDG PET in the diagnosis of neurodegenerative dementia: Comparison with perfusion SPECT and with clinical evaluations lacking nuclear imaging. *Journal of Nuclear Medicine, 45*(4), 594–607.

Snead, O. C. (2008). Neuroimaging and capital punishment. *The New Atlantis, 19*, 35–63.

Soderstrom, H., Hultin, L., Tullberg, M., Wikkelson, C., Ekholm, S., & Forsman, A. (2002). Reduced frontotemporal perfusion in psychopathic personality. *Psychiatry Research, 114*, 81–94.

Sokoloff, L. (2008). The physiological and biochemical bases of functional brain imaging. *Cognitive Neurodynamics, 2*(1), 1–5.

Sommer, I. E., Diederen, K. M., Blom, J., Willems, A., Kushan, L., Slotema, K., . . . Kahn, R. S. (2008). Auditory verbal hallucinations predominantly activate the right inferior frontal area. *Brain: A Journal of Neurology, 131*(12), 3169–3177.

Soyka, M., Koch, W., Möller, H. J., Rüther, T., & Tatsch, K. (2005). Hypermetabolic pattern in frontal cortex and other brain regions in unmedicated schizophrenia patients: Results from a FDG-PET study. *European Archives of Psychiatry and Clinical Neuroscience, 255*(5), 308–312.

Thompson, N. (2006, January–February). My brain made me do it: Breakthroughs in neuroscience are changing our understanding of criminal culpability. That worries a leading neuroscientist—but it shouldn't worry lawyers or judges. *Legal Affairs*, 50–53.

Thornton, K. E., & Carmody, D. P. (2009). Traumatic brain injury rehabilitation: QEEG biofeedback treatment protocols. *Applied Psychophysiology and Biofeedback, 34*(1), 59–68.

Tolias, C., & Sgouros. S. (2006). Initial evaluation and management of CNS injury. Retrieved from http://emedicine.medscape.com/article/434261-overview.

Tot, Ş., Özge, A., Çömelekoglu, Ü., Yazici, K., & Bal, N. (2002). Association of QEEG findings with clinical characteristics of OCD: Evidence of left frontotemporal dysfunction. *Canadian Journal of Psychiatry, 47*(6), 538–545.

Townsend, D. T. (2008). Dual-modality imaging: Combining anatomy and function. *Journal of Nuclear Medicine, 49*, 938–955.

van de Giessen, D., Thompson, J., Rosell, D., Xu, X., Girgis, R., Ehrlich, Y., . . . Siever, L. (2013). Serotonin transporter availability in impulsive aggressive personality disordered patients: A PET study with [¹¹C]DASB. *Journal of Nuclear Medicine, 54*(2), 34.

Varrone, A., & Halldin, C. (2010). Molecular imaging of the dopamine transporter. *Journal of Nuclear Medicine, 51*, 1331–1334.

Wager, T. D., Hernandez, L., Jonides, J., & Lindquist, M. (2007). Elements of functional neuroimaging. In J. T. Cacioppo, L. G. Tassinary, & G. G. Berntson (Eds.), *Handbook of psychophysiology* (4th ed., pp. 19–55). Cambridge, UK: Cambridge University Press.

Weiller, C., May, A., Sach, M., Buhmann, C., & Rijntjes, M. (2006). Role of functional imaging in neurological disorders. *Journal of Magnetic Resonance Imaging, 23*, 840–850.

Weinberger, D. R., Berman, K. F., & Zec, R. F. (1986). Physiologic dysfunction of dorsolateral prefrontal cortex in schizophrenia. I: Regional cerebral blood flow evidence. *Archives of General Psychiatry, 43*, 114–124.

Westbrook, C. (2011). *MRI in practice* (4th ed). West Sussex, UK: Blackwell.

Wintermark, M., Sesay, M., Barbier, E., Borbély, K., Dillon, W.P., Eastwood, J. D., . . . Yonas, H. (2005). Comparative overview of brain perfusion imaging techniques. *Stroke, 36*, 2032–2033.

Wortzel, H. S., Kraus, M. F., Filley, C. M., Anderson, C. A., & Arciniegas, D. B. (2011). Diffusion tensor imaging in mild traumatic brain injury litigation. *Journal of the American Academy of Psychiatry and Law, 39*, 511–523.

Yoshioka, H., & Burns, J. E. (2012). Magnetic resonance imaging of triangular fibrocartilage. *Journal of Magnetic Resonance Imaging, 35*(4), 764–778.

Zemishlany, Z., Alexander, G. E., Prohovnik, I., Goldman, R. G., Mukherjee, S., & Sackheim H. (1996). Cortical blood flow and negative symptoms in schizophrenia. *Neuropsychobiology, 33*, 127–131.

Zimmer, L., & Luxen, A. (2012). PET radiotracers for molecular imaging in the brain: Past, present and future. *NeuroImage, 61*, 363–370.

Zipursky, R. B., Meyer, J. H., & Verhoeff, N. P. (2007). PET and SPECT imaging in psychiatric disorders. *Canadian Journal of Psychiatry, 52*, 146–157.

Chapter 4. Neuropsychological Assessment

Alvarez, J. A., & Emory, E. (2006). Executive function and the frontal lobes: A meta-analytic review. *Neuropsychology Review, 16*(1), 17–42.

American Psychiatric Association. (2000). *Diagnostic and statistical manual of mental disorders* (4th ed., text rev.). Washington, DC: Author.

American Psychiatric Association. (2013). *Diagnostic and statistical manual of mental disorders* (5th ed.). Washington, DC: Author.

Anderson, C. V., Bigler, E. D., & Blatter, D. D. (1995). Frontal lobe lesions, diffuse damage, and neuropsychological functioning in traumatic brain-injured patients. *Journal of Clinical and Experimental Neuropsychology, 17*(6), 900–908.

Archer, R. P., Buffington-Vollum, J. K., Stredny, R. V., & Handel, R. W. (2006). A survey of psychological test use patterns among forensic psychologists. *Journal of Personality Assessment, 87*(1), 84–94.

Atkins v. Virginia, 536 U.S. 304 (U.S. 2002).

Audenaert, K., Brans, B., Van Laere, K., Versijpt, J., Dierckx, R., Lahorte, P., & van Heeringen, K. (2000). Verbal fluency as a prefrontal activation probe: A validation study using [^{99}m]Tc-ECD brain SPET. *European Journal of Nuclear Medicine, 27*(12), 1800–1808.

Barbey, A. K., Colom, R., & Grafman, J. (2013). Dorsolateral prefrontal contributions to human intelligence. *Neuropsychologia, 51*(7), 1361–1369.

Barbey, A. K., Colom, R., Solomon, J., Krueger, F., Forbes, C., & Grafman, J. (2012). An integrative architecture for general intelligence and executive function revealed by lesion mapping. *Brain, 135*(4), 1154–1164.

Barcelo, F. (2001). Does the Wisconsin Card Sorting Test measure prefrontal function? *The Spanish Journal of Psychology, 4*(1), 79–100.

Ben-Porath, Y. S. (2012). *Interpreting the MMPI-2-RF*. Minneapolis: University of Minnesota Press.

Benson, N., Hulac, D. M., & Kranzler, J. H. (2010). Independent examination of the Wechsler Adult Intelligence Scale–Fourth Edition (WAIS–IV): What does the WAIS–IV measure? *Psychological Assessment, 22*(1), 121–130.

Bolinskey, K. P., & Nichols, D.S. (2011). Construct drift in the MMPI-2 Restructured Clinical scales: Further evidence and a possible historic example. *Journal of Clinical Psychology, 67*(9), 907–917.

Bow, J. N., Flens, J. R., & Gould, J. W. (2010). MMPI-2 and MCMI-III in forensic evaluations: A survey of psychologists. *Journal of Forensic Psychology Practice, 10*, 37–52.

Burns v. State, 609 So. 2d 600 (Fla. 1992).

Burns v. State, Case No. SC01-166 (2006).

Caldwell, A. B. (2006). Maximal measurement or meaningful measurement: The interpretive challenges of the MMPI-2 Restructured Clinical (RC) scales. *Journal of Personality Assessment, 87*, 193–201.

Camara, W. J., Nathan, J. S., & Puente, A. E. (2003). Psychological test usage: implications in professional psychology. *Professional Psychology: Research and Practice, 31*, 141–154.

Charter, R. A. (2001). Discrepancy scores of reliabilities of the WAIS-III. *Psychological Reports, 89*, 453–456.

Choca, J., Laatsch, L., Wetzel, L., & Agresti, A. (1997). The Halstead Category Test: A fifty year perspective. *Neuropsychology Review, 7*, 62–75.

Coid, J., Yang, M., Tyrer, P., Roberts, A., & Ullrich, S. (2006). Prevalence and correlates of personality disorder in Great Britain. *The British Journal of Psychiatry, 188*, 423–431.

Conners, C. K., & MHS Staff. (Eds.). (2000). *Conners' Continuous Performance Test II: Computer program for Windows technical guide and software manual.* North Tonawanda, NY: Multi-Health Systems.

Coolican, H. (2005). *Research methods and statistics in psychology.* London: Hodder & Stoughton.

Crick, F. (1994). *The astonishing hypothesis: The scientific search for the soul.* New York: Scribner's.

Dao, T. K., Prevatt, F., & Horne, H. L. (2008). Differentiating psychotic patients from nonpsychotic patients with the MMPI-2 and Rorschach. *Journal of Personality Assessment, 90*(1), 93–101.

Daubert v. Merrell Dow Pharmaceuticals, Inc., 509 U.S. 579, 590 (1993).

Davidson, D. J., Zacks, R. T., & Williams, C. C. (2003). Stroop interference, practice and aging. *Aging Neuropsychology and Cognition, 10*, 85–98.

Delis, D. C., Kaplan, E., & Kramer, J. H. (2001). *Delis–Kaplan executive function system.* New York: Psychological Corporation.

Delis, D. C., Wetter, S. R., Jacobson, M. W., Peavy, G., Hamilton, J., Gongvatana, A., . . . Salmon, D. P. (2005). Recall discriminability: Utility of a new CVLT-II measure in the differential diagnosis of dementia. *Journal of the International Neuropsychological Society, 11*(6), 708–715.

Demakis, G. J. (2004). A meta-analytic review of the sensitivity of the Wisconsin Card Sorting Test to fronto-lateralized frontal brain damage. *Neuropsychology, 17*(2), 255–264.

Demakis, G. J. (2013). Frontal lobe damage and tests of executive processing: A meta- analysis of the Category Test, Stroop Test, and Trail-Making Test. *Journal of Clinical and Experimental Neuropsychology*, *26*(3), 441–450.

Dvorak-Bertsch, J. D., Sadeh, N., Glass, S. J., Thornton, D., & Newman, J. P. (2007). Stroop tasks associated with differential activation of anterior cingulate do not differentiate psychopathic and non-psychopathic offenders. *Personality and Individual Differences*, *42*(3), 585–595.

Dyer, F. J. (2005). Forensic applications of the MCMI-III in light of current controversies. In R. J. Craig (Ed.), *New directions in interpreting the Millon Clinical Multiaxial Inventory-III* (pp. 201–223). New York: Wiley.

Edens, J. F., & Ruiz, M. A. (2008). Identification of mental disorders in an in-patient prison psychiatric unit: Examining the criterion-related validity of the Personality Assessment Inventory. *Psychological Services*, *5*(2), 108–117.

Edwards, M. C, Gardner, E. S., Chelonis, J. J., Schulz, E. G., Flake, R. A., & Diaz, P. F. (2007). Estimates of the validity and utility of the Conners' Continuous Performance Test in the assessment of inattentive and/or hyperactive-impulsive behaviors in children. *Journal of Abnormal Child Psychology*, *35*(3), 393–404.

Fabian, J. M. (2010). Neuropsychological and neurological correlates in violent and homicidal offenders: A legal and neuroscience perspective. *Aggression and Violent Behavior*, *15*(3), 209–223.

Fallows, R. R., & Hilsabeck, R. C. (2012). WAIS-IV visual puzzles in a mixed clinical sample. *Clinical Neuropsychology*, *26*(6), 942–950.

Farmer, R. F., & Chapman, A. L. (2002). Evaluation of DSM–IV personality disorder criteria as assessed by the structured clinical interview for DSM–IV personality disorders. *Comprehensive Psychiatry*, *43*(4), 285–300.

Fassbender, C., Murphy, K., Foxe, J. J., Wylie, G. R., Javitt, D. C., & Robertson, I. H. (2004). A topography of executive functions and their interactions revealed by functional magnetic resonance imaging. *Cognitive Brain Research*, *20*(2), 132–143.

Flynn, J. R. (2007). *What is intelligence?* New York: Cambridge University Press.

Forbey, J. D., & Ben-Porath, Y. S. (2007). A comparison of the MMPI-2 Restructured Clinical (RC) and Clinical Scales in a substance abuse treatment sample. *Psychological Services*, *4*, 46–58.

Gläscher, J., Rudrauf, D., Colom, R., Paul, L. K., Tranel, D., Damasio, H., & Adolphs, R. (2010). Distributed neural systems for general intelligence revealed by lesion mapping. *Proceedings of the National Academy of Science USA*, *107*, 4705–4709.

Golden, C. J. (1978). *Stroop Color and Word Test: A manual for clinical and experimental uses*. Chicago: Skoelting.

Goldstein, B., Obrzut, J. E., John, C., Ledakis, G., & Armstrong, C. L. (2004). The impact of frontal and non-frontal brain tumor lesions on Wisconsin Card Sorting Test performance. *Brain and Cognition*, *54*, 110–116.

Gross, K., Keyes, M. D., & Greene, R. L. (2000). Assessing depression with the MMPI and MMPI-2. *Journal of Personality Assessment*, *75*(3), 464–477.

Grossman, H. J. (1983). *Classification in mental retardation*. Washington, DC: American Association on Mental Deficiency.

Groth-Marnat, G., & Baker, S. (2003). Digit Span as a measure of everyday attention: A study of ecological validity. *Perception and Motor Skills, 97*(3 Pt 2), 1209–1218.

Gruber, S. A., Rogowska, J., Holcomb, P., Soraci, S., & Yurgelun-Todd, D. (2002). Stroop performance in normal control subjects: An fMRI study. *NeuroImage, 16*, 349–360.

Haddy, C., Strack, S., & Choca, J. P. (2005). Linking personality disorders and clinical syndromes on the MCMI-III. *Journal of Personality Assessment, 84*(2), 193–204.

Hanlon, R. E., Brook, M., Stratton, J., Jensen, M., Leah, H., & Rubin, L. H. (2013). Neuropsychological and intellectual differences between types of murderers: Affective/impulsive versus predatory/ instrumental (premeditated) homicide. *Criminal Justice and Behavior.* Advance online publication. doi: 10.1177/0093854813479779

Heaton, R. K., Chelune, G. J., Talley, J. L., Kay, G. G., & Curtiss, G. (1993). *Wisconsin Card Sorting Test manual: Revised and expanded.* New York: Psychological Assessment Resources.

Heaton, R. K., Taylor, M. J., & Manly, J. (2003). Demographic effects and use of demographically corrected norms with the WAIS-III and WMS-III. In D. S. Tulsky, D. H. Saklofske, G. J. Chelune, R. K. Heaton, R. J. Ivnik, R. Bornstein, . . . M. F. Ledbetter (Eds.). *Clinical interpretation of the WAIS-III and WMS-III.* (pp. 181–210). San Diego: Academic Press.

Hesse, M., Guldager, S., & Linneberg, I. (2012). Convergent validity of MCMI-III clinical syndrome scales. *British Journal of Clinical Psychology, 51*, 172–184.

Hester, R. L., Murphy, K., Foxe, J. J., Foxe, D. M., Javitt, D. C., & Garavan, H. (2004). Predicting success: Patterns of cortical activation and deactivation prior to response inhibition. *Journal of Cognitive Neuroscience, 16*(5), 776–785.

Hoelzle, J. B., Nelson, N. W., & Smith, C, A. (2011). Comparison of Wechsler Memory Scale–Fourth Edition (WMS-IV) and Third Edition (WMS-III) dimensional structures: Improved ability to evaluate auditory and visual constructs. *Journal of Clinical and Experimental Neuropsychology, 33*(3), 283–291.

Hom, J. (2003). Forensic neuropsychology: Are we there yet? *Archives of Clinical Neuropsychology, 18*, 827–845.

Jacobs, M. L., & Donders, J. (2007). Criterion validity of the California Verbal Learning Test–Second Edition (CVLT-II) after traumatic brain injury. *Archives of Clinical Neuropsychology, 32*(2), 143–149.

Jurado, M. B., & Rosselli, M. (2007). The elusive nature of executive functions: A review of our current understanding. *Neuropsychology Reviews, 17*, 213–233.

Kalmbach, K. C., & Lyons, P. M. (2006). Ethical issues in conducting forensic evaluations. *Applied Psychology in Criminal Justice, 2*(3), 261–290.

Kaplan, R. M., & Saccuzzo, D. P. (2010). *Psychological testing: Principles, applications, & issues* (8th ed.). Belmont, CA: Wadsworth/Cengage.

Karzmark, P. (2009). The effect of cognitive, personality, and background factors on the WAIS- III Arithmetic subtest. *Applied Neuropsychology, 16*(1), 49–53.

Kaufman, A. S., & Lichtenberger, E. O. (1999). *Essentials of WAIS-III assessment.* New York: Wiley.

Keen v. State, No. W2011-00789-SC-R11-PD—Filed December 20, 2012.

Kirsch, P., Lis, S., Esslinger, C., Gruppe, H., Danos, P., Broll, J., Wiltink, J., & Gallhofer, B. (2006). Brain activation during mental maze solving. *Neuropsychobiology, 54,* 51–58.

Kranzler, H., Kadden, R., Babor, T., Tennen, H., & Rounsaville, B. (1996). Validity of the SCID in substance abuse patients. *Addiction, 91*(6), 859–868.

Kranzler, H., Tennen, H., Babor, T., Kadden, R., & Rounsaville, B. (1997). Validity of the longitudinal, expert, all data procedure for psychiatric diagnosis in patients with psychoactive substance use disorders. *Drug and Alcohol Dependency, 45,* 93–104.

Krikorian, R., & Bartok, J. A. (1998). Developmental data for the Porteus Maze Test. *Clinical Neuropsychology, 12,* 305–310.

Lam, M., Eng, G. K., Rapisarda, A., Subramaniam, M., Kraus, M., Keefe, R. S., & Collinson, S. L. (2013). Formulation of the age-education index: measuring age and education effects in neuropsychological performance. *Psychological Assessment, 25*(1), 61–70.

Lees-Haley, P. R., Iverson, G. L., Lange, R. T., Fox, D. D., & Allen, L. M. (2002). Malingering in forensic neuropsychology: Daubert and the MMPI-2. *Journal of Forensic Neuropsychology, 3*(1–2) [Special issue: Detection of response bias in forensic neuropsychology: Part II], 167–203.

Lezak, M. D., Howieson, D. B., & Loring, D. W. (2004). *Neuropsychological assessment* (4th ed.). New York: Oxford University Press

Lezak, M. D. (1995). *Neuropsychological assessment* (3rd ed.). New York: Oxford University Press.

Lie, C. H., Specht, K., Marshall, J. C., & Fink, G. R. (2006). Using fMRI to decompose the neural processes underlying the Wisconsin Card Sorting Test. *NeuroImage, 30,* 1038–1049.

Lim, J., Oh, I. K., Han, C., Huh, Y. J., Jung, I. K., Patkar, A. A., Steffens, D. C., & Jang, B. H. (2013). Sensitivity of cognitive tests in four cognitive domains in discriminating MDD patients from healthy controls: A meta-analysis. *International Journal of Psychogeriatrics, 25*(9):1543–1557

Lobbestael, J., Leurgans, M., & Arntz, A. (2011). Inter-rater reliability of the Structured Clinical Interview for DSM–IV Axis I Disorders (SCID I) and Axis II Disorders (SCID II). *Clinical Psychology & Psychotherapy, 18*(1), 75–79.

Loonstra, A. S., Tarlow, A. R., & Sellers, A. H. (2001). COWAT metanorms across age, education, and gender. *Applied Neuropsychology, 8*(3), 161–166.

Lopez, M. N., Charter, R. A., & Newman, R. J. (2000). Psychometric properties of the Halstead Category Test. *Clinical Neuropsychology, 14*(2), 157–161.

Loring, D. W., & Bauer, R. M. (2010). Testing the limits: Cautions and concerns regarding the new Wechsler IQ and Memory scales. *Neurology, 74*(8), 685–690.

Luckasson, R., Borthwick-Duffy, S., Buntinx, W. H. E., Coulter, D. L., Craig, E. M., Reeve, A., . . . Tasse, M. J. (2002). *Mental retardation: Definition, classification, and systems of supports* (10th ed.). Washington DC: American Association on Mental Retardation.

Maes, J., Vich, J. & Eling, P. (2006). Learned irrelevance and response perseveration in a total change dimensional shift task, *Brain and Cognition, 62,* 74–79.

Marcopulos, B. A., Morgan, J. E., & Denney, R. L. (2008). Neuropsychological evaluation of competency to proceed. In R. L. Denney, & J. P. Sullivan (Eds.), *Clinical neuropsychology in the criminal forensic setting* (pp. 176–203). New York: Guilford Press.

Mason, J. (2007). Personality assessment in offenders with mild and moderate intellectual disabilities. *British Journal of Forensic Practice, 9*, 31–39.

McCann, J. T. (2002). Guidelines for forensic application of the MCMI-III. *Journal of Forensic Psychology Practice, 2*(3), 55–70.

McDowell, B. D., Bayless, J. D., Moser, D. J., Meyers, J. E., & Paulsen, J. S. (2004). Concordance between the CVLT and the WMS-III word lists test. *Archives of Clinical Neuropsychology, 19*(2), 319–324.

Messina, N., Wish, E., Hoffman, J., & Nemes, S. (2001). Diagnosing antisocial personality disorder among substance abusers: The SCID versus the MCMI-II. *American Journal of Drug and Alcohol Abuse, 27*(4), 699–717.

Miller, B., & Cummings, J. (2007). *The human frontal lobes* (2nd ed.). New York: Guilford Press.

Millon, T., Millon, C., Davis, R., & Grossman, S. (2009). *MCMI-III manual* (4th ed.). Minneapolis: Pearson Education.

Mitchell, D. G., Colledge, E., Leonard, A., & Blair, R. J. (2002). Risky decisions and response reversal: Is there evidence of orbitofrontal cortex dysfunction in psychopathic individuals? *Neuropsychologia, 40*, 2013–2022.

Morey, L. C. (1996). *An interpretive guide to the Personality Assessment Inventory (PAI)*. Odessa, FL: Psychological Assessment Resources.

Morey, L. C. (2007). *Personality Assessment Inventory: Professional manual* (2nd ed.). Odessa, FL: Psychological Assessment Resources.

Nichols, D. S. (2006). The trials of separating bath water from baby: A review and critique of the MMPI-2 restructured clinical scales. *Journal of Personality Assessment, 87*(2), 121–138.

Nyhus, E., & Barcelo, F. (2009). The Wisconsin Card Sorting Test and the cognitive assessment of prefrontal executive functions: A critical update. *Brain and Cognition, 71*, 437–451.

Obonsawin, M. C., Crawford, J. R., Page, J., Chalmers, P., Cochrane, R., & Low, G. (2002). Performance on tests of frontal lobe function reflect general intellectual ability. *Neuropsychologia, 40*(7), 970–977.

Ogilvie, J. M., Stewart, A. L., Chan, R. C. K., & Shum, D. H. K. (2011). Neuropsychological measures of executive function and antisocial behavior: A meta-analysis. *Criminology, 49*(4), 1063–1107.

Osuji, I. J., & Cullum, C. M. (2005). Cognition in bipolar disorder. *Psychiatric Clinics of North America, 28*, 427–441.

Psychological Corporation. (1997). *Wechsler Adult Intelligence Scale–Third Edition, and Wechsler Memory Scale–Third Edition technical manual*. San Antonio, TX: Author.

Rabin, L. A., Barr, W. B., & Burton, L. A. (2005). Assessment practices of clinical neuropsychologists in the United States and Canada: A survey of INS, NAN, and APA Division 40 members. *Archives of Clinical Neuropsychology, 20*(1), 33–65.

Reynolds, C., Price, J., & Niland, J. (2003). Applications of neuropsychology in capital felony (death penalty) defense. *Journal of Forensic Neuropsychology, 3*(4), 89–123.

Riddle, M., & Roberts, A. (1978). Psychosurgery and the Porteus Maze Tests: Review and reanalysis of data. *Archives of General Psychiatry, 35,* 493–497.

Rogers, R., Salekin, R. T., & Sewell, K. W. (1999). Validation of the Millon Multiaxial Inventory for Axis II disorders: Does it meet the Daubert standard? *Law and Human Behavior, 23,* 425–443.

Ross, T. P., Furr, A. E., Carter, S. E., & Weinberg, M. (2006). The psychometric equivalence of two alternate forms of the Controlled Oral Word Association Test. *The Clinical Neuropsychologist, 20,* 414–431.

Rossi, G., Hauben, C., van den Brande, I., & Sloore, H. (2003). Empirical evaluation of the MCMI-III personality disorder scales. *Psychological Reports, 92*(2), 627–642.

Roussy, S., & Toupin, J. (2000). Behavioral inhibition deficits in juvenile psychopaths. *Aggressive Behavior, 26,* 413–424.

Salthouse, T. (2005). Relations between cognitive abilities and measures of executive functioning. *Neuropsychology, 19,* 532–545.

Sánchez-Cubillo, I., Periáñez, J. A., Adrover-Roig, D., Rodríguez-Sánchez, J. M., Ríos-Lago, M., Tirapu, J., & Barceló, F. (2009). Construct validity of the Trail Making Test: Role of task- switching, working memory, inhibition/interference control, and visuomotor abilities. *Journal of the International Neuropsychological Society, 15*(3), 438–450.

Sattler, J. M., & Ryan, J. J. (2009). *Assessment with the WAIS-IV.* San Diego, CA: Sattler.

Shear, M. K., Greeno, C., Kang, J., Ludewig, D., Frank, E., Swartz, H. A., & Hanekamp, M. (2000). Diagnosis of nonpsychotic patients in community clinics. *American Journal of Psychiatry, 157,* 581–587.

Shibuya-Tayoshi, S., Sumitani, S., Kikuchi, K., Tanaka, T., Tayoshi, S., Ueno, S., & Ohmori, T. (2007). Activation of the prefrontal cortex during the Trail-Making Test detected with multichannel near-infrared spectroscopy. *Psychiatry and Clinical Neurosciences, 61*(6), 616–621.

Simmonds, D. J., Fotedar, S., Suskauer, S. J., Pekar, J. J., Denckla, M. B., & Mostofsky, S. H. (2007). Functional brain correlates of response time variability in children. *Neuropsychologia, 45*(9), 2147–2157.

Simms, L. J., Casillas, A., Clark, L. A., Watson, D., & Doebbeling, B. N. (2005). Psychometric evaluation of the Restructured Clinical Scales of the MMPI-2. *Psychological Assessment, 17,* 345–358.

Solanto, M. V., Etefia, K., & Marks, D. J. (2004). The utility of self-report measures and the continuous performance test in the diagnosis of ADHD in adults. *CNS Spectrums, 9*(9), 649–659.

Spreen, O., & Strauss, E. A. (1997). *Compendium of neuropsychological tests.* New York: Oxford University Press.

State v. Burns, No. 87-2014 (Fla. 12th Cir. Ct. order filed Dec. 18, 2000) (Postconviction Order).

State v. Cavalieri, 663 A.2d 96 (1995).

Strauss, E., Sherman, E. M., & Spreen, O. (2006). *A compendium of neuropsychological tests: Administration, norms and commentary* (3rd ed.). New York: Oxford University Press.

Streiner, D. L., & Norman, G. R. (2008). *Health measurement scales: A practical guide to their development and use* (4th ed.). Oxford: Oxford University Press.

Swick, D., Ashley, V., & Turken. U. (2011). Are the neural correlates of stopping and not going identical? Quantitative meta-analysis of two response inhibition tasks. *NeuroImage, 56*(3), 1655–1665.

Tancredi, L., & Brodie, J. (2007). The brain and behavior: Limitations in the legal use of functional magnetic resonance imaging. *American Journal of Law & Medicine, 33*, 271–294.

Taub, G. E., & Benson, N. (2013). Matters of consequence: An empirical investigation of the WAIS-III and WAIS-IV and Implications for addressing the Atkins Intelligence Criterion. *Journal of Forensic Psychology Practice, 13*, 27–48.

Tellegen, A., Ben-Porath, Y. S., Sellbom, M., Arbisi, P. A., McNulty, J. L., & Graham, J. R. (2006). Further evidence on the validity of the MMPI-2 Restructured Clinical (RC) scales: Addressing questions raised by Rogers et al. and Nichols. *Journal of Personality Assessment, 87*, 148–171.

Troyer, A. K. (2000). Normative data for clustering and switching on verbal fluency tasks. *Journal of Clinical and Experimental Neuropsychology, 22*, 370–378.

Uttl, B., Graf, P., & Richter, L. K. (2002). Verbal Paired Associates tests limits on validity and reliability. *Archives of Clinical Neuropsychology, 17*(6), 567–581.

Walker, A. J., Batchelor, J., & Shores, A. (2009). Effects of education and cultural background on performance on WAIS-III, WMS-III, WAIS-R and WMS-R measures: Systematic review. *Australian Psychologist, 44*(4), 216–223.

Wechsler, D. (2009). *Wechsler Memory Scale–Fourth Edition (WMS-IV) technical and interpretive manual.* San Antonio, TX: Pearson.

Weiss, L. W. (2010). Considerations on the Flynn effect. *Journal of Psychoeducational Assessment, 28*(5), 482–493.

Wise, E. A., Streiner, D. L., & Walfish, S. (2010). A review and comparison of the reliabilities of the MMPI-2, MCMI-III, and PAI Presented in their respective test manuals. *Measurement and Evaluation in Counseling and Development, 42*(4), 246–254.

Yates, K. F., & Denney, R. L. (2008). Neuropsychology in the assessment of mental state at the time of the offense. In R. L. Denney, & J. P. Sullivan (Eds.), *Clinical neuropsychology in the criminal forensic setting* (pp. 204–237). New York: Guilford Press.

Chapter 5. The Etiology and Neurobiology of Violence

Afifi, A. K., & Bergman, R. A. (2005). Functional neuroanatomy: Text and atlas (2nd ed.). New York: McGraw-Hill.

Aharoni, E., Vincent, G. M., Harenski, C. L., Calhoun, V. D., Sinnott-Armstrong, W., Gazzaniga, M.S., & Kiehl, K. A. (2013). Neuroprediction of future rearrest. *Proceedings of the National Academy of Sciences, 110*(15), 6223–6228.

Alvarez, J. A., & Emory, E. (2006). Executive function and the frontal lobes: A meta-analytic review. *Neuropsychology Review, 16*(1), 17–42.

Amen, D. G., Hanks, C., Prunella, J. R., & Green, A. (2007). Regional cerebral blood flow in impulsive murderers. *The Journal of Neuropsychiatry & Clinical Neurosciences, 19*, 304–309.

American Psychiatric Association. (2000). Diagnostic criteria for 301.7 Antisocial Personality Disorder. In *Diagnostic and statistical manual of mental disorders* (4th ed., text rev.). Washington, DC: Author. Retrieved from http://behavenet.com/node/21650

American Psychiatric Association. (2000). *Diagnostic and statistical manual of mental disorders* (4th ed., text rev.). Washington, DC: Author.

American Psychiatric Association. (2013). *Diagnostic and statistical manual of mental disorders* (5th ed.). Washington, DC: Author.

Anderson, N. E., & Kiehl, K. A. (2012). The psychopath magnetized: Insights from brain imaging. *Trends in Cognitive Sciences, 16*(1), 52–60.

Aycicegi, A., Dinn, W. M., Harris, C. L., & Erkman, H. (2005). Neuropsychological function in obsessive-compulsive disorder: Effects of comorbid conditions on task performance. *European Psychiatry, 18*(5), 241–248.

Ballard, C., & Corbett, A. (2013). Agitation and aggression in people with Alzheimer's disease. *Current Opinions in Psychiatry, 26*(3), 252–259.

Barkataki, I., Kumari, V., Das, M., Hill, M., Morris, R., O'Connell, P., . . . Sharma, T. (2005). A neuropsychological investigation into violence and mental illness. *Schizophrenia Research, 74*(1), 1–13.

Bearden, C. E., Hoffman, K. M., & Cannon, T. D. (2001). The neuropsychology and neuroanatomy of bipolar affective disorder: A critical review. *Bipolar Disorder, 3*, 106–150.

Blair, R. J. R. (2002). Neurocognitive models of acquired sociopathy and developmental psychopathy. In J. Glickson (Ed.), *The neurobiology of criminal behavior* (pp. 157–186). Boston: Kluwer Academic.

Blair, J., Mitchell, D., & Blair, K. (2005). *The psychopath: Emotion and the brain.* Malden, MA: Blackwell.

Blum, K., Chen, A. L. C., Giordano, J., Borsten, J., Chen, T. J., Hauser, M., . . . Barh, D. (2012). The addictive brain: All roads lead to dopamine. *Journal of Psychoactive Drugs, 44*(2), 134–143.

Bremner, J. D.,Vithilingham, M., Vermetten, E., Nazeer, A., Adil, J., . . . Charney, D. S. (2001). Reduced volume of orbitofrontal cortex in major depression. *Biological Psychiatry, 51*, 273–279.

Broomhall, L. (2005). Acquired sociopathy: A neuropsychological study of executive dysfunction in violent offenders. *Psychiatry, Psychology and Law, 12*(2), 367–387.

Brower, M. C., & Price, B. H. (2001). Neuropsychiatry of frontal lobe dysfunction in violent and criminal behavior: A critical review. *Journal of Neurology Neurosurgery & Psychiatry, 71*, 720–726.

Bufkin, J. L., & Luttrell, V. R. (2005). Neuroimaging studies of aggressive and violent behavior: Current findings and implications for criminology and criminal justice. *Trauma, Violence, & Abuse, 6*(2), 176–191.

Burns, A., Gallagley, A., & Byrne J. (2004). Delirium. *Journal of Neurology Neurosurgery & Psychiatry, 75*, 362–367.

Cardenas, V. A., Samuelson, K., Lenoci, M., Studholme, C., Neylan, T. C., Marmar, C.R., . . . Weiner, M. W. (2011). Changes in brain anatomy during the course of posttraumatic stress disorder. *Psychiatry Research, 193*(2), 93–100.

Caspi, A., Sugden, K., Moffitt, T. E., Taylor, A., Craig, I. W., Harrington, W., . . . Poulton, R. (2003). Influence of life stress on depression: Moderation by a polymorphism in the 5-HTT gene. *Science, 301*, 386–389.

Catafau, A. M. (2001). Brain SPECT in clinical practice. Part I: Perfusion. *Journal of Nuclear Medicine, 42*, 259–271.

Christopher, P. P., McCabe, P. J, & Fisher, W. H. (2012). Prevalence of involvement in the criminal justice system during severe mania and associated symptomatology. *Psychiatric Services, 63*(1), 33–39.

Clark, W. R., & Grunstein, M. (2004). The role of neurotransmitters in human behavior. In *Are we hardwired? The role of genes in human behavior* (pp. 136–157). New York: Oxford University Press.

Coccaro, E. F., Beresford, B., Minar, P., Kaskow, J., & Geracioti, T. (2007). CSF testosterone: Relationship to aggression, impulsivity, and venturesomeness in adult males with personality disorder. *Journal of Psychiatry Research, 41*, 488–492.

Cope, L. M., Shane, M. S., Segall, J. M., Nyalakanti, P. K., Stevens, M. C., Pearlson, G.D., . . . Kiehl, K. A. (2012). Examining the effect of psychopathic traits on gray matter volume in a community substance abuse sample. *Psychiatry Research: Neuroimaging, 204*, 91–100.

Crowell, T. A., Kieffer, K. M., Kugeares, S., & Vanderplog, R. D. (2003). Executive and nonexecutive neuropsychological functioning in antisocial personality disorder. *Cognitive and Behavioral Neurology, 16*(2), 100–109.

Davidson, R. J., Putnam, K. M., & Larson, C. L. (2000). Dysfunction in the neural circuitry of emotion regulation—A possible prelude to violence. *Science, 289*(5479), 591–594.

Davis, M., & Whalen, P. J. (2001). The amygdala: Vigilance and emotion. *Molecular Psychiatry, 6*, 13–34.

De Brito, S. A., & Hodgins, S. (2009). Executive functions of persistent violent offenders: A critical review of the literature. In S. Hodgins, E. Viding, & A. Plodowski (Eds.), *Persistent violent offenders: Neurobiology and rehabilitation* (pp. 167–199). Oxford: Oxford University Press,.

Declercq, F., & Audenaert, K. (2011). Predatory violence aiming at relief in a case of mass murder: Meloy's criteria for applied forensic practice. *Behavioral Sciences and the Law, 29*, 578–591.

de Oliveira-Souza, R., Hare, R. D., Bramati, I. E., Garrido, G. J., Azevedo Ignacio, F., Tovar-Moll, F., & Moll, J. (2008). Psychopathy as a disorder of the moral brain: Fronto-temporo-limbic grey matter reductions demonstrated by voxel-based morphometry. *NeuroImage, 40*(3), 1202–1213.

Eisenberg, D., & Berma, K. (2010). Executive function, neural circuitry, and genetic mechanisms in schizophrenia. *Neuropsychopharmacology, 35*, 258–277.

Eisenegger, C., Naef, M., Snozzi, R., Heinrichs, M., & Fehr, E. (2010). Prejudice and truth about the effect of testosterone on human bargaining behavior. *Nature, 463*, 356–359.

Eldreth, D. A., Matochik, J. A., Cadet, J. L., & Bolla, K. I. (2004). Abnormal brain activity in prefrontal brain regions in abstinent marijuana users. *NeuroImage, 23*, 914–920.

Elliott, F. A. (1992). Violence—The neurologic contribution: An overview. *Archives of Neurology, 49*, 595–603.

Engelborghs, S., Vloeberghs, E., Le Bastard, N., Van Buggenhout, M., Mariën, P., Somers, N., . . . De Deyn, P. P. (2008). The dopaminergic neurotransmitter system is associated with aggression and agitation in frontotemporal dementia. *Neurochemistry International, 52*(6), 1052–1060.

Ersche, K. D., Fletcher, P. C., Roiser, J.P., Fryer, T. D., London, M., Robbins, T. W., & Sahakian, B. J. (2006). Differences in orbitofrontal activation during decision-making between methadone-maintained opiate users, heroin users and healthy volunteers. *Psychopharmacology, 188,* 364–373.

Fazel, S., Lichtenstein, P., Grann, M., Goodwin, G. M., & Långström, N. (2010). Bipolar disorder and violent crime: New evidence from population-based longitudinal studies and systematic review. *Archives of General Psychiatry, 67,* 931–938.

Fazel, S., Philipson, J., Gardiner, L., Merritt, R., & Grann, M. (2009). Neurological disorders and violence: A systematic review and meta-analysis with a focus on epilepsy and traumatic brain injury. *Journal of Neurology, 256,* 1591–1602.

Ferguson, C. J. (2010). Genetic contributions to antisocial personality and behavior: A meta- analytic review from an evolutionary perspective. *Journal of Social Psychology, 150*(2), 160–180.

Ferguson, C. J., Averill, P. M., Rhoades, H., Rocha, D., Gruber, N. P., & Gummattira, P. (2005). Social isolation, impulsivity and depression as predictors of aggression in a psychiatric inpatient population. *Psychiatric Quarterly, 76*(2), 123–137.

Filley, C. M., Price, B. H., Nell, V., Antoinett, T., Morgan, A. S., Bresnahan, J. F., . . . Kelly, J. P. (2001). Toward an understanding of violence: Neurobehavioral aspects of unwarranted physical aggression. *Neuropsychiatry, Neuropsychology, and Behavioral Neurology, 14,* 1–4.

Fischer, M., Barkley, R. A., Smallish, L., & Fletcher, K. (2002). Young adult follow-up of hyperactive children: Self-reported psychiatric disorders, co-morbidity, and the role of childhood conduct problems and teen CD. *Journal of Abnormal Child Psychology, 30,* 463–475.

Fishbein, D. (2000). Neuropsychological function, drug abuse, and violence: A conceptual framework. *Criminal Justice and Behavior, 27*(2), 139–159.

Flaks, M. K., Malta, S. M., Almeida, P. P., Bueno, O. F., Pupo, M. C., Andreoli, S. B., . . . Bressan, R. A. (2014). Attentional and executive functions are differentially affected by post-traumatic stress disorder and trauma. *Journal of Psychiatric Research, 48*(1), 32–39.

Fowler, J. S., Volkow, N. D., Kassed, C. A., & Chang, L. (2007, April). Imaging the addicted human brain. *Science & Practice Perspectives,* 4–16.

Franklin, T. R., Acton, P. D., Maldjian, J. A., Gray, J. D., Croft, J. R., Dackis, C. A., . . . Childress, A. R. (2002). Decreased gray matter concentration in the insular, orbitofrontal, cingulate, and temporal cortices of cocaine patients. *Biological Psychiatry, 51,* 134–142.

Friedel, R. O. (2004). Dopamine dysfunction in borderline personality disorder: A hypothesis. *Neuropsychopharmacology, 29,* 1029–1039.

Fujiwara, E., Brand, M., Borsutzky, S., Steingass, H., & Markowitsch, H. J. (2008). Cognitive performance of detoxified alcoholic Korsakoffs syndrome patients remains stable over two years. *Journal of Clinical and Experimental Neuropsychology, 30*(5), 576–587.

Fuster, J. (1997). *The prefrontal cortex.* Philadelphia: Lippincott-Raven.

Galani, V. J., & Rana, D. G. (2011). Depression and antidepressants with dopamine hypothesis: A review. *International Journal of Pharmaceutical Frontier Research*, *1*(2), 45–60.

Gerra, G., Avanzini, P., Zaimovic, A., Fertonani, G., Caccavari, R., Delsignore, R., . . . Brambilla, F. (1996). Neurotransmitter and endocrine modulation of aggressive behavior and its components in normal humans. *Behavioral Brain Research*, *81*, 19–24.

Gerra, G., Zaimovic, A., Avanzini, P., Chittolini, B., Giucastro, G., Caccavari, R., . . . Brambilla, F. (1997). Neurotransmitter neuroendocrine responses to experimentally induced aggression in humans: Influence of personality variable. *Psychiatry Research*, *66*, 33–43.

Glenn, A. L., Raine, A., & Schug, R. A. (2009). The neural correlates of moral decision-making in psychopathy. *Molecular Psychiatry*, *14*(1), 5–6.

Goethals, I., Audenaert, K., Jacobs, F., Van den Eynde, F., Bernagie, K., Kolindou, A., . . . Van Herringen, C. (2005). Brain perfusion SPECT in impulsivity-related personality disorders. *Behavioral Brain Research*, *157*, 187–192.

Goldberg, E. (2001). *The executive brain: Frontal lobes and the civilized mind*. New York: Oxford University Press.

Golden, C. J., Peterson-Rohne, A., & Gontkovsky, S. T. (1996). Neuropsychological correlates of violence and aggression: A review of the clinical literature. *Aggression and Violent Behavior*, *1*(1), 3–25.

Goldsmith, D., & Bartusiak, M. (2006). *E = Einstein: His life, his thought and his influence on our culture*. New York: Sterling.

Goldstein, R. Z., & Volkow, N. D. (2002). Drug addiction and its underlying neurobiological basis: Neuroimaging evidence for the involvement of the frontal cortex. *American Journal of Psychiatry*, *159*(10), 1642–1652.

Goodman, M., & New, A. (2000). Impulsive aggression in borderline personality disorder. *Current Psychiatry Reports*, *2*, 56–61.

Grant, S., Contoreggi, C., & London, E. D. (2000). Drug abusers show impaired performance in a laboratory test of decision making. *Neuropsychologia*, *38*, 1180–1187.

Graz, C., Etschel, E., Schoech, H., & Soyka, M. (2009). Criminal behaviour and violent crimes in former in-patients with affective disorder. *Journal of Affective Disorders*, *117*(1–2), 98–103.

Gregory, S., Ffytche, D., Simmons, A., Kumari, V., Howard, M., Hodgins, S., Blackwood, N. (2012). The antisocial brain: psychopathy matters: A structural MRI investigation of antisocial male violent offenders. *Archives of General Psychiatry*, *69*(9), 962–972.

Hanlon, R. E., Brook, M., Stratton, J., Jensen, M., Leah H., & Rubin, L. H. (2013). Neuropsychological and intellectual differences between types of murderers: Affective/impulsive versus predatory/ instrumental (premeditated) homicide. *Criminal Justice and Behavior*. Advance online publication. doi: 10.1177/0093854813479779

Hawkins, K. A. & Trobst, K. K. (2000). Frontal lobe dysfunction and aggression: Conceptual issues and research findings. *Aggression and Violent Behavior*, *5*(2), 147–157

Hayempour, B. J., Cohen, S., Newberg, A., & Alavi, A. (2013). Neuromolecular imaging instrumentation demonstrating dysfunctional brain function in schizophrenic patients. *Journal of Alzheimer's Disease and Parkinsonism*, 3, 114.

Herholz, K., Langen K. J., Schiepers C., & Mountz J. M. (2012). Brain tumors. *Seminars in Nuclear Medicine, 42*, 356–370.

Hermann, D., Sartorius, A., Welzel, H., Walter, S., Skopp, G., Ende, G., & Mann, K. (2007). Dorsolateral prefrontal cortex N-acetylaspartate/total creatine (NAA/tCr) loss in male recreational cannabis users. *Biological Psychiatry, 61*(11), 1281–1289.

Herrero, O., Escorial, S., & Colom, R. (2010). Basic executive processes in incarcerated offenders. *Personality & Individual Differences, 48*(2), 133–137.

Herrmann, N., Lanctôt, K. L., & Khan, L. R. (2004). The role of norepinephrine in the behavioral and psychological symptoms of dementia. *The Journal of Neuropsychiatry & Clinical Neurosciences, 16*, 261–276.

Ito, M., Okazaki, M., Takahashi, S., Muramatsu, R., Kato, M., & Onuma, T. (2007). Subacute postictal aggression in patients with epilepsy. *Epilepsy Behavior, 10*, 611–614.

Jacobs, A. H., Winkler, A., Castro, M. G., & Lowenstein, P. (2005). Human gene therapy and imaging in neurological diseases. *European Journal of Nuclear Medicine and Molecular Imaging, 32*, S358–S383.

Jones, S. H., & Bentall, R. P. (2006). *The psychology of bipolar disorder.* Oxford: Oxford University Press.

Josephs, K. A., Whitwell, J. L., Weigand, S. D., Senjem, M. L., Boeve, B. F., Knopman, C. R., . . . Petersen, R. C. (2011). Predicting functional decline in behavioral variant frontotemporal dementia. *Brain, 134*(2), 432–448.

Kalechstein, A. D., Newton, T. F., & Green, M. (2003). Methamphetamine dependence is associated with neurocognitive impairment in the initial phases of abstinence. *The Journal of Neuropsychiatry & Clinical Neuroscience, 15*, 215–220.

Kanahara, N., Sekine, Y., Haraguchi, T., Uchida, Y., Hashimoto, K., Shimizu, E., & Iyo, M. (2013). Orbitofrontal cortex abnormality and deficit schizophrenia. *Schizophrenia Research, 143*, 246–252.

Kandel, E. R., & Freed, D. (1989). Frontal-lobe dysfunction and antisocial behavior: A review. *Journal of Clinical Psychology, 45*(3), 404–413.

Kandel, E. R., Schwartz, J. H., & Jessell, T. M. (2000). *Principles of neural science* (4th ed.). New York: McGraw-Hill.

Karl, A., Schaefer, M., Malta, L. S., Dorfel, D., Rohleder, N., & Werner, A. (2006). A meta-analysis of structural brain abnormalities in PTSD. *Neuroscience and Biobehavioral Reviews, 30*, 1004–1031.

Kessler, R. C., Berglund, P., Demler, O., Jin, R., Merikangas, K. R., & Walters, E. E. (2005). Lifetime prevalence and age-of-onset distributions of DSM-IV disorders in the National Comorbidity Survey Replication. *Archives of General Psychiatry, 62*, 593–602.

Ketter, T. A., Kimbrell, T. A., George, M. S., Dunn, R.T., Speer, A. M., Benson, B. E., . . . Post, R. M. (2001). Effects of mood and subtype on cerebral glucose metabolism in treatment-resistant bipolar disorder. *Biological Psychiatry, 49*, 97–109.

Kim, S. J., Lyoo, I. K., Hwang, J., Chung, A., Hoon, S. Y, Kim, J., . . . Renshaw, P. F. (2006). Prefrontal grey-matter changes in short-term and long-term abstinent methamphetamine abusers. *International Journal of Neuropsychopharmacology, 9*, 221–228.

Krakowski, M. (2003). Violence and serotonin: Influence of impulse control, affect regulation, and social functioning. *The Journal of Neuropsychiatry & Clinical Neuroscience, 15*(3), 294–305.

Kwentus, J. A., Hart, R. P. Peck, E. T., & Kornstein, S. (1985). Psychiatric complications of closed head trauma. *Psychosomatics, 26*(1), 8–17.

Lahey, B. B., Loeber, R., Burke, J. D., & Applegate, B. (2005). Predicting future antisocial personality disorder in males from a clinical assessment in childhood. *Journal of Consulting and Clinical Psychology, 73*(3), 389–399.

Langevin, R., & Curnoe, S. (2008). Are mentally retarded and learning disordered overrepresented among sex offenders and paraphilics? *International Journal of Offender Therapy and Comparative Criminology, 52*(4), 401–415.

León-Carrión, J., & Ramos, F. J. (2003). Blows to the head during development can predispose to violent criminal behaviour: Rehabilitation of consequences of head injury is a measure for crime prevention. *Brain Injury, 17*(3), 207–216.

Leung D. K., & Van Heertum, R. L (2009). Interventional nuclear brain imaging. *Seminars in Nuclear Medicine, 39*, 195–203.

Lezak, M. D. (1995). *Neuropsychological assessment* (3rd ed.). New York: Oxford University Press.

Lichter, D. G., & Cummings, J. L. (Eds.). (2001). *Frontal-subcortical circuits in psychiatric and neurological disorders.* New York: Guilford Press.

Linnoila, M., Virkkunen, M., Scheinin, M., Nuutila, A., Rimon, R., & Goodwin, F. K. (1983). Low cerebrospinal fluid 5-hydroxyindoleacetic acid concentration differentiates impulsive from nonimpulsive violent behavior. *Life Sciences, 33*, 2609–2614.

Manning, V., Wanigaratne, S., Best, D., Hill, R. G., Reed, L. J., Ball, D., . . . Strang, J. (2008). Changes in neuropsychological functioning during alcohol detoxification. *European Addiction Research, 14*(4), 226–233.

Marsh, L., & Krauss, G. L. (2000). Aggression and violence in patients with epilepsy. *Epilepsy Behavior, 1*(3), 160–168.

Marsh, N. V., & Martinovich, W. M. (2006). Executive dysfunction and domestic violence. *Brain Injury, 20*(1), 61–66.

Martino, D. J., Bucay, D., Butman, J. T., & Allegri, R.F. (2007). Neuropsychological frontal impairments and negative symptoms in schizophrenia. *Psychiatry Research, 152*(2–3), 121–128.

Martins, S., & Fernandes, L. (2012). Delirium in elderly people: A review. *Frontiers in Neurology, 3*(101), 1–12.

McCloskey, M. S., Berman, M. E., Noblett, K. L., & Coccaro, E. F. (2006). Intermittent explosive disorder-integrated research diagnostic criteria: Convergent and discriminant validity, *Journal of Psychiatry Research, 40*, 231–242.

McClosky, M. S., Phan, K. L., & Coccaro, E. (2005). Neuroimaging and personality disorders. *Current Psychiatry Reports, 7*, 65–72.

McDonald, C. R., Swartz, B. E., Halgren, E., Patell, A., Daimes, R., & Mandelkern, M. (2006). The relationship of regional frontal hypometabolism to executive function: A resting fluorodeoxyglucose PET study of patients with epilepsy and healthy controls. *Epilepsy & Behavior, 9*, 58–67.

Meagher, D. (2001). Delirium: the role of psychiatry. *Advances in Psychiatric Treatment, 7*, 433–442.

Meloy, J. R. (2006). Empirical basis and forensic application of affective and predatory violence. *Australian and New Zealand Journal of Psychiatry, 40*, 539–547.

Mendez, M. F., & Kremen, S. A. (2012). Delirium. In R. Daroff, G. Fenichel, J. Jankovic, & J. Mazziotta (Eds.), *Bradley's neurology in clinical practice* (6th ed.,pp. 26–37). Philadelphia: Elsevier Saunders.

Mesulam, M. M. (2002). The human frontal lobes: Transcending the default mode through contingent encoding. In D. T. Stuss & R. T. Knight (Eds.), *Principles of frontal lobe function* (pp. 8–30). Oxford: Oxford University Press.

Meyer-Lindenberg, A., Buckholtz, J. W., Kolachana, B., Hariri, A., Pezawas, L., Blasi, G., . . . Weinberger, D. R. (2006). Neural mechanisms of genetic risk for impulsivity and violence in humans. *Proceedings of the National Academy of Science USA, 103*, 6269–6274.

Middleton, F. A., & Strick, P. L. (2002). Basal-ganglia projections to the prefrontal cortex of the primate. *Cerebral Cortex, 12*(9), 926–935.

Minzenberg. M. J., Fan, J., New, A. S., Tang, C. Y., & Siever, L. J. (2007). Fronto-limbic dysfunction in response to facial emotion in borderline personality disorder: an event- related fMRI study. *Psychiatry Research, 155*, 231–243.

Morgan, A. B., & Lilienfeld, S. O. (2000). A meta-analytic review of the relationship between antisocial behavior and neuropsychological measures of executive function. *Clinical Psychology Review, 20*(1), 113–136.

Motzkin, J. C., Newman, J. P., Kiehl, K. A., & Koenigs, M. (2011). Reduced prefrontal connectivity in psychopathy. *The Journal of Neuroscience, 31*, 17348–17357.

Müeller, J. L., Gänssbauer, S., Sommer, M., Döhnel, K., Weber, T., Schmidt-Wilcke, T., &, Hajak, G. (2008). Gray matter changes in right superior temporal gyrus in criminal psychopaths: Evidence from voxel-based morphometry. *Psychiatry Research: Neuroimaging, 163*(3), 213–222.

Narayan, V. M., Narr, K. L., Kumari, V., Woods, R. P., Thompson, P. M., Toga, A.W., & Sharma, T. (2007). Regional cortical thinning in subjects with violent antisocial personality disorder or schizophrenia. *American Journal of Psychiatry, 164*, 1418–1427.

Neary D., Snowden, J. S., & Mann, D. M. (2000). Classification and description of frontotemporal dementias. *Annals of the New York Academy of Science, 920*, 46–51.

Newton, P. (2009, January 29). The anatomy of posttraumatic stress disorder. *Psychology Today*. Retrieved from http://www.psychologytoday.com/blog/mouse-man/200901/the-anatomy-post- traumatic-stress-disorder

Ogilvie, J. M., Stewart, A. L., Chan, R. C. K., & Shum, D. H. K. (2011). Neuropsychological measures of executive function and antisocial behavior: A meta-analysis. *Criminology, 49*, 1063–1107.

Passingham, R. E. & Wise, S. P. (2012). *The neurobiology of the prefrontal cortex: Anatomy, evolution, and the origin of insight*. Oxford: Oxford University Press.

Pennington, B. F., & Ozonoff, S. (1996). Executive functions and developmental psychopathology. *Journal of Child Psychology and Psychiatry, 37*(1), 51–87.

Petrides, M., & Pandya, D. N. (2002). Association pathways of the prefrontal cortex and functional observations. In D.T. Stuss & R. T. (Eds.), *Principles of frontal lobe function* (pp. 31–50). Oxford: Oxford University Press.

Potkin, S. G., Alva, G., Fleming, K., Anand, R., Keator, D., Carreon, D., . . . Fallon, J. H. (2002). A PET study of the pathophysiology of negative symptoms in schizophrenia. *American Journal of Psychiatry, 159*, 227–237.

Pradhan, B. K., Chakrabarti, S., Nehra, R., & Mankotia, A. (2008). Cognitive functions in bipolar affective disorder and schizophrenia: Comparison. *Psychiatry and Clinical Neurosciences, 62*(5), 515–525.

Raine, A., Lencz, T., Bihrle, S., LaCasse, L., & Colletti, P. (2000). Reduced prefrontal gray matter volume and reduced autonomic activity in antisocial personality disorder. *Archives of General Psychiatry, 57*(2), 119–127.

Raine, A., Meloy, J., Bihrie, J, Stoddard, L., La Casse, L., & Buchsbaum, M. (1998). Reduced prefrontal and increased subcortical brain functioning assessed using positron emission tomography in affective and predatory murderers. *Behavioral Sciences and the Law, 16*, 329–332.

Raine, A., & Yang, Y. (2006). Neural foundations to moral reasoning and antisocial behavior. *Social Cognitive & Affective Neuroscience, 1*(3), 203–213.

Rosen, H. J., Gorno-Tempini, M. L., Goldman, W. P., Perry, R. J., Schuff, N., Weiner, M., . . . Miller, B. L. (2002). Patterns of brain atrophy in frontotemporal dementia and semantic dementia. *Neurology, 58*(2), 198–208.

Rosen, H. J., Hartikainen, K. M., Jagust, W., Kramer, J. H., Reed, B. R., Cummings, J. L., . . . Miller, B. L. (2002). Utility of clinical criteria in differentiating frontotemporal lobar degeneration (FTLD) from AD. *Neurology, 58*, 1608–1615.

Roth, R., Koven, N., Randolph, J., Flashman, L., Pixley, H., Ricketts, S., . . . Saykin, A. (2006). Functional magnetic resonance imaging of executive control in bipolar disorder. *Neuroreport, 17*(11), 1085–1089.

Rylands, A. J., Hinz, R., Jones, M., Holmes, S. E., Feldmann, M., Brown, G., . . . Talbot, P. S. (2012). Pre- and postsynaptic serotonergic differences in males with extreme levels of impulsive aggression without callous unemotional traits: A positron emission tomography study using 11C-DASB and 11C-MDL100907. *Biological Psychiatry, 72*, 1004–1011.

Samuelson, K. W., Neylan, T. C., Lenoci, M., Metzler, T. J., Cardenas, V., Weiner, M. W., & Marmar, C. R. (2009). Longitudinal effects of PTSD on memory functioning. *Journal of the International Neuropsychological Society, 15*, 853–861.

Sansone, R. A., & Sansone, L. A. (2009). Borderline personality and criminality. *Psychiatry (Edgemont), 6*, 16–20.

Sapolsky, R. M., Gunn, J. A., Gunn, C., Siegel, A., Grafman, A., Blake, P., . . . Schmidle, R. E. (2013). *Topics in the neurobiology of aggression: Implications to deterrence*. Washington, DC: Pentagon Press.

Schuff, N., Neylan, T. C., Fox-Bosetti, S., Lenoci, M., Samuelson, K. W., Studholme, C., . . . Weiner, M. W. (2008). Abnormal N-acetylaspartate in hippocampus and anterior cingulate in posttraumatic stress disorder. *Psychiatry Research, 162*, 147–157.

Seethalakshmi, R., Parkar, S. R., Nair, N., Batra, S. A., Pandit, A. G., Adarkar, S. A., . . . Moghe, S. H. (2007). Regional brain metabolism in schizophrenia: The influence of antipsychotics. *Journal of Postgraduate Medicine, 53,* 241–246.

Seo, D., Patrick, C. J., & Kennealy, P. J. (2008). Role of serotonin and dopamine system interactions in the neurobiology of impulsive aggression and its comorbidity with other clinical disorders. *Aggressive and Violent Behavior, 13*(5), 383–395.

Siegel, A. (2005). *The neurobiology of aggression and rage.* Boca Raton, FL: CRC Press.

Siever, L. J. (2008). Neurobiology of aggression and violence. *American Journal of Psychiatry, 165,* 429–442.

Soloff, P. H., Meltzer, C. C., Becker, C., Greer, P. J., Kelly, T. M., & Constantine, D. (2003). Impulsivity and prefrontal hypometabolism in borderline personality disorder. *Psychiatry Research, 123,* 153–163.

Spaletta, G., Troisi, A., Alimenti, S., diMichele, F., Pau, F., Pasini, A., & Caltagironi, C. (2001). Reduced prefrontal cognitive activation associated with aggression in schizophrenia. *Schizophrenia Research, 50*(1–2), 134–135.

Stein, D. J., Trestman, R. L., Mitropoulou, V., Coccaro, E. F., Hollander, E., & Siever, L. J. (1996). Impulsivity and serotonergic function in compulsive personality disorder. *The Journal of Neuropsychiatry & Clinical Neurosciences, 8*(4), 393–398.

Stevens, M. C., Kaplan, R. F., & Hesselbrock, V. M. (2003). Executive-cognitive functioning in the development of antisocial personality disorder. *Addictive Behaviors, 28*(2), 285–300.

Storandt, M. (2008). Cognitive deficits in the early stages of Alzheimer's disease. *Current Directions in Psychological Science, 17*(3), 198–202.

Swann, A. C., Lijffijt, M., Lane, S. D., Cox, B., Steinberg, J. L., & Moeller, F. G. (2013). Norepinephrine and impulsivity: effects of acute yohimbine. *Psychopharmacology, 6,* 229(1), 83–94.

Swann, A. C. (2003). Neuroreceptor mechanisms of aggression and its treatment. *Journal of Clinical Psychiatry, 64*(4), 26–35.

Tateno, A., Jorge, R. E., & Robinson, R. G. (2003). Clinical correlates of aggressive behavior after traumatic brain injury. *The Journal of Neuropsychiatry & Clinical Neurosciences, 15,* 155–160.

Taylor, W. D., Steffens, D. C., McQuoid, D. R., Payne, M. E., Lee, S.H., Lai, T.J., & Krishnan, K. R. (2003). Smaller orbital frontal cortex volumes associated with functional disability in depressed elders. *Biological Psychiatry, 53,* 144–149.

Teten, A. L., Sharp, C., Stanford, M. S., Lake, S. L., Raine, A. & Kent, T. A. (2011). Correspondence of aggressive behavior classifications among young adults using the Impulsive/Premeditated Aggression Scale and the Reactive Proactive Questionnaire. *Personality and Individual Differences, 50,* 279–285.

Tremblay, R. E., Hartup, W. W., & Archer, J. (Eds.). (2005). *Developmental origins of aggression.* New York: Guilford Press.

van den Heuvel, O. A., Veltman, D. J., Groenewegen, H. J., Cath, D. C., van Balkom, A. J., van Hartskamp, J., . . . van Dyck, R. (2005). Frontal-striatal dysfunction during planning in obsessive-compulsive disorder. *Archives of General Psychiatry, 62*(3), 301–310.

van Elst, L. T., Hesslinger, B., Thiel, T., Geiger, E., Haegele, K., Lemieux, L., . . . Ebert, D. (2003). Frontolimbic brain abnormalities in patients with borderline personality disorder: A volumetric magnetic resonance imaging study. *Biological Psychiatry, 54,* 163–171.

Vassos, E., Collier, D. A., & Fazel, S. (2013). Systematic meta-analyses and field synopsis of genetic association studies of violence and aggression. *Molecular Psychiatry.* Advance online publication. http://www.ncbi.nlm.nih.gov/pubmed/23546171

Verdejo-García, A., & Pérez-García, M. (2007). Profile of executive deficits in cocaine and heroin polysubstance users: common and differential effects on separate executive components, *Psychopharmacology (Berlin), 190,* 517–530.

Villano, J. L., Mlinarevich, N., Watson, K. S., Engelhard, H. H., & Anderson-Shaw, L. (2009). Aggression in a patient with primary brain tumor: Ethical implications for best management. *Journal of Neurooncology, 94*(2), 293–296.

Volkow, N. D., Wang, G.-J., Franceschi, D., Fowler, J. S., Thanos, P. K., Maynard, L., . . ., Li, T. K. (2006). Low doses of alcohol substantially decrease glucose metabolism in the human brain. *NeuroImage, 29,* 295–301.

Watson, D. B. (1996). Opening the door—looking back to move forward. *Canadian Journal of Psychiatry, 41,* 543–548.

Weinshenker, N. J., & Siegel, A. (2002). Bimodal classification of aggression: Affective defense and predatory attack. *Aggression and Violent Behavior, 7*(3), 237–250.

Weniger, G., Lange, C., Sachsse, U., & Irle, E. (2008). Amygdala and hippocampal volumes and cognition in adult survivors of childhood abuse with dissociative disorders. *Acta Psychiatrica Scandinavica, 118,* 281–290.

Wenk, G. L. (2003). Neuropathologic changes in Alzheimer's disease. *Journal of Clinical Psychiatry, 64*(9), 7–10.

Williams, W. H., Mewse, A. J., Tonks, J., Mills, S., Burgess, C. N., & Cordan, G. (2010). Traumatic brain injury in a prison population: Prevalence and risk for re-offending. *Brain Injury, 24,* 1184–1188.

Wortzel, H. S., & Arciniegas, D. B. (2010). Combat veterans and the death penalty: A forensic neuropsychiatric perspective. *Journal of the American Academy of Psychiatry and Law, 38,* 407–414.

Yang, Y., Raine, A., Colletti, P., Toga, A. W., & Narr, K. L. (2009). Abnormal temporal and prefrontal cortical gray matter thinning in psychopaths. *Molecular Psychiatry, 14*(6), 561–562.

Yehuda, R., Tischler, L., Golier, J. A., Grossman, R., Brand, S. R., Kaufman, S., & Harvey, P. D. (2006). Longitudinal assessment of cognitive performance in Holocaust survivors with and without PTSD. *Biological Psychiatry, 60,* 714–721.

Chapter 6. Violence and the Adolescent Brain

Adleman, N., Menon, V., Blasey, C., White, C., Warsofsky, I., Glover, G., & Reiss, A. (2002). A developmental fMRI study of the Stroop Color-Word task. *Neuroimage, 16,* 61–75.

Anderson, V., Anderson, P. J., Jacobs, R., & Spencer-Smith, M. (2008). Development and assessment of executive function: From preschool to adolescence. In V. Anderson, R. Jacobs, & P. J. Anderson (Eds.), *Executive functions and the frontal lobes: A lifespan perspective* (pp. 123–154). New York: Psychology Press.

Andrews-Hanna, J. R., Mackiewicz Seghete, K. L., Claus, E. D., Burgess, G. C., Ruzic, L., & Banich, M. T. (2011). Cognitive control in adolescence: Neural underpinnings and relation to self-report behaviors. *PLoS One, 6*(6), e21598.

APA Amicus Curiae Brief. (1989). No. 88-805.

Aristotle. (1954). Rhetoric. (W. Rhys Roberts, Trans.). Retrieved April, 8, 2013, from: http://classics.mit.edu/Aristotle/rhetoric.html (Original work published 350 BC)

Aronson, J. D. (2009). Neuroscience and juvenile justice. *Akron Law Review, 42*, 917–930.

Asato, M. R., Terwilliger, R., Woo, J., & Luna, B. (2010). White matter development in adolescence: A DTI study. *Cerebral Cortex, 20*, 2122–2131.

Atkins v. Virginia, 536 U.S. 304 (2002).

Barnea-Goraly, N., Menon, V., Eckert, M., Tamm, L., Bammer, R., Karchemskiy, A., . . . Reiss, A. L. (2005). White matter development during childhood and adolescence: a cross-sectional diffusion tensor imaging study. *Cerebral Cortex, 15*(12), 1848–1854.

Blakemore, S. J., & Robbins, T. W. (2012). Decision-making in the adolescent brain. *Nature Neuroscience, 15*, 1184–1191.

Buss, E. (2009). Rethinking the connection between developmental science and juvenile justice. *University of Chicago Law Review, 76*, 493–515.

Casey, B. J., Epstein, J. N., Buhle, J., Liston, C, Davidson, M. C., Tonev, S. T., . . . Glover, G. (2007). Frontostriatal connectivity and its role in cognitive control in parent-child dyads with ADHD. *American Journal of Psychiatry, 164*(11), 1729–1736.

Casey, B. J., Giedd, J. N., & Thomas, K. M. (2000). Structural and functional brain development and its relation to cognitive development. *Biological Psychology, 54*, 241–257.

Casey, B. J., & Jones, R. M. (2010). Neurobiology of the adolescent brain and behavior. *Journal of the American Academy of Child & Adolescent Psychiatry, 49*(12), 1189–1285.

Cauffman, E., & Steinberg, L. (2000). (Im)maturity and judgment in adolescence: Why adolescents may be less culpable than adults. *Behavioral Sciences & the Law, 18*, 741–760.

Chein, J., Albert, D., O'Brien, L., Uckert, K., & Steinberg, L. (2011). Peers increase adolescent risk taking by enhancing activity in the brain's reward circuitry. *Developmental Science, 14*(2), F1–F10.

Constable, R. T., Ment, L. R., Vohr, B. R., Kesler, S. R., Fulbright, R. K., Lacadie, C.,. .. Reiss, A. R. (2008). Prematurely born children demonstrate white matter microstructural differences at 12 years of age, relative to term control subjects: An investigation of group and gender effects. *Pediatrics, 121*(2), 306–316.

Damasio, A. R., & Anderson, S. W. (2003). The frontal lobes. In K. M. Heilman & E. Valenstein (Eds.), *Clinical neuropsychology* (4th ed., pp. 404–446). New York: Oxford University Press.

Ermer, E., Cope, L. M., Nyalakanti, P. K., Calhoun, V. D., & Kiehl, K. A. (2013). Aberrant paralimbic gray matter in incarcerated male adolescents with psychopathic traits. *Journal of the American Academy of Child & Adolescent Psychiatry, 52,* 94–103.

Eshel, N., Nelson, E. E., Blair, R. J., Pine, D. S., & Ernst, M. (2007). Neural substrates of choice selection in adults and adolescents: Development of the ventrolateral prefrontal and anterior cingulate cortices. *Neuropsychologia, 45*(6), 1270–1279.

Feld, B. C. (2003). Competence Culpability, and punishment: implications of Atkins for executing and sentencing adolescents. *Hofstra Law Review, 32*(1), 463–522.

Feld, B. C. (2007). Unmitigated punishment: Adolescent criminal responsibility and LWOP sentences. *Journal of Law and Family Studies, 10*(1), 11.

Fields, D. (2008). White matter. *Scientific American, 298*(3), 54–61.

Finger, E. C., Marsh, A., Blair, K. S., Majestic, C., Evangelou, I., Gupta, K., . . . Blair R.J. (2012). Impaired functional but preserved structural connectivity in limbic white matter tracts in youth with conduct disorder or oppositional defiant disorder plus psychopathic traits. *Psychiatry Research: Neuroimaging, 202,* 239–244.

Giedd, J. N. (2004). Structural magnetic resonance imaging of the adolescent brain. *Annals of the New York Academy of Science, 1021,* 77–85.

Giedd, J. N., & Rapoport, J. L. (2010). Structural MRI of pediatric brain development: What have we learned and where are we going? *Neuron, 67*(5), 728–734.

Glannon, W. (2005). Neurobiology, neuroimaging, and free will. *Midwest Studies in Philosophy, 29*(1), 68–82.

Gnaber, S. A., & Yurgelun-Todd, D. A. (2006). Neurobiology and the law: A role in juvenile justice? *Ohio State Journal of Criminal Law, 3,* 321–340.

Gogtay, N., & Thompson, P. M. (2010). Mapping gray matter development: Implications for typical development and vulnerability to psychopathology. *Brain and Cognition, 72,* 6–15.

Gogtay, N., Giedd, J. N., Lusk, L., Hayashi, K. M., Greenstein, D., Vaituzis, A. C., Nugent, T. F., Herman, D. H., Clasen, L. S., Toga, A. W., Rapoport, J. L., & Thompson, P. M. (2004). Dynamic mapping of human cortical development during childhood through early adulthood. *Proceedings of the National Academy of Sciences, 101*(21), 8174-8179.

Goldberg, E. (2001). *The executive brain: Frontal lobes and the civilized mind.* New York: Oxford University Press.

Graham v. Florida, 130 S. CT. 2011 (2010).

Grosbras, M., Jansen, M., Leonard, G., McIntosh, A., Osswald. K., Poulsen, C., . . . Paus, T. (2007). Neural mechanisms of resistance to peer influence in early adolescence. *Journal of Neuroscience, 27*(30), 8040–8045.

Hodgson v. State of Minnesota, 853 F.2d 1452 (1989).

Huebner, T., Vloet, T. D., Marx, I., Konrad, K., Fink, G. R., Herpertz, S. C., & Herpertz- Dahlmann, B. (2008). Morphometric brain abnormalities in boys with conduct disorder. *Journal of the American Academy of Child & Adolescent Psychiatry, 47*(5), 540–547.

In re Stanford, 537 U.S. 968, 971 (2002).

Jackson v. Hobbs, No. 10-9647 (2012).

Lebel, C., Walker, L., Leemans, A., Phillips, L., & Beaulieu, C. (2008). Microstructural maturation of the human brain from childhood to adulthood. *Neuroimage, 40*(3), 1044–1055.

Liptak, A. (2005). Locked away forever. *The New York Times Upfront.* Retrieved from http://teacher.scholastic.com/scholasticnews/indepth/upfront/features/index.asp?article=f0130a

Luna, B., Padmanabhan, A., & O'Hearn, K. (2010). What has fMRI told us about the development of cognitive control through adolescence? *Brain and Cognition, 72*(1), 101–113.

Maroney, T. A. (2011). Adolescent brain science after *Graham v. Florida. Notre Dame Law Review, 86*(2), 765–794.

Miller v. Alabama, 567 U.S. ___ (2012).

Monahan, K. C., Steinberg, L., & Cauffman, E. (2009). Affiliation with antisocial peers, susceptibility to peer influence, and antisocial behavior during the transition to adulthood. *Developmental Psychology, 45*(6), 1520–1530.

Nelson, E. E., Leibenluft, E., McClure, E. B., & Pine, D. S. (2005). The social re-orientation of adolescence: a neuroscience perspective on the process and its relation to psychopathology. *Psychological Medicine, 35*, 163–174.

Passamonti, L., Fairchild, G., Fornito, A., Goodyer, I. M., Nimmo-Smith, I., Hagan, C. C., & Calder, A. J. (2012). Abnormal anatomical connectivity between the amygdala and orbitofrontal cortex in conduct disorder. *PloS One, 7*, e48789.

Paus, T., Toro, R., Leonard, G., Lerner, J., Lerner, R., Perron, M., . . . Steinberg, L. (2008). Morphological properties of the action-observation cortical network in adolescents with low and high resistance to peer influence. *Social Neuroscience, 3*(3–4), 303–316.

Paus, T., Zijdenbos, A., Worsley, K., Collins, D. L., Blumenthal, J., Giedd, J. N., . . . Evans, A. C. (1999). Structural maturation of neural pathways in children and adolescents: In vivo study. *Science, 283*, 1908–1911.

Roper v. Simmons, 543 U.S. 551 (2005).

Sarkar, S., Craig, M., Catani, M., Dell'Acqua, F., Fahy, T., Deeley, Q., & Murphy, D. G. (2013). Frontotemporal white-matter microstructural abnormalities in adolescents with conduct disorder: A diffusion tensor imaging study. *Psychological Medicine, 43*, 401–411.

Scott, E. S., & Steinberg, L. (2003). Blaming youth. *Texas Law Review, 81*, 799–840.

Scott, E. S., & Steinberg, L. (2008). Adolescent development and the regulation of youth crime. *The Future of Children, 18*(2), 15–33.

Simmons v. Roper, 112 S.W.3d 397, 399 (Mo. 2003) (en banc).

Snead, O. C. (2008). Neuroimaging and capital punishment. *The New Atlantis: A Journal of Technology and Society, 19*, 35–63.

Sowell, E. R., Thompson, P. M., Tessner, K. D., & Toga. A. W. (2001). Mapping continued brain growth and gray matter density reduction in dorsal frontal cortex: Inverse relationships during post-adolescent brain maturation. *Journal of Neuroscience, 21*(22), 8819–8829.

Sowell, E. R., Trauner, D. A., Gamst, A., & Jernigan, T. L. (2002). Development of cortical and subcortical brain structures in childhood and adolescence: A structural MRI study. *Developmental Medicine and Child Neurology, 44,* 4–16.

Spear, L. P. (2010). *The behavioral neuroscience of adolescence.* New York: Norton.

State v. Simmons, 944 S. W. 2d 165, 169 (en banc), cert. denied, 522 U. S. 953 (1997).

Steinberg L. (2003). Is decision making the right framework for research on adolescent risk taking? In D. Romer (Ed.), *Reducing adolescent risk: Toward an integrated approach* (pp. 18–24). Thousand Oaks, CA: SAGE.

Steinberg, L. (2007). Risk taking in adolescence: New perspectives from brain and behavioral science. *Current Directions in Psychological Science, 16,* 55–59.

Steinberg, L. (2008). Adolescent development and juvenile justice. *Annual Review of Clinical Psychology, 5,* 47–73.

Steinberg, L. (2010). A behavioral scientist looks at the science of adolescent brain development. *Brain and Cognition, 72*(1), 160–164.

Steinberg, L., Albert, D., Cauffman, E., Banich, M., Graham, S., & Woolard, J. (2008). Age differences in sensation seeking and impulsivity as indexed by behavior and self-report: Evidence for a dual systems model. *Developmental Psychology, 44,* 1764–1778.

Steinberg, L., Cauffman, E., Woolard, J., Graham, S., & Banich, M. (2009). Are adolescents less mature than adults? Minors' access to abortion, the juvenile death penalty, and the alleged APA "flip-flop." *American Psychologist, 64*(7), 583–594.

Steinberg, L., & Haskins, R. (2008). Keeping adolescents out of prison. *Brookings Institution Policy Brief* (Fall), 1–7.

Steinberg, L., & Monahan, K. C. (2007). Age differences in resistance to peer influence. *Developmental Psychology, 43*(6), 1531–1543.

Sturman, D. A., & Moghaddam, B. (2011). The neurobiology of adolescence: Changes in brain architecture, functional dynamics, and behavioral tendencies. *Neuroscience Biobehavioral Review, 35*(8), 1704–1712.

Stuss, D. T., & Knight, R. T. (2013). *Principles of frontal lobe function* (2nd ed.). New York: Oxford University Press.

Taylor-Thompson, K. (2003). Children, crime, and consequences: juvenile justice in America: States of mind/state of development. *Stanford Law & Policy Review, 14,* 143, 152.

Warr M. (2002). *Companions in crime: The social aspects of criminal conduct.* New York: Cambridge University Press.

Zimring, F. E. (2000). Penal proportionality for the young offender. In T. Grisso & R. G. Schwartz (Eds.), *Youth on trial: Developmental perspective on juvenile justice* (p. 271–290). Chicago: University of Chicago Press.

Chapter 7. The Admissibility of Scientific Evidence

American Psychiatric Association. (2000). *Diagnostic and statistical manual of mental disorders* (4th ed., text rev.). Washington, DC: Author.

Applebaum, P. S. (2009). Law & psychiatry: Through a glass darkly: Functional neuroimaging evidence enters the courtroom. *Psychiatric Services, 60*(1), 21–23.

Ballantine's Law Dictionary. (2010). Lawyers Cooperative Pub. Rochester: NY.

Barkataki, I., Kumari, V., Das, M., Hill, M., Morris, R., O'Connell, O. O., ... Sharma, T. (2005). A neuropsychological investigation into violence and mental illness. *Schizophrenia Research, 74*, 1–13.

Baskin, J. H., Edersheim, J. G., & Price, B. H. (2007). Is a picture worth a thousand words? Neuroimaging in the courtroom. *American Journal of Law & Medicine, 33*(2–3), 239–269.

Bernstein, D. E. (2001). Frye, Frye, again: The past, present, and future of the General Acceptance Test. George Mason Law & Economics Research Paper, No. 01-07. Retrieved from http://dx.doi.org/10.2139/ssrn.262034

Brower, M. C., & Price, B. H. (2001). Neuropsychiatry of frontal lobe dysfunction in violent and criminal behavior: A critical review. *Journal of Neurology, Neurosurgery & Psychiatry, 71*, 720–726.

Bufkin, J. L., & Lutrell, V. R. (2005). Neuroimaging studies of aggressive and violent behavior: Current findings and implications for criminology and criminal justice. *Trauma, Violence, & Abuse, 6*(2), 176–191.

Carmichael v. Samyang Tire, Inc., 923 F. Supp. 1514 (S.D. Ala. 1996).

Carmichael v. Samyang Tire, Inc., 131 F.3d 1433 (11th Cir. 1997).

Dahir, V., Richardson, J. T., Ginsburg, G. P., Gatowski, S. I., Dobbin, S. A., & Merlino, M. L. (2005). Judicial application of *Daubert* to psychological syndrome and profile evidence: A research note. *Psychology, Public Policy, and Law, 11*(1), 62–82.

Daubert v. Merrell Dow Pharmaceuticals, Inc., 509 U.S. 579, 590 (1993).

Dreyfuss, R. C. (1995). Is science a special case? The admissibility of scientific evidence after *Daubert v. Merrill Dow. Texas Law Review, 73*, 1779.

Erickson, S. K. (2010). Blaming the brain. *Minnesota Journal of Law, Science & Technology, 11*(1), 27–77.

Faigman, D. L. (2000). *Legal alchemy: The use and misuse of science in the law.* New York: W. H. Freeman.

Filley, C. M., Price, B. H., Nell, V., Antoinett, T., Morgan, A. S., Bresnahan, J. F., ... Kelly, J. P. (2001).Toward an understanding of violence: Neurobehavioral aspects of unwarranted physical aggression. *Neuropsychiatry, Neuropsychology, and Behavioral Neurology, 14*, 1–4.

Frye v. United States, 293 F.103 (1923).

Gatowski, S. I., Dobbin, S. A., Richardson, J. T., Ginsburg, G. P., Merlino, M. L., & Dahir, V. (2001). Asking the gatekeepers: A national survey of judges on judging expert evidence in a post-Daubert world. *Law and Human Behavior, 25*, 433–458.

General Electric Co. v. Joiner. 522 U.S. 136 (1997).

Gier v. Educational Service Unit No. 16 (845 F.Supp. 1342, 1351-52, D.Neb. 1994).

Gier v. Educational Service Unit No. 16 (66 F.3d 940, 8th Cir. 1995).

Joiner v. General Electric Company, 78 F.3d 524 (11th Cir. 1996), cert. granted, 117 S. Ct. 1243 (1997).

Kant Immanuel. Translated by Norman Kemp Smith. London: Macmillan, 1929. (Original work published 1785).

Learned Hand (1902). Expert testimony, historical and practical considerations regarding expert testimony. *Harvard Law Review, 15,* 40.

Logothetis, N. K. (2008). What we can do and what we cannot do with fMRI. *Nature, 453*(7197), 869–878.

Lopez, S. (2004). Satisfying the judicial gatekeeper: Assessing legal standards for the reliability of expert testimony. *University of California Irvine Law Forum Journal, 2,* 70–122.

Merlino, M. L., Murray, C. I., & Richardson, J. T. (2008). Judicial gatekeeping and the social construction of the admissibility of expert testimony. *Behavioral Sciences and the Law, 26,* 187–206.

Mobbs, D., Lau, H. C., Jones, O. D., & Frith, C.D. (2007). Law, responsibility, and the brain. *Biology, 5*(4), 693–700.

Pridmore, S., Chambers, A., & McArthur, M. L. (2005). Neuroimaging in psychopathy. *Australian and New Zealand Journal of Psychiatry, 39*(10), 856–865.

Pustilnik, A. C. (2009). Violence on the brain: A critique of neuroscience in criminal law. *Wake Forest Law Review, 44,* 183.

Raine, A., Buchsbaum, M. S., Stanley, J., Lottenberg, S., Abel, L., & Stoddard, S. (1994). Selective reductions in prefrontal glucose metabolism in murderers. *Biological Psychiatry, 36,* 365–373.

Raine, A., Lencz, T., Bihrle, S., LaCasse, L., & Colletti, P. (2000). Reduced prefrontal gray matter volume and reduced autonomic activity in antisocial personality disorder. *Archives of General Psychiatry, 57*(2), 119–127.

Roper v. Simmons, 543 U.S. 551 (2005).

State v. Foret (628 So.2d 1116, 1127, La. 1993).

United States v. Burnett, 579 F.3d 129 (1st Cir., 2009).

United States v. Messino, 181 F.3d 826, 829-30 (7th Cir. 1999).

United States v. Montgomery, 635 F.3d, 1074 (8th Cir., 2011).

Vickers, L. (2005). Daubert, critique and interpretation: What empirical studies tell us about the application of Daubert. *University of San Francisco Law Review, 40,* 109.

Vidmar, N., Lempert, R. O., Diamond, S. S., Hans, V. P., Landsman, S., MacCoun, R., . . . Horowitz, I. (2000). Amicus brief: *Kumho Tire v. Carmichael. Law and Human Behavior, 24,* 387–400.

Zink v. State, 278 S.W.3d 170 (Mo. 2009).

Chapter 8. The Issue of Evidentiary Reliability

Aharoni, E., Funk, C., Sinnott-Armstrong, W., & Gazzaniga, M. (2008). Can neurological evidence help courts assess criminal responsibility? Lessons from law and neuroscience. *Annals of the New York Academy of Sciences, 1124,* 145–160.

Anderson, B. M., Stevens, M. C., Meda, S., Jordan, K., Calhoun, V. D., & Pearlson, G. D. (2011). Functional imaging of cognitive control during acute alcohol intoxication. *Alcoholism Clinical Experimental Research, 35*(1), 156–165.

Atkins v. Virginia, 536 U.S. 304, 351 (2002).

Babikian, T., Boone, K., Lu, P., & Arnold, G. (2006). Sensitivity and specificity of various Digit Span scores in the detection of suspect effort. *The Clinical Neuropsychologist, 20*(1), 145–159.

Baer, R. A., & Miller, J. (2002). Underreporting of psychopathology on the MMPI-2: A meta-analytic review. *Psychological Assessment, 14*(1), 16–26.

Baskin, J. H., Edersheim, J. G., & Price, B. H. (2007). Is a picture worth a thousand words? Neuroimaging in the courtroom. *American Journal of Law & Medicine, 33*, 239–269.

Bennett, C. M., & Miller, M. B. (2010). How reliable are the results from functional magnetic resonance imaging? *Annals of the New York Academy of Sciences, 1191*, 133–155.

Binder, J. R., Frost, J. A., Hammeke, T. A., Bellgowan, P. S., Rao, S. M., & Cox, R. W. (1999). Conceptual processing during the conscious resting state: A functional MRI study. *Journal of Cognitive Neuroscience, 11*, 80–95.

Blackstone, W. (1979). *Commentaries on the laws of England: A facsimile edition with introductions by Stanley N. Katz.* Chicago: University of Chicago.

Borg, J., Holm, L., Cassidy, J. D., Peloso, P. M., Carroll, L. J., von Holst, H., & Ericson, K. (2004). Diagnostic procedures in mild traumatic brain injury: Results of the World Health Organization Collaborating Centre Task Force on mild traumatic brain injury. *Journal of Rehabilitative Medicine, 43*, 61–75.

Brammer, R. (1997). Case conceptualization strategies: The relationship between psychologists' experience levels, academic training, and mode of clinical inquiry. *Educational Psychology Review, 9*, 333–351.

Breau, D. L., & Brook, B. (2007). "Mock" mock juries: A field experiment on the ecological validity of jury simulations. *Law and Psychology Review, 31*, 77–92.

Breyer, S. (2011). Introduction. In *Reference manual on scientific evidence* (3rd ed., pp. 1–11). Washington, DC: National Academies Press.

Brodie, J. D. (1996). Imaging for the clinical psychiatrist: Facts, fantasies, and other musings [editorial]. *American Journal of Psychiatry, 153*, 145–149.

Bryman, A. (2012). *Social research methods* (4th ed.). New York: Oxford University Press.

Butcher, J. N. (2002). *Clinical personality assessment: Practical approaches. Vol. 2 of Oxford Textbooks in Clinical Psychology* (pp. 76–95). New York: Oxford University Press.

Canli, T., & Amin, Z. (2002). Neuroimaging of emotion and personality: Scientific evidence and ethical considerations. *Brain and Cognition, 50*(3), 414–431.

Cecil, J. S. (2005). Ten years of judicial gatekeeping under *Daubert. American Journal of Public Health, 95*(1), 74–80.

Chapple v. Ganger, 851 F. Supp 1481 (E. D. Wash. 1999).

Daubert v. Merrell Dow Pharmaceuticals, Inc., 509 U.S. 579, 590 (1993).

Dawes, R. M. (2001). *Everyday irrationality: How pseudo-scientists, lunatics, and the rest of us systematically fail to think rationally.* Boulder, CO: Westview Press.

Feigenson, N. (2006). Brain imaging and courtroom evidence: On the admissibility and persuasiveness of fMRI. *International Journal of Law in Context, 2*(3), 233–255.

Finn, S. E., & Kamphuis, J. H. (1995). What a clinician needs to know about base rates. In J. N. Butcher (Ed.), *Clinical personality assessment: Practical approaches* (pp. 224–235). New York: Oxford University Press.

Fowler, J. S., Volkow, N. D., Logan, J., Wang, G. J., MacGregor, R. R., Schyler, D., . . . Patlak, C. (1994). Slow recovery of human brain MAO B after L-deprenyl (Selegeline) withdrawal. *Synapse, 18*, 86–93.

Fox, P. T., & Friston, K. J. (2012). Distributed processing; distributed functions? *NeuroImage, 61*(2), 407–426.

Groenier, M., Pieters, J. M., Hulshof, C. D., Wilhelm, P., & Wittem, C. L. M. (2008). Psychologists' judgements of diagnostic activities: Deviations from a theoretical model. *Clinical Psychology & Psychotherapy, 15*, 256–265.

Gurley, J. R., & Marcus, D. K. (2008). The effects of neuroimaging and brain injury on insanity defenses. *Behavioral Sciences and the Law, 26*, 85–97.

Henson, R. (2006). Forward inference using functional neuroimaging: Dissociations versus associations. *Trends in Cognitive Sciences, 10*(2), 64–69.

Hofman, P. A., Stapert, S. Z., van Kroonenburgh, M. J., Jolles, J., de Kruijk, J., & Wilmink, J. T. (2001). MR imaging, single-photon emission CT, and neurocognitive performance after mild traumatic brain injury. *American Journal of Neuroradiology, 22*, 441–449.

Hom, J. (2008). Response to Bigler (2007): The sky is not falling. *Archives of Clinical Neuropsychology, 23*(1), 125–128.

Horwitz, J. E., Lynch, J. K., McCaffrey, R. J., & Fisher, J. M. (2008). Screening for neuropsychological impairment using Reitan and Wolfson's preliminary neuropsychological test battery. *Archives of Clinical Neuropsychology, 23*(4), 393–398.

Hughes, D. G., Jackson, A., Mason, D. L., Berry, E., Hollis, S., & Yates, D. W. (2004). Abnormalities on magnetic resonance imaging seen acutely following mild traumatic brain injury: Correlation with neuropsychological tests and delayed recovery. *Neuroradiology, 46*, 550–558.

Hutzler, F. (2014). Reverse inference is not a fallacy per se: Cognitive processes can be inferred from functional imaging data. *NeuroImage, 84*(1), 1061–1069.

Jones, O. D., Buckholtz, J., Schall, J. D., & Marois, R. (2009). Brain imaging for legal thinkers: A guide for the perplexed. *Stanford Technology Law Review 5*. Vanderbilt Public Law Research Paper No. 10-09. Retrieved from http://ssrn.com/abstract=1563612

Kamphuis, J. H., & Finn, S. E. (2002). Implementing base rates in daily clinical decision making. In J. N. Butcher (Ed.), *Clinical personality assessment* (2nd ed., pp. 257–268). New York: Oxford University Press.

Khoshbin L., & Khoshbin, S. (2007). Imaging the mind, minding the image: An historical introduction to brain imaging and the law. *American Journal of Law & Medicine, 33*(2–3), 171–192.

Kim, N. S., & Ahn, W. (2002). Clinical psychologists' theory-based representations of mental disorders predict their diagnostic reasoning and memory. *Journal of Experimental Psychology: General, 131*, 451–476.

Kim, Y. K., Lee, D. S., Lee, S. K., Chung, C. K., Chung, J., & Lee, M. C. (2002). 18F-FDG PET in localization of frontal lobe epilepsy: Comparison of visual and SPM analysis. *Journal of Nuclear Medicine, 43*, 1167–1174.

Knight, D., Smith, C., Cheng, D., Stein, E., & Helmstetter, F. (2004). Amygdala and hippocampal activity during acquisition and extinction of human fear conditioning. *Cognitive, Affective and Behavioral Neuroscience, 4,* 317–325.

Larrabee, G. J. (2008). Aggregation across multiple indicators improves the detection of malingering: Relationship to likelihood ratios. *The Clinical Neuropsychologist, 22,* 666–679.

Last, J. (2001). *A dictionary of epidemiology* (4th ed.). New York: Oxford University Press.

Lezak, M. D. (1995). *Neuropsychological assessment* (3rd ed.). New York: Oxford University Press.

Meehl, P. E., & Rosen, A. (1955). Antecedent probability and the efficiency of psychometric signs, patterns, or cutting scores. *Psychological Bulletin, 52,* 194–216.

Meyer, G. J., Finn, S. E., Eyde, L. D., Kay, G. G., Moreland, K. L., Dies, . . . Reed, G. M. (2001). Psychological testing and psychological assessment: A review of evidence and issues. *American Psychologist, 56*(2), 128–165.

Moreno, J. (2009). The future of neuroimaged lie detection and the law. *Akron Law Review, 42,* 717–734.

Müller, J. L., Sommer, M., Döhnel, K., Weber, T., Schmidt-Wilcke, T., & Hajak, G. (2008). Disturbed prefrontal and temporal brain function during emotion and cognition interaction in criminal psychopathy. *Behavioral Science and the Law, 26*(1), 131–150.

Poldrack, R. A. (2006). Can cognitive processes be inferred from neuroimaging data? *Trends in Cognitive Sciences, 10,* 59–63.

Poldrack, R. A. (2008). The role of fMRI in cognitive neuroscience: Where do we stand? *Current Opinion in Neurobiology, 18,* 223–227.

Poldrack, R. A. (2011). Inferring mental states from neuroimaging data: from reverse inference to large-scale decoding. *Neuron, 72,* 692–697.

Pope, K. S., & Vasquez, M. J. (2005). In *How to survive and thrive as a therapist: Information, ideas, and resources for psychologists in practice* (pp. 95–100). Washington, DC: American Psychological Association.

Pratt, B. (2005). Soft science in the courtroom? The effects of admitting neuroimaging evidence into legal proceedings. *Penn Bioethics Journal, 1*(1), 1–3.

Pustilnik, A. C. (2009). Violence on the brain: a critique of neuroscience in criminal law. *Wake Forest Law Review, 44,* 183.

*Quick v. State.*Tex. App. LEXIS 680 (2011).

Reeves, D. R., Mills, M. J., Billick, S. B., & Brodie, J. D. (2003). Limitations of brain imaging in forensic psychiatry. *Journal of the American Academy of Psychiatry and Law, 31*(1), 89-86.

Roberts, A. (2007). Note, everything new is old again: Brain fingerprinting and evidentiary analogy. *Yale Journal of Law and Technology, 9,* 234–266. Retrieved from http://ssrn.com/abstract=1784359

Rogers, R. (1997). Introduction. In R. Rogers (Ed.), *Clinical assessment of malingering and deception* (pp. 1–19). New York: Guilford Press.

Rogers, R., Salekin, R. T., & Sewell, K. W. (1999). Validation of the Millon Clinical Multiaxial Inventory for Axis II disorders: Does it meet the Daubert standard? *Law and Human Behavior, 23,* 425–443.

Rosenfeld, B., Green, D., Pivovarova, E., Dole, T., & Zapf, P. (2010). What to do with contradictory data? Approaches to the integration of multiple malingering measures. *International Journal of Forensic Mental Health,* *9*(2), 63–73.

Rosenfeld, B., Sands, S. A., & van Gorp, W. G. (2000). Have we forgotten the base rate problem? Methodological issues in the detection of distortion. *Archives of Clinical Neuropsychology, 15*(4), 349–359.

Rosenhan, D. L. (1973). On being sane in insane places. *Science, 179,* 250–258.

Russell, E. W., Russell, S. L. K., & Hill, B. D. (2005). The fundamental psychometric status of neuropsychological batteries. *Archives of Clinical Neuropsychology, 20*(6), 785–794.

Sagan, C. (1997). *The demon-haunted world—Science as a candle in the dark.* New York: Ballantine Books.

Samuel, R. Z., & Mittenberg, W. (2005). Determination of malingering in disability evaluations. *Primary Psychiatry, 12*(12), 60–68.

Saxe, L., & Ben-Shakhar, G. (1999). Admissibility of polygraph tests: The application of scientific standards post-*Daubert*. *Psychology, Public Policy, and Law, 5*(1), 203–223.

Schauer, F. (2010). Neuroscience, lie-detection, and the law: Contrary to the prevailing view, the suitability of brain-based lie-detection for courtroom or forensic use should be determined according to legal and not scientific standards. *Trends in Cognitive Science, 14*(3), 101–103.

Skeem, J. L., Louden, J. E., & Evans, J. (2004). Venirepersons's attitudes toward the insanity defense: Developing, refining, and validating a scale. *Law and Human Behavior, 28*(6), 623–648.

Snead, C. (2007). Neuroimaging and the "complexity" of capital punishment. *New York University Law Review, 82*(5), 1265–1339.

Soderlund, H., Grady, C. L., Easdon, C., & Tulving, E. (2007). Acute effects of alcohol on neural correlates of episodic memory encoding. *Neuroimage, 35*(2), 928–939.

Spitzer, R. L. (1976). More on pseudoscience in science and the case for psychiatric diagnosis. *Archives of General Psychology, 33,* 459–470.

Stark, C., & Squire, L. (2001). When zero is not zero: The problem of ambiguous baseline conditions in fMRI. *Proceedings of the National Academy of Science, 98*(22), 12760–12766.

Sweet, J. J., Nelson, N. W., & Moberg, P. J. (2006). The TCN/AACN 2005 "salary survey": Professional practices, beliefs, and incomes of U.S. neuropsychologists. *Clinical Neuropsychology, 20,* 325–364.

Trowbridge, B. C., & Schutte, J. W. (2007). Some problems inherent in neuropsychological testing. *American Journal of Forensic Psychology, 25*(2), 5–34.

United States v. Flaherty, U.S. App. LEXIS 6930 (9th Cir. Nev. 2008).

United States v. Gigante, 987 F.Supp. 143, 146 (E.D.N.Y.1996).

United States v. Gigante, 982 F.Supp. 140, 159 (E.D.N.Y.1997).

Vallabhajosula, B., and van Gorp, W. (2001). Post-Daubert admissibility of scientific evidence on malingering of cognitive deficits. *Journal of the American Academy of Psychiatry and Law, 29,* 207–215.

Van Horn, J. D., Yanos, M., Schmitt, P. J., & Grafton, S. T. (2006). Alcohol-induced suppression of BOLD activity during goal-directed visuomotor performance. *Neuroimage, 31*(3), 1209–1221.

Vloet, T., Konrad, K., Huebner, T., Herpertz, S., & Herpertz-Dahlmann, B. (2008). Structural and functional MRI findings in children and adolescents with antisocial behavior. *Behavioral Science and the Law, 26*(1), 99–111.

Volkow, N. D., Fowler, J. S., Wolf, A. P., Hitzemann, R., Dewey, S., Bendriem, B., . . . Hoff, A. (1991). Changes in brain glucose metabolism in cocaine dependence and withdrawal. *American Journal of Psychiatry, 148*(5), 621–626.

Volkow, N. D., Ma, Y., Zhu, W., Fowler, J. S., Li, J., Rao, M., . . . Wang, G. J. (2008). Moderate doses of alcohol disrupt the functional organization of the human brain. *Psychiatry Research, 162*(3), 205–213.

Wardlaw, J. M., O'Connell, G., Shuler, K., DeWilde, J., Haley, J., Escobar, O., . . . Schafer, B. (2011). "Can it read my mind?"—What do the public and experts think of the current (mis)uses of neuroimaging? *PLoS ONE* 6(10): e25829.

Chapter 9. Malingering and its Assessment

Aamodt, M. G., & Custer, H. (2006). Who can best catch a liar? A meta-analysis of individual differences in detecting deception. *Forensic Exam, 15*, 6–11.

Abe, N., Suzuki, M., Mori, E., Itoh, M., & Fujii, T. (2007). Deceiving others: Distinct neural responses of the prefrontal cortex and amygdala in simple fabrication and deception with social interactions. *Journal of Cognitive Neuroscience, 19*(2), 287–295.

Abe, N., Suzuki, M., Tsukiura, T., Mori, E., Yamaguchi, K., Itoh, M., & Fujii, T. (2006). Dissociable roles of prefrontal and anterior cingulate cortices in deception. *Cerebral Cortex, 16*, 192–199.

Adelsheim, C. (2011). Functional Magnetic Resonance Detection of Deception: Great as Fundamental Research, Inadequate as Substantive Evidence. *Mercer Law Review, 62*, 885–908.

Adelson, R. (2004). Detecting deception. *Monitor on Psychology, 37*(7), 70.

Aguerrevere, L. E., Greve, K. W., Bianchini, K. J., & Ord, J. S. (2011). Classification accuracy of the Millon Clinical Multiaxial Inventory-III modifier indices in the detection of malingering in traumatic brain injury. *Journal of Clinical and Experimental Neuropsychology, 33*(5), 497–504.

Allen, L., Bigler, E. D., Larson, J., Goodrich-Hunsaker, N. J., & Hopkins, R. O. (2007). Functional neuroimaging evidence for high effort on the Word Memory Test in the absence of external incentives. *Brain Injury, 21*(13–14), 1425–1428.

Alwes, Y. R., Clark, J. A., Berry, D. T. R., & Granacher, R. P. (2008). Screening for feigning in a civil forensic setting. *Journal of Clinical and Experimental Neuropsychology, 30*(2), 1–8.

American Psychiatric Association. (2000). *Diagnostic and statistical manual of mental disorders* (4th ed., text rev.). Washington, DC: Author.

Bagby, M., Nicholson, R., Bacchiochi, J., Ryder, A., & Bury, A. (2002). Predictive capacity of the MMPI-2 and PAI validity scales and indexes to detect coached and uncoached feigning. *Journal of Personality Assessment, 2*, 69–86.

Baity, M. R., Siefert, C. J., Chambers, A., & Blais, M. A. (2007). Deceptiveness on the PAI: A study of naive faking with psychiatric inpatients. *Journal of Personality Assessment, 88*(1), 16–24.

Ben-Porath, Y. S. (2012). *Interpreting the MMPI-2-RF*. Minneapolis: University of Minnesota Press.

Bianchini, K. J., Mathias, C. W., & Greve, K. W. (2001). Symptom validity testing: A critical review. *The Clinical Neuropsychologist, 15*(1), 19–45.

Binder, L. M. (2002). The Portland Digit Recognition Test: A review of validation data and clinical use. *Journal of Forensic Neuropsychology, 2*, 27–41.

Binder, L. M., & Rohling, M. (1996). Money matters: A meta-analytic review of the effects of financial incentives on recovery after closed-head injury. *American Journal of Psychiatry, 153*, 7–10.

Binks, P. G., Gouvier, W. D., & Waters, W. F. (1996). Malingering detection with the Dot Counting Test. *Archives of Clinical Neuropsychology, 12*, 41–46.

Bles, M., & Haynes, J. D. (2008). Detecting concealed information using brain-imaging technology. *Neurocase, 14*(1), 82–92.

Boccaccini, M. T., Murrie, D. C., & Duncan, S. A. (2006). Screening for malingering in a criminal-forensic sample with the Personality Assessment Inventory. *Psychological Assessment, 18*(4), 415–423.

Bounds, T. A. (2005). The test of memory malingering: Detection of malingered cognitive deficits in a criminal forensic population. *Dissertation Abstracts International: Section B: The Sciences and Engineering, 65*(10-B), 5388.

Brennan, A. M., & Gouvier, W. D. (2006). Are we honestly studying malingering? A profile and comparison of simulated and suspected malingerers. *Applied Neuropsychology, 13*(1), 1–11.

Brockhaus, R., & Merten, T. (2004). Neuropsychologische diagnostik suboptimalen leistungsverhaltens mit dem Word Memory Test. *Nervenarzt, 75*, 882–887.

Bush, S. S., Ruff, R. M., Troster, A. I., Barth, J. T., Koffler, S. P., Pliskin, N. H., . . . Silver, C. H. (2005). Symptom validity assessment: Practice issues and medical necessity. *Archives of Clinical Neuropsychology, 20*, 419–426.

Butcher, J. N., Arbisi, P. A., Atlis, M. M., & McNulty, J. L. (2003). The construct validity of the Lees-Haley Fake Bad Scale. Does this scale measure somatic malingering and feigned emotional distress? *Archives of Clinical Neuropsychology, 18*, 473–485.

Cato, M. A., Brewster, J., Ryan, T., & Guiliano, A. (2002). Coaching and the ability to simulate mild traumatic brain-injury symptoms. *The Clinical Neuropsychologist, 16*, 524–535.

Chesterman, L. P., Terbeck, S., & Vaughan, F. (2008). Malingered psychosis. *Journal of Forensic Psychiatry & Psychology, 19*(3), 275–300.

Christ, S. E., Van Essen, D. C., Watson, J. M., Brubaker, L., & McDermott, K. B. (2009). The Contributions of prefrontal cortex and executive control to deception: Evidence from activation likelihood estimate meta-analyses. *Cerebral Cortex, 19*, 1557–1566.

Clegg, C., Fremouw, W., & Mogge, N. (2009). Utility of the Structured Inventory of Malingered Symptomatology (SIMS) and the Assessment of Depression Inventory (ADI) in screening for malingering among outpatients seeking to claim disability. *Journal of Forensic Psychiatry & Psychology, 20*(2), 239–254.

Coleman, R. D., Rapport, L. J., Millis, S. R., Ricker, J. H., & Farchione, T. J. (1998). Effects of coaching on detection of malingering on the California Verbal Learning Test. *Journal of Clinical and Experimental Neuropsychology, 20,* 201–210.

Conroy, M. A., & Kwartner, P. P. (2006). Malingering. *Applied Psychology in Criminal Justice, 2*(3), 29–51.

Curtis, K. L., Greve, K. W., Bianchini, K. J., & Brennan, A. (2006). California Verbal Learning Test indicators of malingered neurocognitive dysfunction: Sensitivity and specificity in traumatic brain injury. *Assessment, 13*(1), 46–61.

Curtiss, G., & Vanderploeg, R. D. (2000). Prevalence rates for neuropsychological malingering indexes in traumatic brain injury. *Division of Clinical Neuropsychology: Newsletter, 40*(18), 9–13.

Daubert, S. D., & Metzler, A. E. (2000). The detection of fake-bad and fake-good responding on the Millon Clinical Multiaxial Inventory III. *Psychological Assessment, 12,* 418–424.

Daubert v. Merrell Dow Pharmaceuticals, Inc., 509 U.S. 579, 590 (1993).

DeClue, G. (2002). Feigning does not equal malingering: A case study. *Behavioral Science and the Law, 20,* 716–726.

Delain, S. L., Stafford, K. P., & Ben-Porath, Y. S. (2003). Use of the TOMM in a criminal court forensic assessment setting. *Assessment, 10*(4), 370–381.

Delis, D. C., Kramer, J. H., Kaplan, E. & Ober, B. A. (2000). *California Verbal Learning Test—Second Edition, Adult Version.* San Antonio, TX: Psychological Corporation.

Dell'Anno, C. S., & Shiva, A. (2006). An aspect of mental illness and violence: The relationship between the severity of criminal charges and psychopathology. *The New School Psychology Bulletin, 4*(1), 44–61.

Drob, S. L., Meehan, K. B., & Waxman, S. E. (2009). Clinical and Conceptual Problems in the Attribution of Malingering in Forensic Evaluations. *Journal of the American Academy of Psychiatry and Law, 37,* 98–106.

Dunn, T. M., Shear, P. K., Howe, S., & Ris, M. D. (2003). Detecting neuropsychological malingering: Effects of coaching and information. *Archives of Clinical Neuropsychology, 18*(2), 121–134.

Edens, J. F., Hart, S. D., Johnson, D. W., Johnson, J. K., & Oliver, M. E. (2000). Use of the Personality Assessment Inventory to assess psychopathy in offender population. *Psychological Assessment, 12,* 132–193.

Ellwanger, J., Tenhula, W. N., Rosenfeld, J. P., & Sweet, J. J. (1999). Identifying simulators of cognitive deficit through combined use of neuropsychological test performance and event-related potentials. *Journal of Clinical and Experimental Neuropsychology, 21*(6), 866–879.

Essig, S. M., Mittenberg, W., Petersen, R. S., Strauman, S., & Cooper, J. T. (2001). Practices in forensic neuropsychology: Perspectives of neuropsychologists and trial attorneys. *Archives of Clinical Neuropsychology, 16,* 271–291.

Farkas, M. R., Rosenfeld, B., Robbins, R., & van Gorp, W. (2006). Do tests of malingering concur? Concordance among malingering measures. *Behavioral Sciences & the Law, 24,* 659–671.

Fox, D. (2009). The right to silence as protecting mental control. *Akron Law Review, 42,* 763–801.

Frederick, R. (2002). A review of Rey's strategies for detecting malingered neuropsychological impairment. *Journal of Forensic Neuropsychology, 2*, 1–25.

Frederick, R. I. (1997). *Validity Indicator Profile manual.* Minnetonka, MN: NCS Assessments.

Frederick, R. I., Crosby, R. D., & Wynkoop, T. F. (2000). Performance curve classification of invalid responding on the Validity Indicator Profile. *Archives of Clinical Neuropsychology, 15*, 281–300.

Frederick, R. I., & Foster, H. (1991). Multiple measures of malingering on a forced-choice test of cognitive ability. *Psychological Assessment, 3*, 596–602.

Gaetz, M., & Bernstein, D. M. (2001). The current status of electrophysiologic procedures for the assessment of mild traumatic brain injury. *Journal of Head Trauma Rehabilitation, 16*, 386–405.

Ganis, G., Rosenfeld, J. P., Meixner, J., Kievit, R. A., & Schendan, H. E. (2011). *NeuroImage, 55*, 312–319.

Gebart-Eaglemont, J. E. (2001). Review of the Validity Indicator Profile. In B. S. Plake and J. C. Impara (Eds.). *The Fourteenth Mental Measurements Yearbook* (pp. 125–145). Lincoln, NE: Buros Institute of Mental Measurements.

Gerard, E. (2008). Waiting in the wings? The admissibility of neuroimagery for lie detection. *Developments in Mental Health Law, 27*, 1–32.

Gierok, S. D., Dickson, A. L., & Cole, J. A. (2005). Performance of forensic and non-forensic adult psychiatric inpatients on the Test of Memory Malingering. *Archives of Clinical Neuropsychology, 20*, 755–760.

Gonzalez-Andino, S. L., Blanke, O., Lantz, G., Thut, G., & Grave de Peralta Menendez, R. (2001). The use of functional constraints for the neuroelectromagnetic inverse problem: Alternatives and caveats. *International Journal of Bioelectromagnetism, 3*, 1–17.

Green, D., & Rosenfeld, B. (2011). Evaluating the gold standard: A review and meta-analysis of the Structured Interview of Reported Symptoms. *Psychological Assessment, 23*(1), 95–107.

Green, D., Rosenfeld, B., & Belfi, B. (2013). New and improved? A comparison of the original and revised versions of the Structured Interview of Reported Symptoms. *Assessment, 20*(2), 210–218.

Green, P. (2003). *Word Memory Test for Windows: User's manual and program.* Edmonton, Alberta: Author. (Revised 2005)

Green, P., Lees-Haley, P., & Allen, L. (2002). Word Memory Test and the validity of neuropsychological test scores. *Journal of Forensic Neuropsychology, 2*(3–4), 97–24.

Greene, R. L. (2000). *The MMPI-2: An interpretive manual* (2nd ed.). Boston: Allyn and Bacon.

Greve, K. W., & Bianchini, K. J. (2006). Classification accuracy of the Portland Digit Recognition Test in traumatic brain injury: Results of a known-groups analysis. *Clinical Neuropsychologist, 20*(4), 816–830.

Greve, K. W., Ord, J., Curtis, K. L., Bianchini, K. J., & Brennan, A. (2008). Detecting malingering in traumatic brain injury and chronic pain: A comparison of three forced-choice symptom validity tests. *Clinical Neuropsychologist, 22*(5), 896–918.

Groth-Marnat, G. (1997). *Handbook of psychological assessment* (3rd ed.). New York: Wiley.

Guy, L. S., Kwartner, P. P., & Miller, H. A. (2006). Investigating the M-FAST: psychometric properties and utility to detect diagnostic specific malingering. *Behavioral Sciences and the Law, 24*(5), 687–702.

Haines, M. E., & Norris, M. P. (1995). Detecting the malingering of cognitive deficits: An update. *Neuropsychology Review, 5*(2), 125–148.

Harrington v. State, Case No. PCCV 073247. Iowa District Court for Pottawattamie County, 2001.

Hilsabeck, R. C., LeCompte, D. C., Marks, A. R., & Grafman, J. (2001). The Word Completion Memory Test (WCMT): A new test to detect malingered memory deficits. *Archives of Clinical Neuropsychology, 16*, 669–677.

Hugo, V. (1862). *Les Miserables*, pt. 2, bk. 7, ch. 3.

Hunt, S., Root, J. C., & Bascetta, B. L. (2013). Effort testing in schizophrenia and schizoaffective disorder: Validity Indicator Profile and Test of Memory Malingering performance characteristics. *Archives of Clinical Neuropsychology, 29*(2), 164–172.

Iverson, G. L. (2003). Detecting malingering in civil forensic evaluations. In A. M. Horton Jr. & L. C. Hartlage (Eds.), *Handbook of forensic neuropsychology* (pp. 137–177). New York: Springer.

Iverson, G. L., & Tuslky, D. S. (2003). Detecting malingering on the WAIS-III: Unusual digit span performance patterns in the normal population and in clinical groups. *Archives of Clinical Neuropsychology, 18*(1), 1–9.

Jacoby, L. L. (1991). A process dissociation framework: Separating automatic from intentional uses of memory. *Journal of Memory and Language, 30*, 513–541.

Jelicic, M., Ceunen, E., Peters, M. J., & Merckelbach, H. (2011). Detecting coached feigning using the Test of Memory Malingering (TOMM) and the Structured Inventory of Malingered Symptomatology (SIMS). *Journal of Clinical Psychology, 67*(9), 850–855.

Jiang, W., Liu, H., Liao, J., Ma, X., Rong, P., Tang, Y., & Wang W. (2013). A functional MRI study of deception among offenders with antisocial personality disorders. *Neuroscience, 244*, 90–98.

Jones, A. (2013a). Test of memory malingering: cutoff scores for psychometrically defined malingering groups in a military sample. *Clinical Neuropsychology, 27*(6), 1043–1059.

Jones, A. (2013b). Victoria Symptom Validity Test: Cutoff scores for psychometrically defined malingering groups in a military sample. *Clinical Neuropsychology, 27*(8), 1373–1394.

Keary, T. A., Frazier, T. W., Belzile, C. J., Chapin, J. S., Naugle, R. I., Najm, I. M., & Busch, R. M. (2013). Working memory and intelligence are associated with Victoria Symptom Validity Test hard item performance in patients with intractable epilepsy. *Journal of the International Neuropsychological Society, 19*(3), 314–323.

Kruesi, M. J. P., & Casanova, M. F. (2006). White matter in liars. *The British Journal of Psychiatry, 188*, 293–294.

Kucharski, L. T., Duncan, S., Egan, S. S., & Falkenbach, D. M. (2006). Psychopathy and malingering of psychiatric disorder in criminal defendants. *Behavioral Science & the Law, 24*(5), 633–644.

Kucharski, L. T., Falkenbach, D. M., & Duncan, S. (2004). Antisocial personality disorder and malingering. Paper presented at the annual meeting of the American Academy of Psychiatry and the Law, Phoenix, AZ (October).

Kucharski, L. T., Toomey, J. P., Fila, K., & Duncan, S. (2007). Detection of malingering of psychiatric disorder with the Personality Assessment Inventory: An investigation of criminal defendants. *Journal of Personality Assessment, 88*(1), 25–32.

Lamb, D. G., Berry, D. T. R., Wetter, M. W., & Baer, A. (1994). Effects of two types of information on malingering of closed head-injury on the MMPI-2: An analog investigation. *Psychological Assessment, 6,* 8–13.

Langleben, D. D., Schroeder, L., Maldjian, J. A., Gur, R. C., McDonald, S., Ragland, J.D., . . . Childress, A. R. (2002). Brain activity during simulated deception: An event-related functional magnetic resonance study. *NeuroImage, 15,* 727–732.

Larrabee, G. J. (2003). Detection of symptom exaggeration with the MMPI-2 in litigants with malingered neurocognitive dysfunction. *The Clinical Neuropsychologist, 17,* 54–68.

Larrabee, G. J., Greiffenstein, M. F., Greve, K. W., & Bianchini, K. J. (2007). Refining diagnostic criteria for malingering. In G. J. Larrabee (Ed.), *Assessment of malingered neuropsychological deficits* (pp. 334–371). New York: Oxford University Press.

Lee, G. P., Lohring, D. W., & Martin, R. C. (1992). Rey's 15-item Visual Memory Test for the detecting of malingering: Normative observations on patients with neurological disorders. *Psychological Assessment, 4,* 43–46.

Lee, T. M., Liu, H. L., Tan, L. H., Chan, C. C., Mahankali, S., Feng, C. M., . . . Gao, J. H. (2002). Lie detection by functional magnetic resonance imaging. *Human Brain Mapping, 15,* 157–164.

Lezak, M. D. (1995). *Neuropsychological assessment* (3rd ed.). New York: Oxford University Press.

Lezak, M. D., Howieson, D. B., & Loring, D. W. (2004). *Neuropsychological assessment* (4th ed.). New York: Oxford University Press.

Libet, B. (2002). The timing of mental events: Libet's experimental findings and their implications. *Consciousness and Cognition, 11,* 291–299.

Marchewka, A., Jednorog, K., Falkiewicz, M., Szeszkowski, W., Grabowska, A., & Szatkowska, I. (2012). Sex, lies and fMRI—gender differences in neural basis of deception. *PloSOne, 7*(8), e43076.

Mathias, C. W., Greve, K. W., Bianchini, K. J., Houston, R. J., & Crouch, J. A. (2002). Detecting malingered neurocognitive dysfunction using the reliable digit span in traumatic brain injury. *Assessment, 9,* 301–308.

McCabe, D. P., Castel, A. D., & Rhodes, M. G. (2011). The influence of fMRI lie detection evidence on juror decision-making. *Behavioral Sciences and the Law, 29*(4), 566–577.

McCaffrey, R. J., O'Bryant, S. E., Ashendorf, L., & Fisher, J. M. (2003). Correlations among the TOMM, Rey-15, and MMPI-2 validity scales in a sample of TBI litigants. *Journal of Forensic Neuropsychology, 3*(3), 45–54.

Merckelbach, H., & Smith, G.P. (2003). Diagnostic accuracy of the Structured Inventory of Malingered Symptomatology (SIMS) in detecting instructed malingering. *Archives of Clinical Neuropsychology, 18,* 145–152.

Merten, T., Bossink, L., & Schmand, B. (2007). On the limits of effort testing: Symptom validity tests and severity of neurocognitive symptoms in non-litigant patients. *Journal of Clinical and Experimental Neuropsychology, 29*(3), 308–318.

Meyers, J. E., & Volbrecht, M. E. (2003). A validation of multiple malingering detection methods in a large clinical sample. *Archives of Clinical Neuropsychology, 18*(3), 261–276.

Miears v. State, Nos. 04-11-00531-CR, 04-11-00532-CR & 04-11-0533-CR (4th Ct. Appeals, 2013).

Miller, H. (2001). *Manual for the Miller Forensic Assessment of Symptoms Test (M-FAST)*. Odessa, FL: Psychological Assessment Resources.

Miller, H., Guy, L., & Davila, M. (2000). Utility of the M-FAST: Detecting malingering with disability claimants. Poster presented at the 109th annual conference of the American Psychological Association, San Francisco, CA.

Millis, S. R., & Kler, S. (1995). Limitations of the Rey Fifteen-Item Test in the detection of malingering. *The Clinical Neuropsychologist, 9*, 241–244.

Millon, T., Davis, R., & Millon, C. (1997). *The Millon Clinical Multiaxial Inventory-III manual* (2nd ed.). Minneapolis: National Computer Systems.

Mittenberg, W., Fichera, S., Zielinski, R., & Heilbronner, R. (1995). Identification of malingered head injury on the Wechsler Adult Intelligence Scale–Revised. *Professional Psychology: Research and Practice, 26*, 491–498.

Mochizuki, Y., Oishi, M., & Takasu, T. (2001). Correlations between P300 components and regional cerebral blood flows. *Journal of Clinical Neuroscience, 8*(5), 407–410.

Morey, L. C. (1996). *An interpretive guide to the Personality Assessment Inventory (PAI)*. Odessa, FL: Psychological Assessment Resources.

Morey, L. C. (2003). *Essentials of PAI Assessment*. New York: Wiley.

Morey, L. C., & Lanier, V. M. (1998). Operating characteristics of six response distortion indicators for the Personality Assessment Inventory. *Assessment, 5*, 203–214.

Nelson, N., Sweet, J., & Demakis, G. (2006). Meta-Analysis of the MMPI-2 Fake Bad Scale: Utility in forensic practice. *Clinical Neuropsychologist, 20*(1), 39–58.

O'Bryant, S. E., Gavett, B. E., McCaffrey, R. J., O'Jile, J.R., Huerkamp, J. K., Smitherman, T.A., & Humphreys, J. D. (2008). Clinical utility of trial 1 of the Test of Memory Malingering (TOMM). *Applied Neuropsychology, 15*(2), 113–116.

Pardo, M. S. (2006). Neuroscience evidence, legal culture, and criminal procedure. *American. Journal of Criminal Law, 33*, 301–337.

Pollen, D. A. (2004). Brain stimulation and conscious experience. *Consciousness and Cognition, 13*, 626–645.

Powell, M. R., Gfeller, J. D., Hendricks, B. L., & Sharland, M. (2004). Detecting symptom- and test-coached simulators with the Test of Memory Malingering. *Archives of Clinical Neuropsychology, 19*, 693–702.

Poythress, N. G., Edens, J. F., & Watkins, M. M. (2001). The relationship between psychopathic personality features and malingering of major mental illness. *Law and Human Behavior, 25*(6), 567–582.

Rabin, L. A., Barr, W. B., & Burton, L. A. (2005). Assessment practices of clinical neuropsychologists in the United States and Canada: A survey of INS, NAN, and Division 40 members. *Archives of Clinical Neuropsychology, 10*, 33–65.

Reinvang, I., Nordby, H., & Nielsen, C. S. (2000). Information processing deficits in head injury assessed with ERPs reflecting early and late processing stages. *Neuropsychologia, 38*, 995–1005.

Resnick, P. J. (1994). Malingering. In R. Rosner (Ed.), *Principles and practice of forensic psychiatry* (pp. 417–426). New York: Chapman & Hall.

Resnick, P. J. (1999). The detection of malingered psychosis. *Psychiatric Clinics of North America, 22*(1), 159–172.

Reznek, L. (2005). The Rey 15-Item Memory Test for malingering: A meta-analysis. *Brain Injury, 19*(7), 539–543.

Rogers, R., Bagby, R. M., & Dickens, S. E. (1992). *Structured Interview of Reported Symptoms: Professional manual*. Odessa, FL: Psychological Assessment Resources.

Rogers, R., Harrell, E. H., & Liff, C. D. (1993). Feigning neuropsychological impairment: A critical review of methodological and clinical considerations. *Clinical Psychology Review, 13*, 255–274.

Rogers, R., Sewell, K. W., Morey, L. C., & Ustad, K. L. (1996). Detection of feigned mental disorders on the Personality Assessment Inventory: A discriminant analysis. *Journal of Personality Assessment, 67*, 629–640.

Rogers, R. (1997). Introduction. In R. Rogers (Ed.). Clinical assessment of malingering and deception (pp. 1–19). New York: Guilford Press.

Rogers, R., Ustad, K. L., & Salekin, R. T. (1998). Convergent validity of the Personality Assessment Inventory: A study of emergency referrals in a correctional setting. *Assessment, 5*, 3–12.

Rogers, R., & Cruise, K. R. (1998). Assessment of malingering with simulation designs: Threats to external validity. *Law and Human Behavior, 22*, 273–285.

Rogers, R., & Bender, S. D. (2003). Evaluation of malingering and deception. In I. B. Weiner (Series Ed.) & A. M. Goldstein (Vol. Ed.), *Handbook of psychology: Vol. 11*. Forensic psychology (pp. 109–129). New York: Wiley.

Rogers, R. Sewell, K. W., Martin, M. A., & Vitacco, M. J. (2003). Detection of feigned mental disorders: A meta-analysis of the MMPI-2 and malingering. *Assessment, 10*, 160–177.

Rogers, R., & Correa, A. (2008). Determinations of malingering: Evolution from case-based methods to detection strategies. *Psychiatry, Psychology, and Law, 15*(2), 213–223.

Rogers, R., Gillard, N. D., Berry, D. T. R., & Granacher, R. P. (2011). Effectiveness of the MMPI- 2-RF Validity scales for feigned mental disorders and cognitive impairment: A known-groups study. *Journal of Psychopathology and Behavioral Assessment, 33*(3), 355–367.

Root, J. C., Robbins, R. N., Chang, L., & van Gorp, W. G. (2006). Detection of inadequate effort on the California Verbal Learning Test–Second Edition: Forced choice recognition and critical item analysis. *Journal of the International Neuropsychological Society, 12*(5), 688–696.

Rose, F. E., Hall, S., Szalda-Petreem, A. D., & Bach, P. J. (1998). A comparison of four tests of malingering and the effects of coaching. *Archives of Clinical Neuropsychology, 13*, 349–363.

Rosenfeld, J. P., Sweet, J. J., Chuang, J., Ellwanger, J., & Song, L. (1996). Detection of simulated malingering using forced choice recognition enhanced with event-related potential recording. *The Clinical Neuropsychologist, 10*(2), 163–179.

Rosenhan, D. (1973). On being sane in insane places. *Science, 179*(4070), 250–258.

Rowe, D. L. (2005). A framework for investigating thalamocortical activity in multistage information processing. *Journal of Integrative Neuroscience, 4,* 5–26.

Rusconi, E., & Mitchener-Nissen, T. (2013). Prospects of functional magnetic resonance imaging as lie detector. *Frontier in Human Neuroscience, 7*(594), 1–12.

Rüsseler, J., Brett, A., Klaue, U., Sailer, M., & Münte, T. F. (2008). The effect of coaching on the simulated malingering of memory impairment. *BioMedicalCentral, Neurology, 8*(1), 37.

Saxe, L., & Ben-Shakhar, G. (1999). Admissibility of polygraph tests: The application of scientific standards post-*Daubert. Psychology, Public Policy, and Law, 5*(1), 203–223.

Schoenberg, M. R., Dorr, D., & Morgan, C. D. (2003). The ability of the Millon Clinical Multiaxial Inventory–Third Edition to detect malingering. *Psychological Assessment, 15,* 198–204.

Schwarz, L. R., Gfeller, J. D., & Oliveri, M. V. (2006). Detecting feigned impairment with the Digit Span and Vocabulary subtests of the Wechsler Adult Intelligence Scale–Third Edition. *The Clinical Neuropsychologist, 20,* 741–753.

Sellbom, M., & Bagby, R. M. (2008). Validity of the MMPI-2-RF (restructured form) L-r and K-r scales in detecting underreporting in clinical and nonclinical samples. *Psychological Assessment, 20*(4), 370–376.

Sellbom, M., Ben-Porath, Y. S., & Stafford, K. P. (2007). A comparison of measures of psychopathic deviance in a forensic setting. *Psychological Assessment, 19,* 430–436.

Sellbom, M., Toomey, A., Wygant, D., Kucharski, L.T., & Duncan, S. (2010). Utility of the MMPI-2-RF (Restructured Form) Validity scales in detecting malingering in a criminal forensic setting: A known-groups design. *Psychological Assessment, 22,* 22–31.

Sharland, M. J. and Gfeller, J. D. (2007). A survey of neuropsychologists' beliefs and practices with respect to the assessment of effort. *Archives of Clinical Neuropsychology, 22*(2), 213–223.

Simon, M. J. (2007). Performance of mentally retarded forensic patients on the Test of Memory Malingering. *Journal of Clinical Psychology, 63*(4), 339–344.

Slick, D., Hopp G., Strauss E., & Thompson, G. B. (1997). *Victoria Symptom Validity Test version 1.0: Professional manual.* Odessa, FL: Psychological Assessment Resources.

Slick, D. J., Sherman, E. M. S., & Iverson, G. L. (1999). Diagnostic criteria for malingered neurocognitive dysfunction: Proposed standards for clinical practice and research. *The Clinical Neuropsychologist, 13,* 545–561.

Smith, G. P., & Burger, G. K. (1997). Detection of malingering: Validation of the Structured Inventory of Malingered Symptomatology (SIMS). *Journal of the Academy of Psychiatry and the Law, 25,* 180–183.

Spence, S. A., Crimlisk, H. L., Cope, H., Ron, M. A., & Grasby, P. M. (2000). Discrete neurophysiological correlates in prefrontal cortex during hysterical and feigned disorder of movement. *Lancet, 355*, 1243–1244.

Spence, S. A., Farrow, T. F., Herford, A. E., Wilkinson, I. D., Zheng, Y., & Woodruff, P. W. (2001). Behavioural and functional anatomical correlates of deception in humans. *Neuroreport, 12*, 2849–2853.

State v. Mary Doherty, 2 Overt. Tenn. Rep. 79 (1806).

Stenclik, J. H., Miele, A. S., Silk-Eglit, G., Lynch, J. K., & McCaffrey, R. J. (2013). Can the sensitivity and specificity of the TOMM be increased with differential cutoff scores? *Applied Neuropsychology: Adult, 20*(4), 243–248.

Strauss, E., Hultsch, D. F., Hunter, M., Slick D. J., Patry, B., & Levy-Bencheton, J. (2000). Using intraindividual variability to detect malingering in cognitive performance. *The Clinical Neuropsychologist, 14*, 420–432.

Strauss, E., Slick, D. J., Levy-Bencheton, J., Hunter, M., MacDonald, S. W. S., & Hultsch, D. F. (2002). Intraindividual variability as indicators of malingering of head injury. *Archives of Clinical Neuropsychology, 17*, 423–444.

Suhr, J. A., & Gunstad, J. (2000). The effects of coaching on the sensitivity and specificity of malingering measures. *Archives of Clinical Neuropsychology, 15*, 415–424.

Suhr, J. A., & Gunstad, J. (2007). Coaching and malingering: A review. In G. J. Larrabee (Ed.), *Assessment of malingered neuropsychological deficits* (pp. 287–310). New York: Oxford University Press.

Sweet, J. J., Wolfe, P., Sattlberger, E., Numan, B., Rosenfeld, J. P., & Clingerman, S. (2000). Further investigation of traumatic brain injury versus insufficient effort with the California Verbal Learning Test. *Archives of Clinical Neuropsychology, 15*, 105–113.

Tardiff, H. P., Barry, R. J., & Johnstone, S. J. (2002). Event-related potentials reveal processing differences in honest vs. malingered memory performance. *International Journal of Psychophysiology, 46*, 147–158.

Tombaugh, T. N. (1996). *Test of Memory Malingering (TOMM)*. New York: Multi-Health Systems.

Tombaugh, T. N. (1997). The Test of Memory Malingering (TOMM): Normative data from cognitively intact and cognitively impaired individuals. *Psychological Assessment, 9*, 260–268.

Trueblood, W. (1994). Qualitative and quantitative characteristics of malingered and other invalid WAIS-R and clinical memory data. *Journal of Clinical and Experimental Neuropsychology, 16*, 597–607.

United States v. Gigante, 925 F. Supp. 967, 968 (E.D.N.Y. 1996).

United States v. Gigante, 982 F. Supp. 140, 159 (E.D.N.Y. 1997).

United States v. Greer, 158 F.3d 228 (1998).

Vagnini, V. L., Berry, D. T. R., Clark, J. A. & Jiang, Y. (2008). New measures to detect malingered neurocognitive deficit: Applying reaction time and event-related potentials. *Journal of Clinical and Experimental Neuropsychology, 30*(7), 766–776.

Vallabhajosula, B., & van Gorp, W. (2001). Post-Daubert admissibility of scientific evidence on malingering of cognitive deficits. *Journal of the American Academy of Psychiatry and Law, 29*, 207–215.

Weinborn, M., Orr, T., Woods, S. P., Conover, E., & Feix, J. (2003). A validation of the Test of Memory Malingering in a forensic psychiatric setting. *Journal of Clinical and Experimental Neuropsychology, 25,* 979–990.

Weiss, R. A., Rosenfeld, B., & Farkas, M. R. (2011). The utility of the structured interview of reported symptoms in a sample of individuals with intellectual disabilities. *Assessment, 18*(3), 284–290.

Williamson, D. J., Green, P., Allen, L., & Rohling, M. L. (2003). Evaluating effort with the Word Memory Test and Category Test—or not: Inconsistencies in a compensation-seeking sample. *Journal of Forensic Neuropsychology, 3,* 19–44.

Wisdom, N. M., Callahan, J. L., & Shaw, T. G. (2010). Diagnostic utility of the Structured Inventory of Malingered Symptomatology to detect malingering in a forensic sample. *Archives of Clinical Neuropsychology, 25*(2), 118–125.

Woodruff, W. A. (2010). Functional magnetic resonance imaging to detect deception: Not ready for the courtroom. Retrieved from http://ssrn.com/abstract=1809761

Yang, Y., Raine, A., Lencz, T., Bihrle, S., Lacasse, L., & Colletti P. (2005). Prefrontal white matter in pathological liars. *The British Journal of Psychiatry, 187,* 320–325.

Yang, Y., Raine, A., Narr, K. L., Lencz, T., LaCasse, L., Colletti, P., & Toga, A. W. (2007). Localisation of increased prefrontal white matter in pathological liars. *The British Journal of Psychiatry, 190,* 174–175.

Chapter 10. Neuroscience and the Law

Allen v. Hickman, 407 F.Supp.2d 1098 (N.D. Cal. 2005).

Ake v. Oklahoma, 470 U.S. 68 (1985).

Appelbaum, P. S. (2009). Law and psychiatry: Through the glass darkly: Functional neuroimaging evidence enters the courtroom. *Psychiatric Services, 60,* 21–23.

Aronson, J. D. (2010). The law's use of brain evidence. *Annual Review of Law and Social Science, 6,* 93–108.

Awkal v. Mitchell, 559 F.3d 456 (6th Cir. 2009).

Barth, A. S. (2007). A double-edged sword: The role of neuroimaging in federal capital sentencing. *American Journal of Law & Medicine, 33,* 501–522.

Baxter v. Temple, 949 A. 2d 167 (NH 2008).

Brown, T., & Murphy, E. (2010). Through a scanner darkly: Functional neuroimaging as evidence of a criminal defendant's past mental states. *Stanford Law Review, 62*(4), 1119–1208.

Buchanan, A. (2004). Mental capacity, legal competence and consent to treatment. *Journal of the Royal Society of Medicine, 97,* 415–420.

Commonwealth v. Morales, No. 2143 (Phila C.P. Apr. 30, 2004).

Commonwealth v. Pirela, 510 Pa. 43, 507 A.2d 23 (1986).

Crook v. State, 813 So.2d 68, 69 (Fla.2002).

Daubert v. Merrell Dow Pharmaceuticals, 509 U.S. 579 (1993).

Davis v. State, No. 49A05-1109-CR-459 (Ct. of App. 2012).

Dunlap v. Commonwealth of Kentucky, No. 2010–SC–000226–MR (2013).

Dusky v. United States, 362 U.S. 402 (1960).

Erickson, S. K. (2010). Blaming the brain. *Minnesota Journal of Law, Science & Technology, 11*, 27–77.

Ferguson v. Florida Department of Corrections, No. 12-15422 (2013).

Ferguson v. State, 593 So. 2d 508 (Fla. 1992).

Ferguson v. State, 789 So. 2d 306, 308 (Fla. 2001).

Ford v. Wainwright, 477 U.S. 399 (1986).

Forrest v. State, 290 S.W.3d 704 (Mo. banc 2009).

Frye v. United States, 293 F. 1013 (D.C. Cir. 1923).

Garner v. Mitchell, 502 F.3d 394 (6th Cir. 2007).

Gregory, T. (2009, November 8). Jeanine Nicarico murder case: Brian Dugan sentencing focuses on psychopathy. *Chicago Tribune.* Retrieved June 16, 2013, from: articles.chicagotribune.com/2009-11-08/news/0911070221_1_brian . . .

Gurley, J. R., & Marcus, D. K. (2005, March). Phineas Gage on trial: The effects of neuroimaging and brain injury on decisions of insanity. Paper presented at the American Psychology-Law Society Conference. La Jolla, CA.

Holloway v. U.S., 148 F.2d 665 (DC Cir. 1945).

Hughes, V. (2010). Science in court: Head case. *Nature, 464*, 340–342.

Hughes v. South Carolina, 529 U.S. 1025, 120 S.Ct. 1434, 146 L.Ed.2d 323 (2000).

Hughes v. State, No. 26115 (2006).

Hyman, H. H., Cobb, W. J., Feldman, J. J., Hart, C. W., & Stember, C. H. (1954). *Interviewing in social research.* Chicago: University of Chicago Press.

Indiana v. Edwards, 128 S. CT. 2379 (2008).

Jackson v. Calderon, 21 F.3d 1149 (9th Cir 2000) (aff'd in *People v. Jackson*, 199 P.3d 1098 (Cal. 2009).

Lamparello, A. (2011). Neuroscience, brain damage, and the criminal defendant: Who does it help and where in the criminal proceeding is it most relevant? *Rutgers Law Record, 39*, 161–180.

Lockett v. Ohio, 438 U.S. 586, 604 (1978).

McNamara v. Borg, 923 F.2d 862 (9th Cir. 1991).

Moriarty, J. C. (2008). Flickering admissibility: neuroimaging evidence in the U.S. courts. *Behavioral Science and the Law, 26*, 29–49.

Panetti v. Dretke, 401 F. Supp. 705, 711 (W.D. Tex. 2004).

Panetti v. Dretke, 448 F. 3d 815 (5th Cir. 2006).

Panetti v. Quarterman, 551 U.S. 930, 127 S.Ct. 2842, 168 L.Ed.2d 662 (2007).

People v. Goldstein, 14 A.D.3d 32, 786 N.Y.S.2d 428 (N.Y. App. Div. 2004).

People v. Goldstein, 6 N.Y.3d 119 (N.Y. App. Div. 2005).

People v. Jones, 210 A.D.2d. 904 (N.Y. App. Div. 1994).

People v. Lee, 2011 WL 651850 (Cal. 2011).

People v. Phillips, Index 41, NYLJ 1202488522930 (Ct. of App., decided March 29, 2011).

People v. Protsman, 105 Cal. Rptr. 2d 819, 822-23 (Ct. App. 2001).

People v. Yum, 3 Cal. Rptr. 3d 855, 857 (Ct. App. 2003).

People v. Weinstein, 591 N.Y.S.2d 715 (Sup. Ct. 1992).

People v. White, 117 Cal. App. 3d 270, 172 Cal. Rptr. 612 (Cal. Ct. App. 1981).

People v. Wilson, 732 N.E.2d 498, 502 (Ill. 2000).

Perlin, M. L. (2010). Neuroimaging and competency to be executed after Panetti. NYLS Legal Studies Research Paper No. 09/10, #20. Retrieved from http://ssrn.com/abstract=1557753

Persaud, V. (2013, January 17). Bargo's trial in Seath Jackson murder postponed until August. *Ocala StarBanner.* Retrieved from http://www.ocala.com/article/20130117/ARTICLES/130119726?tc=ar

Pogash, C. (2003, November 23). Myth of the Twinkie defense. *San Francisco Chronicle*, p. D-1.

Quick v. State of Texas, Texas App. NO. 01-09-01127-CR (2011).

Reeves, D., Mills, M. J., Billick, S. B., & Brodie, J. D. (2003). Limitations of brain imaging in forensic psychiatry. *Journal of the American Academy of Psychiatry and Law, 31*, 89–96.

Risinger, D. M., Saks, M. J., Thompson, W. C., & Rosenthal, R. (2002). The Daubert/Khumo implications of observer effects in forensic science: Hidden problems of expectation and suggestion. *California Law Review, 90*, 1–56.

Rogers v. State, 783 So.2d 980 (Fla. 2001).

Samayoa v. Ayers, 2011 WL 1226375 (9th Cir. 2011).

Schweitzer, N. J., & Saks, M. J. (2011). Neuroimage evidence and the insanity defense. *Behavioral Sciences and the Law, 29*, 592–607.

Sears v. State, 268 Ga. 759, 493 S.E.2d 180 (1997).

Sears v. Upton, 561 U. S. _____ (2010).

Simmons v. South Carolina, 512 U.S. 154,169 (1994).

Singleton v. State, 313 S.C. at 83, 437 S.E.2d at 58 (1993).

Snead, O. C. (2007). Neuroimaging and the complexity of capital punishment. *New York University Law Review, 82*, 1265–1339.

Society of Nuclear Medicine Brain Imaging Council. (1996). Ethical clinical practice of functional brain imaging. *Journal of Nuclear Medicine, 37*, 1256–1259.

Solesbee v. Balkcom, 339 U.S. 9 (1950).

State v. Anderson, 79 S.W.3d 420 (Mo. 2002).

State v. Carreiro, NO. CA2011-12-236, 2013-Ohio-1103 (2013).

State v. Delahanty, 2011 WL 1327986 (Ariz. 2011).

State v. Downs, 361 S.C. 141, 604 S.E.2d 377 (2004).

State v. Ferguson, No. 04-2012-CA- 507, op. at 1, 17 (Fla. Cir. Ct. Oct. 12, 2012).

State v. Forrest, 183 S.W.3d 218 (Mo. banc 2006).

State v. Griffin, 273 Conn. 266, 869 A.2d 640 (2005).

State v. Hall, 752 N.E.2d 318, 320-26 (Ohio Ct. App. 2001).

State v. Hughes, 336 S.C. 585, 521 S.E.2d 500 (1999), cert denied.

State v. Mears, 749 A.2d 600, 605-06 (Vt. 2000).

State v. Stanko, 376 S.C. 571, 573, 658 S.E.2d 94, 95 (2008).

Strickland v. Washington, 466 U.S. 668, 687-88, 104 S.Ct. 2052, 80 L.Ed.2d 674, (1984).

Stone, A. A. (1984). The Trial of John Hinckley. In *Law, Psychiatry and Morality* (pp. 77–98). New York: Donnelly.

Tancredi, L., & Brodie, J. (2007). The brain and behavior: Limitations in the legal use of functional magnetic resonance imaging. *American Journal of Law & Medicine, 33*(2–3), 271–294.

Taylor, S. Jr. (1982, June 4). Hinckley's brain is termed normal. *New York Times*, p. A21.

Trapp v. Spencer, 479 F.3d 53 (1st Cir. 2007).

United States v. Eff, 461 F. Supp. 2d 529 (E.D.Tex. 2006).
United States v. Hinckley, 525 F. Supp. 1342, 1348 (D.D.C. 1981).
United States v. Llera Plaza, 179 F.Supp.2d 464, 487 (E.D. Pa. 2001).
United States v. Pineyro, 372 F.Supp.2d, 133 (D. Mass 2005).
United States v. Sandoval-Mendoza, 472 F.3d 645 (9th Cir. 2006).
Vincent, N. A. (2011). Neuroimaging and responsibility assessments. *Neuroethics*, 4(1), 35–49.
Ward v. Sternes, 334 F.3d 696 (7th Cir. 2003).
Washington v. Marshall, 144 Wn.2d 266 (Wa. Sup. Ct. 2001).
Zink v. State, 278 S.W.3d 170 (Mo. 2009).

Chapter 11. Linking Brain Function and Behavior

Aspinwall, L. G., Brown, T. R., & Tabery, J. (2012). The double-edged sword: Does biomechanism increase or decrease judges' sentencing of psychopaths? *Science*, 337(6096), 846–849.
Brown, G. G., & Eyler, L. T. (2006). Methodological and conceptual issues in functional magnetic resonance imaging: Applications to schizophrenia research. *Annual Review of Clinical Psychology*, 2, 51–81.
Brown, T., & Murphy, E. (2010). Through a scanner darkly: Functional neuroimaging as evidence of a criminal defendant's past mental states. *Stanford Law Review*, 62, 1119–1208.
Burton, P. R. S., & Chamberlain, J. R. (2010). Competence to waive Miranda rights. *Journal of the American Academy of Psychiatry and the Law*, 38(2), 280–282.
Compton, E. S. (2010). Not guilty by reason of neuroimaging: The need for cautionary jury instructions for neuroscience evidence in criminal trials. *Vanderbilt Journal of Entertainment and Technology Law*, 12(2), 333–354.
Daubert v. Merrell Dow Pharmaceuticals, Inc., 509 U.S. 579, 597 (1993).
Dusky v. United States, 362 U.S. 402 (1960).
Gurley, J. R., & Marcus, D. K. (2008). The effects of neuroimaging and brain injury on insanity defenses. *Behavioral Sciences and the Law*, 26(1), 85–97.
James, W. (1890). *The principles of psychology*. New York: Holt and Co.
Kulynych, J. (1997). Psychiatric neuroimaging research: A high-tech crystal ball? *Stanford Law Review*, 49, 1249–1270.
Lavergne, G. M. (1997). *A sniper in the tower: The Charles Whitman murders*. Denton: University of North Texas Press.
Martell, D. (1992). Forensic neuropsychology and the criminal law. *Law and Human Behavior*, 16, 313–336.
Melton, G. (1997). *Psychological evaluations for the courts: A handbook for mental health professionals and lawyers* (2nd ed.). New York: Guilford Press.
Moberg, P. J., & Kniele, K. (2006). Evaluation of competency: Ethical considerations for neuropsychologists. *Applied Neuropsychology*, 13(2), 101–114.
Moriarty, J. (2009). Visions of deception: Neuroimages and the search for the truth. *Akron Law Review*, 42, 739–762.

Mossman, D., Noffsinger, S. G., Ash, P., Frierson, R. L., Gerbasi, J., Hackett, M., . . . American Academy of Psychiatry and the Law. (2007). AAPL practice guideline for the forensic psychiatric evaluation of competence to stand trial. *Journal of the American Academy of Psychiatry and the Law, 35*(4), S3–S72.

Nestor, P. G., Daggett, D., Haycock, J., & Price, M. (1999). Competence to stand trial: A neuropsychological inquiry. *Law and Human Behavior, 23*, 397–412.

Nicholson, R. A., & Kugler, K. E. (1991). Competent and incompetent criminal defendants: A quantitative review of comparative research. *Psychology Bulletin, 109*, 355–370.

Pinals, D. A., Tillbrook, C. E., & Mumley, D. L. (2006). Practical application of the MacArthur Competence Assessment Tool–Criminal Adjudication (MacCAT-CA) in a public sector forensic setting. *Journal of the American Academy of Psychiatry and the Law, 34*(2), 179–188.

Reeves, D., Mills, M. J., Billick, S. B., & Brodie, J. D. (2003). Limitations of brain imaging in forensic psychiatry. *Journal of the American Academy of Psychiatry and Law, 31*, 89–96.

Rogers v. State, 783 So.2d 980 (Fla. 2001).

Schwarz, C. (2009). Irreconcilable differences: Mens rea and mental illness. Retrieved from uwp.duke.edu/uploads/assets/Schwarz_09.pdf

Sinnott-Armstrong, W., Roskies, A., Brown, T., & Murphy, E. (2008). Brain images as legal evidence. *Episteme, 5*, 359–373.

Smith v. Anderson, 402 F.3d 718 (6th Cir. 2005).

Stafford, K. P., & Sellbom, M. O. (2012). Competency to stand trial. In R. Otto (Ed.), *Handbook of psychology: Vol. 11*, Forensic psychology (pp. 412–439). New York: Wiley.

State v. Reid, 213 S.W.3d 792 (Ten. 2006).

Stuss, D. T., & Knight, R. T. (2002). *Principles of frontal lobe function*. New York: Oxford University Press.

United States v. Pohlot, 827 F.2d 889, 890 (3d Cir. 1987).

Valeo, T. (2012). Legal-ease: Is neuroimaging a valid biomarker in legal cases? *Neurology Today, 12*(8), 38–40.

Whitman, C. (1966, July 31). Whitman letter: The Whitman Archives. *Austin American- Statesman*.

Zapf, P. (2011). Politics and incompetence: The Luke Wright case. Retrieved from http://www.clinicalforensicpsychology.org/luke-wright-found-competent-to . . .

Chapter 12. A Cautionary Tale

Alavi, A., Mavi, A., Basu, S., & Fischman, A. (2007). Is PET-CT the only option? *European Journal of Nuclear Medicine and Molecular Imaging, 34*(6), 819–821.

Appelbaum, P. S. (2009). Through a glass darkly: Functional neuroimaging evidence enters the courtroom. *Psychiatric Services, 60*(1), 21–213.

Bandes, S. A. (2008). Framing wrongful convictions. *Utah Law Review, 5*, 11.

Bandes, S. A. (2010). The promise and pitfalls of neuroscience for criminal law and procedure. *Ohio State Journal of Criminal Law, 8*, 119–122.

Barak, G. (1998). *Integrating Criminologies.* Boston: Allyn and Bacon.

Baskin, J. H., Edersheim, J. G., & Price, B. H. (2007). Is a picture worth a thousand words? Neuroimaging in the courtroom. *American Journal of Law & Medicine, 33,* 239–269.

Batts, S. (2009). Brain lesions and their implications in criminal responsibility. *Behavioral Sciences and the Law, 27,* 261–272.

Bennett, C. M., & Miller, M. B. (2010). How reliable are the results from functional magnetic resonance imaging? *Annals of the New York Academy of Science, 1191,* 133–155.

Blakemore, C. (2005). Harveian oration: In celebration of cerebration. *Lancet, 366,* 2035–2059.

Brower, M. C., & Price, B. H. (2000). Epilepsy and violence: When is the brain to blame? *Epilepsy and Behavior, 1*(3):145–149.

Brown, T., & Murphy, E. (2010). Through a scanner darkly: Functional neuroimaging as evidence of a criminal defendant's past mental states. *Stanford Law Review 62*(4), 1119–1208.

Button, K. S., Ioannidis, J. P., Mokrysz, C., Nosek, B.A., Flint, J., Robinson, E. S., & Munafò, M. R. (2013). Power failure: Why small sample size undermines the reliability of neuroscience. *Nature Reviews Neuroscience, 14*(5), 365–376.

Case Western Reserve University. (2013, July 10). Fundamental problem for brain mapping. *Science Daily.* Retrieved from http://www.sciencedaily.com/releases/2013/07/130710114221.htm

Catana, C., Drzezga, A., Heiss, W. D., & Rosen, B. R. (2012). PET/MRI for neurologic applications. *Journal of Nuclear Medicine, 53,* 1916–1925.

Chatterjee, A. (2005). A madness to the methods in cognitive neuroscience? *Journal of Cognitive Neuroscience, 17,* 847–849.

Chorvat, T., & McCabe, K. (2006). The brain and the law. In S. Zeki & O. Goodenough (Eds.), *Law and the brain* (pp. 113–131). New York: Oxford University Press.

Compton, E. S. (2010). Not guilty by reason of neuroimaging: The need for cautionary jury instructions for neuroscience evidence in criminal trials. *Vanderbilt Journal of Entertainment and Technology Law, 12,* 333–355.

Daubert v. Merrell Dow Pharmaceuticals, Inc., 509 U.S. 579, 590 (1993).

Duke University. (2013, March 28). Brain scans might predict future criminal behavior. *Science Daily.* Retrieved from http://www.sciencedaily.com / releases/2013/03/130328125319.htm

Fallon, J. (2013). *The psychopath inside: A neuroscientist's personal journey into the dark side of the brain.* New York: Penguin.

Farah, M. J., & Gillihan, S. J. (2012). Diagnostic brain imaging in psychiatry: Current uses and future prospects. *Virtual Mentor, 14*(6), 464–471.

Friston, K. J., & Price, C. J. (2003). Degeneracy and redundancy in cognitive anatomy. *Trends in Cognitive Science, 7,* 151–152.

Ganis, G., & Kosslyn, S. M. (2002). Neuroimaging. In *Encyclopedia of the Human Brain* (Vol. 3, pp. 493–505). San Diego, CA: Academic Press.

Garibotto, V., Heinzer, S., Vulliemoz, S., Guignard, R., Wissmeyer, M., Seeck, M., . . . Vargas, M. I. (2013). Clinical applications of Hybrid PET/MRI in neuroimaging. *Clinical Nuclear Medicine, 38*(1), e13–e18.

Gazzaniga, M. S. (2006). *The ethical brain: The science of our moral dilemmas.* New York: Harper Perennial.

Heilbrun, K. (1992). The role of psychological testing in forensic assessment. *Law and Human Behavior, 16*, 257–272.

Heilbrun, K., Marczyk, G., DeMatteo, D., & Goldstein, A. M. (2008). Standards of practice and care in forensic mental health assessment: Legal, professional, and principles-based considerations. *Psychology, Public Policy, and Law, 14*, 1–26.

Hicks, J. W. (2004). Ethnicity, race, and forensic psychiatry: Are we color-blind? *Journal of the American Academy of Psychiatry and the Law, 32*(1), 21–33.

Hotz. R. (2009, January 16). The brain, your honor, will take the witness stand. *The Wall Street Journal.*

Hyman, S. E. (2007). *Neuroethics: At age 5, the field continues to evolve.* The 2007 Progress Report on Brain Research. New York: Dana Press.

Ioannidis, J. (2008). Why most discovered true associations are inflated. *Epidemiology, 19*, 640–648.

Judenhofer, M. S., Wehrl, H. F., Newport, D.F., Catana, C., Siegel, S.B., Becker, M., . . . Pichler, B. J. (2008). Simultaneous PET-MRI: a new approach for functional and morphological imaging. *Nature Medicine, 14*(4), 459–465.

Kalmbach, K. C. & Lyons, P. M. (2006). Ethical Issues in Conducting Forensic Evaluations. *Applied Psychology in Criminal Justice, 2*(3), 261–290.

Kriegeskorte, N., Lindquist, M. A., Nichols, T. E., Poldrack, R. A., & Vul, E. (2010). Everything you never wanted to know about circular analysis, but were afraid to ask. *Journal of Cerebral Blood Flow & Metabolism, 30*(9), 1551–1557.

Martell, D. A. (2009). Neuroscience and the law: Philosophical differences and practical constraints. *Behavioral Sciences and the Law, 27*, 123–136.

Morcom, A. M., & Fletcher, P. C. (2007). Does the brain have a baseline? Why we should be resisting a rest. *Neuroimage, 37*(4), 1073–1082.

Morse, S. J. (2006). Brain overclaim syndrome and criminal responsibility: A diagnostic note. *Ohio State Journal of Criminal Law, 3*, 397.

Morse, S. J. (2004). New neuroscience, old problems. In B. Garland (Ed.), *Neuroscience and the law: Brain, mind, and the scales of justice* (pp. 157–198). New York: Dana Press.

Nugent, K. M. (2009). Neuroimaging in criminal trials: Evidentiary and constitutional concerns. Retrieved from http://works.bepress.com/kristen_nugent/4

Oullier, O. (2012). Clear up this fuzzy thinking on brain scans. *Nature, 483*, 7.

Pardo, M. S., & Patterson, D. (2010). Philosophical foundations of law and neuroscience. *University of Illinois Law Review, 2010*(4), 1211–1250.

Paterson, L. M., Tyacke, R. J., Nutt, D. J., & Knudsen, G. M. (2010). Measuring endogenous 5-HT release by emission tomography: promises and pitfalls. *Journal of Cerebral Blood Flow & Metabolism, 30*(10), 1682–1706.

Raine, A. (2002). The biological basis of crime. In J. Q. Wilson & J. Petersilia (Eds.), *Crime: Public policies for crime control* (pp. 43–74). Oakland, CA: ICS Press.

Sarter, M., Bruno, J. P., & Parikh, V. (2007). Abnormal neurotransmitter release underlying behavioral and cognitive disorders: Toward concepts of dynamic and function-specific dysregulation. *Neuropsychopharmacology, 32*, 1452–1461.

Shen, L. H., Liao, M. H., & Tseng, Y. C. (2012). Recent advances in imaging of dopaminergic neurons for evaluation of neuropsychiatric disorders. *Journal of Biomedicine and Biotechnology.* http://dx.doi.org/10.1155/2012/259349

Silva, J. A. (2013). The relevance of neuroscience to forensic psychiatry. *Journal of the American Academy of Psychiatry and the Law, 35*(1), 6–9.

Simmons, J. P., Nelson, L. D., & Simonsohn, U. (2011). False positive psychology: Undisclosed flexibility in data collection and analysis allows presenting anything as significant. *Psychological Science, 22*, 1359–1366.

Snead, O. C. (2007). Neuroimaging and the "complexity" of capital punishment. *New York University Law Review, 82*, 1265–1338.

Snowden, J. (2010). Neuropsychological advances in our understanding and classification of the dementias. *Journal of Neurology, Neurosurgery, & Psychiatry, 81*(10), e4 doi:10.1136.

Stark, C. E., & Squire, L. R. (2001). When zero is not zero: The problem of ambiguous baseline conditions in fMRI. *Proceedings of the National Academy of Science USA, 98*(22), 12760–12766.

Todd, M., Nystrom, L., & Cohen, J. (2013). Confounds in multivariate pattern analysis: Theory and rule representation case study. *Neuroimage, 77*, 157–165.

Treadway Johnson, M., Krafka, C., & Cecil, J. S. (2000). Expert testimony in federal civil trials: A preliminary analysis. Washington, DC: Federal Judicial Center. Retrieved from http://www.fjc.gov/public/pdf.nsf/lookup/exptesti.pdf/$file/exptesti.pd

United States v. Alexander, 526 F.2d 161, 168 (8th Cir. 1975).

United States v. Williams, 2009 U.S. Dist. LEXIS 13472 (D. Haw.2009).

Uttal, W. R. (2012). *Reliability in cognitive neuroscience: A meta-meta analysis.* Cambridge, MA: MIT Press.

von Schulthess, G. K., Kuhn, F. P., Kaufmann, P., & Veit-Haibach, P. (2013). Clinical positron emission tomography/magnetic resonance imaging applications. *Seminars in Nuclear Medicine, 43*(1), 3–10.

Vul, E., Harris, C., Winkielman, P., & Pashler, H. (2009). Puzzlingly high correlations in fMRI studies of emotion, personality, and social cognition. *Perspectives on Psychological Science, 4*, 274–290.

Wager, T. D., Hernandez, L., & Lindquist, M. A. (2009). Essentials of functional neuroimaging. In G. G. Berntson & J. T. Cacioppo (Eds.), *Handbook of neuroscience for the behavioral sciences* (pp. 152–197). Hoboken, NJ: Wiley.

Walsh, A., & Hemmens, C. (2010). *Introduction to Criminology: A Text/Reader.*

Weisberg, D. S., Keil, F. C., Goodstein, J., Rawson, E., & Gray, J. R. (2008). The seductive allure of neuroscience explanations. *Journal of Cognitive Neuroscience, 20*, 470–477.

Yarkoni T. (2007). Big correlations in little studies. *Perspectives in Psychological Science, 4*, 294–298.

Yarkoni, T., Poldrack, R. A., Van Essen, D. C., & Wager, T. D. (2010). Cognitive neuroscience 2.0: Building a cumulative science of human brain function. *Trends in Cognitive Science, 14*(11), 489–496.

Zaidi, H., & Mawlawi, O. (2007). Simultaneous PET/MR will replace PET/CT as the molecular multimodality imaging platform of choice. *Medical Physics, 34*(5), 1525–1528.

Zimmer, C. (2004). *Soul made flesh: The discovery of the brain—and how it changed the world.* New York: Free Press.

Index